CRITICAL GESTURES

WRITINGS ON DANCE AND CULTURE

ANN DALY

WESLEYAN UNIVERSITY PRESS · *Middletown, Connecticut*

♾ The paper used in this publication meets the requirements
of the American National Standard for Information Sciences — Permanence
of Paper for Printed Library Materials, ANSI Z39.48–1984

Library of Congress Cataloging-in-Publication Data

Daly, Ann, 1959-
  Critical gestures : writings on dance and culture / Ann Daly.
    p. cm.
Includes index.
  ISBN 0-8195-6565-2 (cloth : alk. paper) — ISBN 0-8195-6566-0 (pbk. :
alk. paper)
  1. Modern dance—Social aspects. 2. Feminism and dance. 3. Dance
criticism. I. Title.
  GV1783 .D35 2002
  792.8–dc21   2002010172

CRITICAL GESTURES WITHDRAWN

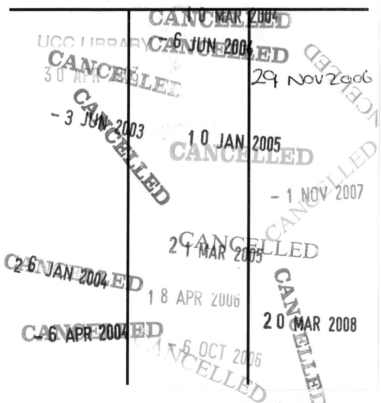

For all my teachers, beginning with my parents,
Claire and Edwin Daly.

CONTENTS

CONTENTS

PERFORMANCES

IMAGES AND EXHIBITS

BOOKS

INTRODUCTION

INTRODUCTION

WHY ELSE would anyone practice criticism, except for love? I didn't fall in love with dance as a ballerina wannabe, which is the more usual story. I fell in love with dance as a journalism major in college, when I attended my first dance performance. It was Pittsburgh Ballet Theatre's *Romeo and Juliet*, and most of all I was eager to see how they could possibly tell the tale without words. By my sophomore year I decided to become a dance critic, for two reasons. First, because in dance I had discovered my own peculiar susceptibility, to bodies that speak without talking. I got it. Dance totally absorbed me, all of me—intellectually, emotionally, kinesthetically. Second, because it was obviously impossible to write about.

So I enrolled in dance classes and cross-registered for dance history courses. I volunteered at Pittsburgh Ballet Theatre, where I sat in on classes and rehearsals. Thanks to People Express airline, I could fly home weekends from Pittsburgh to New Jersey to catch my first glimpse of Merce Cunningham at the McCarter Theatre in Princeton or Suzanne Farrell and Peter Martins at the New York City Ballet. I clipped dance reviews from the *New York Times* and the *New Yorker* and taped them into huge three-ring binders.

I had stumbled across the *New Yorker* in high school, amidst the library's shelves of current periodicals. A single "Talk of the Town" piece, recounting a milkman's rounds, claimed me for nonfiction. I aspired to write so well—with such seemingly transparent apprehension—as to render a milkman's rounds worth a dozen column inches.

For me, writing has always been "about" something. I studied literature, then art, then dance, and paused here. Dance seemed far afield from my academically oriented upbringing, but, then again, I had been a mad fan of high school wrestling and professional tennis. These sports, like dance, require a convergence of mind and body. As games of solo strategy, they depend upon a player's sensitivity to dynamic interplay. One's stroke, or one's move on the mat, happens in response to and anticipation of the opponent's. Decisions become coincident with action. In sports this sense of palpable necessity is known as "the zone." In dance, it's called "presence." Observing how the body thinks and the mind moves remains my unexhausted fascination.

What was it about that *New Yorker* piece? It showed me what writing can achieve: that, by deeply and devotedly observing the world, the writer enlarges that world. Dance gives us the world under glass. Because it is enclosed, dance is easier to see than the apparent randomness and infinity of everyday life. At the same time, it is also harder to see because of its semantic density. Dance is distilled social relations, writ large and buck naked. As such, it magnifies questions of identity and culture. Dance can register our faintest tremors, revealing the unruly desires and gaping vulnerabilities that we spend so much energy trying to hide, and deny.

I am a person of language and logic in thrall to the murmurs of the body. They alert me to my remote sensations, relieve my too-rational habits, and remind me of my damped desires. Unlocking the dance is tantamount to unlocking myself. Some people challenge themselves in extreme sports. For me, it's experimental dance. Can I fine-tune myself to a new expressive frequency? Can I bring to this dance what it needs in order to be seen? In the process, I become more visible to myself.

My primal scene of criticism came in the seventh grade, in religion class at St. Christopher School in Parsippany, New Jersey. We were assigned an essay on an article of our choice from the diocesan newspaper; in order to avoid the subject at hand, I picked a music review of Roberta Flack's "Killing Me Softly." I was astonished by how much the reviewer could find to discuss in a three-minute pop song and how much more interesting it then became to me. That review—a close reading of the lyrics—initiated me into the twin towers of criticism: identification and interpretation. It taught me that there is a universe of significance in a song and that this significance is called into being by an empathic writer/commentator: the critic.

Flack's plaintive phrasing is easy to recall. With it, she transforms the song from adolescent infatuation into performance theory. She captures the critic's exquisite longing—both painful and pleasurable—for the performer who sings a good song, who has a style. And when the critic is seduced by the performer, or, perhaps more accurately, by her own desire to perfectly possess that style, she experiences immanent obliteration. "Killing Me Softly" is an allegory of critical erotics.

When I'm anxious, I organize. If my desktop is in order, anyone else's will do. Criticism, not dissimilarly, is about sorting out the morass of perception into something orderly and interesting. It's about discerning relationships and making meaning. A dance critic must listen long and hard to a dance (at least, to an experimental dance) in order to discover how it needs to be understood. In this sense, criticism takes a deferential position. After all, I'm not the topic of conversation, the dance is. And yet here I am center stage, proffering what I saw, what I felt, and what I thought. Criticism is the practice of appearing to disappear.

Experience ripens the critical sensibility—its eye, its ground for understanding, its accumulated knowledge, its personal voice. If youthful criticism gains by its fresh perspective—the expansiveness of the beginner's mind—mature criticism gains by its complexity and self-assurance. After twenty years, it is still the beginner's mind that appeals to me. That's the flow I seek in critical practice, when an unfamiliar performance requires me to find or create new pathways out into the world.

I find it difficult to try to separate the perceiving from the writing, because it's in the writing that I figure out what I know about a dance. At some point, the dance becomes a prompt for the words. I love it when the words take the lead. With eyes closed, I feel them approaching, their weight and rhythms taking form and taking possession. I write about dance because I prefer verbs, and moving targets. I thrill to sentence structure: syntax is, after all, about moveable parts.

The dancing I love best is the kind that's so physical it becomes metaphysical. Some years ago I tortuously belabored the point in a conference paper I delivered. Afterward, a fellow panelist's husband—he had attended our session—approached me. "Of course," he said. "I only look at the dancers' bodies when there's nothing else to see."

I like to watch, and I love to learn. In dance I found an experience that engages my eyes and mind equally. Dance provided me with a way to analyze gender representation and to research American cultural history. I've learned about all kinds of beauty and about power—the power of illusion as well as the illusion of power. As a cultural practice, dance yields endless material for both the journalist and the scholar. I've never given up either writing practice, trained as I am in both of them, and over time I have worked to hybridize their respective strengths, the clarity of journalism with the rigor of scholarship.

Despite the clarity, despite the rigor, the words fail. Encountering the ineffable, the words fail to deliver my experience of it. From the beginning, this paradox was the better part of my attraction to dance criticism. Initially I was invigorated by the writerly challenge, which I must have expected to someday overcome; nowadays, I can more ably refuse the impossible burden of translation, although the sense of dispossession lingers. I read a lot of Artaud. "All true feeling is in reality untranslatable. To express it is to betray it. But to translate it is to dissimulate it. True expression hides what it makes manifest.... This is why true beauty never strikes us directly. The setting sun is beautiful because of all it makes us lose." [1]

Choreographer Neil Greenberg once suggested to me that dance criticism is an attempt to stave off such loss, because the dance critic, whose passion is for the fleeting, unrepeatable moment, insists on trying to repeat it. But I don't think that dance is any more fleeting and unrepeatable than any other aesthetic experience, and I don't think that criticism marks a discontinuity with the dance. Criticism is a gesture that carries the dance beyond its curtain time, extending it to readers near and far, present and future. Criticism transfigures dance into a much larger, discursive existence. (For Allan Kaprow, even Happenings remained in circulation as "leftover thoughts in the form of gossip." [2])

Ultimately, the critical gesture is the best we can ever hope for: that someone will pay attention. I lean in, the dancer's double and the reader's surrogate, offering myself to be written upon by the dance and, in turn, to write it. I partake in what Merleau-Ponty calls the "flesh of the world." His description of perception is as accurate an account of the critical act as I have found: "[I] *follow with my eyes* the movements and the contours of the things themselves, this magical relation, this pact between them and me according to which I lend them my body in order that they inscribe upon it and give me their resemblance."[3] From a distance, the critic is poised, porous, and, as Deb Margolin correctly suspects, wanting to touch and be touched. It is a surpassing gesture, like Pollock's excursive stroke, the one that touches without making contact.

THE ARTICLES reprinted here were published between 1985 and 2001. They have not been substantively revised or updated. I want them to remain as they were originally written, despite the temptation of hindsight, just as I want to refuse the tidy distinction between scholarship and journalism. The value of these writings, as I see it, stretches beyond the reach of any given piece, to the larger tales they tell as a collection. These reviews and articles and interviews and essays constitute an autobiography of sorts, of a writer's fondnesses and vulnerabilities. They recount how, during the 1980s and 1990s, choreographers expanded their attention from formal to social concerns. And then, too, they plot the transformation of dance studies in the academy from historical documentation to cultural criticism. My commitment to feminist critical theory is chronicled from first flush to second thoughts.

The book is organized as a triptych: "Writing Dance," "Making History," and "Theorizing Gender." "Writing Dance" includes pieces that directly engage the art, whether in the form of a concert, book, or exhibit. My research on Isadora Duncan is gathered in "Making History." "Theorizing Gender" charts the trajectory of my engagement with feminist critical theory. Insofar as this boundary-making fails (there is an essay on Duncan in the gender theory section; feminist theory shows up regularly in the reviews; and both the historical and theoretical work depends upon critical practice), I succeed in making my point that the project of criticism exceeds disciplinary and methodological allegiances. The categories of "criticism," "history," and "theory" are but three incarnations of the same quest for meaning.

On my own journey, I have benefited from the generosity of a lifetime of teachers, editors, colleagues, artists, friends, and family members. To them I offer my profound gratitude.

To the high school teachers and university professors who inspired, encouraged, and taught me to write: Ms. Holub, Mrs. Abitabilo, and Linda Lee at Parsippany Hills High School; to Mrs. Ingram, Mr. K., Professor McCarthy, Mrs. Parker, and Mrs. Peterson at Duquesne University. Especially to Mrs. Parker, who used my first paper in honors English as an in-class example of how-not-to. She wrote at the end of that paper: "Never sacrifice clarity, accuracy, meaning, for writing which sounds good, intelligent, knowledgeable. Remember that the purpose of language is to convey/reveal truth, not to obfuscate and confuse."

To Selma Odom, at York University, whose precision and elegance of thought has sustained me since the very beginning, when I enrolled in her two-semester tour de force, "History and Theory of Dance Criticism." Twenty years later, she provided insightful comments on this manuscript.

To Marcia B. Siegel, at New York University, a devoted and demanding mentor. To put it starkly: she taught me how to see dance, and how to write about it. Her work continues to inspire me, and her comments on this manuscript challenged me—as always—to go further and deeper.

To my other professors at NYU's Department of Performance Studies: Barbara Kirshenblatt-Gimblett, who taught me to read; Peggy Phelan, who taught me to theorize; and Richard Schechner, who taught me to argue. Kate Davy initiated me into feminist critical theory, and Deborah Jowitt introduced me to Martha Graham and modern dance history.

To my editors and fellow writers at the *Pittsburgh Press,* especially Ann Butler and Jim Davidson. They exemplified for me at a formative moment of my career the highest professional standards as writers and reporters.

To my subsequent editors, for offering me those golden opportunities to write: Robert Boyd, Joan Catapano, Louis Dubose, Steven Durland, Marianne Goldberg, Annette Grant, Kim Grover Haskin, Will Joyner, Michael King, Julie Malnig, Bonnie Marranca, Carol Martin, Gerald Myers, Ann Nugent, Mariellen R. Sandford, Richard Schechner, Laurence Senelick, Suzanna Tamminen, Alexandra Tomalonis, and Elizabeth Zimmer. To Richard Schechner I owe a special debt, for cultivating my scholarship over many years and providing such an honored and congenial place as *TDR: The Journal of Performance Studies* to publish it.

To Suzanna Tamminen, editor at Wesleyan University Press, for making a reality out of my vague gestures toward this collection.

To my colleagues at the University of Texas at Austin: Oscar G. Brockett, Charlotte Canning, Jill Dolan, and Stacy Wolf. They provide the good-humored intellectual community that every critic/scholar needs in order to thrive. To Theatre and Dance Chair Richard Isackes, for awarding me a Dean's Fellowship in Spring 2001, when this volume was prepared. The university has provided consistent support for my research and writing, through grants from the Vice President for Research, the College of Fine Arts, the Theatre and Dance Department, and the Morton Brown Fund.

To my friends-turned-colleagues and colleagues-turned-friends, a dependable and delightful source of writerly support: Lynn Garafola, Saundra Goldman, Deb Margolin, Carol Martin, Leslie Satin, and Jon Whitmore. Nicole Plett went so far as to read and provide trenchant commentary on the introduction to this collection.

To the many choreographers, dancers, performers, and artists who make my work possible, and worthwhile. Especially Pina Bausch, Bill T. Jones, and Ralph Lemon, who granted me such generous access to their work. Deborah Hay is a remarkable artist and friend who keeps me awake and playing.

To the photographers who contributed their vision to these pages, especially Emma Dodge Hanson. And to Joann McNamara, for her probing interview questions.

To Ross Baldick, for reminding me what is truly important.

To my parents, gone all too soon. Their belief in me made all the difference.

—August 2001

LOOKING UNDERNEATH
THE ITCH TO CRITICIZE

Deb Margolin has poised herself at the brink this time. Not that the performance artist has ever shied from charged material—pregnancy, being Jewish, a collaboration entitled *Lesbians Who Kill*. But an artist, taking on the subject of criticism? She might as well rush headlong into a hungry propeller.

"I'm scared to death," she acknowledges. "I'm terrified that the critics are going to hate it. But, ever forward."

Critical Mass, which opened 27 February and runs Thursday through next Sunday at P.S. 122 in the East Village, theatricalizes Ms. Margolin's struggle to understand the all-too-human impulse to criticize. Her starting point is a biting left-handed compliment she received several years ago about her unusually handsome son, who was then two: "God is good! That a person who looks like you could have a child who looks like that!" The remark, she says, flexed the same "muscles of hope" she had developed as a child in defensive response to her "very critical" mother. (Talking, for Ms. Margolin, seems to involve absorbing the world through her own critical eye, then squeezing it out through her pores in a language so sinewy it almost aches.)

In *Critical Mass*, directed by Jamie Leo, Ms. Margolin attributes the impulse to criticize to the fear of death and the fear of God but mostly to the fear of beauty. "I want to go inside that terror," says the author, forty-three. "Perhaps one of the reasons it compels me so much is that I was raised inside the needle point of that terror, and because I continue to see its evidence in larger, more diffuse form. I see it in sexism. That's fear of beauty."

Criticism, Ms. Margolin proposes, is a substitute for the need to touch and be touched; it turns nasty when the object of desire beckons beyond reach: "So instead, you try to make it smaller, or make it go away, because unrequited desire is an unbearable burden sometimes."

Ms. Margolin, who is married and has two small children, grew up in Westchester County and majored in English at New York University. She began making her reputation as a writer and performer in the burgeoning downtown performance scene of the 1980s. A founding member of the feminist Split Britches Theater Company, she started creating solo pieces in 1987.

Last spring she performed a monologue entitled *O Wholly Night and Other Jewish Solecisms*, commissioned by the Jewish Museum in Manhattan; three years ago she presented four monologues called *Of Mice, Bugs and Women*. Today, she rides the Red and Tan bus line into Port Authority in Manhattan "from some distant and bizarre community in New Jersey."

At least that's the way she describes Montvale in *Critical Mass,* a bulging collage of monologues, stage business, and scenes in which six actors, including the author, play a revolving cast of characters, anchored by a Performer and a Theater Critic. They reenact the Holy Family in the manger; they watch a television show, "Critically Incorrect"; the Performer fends off her nagging mother as well as an attack of makeup artists; the Theater Critic visits a psychiatrist. Even the "God is good" woman gets her say ("I don't even know why, but there's a scream running down the center of me like hot sap from deep inside a maple tree!").

Although criticism is just a pretext for Ms. Margolin's obsessions with death, beauty, time, God, sex, and desire (What else is there to talk about?), smack in the middle of the stage sits the Theater Critic, in a chair marked "Reserved," scribbling furiously and crunching a candy wrapper. He is an obvious conceit through which Ms. Margolin explores the complex motivations behind any critical act. But in truth, she says, "we are all critics."

—*New York Times,* 1997

WRITING ABOUT DANCE

An Urgent, High-Profile Opportunity

IT IS THE nature of panel discussions to raise more questions than they answer, and the "German and American Modern Dance: Yesterday and Today" symposium held 8 November 1985 at Goethe House New York was no exception. The "Today" session in particular was a diffuse, emotionally charged exchange. The massively hyped appearances of Pina Bausch, Reinhild Hoffmann, Susanne Linke, and Mechthild Grossmann at the Brooklyn Academy of Music in Fall 1985 polarized the American and German critical and intellectual communities in what became almost a matter of nationalistic self-righteousness.

The panel discussion inevitably crisscrossed over many fundamental issues that were left unprobed: the capacity of movement to express a range of things other than emotion, the capacity of dance to connote, the nature of the relation between reading dance patterns and reading everyday interaction, the relation between form and content, what constitutes form and structure, the lingering influence of modernism on current American dance, the distinction between realism and naturalism, the influence of German neo-expressionist artists on tanztheater, whether or not there are absolute aesthetic values across cultures, and the way culture shapes our ability to read movement.

Ideally, the Goethe House symposium would be a springboard for extended discourse on these issues where they can best be pursued—in print. Tanztheater has presented American dance scholars and critics with an urgent, high-profile opportunity unavailable since the rise of formalism two decades ago to probe some fundamentals of dance aesthetics. In the early 1970s, writers riding the crest of the dance boom regularly decried the lack of dance literature and the generally accepted notion of dance as a field for sensual but not intellectual inquiry. Despite their efforts, dance aesthetics has taken a backslide, along with the dance boom.

Today, the potential growth of dance scholarship and criticism is thwarted by a near absence of publishing opportunities. Some of our most brilliant writers cannot find willing book publishers. If the space in American journals for one-shot reviews is slim, the space for analysis is downright anorexic. *Ballet News* folded in March, and *Dance Magazine* is overrun with personality pieces and fashion tips. The quarterly *Ballet Review*—the most serious and valuable of American dance journals—tends toward interviews and historical pieces. The debate over contemporary dance is left to the daily press, which, according to a survey conducted by Marcia B. Siegel for the 1984 Dance Critics Association Conference, is devoting much more space to promotional features than reviews. But overnight reviews can only go so far; the best they can do in such short time and space is to deal with the performance at hand. A dance literature cannot be developed without think pieces and essays, which are a seriously endangered species in this country. The dance source most often quoted nowadays is the West German *Ballett International,* whose unabashedly intellectual (and partisan) essays on tanztheater no doubt contributed to the form's rise and notoriety.

It's not just the lack of publishing opportunities that is strangling the dance discipline as an intellectual endeavor. Working hand in hand with the lowly position of dance in American culture at large is a lack of training for dance scholars and critics. The situation is a catch-22. Graduate degrees that go beyond dance history and technical training to analysis and aesthetics in a broad cultural context have been available for a very short time in a very few places, and, as a result, the field of candidates with the requisite Ph.D.s to expand existing graduate programs or start new ones is still slim pickins. Though the situation is slowly improving, dance is still nowhere as established a field as theater.

Dance is a discipline that still hasn't made contact with major twentieth-century thought such as semiotics and deconstruction. It is a discipline where you can still find Curt Sachs's work being taught as fact rather than discredited theory, where you can find an article in the prestigious *Smithsonian* magazine heralding everyday movement as a current trend rather than a twenty-year-old innovation on the way out. Dance is a discipline that has been so busy trying to recapture its past that it often overlooks the challenges of the present.

The narrow scope of dance thinking isolates it from the rest of the arts and the culture, only reinforcing dance's bottom-rung status. A number of respected, general interest journals regularly cover the arts, but not even a handful of them include dance. Some scholars believe that the only way to break out of this dance "ghetto" is to embed dance in theater and other performance genre thinking. That, however, would only subsume dance before it gains its own authority. One way it can make some progress now is for writers to pursue the issues raised by the Goethe House panel discussion. Selma Jeanne Cohen, David Best, and Nelson Goodman have already broken important ground in dance aesthetics, but too few are working this fertile territory.

TDR is a journal where writers can cultivate a dance literature. We are looking for creative, expansive, rigorous thinking about dance. Rigorous but still very much in touch with the sensuous experience of movement. *TDR* aims to engage its writers and readers in an ongoing discourse on dance, beginning with this call for articles and a special "Movement Analysis" issue planned for next year.

—*TDR: The Journal of Performance Studies,* 1986

REVIEW: DIANA THEODORES'S *FIRST WE TAKE MANHATTAN*, JILL JOHNSTON'S *MARMALADE ME*, AND LYNNE CONNER'S *SPREADING THE GOSPEL OF THE MODERN DANCE*

D ANCE CRITICISM in this country has rarely been considered a literary practice, so it's no surprise that the genre has barely established a literature of its own. We have a very modest library of anthologies by twentieth-century critics, ranging from pioneers such as H. T. Parker, Carl Van Vechten, and Lincoln Kirstein (John Martin's reviews remain uncollected) through to contemporaries such as Arlene Croce, Deborah Jowitt, and Marcia B. Siegel. But only Edwin Denby and Jill Johnston are generally acknowledged as serious writers, rather than just dance critics. Denby was a poet, and his reviews and essays reflect that penetrating and imaginative sensibility. Johnston, caught up in the experimental blast of the early 1960s, pressed the limits of criticism by treating it as a primary, rather than secondary, literary genre.

Wesleyan University Press has reissued *Marmalade Me* (1998), Johnston's classic collection of *Village Voice* reviews from the 1960s. In addition, two recent academic studies have significantly forwarded American dance criticism as a practice to be documented, theorized, and critiqued.

This trio of books, along with a much larger number of dust-gathering theses and dissertations, bespeaks an impatient longing for recognition from the larger domains of art and criticism. Judging from the choices in Maurice Berger's *The Crisis of Criticism*,[1] however, that validation remains but a schoolgirl fantasy. This anthology (which inspired a *New York Times* article exploring the decline of American arts criticism[2]) was prompted by Arlene Croce's infamous temper tantrum about Bill T. Jones's *Still/Here* in the *New Yorker* back in 1995. ("Discussing the Undiscussable" was Croce's way of taking her marbles and going home, because artists had dared to move from the 1950s to the 1990s without requesting her permission.[3]) None of the respondents in the volume is a dance critic. The good news is, we've caught the attention of bell hooks and Homi Bhabha. The bad news is, we'll for a long time be known as the folks who gave the world "victim art."

Of the three volumes, Lynne Conner's *Spreading the Gospel of the Modern Dance: Newspaper Dance Criticism in the United States, 1850–1934* (University of Pittsburgh Press, 1997) speaks most potently to the uncertain and uneasy relations between today's critics and choreographers, despite the fact that it examines the historical period furthest removed from ours. Conner treats that period of dance criticism as an institutional practice and defines dance as a community. If Croce's diatribe proved anything, it was that contemporary dance has lost any sense of community in which criticism claims a necessary function. (Certainly, the journalistic "general readership" has no use for it.) Conner's refiguring of modern dance as a discursive practice produced by a "reciprocal relationship" (109) between choreographer and critic provides us with a precedent for rethinking and reclaiming the relevance of criticism, not as a measuring rod apart, but as part of the same project.

Although Conner tackles a large expanse of time, her primary focus is 1927 to 1934, when critics and choreographers such as John Martin and Martha Graham were symbiotic partners in the invention of modern dance. Conner historicizes the situation effectively by tracing the evolving practices of newspaper dance coverage, including detailed analyses of its beginnings on the music pages and the work of pioneering critics H. T. Parker and Carl Van Vechten. She goes on to examine the generic shift from the dance column (a grab bag of listings, announcements, discussion, and audience education) to what we recognize today as dance criticism.

The first full-time critics—Martin at the *New York Times,* Mary F. Watkins at the *New York Herald Tribune,* and Lucile Marsh at the *New York World*—did not position themselves as "outsiders" writing for a faceless "readership." Rather, they were "insiders" writing to and for their own self-selected community, which included the dancers and choreographers about whom they wrote. Conner coins a third category of criticism, which she terms "prescriptive," to add to the usual distinction between "descriptive" and "evaluative" criticism:

> Like their dancing counterparts, these founding critics shared two defining similarities: they rejected the idea that they were writing a subspecies of music criticism; and they rejected traditional standards of journalistic objectivity in favor of a prescriptive and often proactive methodology. Despite their residencies on the music page, by the 1928 fall season each columnist was writing directly to the dance community (offering advice on everything from concert etiquette to how to structure their seasons) and *for* the dance community (taking up a number of causes on the dance community's behalf). Hired to report on the dance community in New York City, they quickly became members of that community, writing columns that functioned as instruments for the dissemination of ideas, information, and news to the early practitioners of the modern dance. (97; emphasis in original)

By 1930 they were writing on-the-night reviews, "with identifiable methodologies, styles, and theoretical agendas" (112).

The strength of the book is in Conner's close analysis of the material conditions of newspaper practice: what gets covered, how (report or review), by whom, in what section. She unravels the economic, social, and political forces at work, and demonstrates how tone, style, length, authorship (signed or unsigned), and even type of headline factored into the change from objective reporting to subjective advocacy.

Working within that prescriptive mode, critics succeeded in forging a vocabulary for describing modern dance as well as a theory for understanding it. By 1934, however, dance criticism had become professionalized and the ideal of critical advocacy replaced with that of canonical standards. There came a strong backlash against the partisanship epitomized by Martin, now the only remaining full-time dance critic on a New York City daily. "After 1934, the balance shifted," Conner concludes, "the line of development diverged, and the relationship between art form and critical discourse obscured. But that is another story" (132).

Conner tells her story admirably, but it's not the whole story. There remains the "other" modern dance community that lost out in the polemical war between Graham/Martin formalism and politically committed choreographers such as Jane Dudley and critic Edna Ocko. Their work has only recently been theorized by Susan Manning and documented by Ellen Graff. *Spreading the Gospel* is indeed required reading on the history of modern dance, but it needs to be read in tandem with Manning's *Ecstasy and the Demon* and Graff's *Stepping Left.*[4]

Diana Theodores's book resumes the story of dance criticism in New York a quarter century later, with Arlene Croce, Nancy Goldner, Deborah Jowitt, and Marcia B. Siegel. The title sets the tone: *First We Take Manhattan: Four American Women and the New York School of Dance Criticism* (Harwood Academic Publishers, 1996) aims to retrieve the glory of this "Golden Age of Dance." The notion of a "New York School" of dance criticism is an obvious bid for legitimation and the project an implicit rebuttal to what Theodores rightly observes as "the more current argument, that descriptive criticism is minimalist, impressionist or anti-theoretical" (54) and the fact that this formalist body of work from the 1970s has been "relegated to an irrelevant status" (57). She wants to restore Croce et al. to the pantheon:

> They created a new critical dance language, a new rigor of investigation in responding to dance, and an aesthetic sensibility so persuasive and influential that a whole generation of dance viewers and critics alike, from the late 1960s to the end of the 1980s, marveled at the prolific and profound nature of the *Golden Age of Dance* in New York. . . . The championing of the *American classicists*, the *permission* to be passionate and majestically subjective in dance criticism, the prolonged attention to description and analysis—the virtual inhaling of dances, and the reading of dances for what they in themselves could offer up for meaning, for theory, for contextual considerations—these things were their legacy. (1; emphasis in original)

Unfortunately, Theodores's reach surpasses her grasp. It is precisely because I agree that these critics are so significant that I find the volume disappointing in the depth and breadth of the analysis it musters to make the case. A tad too enamored of her subjects, the author asserts more than her analysis will support, especially when she looks at the critics "as women."

Working independently of each other (with the exception of Siegel and Jowitt, who are close colleagues and friends), these four dance critics stood at the center of the efflorescence of dance criticism from 1965 to 1985. Croce founded *Ballet Review* in 1965 and began writing for the *New Yorker* in 1973; Goldner covered dance for the *Nation* and the *Christian Science Monitor;* Jowitt started writing for the *Village Voice* in 1967, and remains there; Siegel edited *Dance Scope* from 1963 to 1966 and then wrote for publications such as the *Soho Weekly News,* the *Hudson Review,* and *New York Magazine.*

Theodores spends the first half of the book providing background on the formalist milieu marked by Denby and George Balanchine (the ballet equivalent of the Martin-Graham partnership), in order then to set up the "New York School" as a kind of manifest destiny of the classical tradition. As a result, the critics' similarities tend to be overstated, at the expense of their important and enlivening differences.

The latter half of the book is devoted to "files" on the individual critics, whose own voices begin to emerge. Unfortunately, Theodores depends more on content than literary analysis to animate her subjects' writings. Alongside *First We Take Manhattan,* I was reading Clifford Geertz's *Works and Lives: The Anthropologist As Author*—a brilliant close reading of landmark ethnography.[5] What Geertz has done for Levi-Strauss, Evans-Pritchard, Malinowski, and Benedict, someone still needs to do for Croce, Goldner, Jowitt, and Siegel.

Theodores argues that they established what she calls, after Croce, a "critical repertory," which is an idiosyncratic way of describing canon formation, based on the critical functions of comparison and judgement. Without explicitly saying so, Theodores employs the paradigm of connoisseurship, in which the "great works" are inscribed into literacy.

First We Take Manhattan raises more questions than it could potentially answer, not only because the question of what constitutes a "school" is never problematized, but also because it forestalls its story in 1985. It ignores what has happened to these critics (Croce's "victim art" controversy is mentioned only in passing), which would reveal so much more about the "Golden Age." We could use our distance from that era to ask pertinent questions about then, and now. Why, for example, is Croce no longer reviewing dance? Why did Siegel turn to world dance? Why don't we have such strong critical voices in journalism anymore?

When Theodores concludes that "the spirit of their mission, both celebratory and prudent, has yielded a critical repertory" (161), I wonder: Of what use is that critical repertory today—as style, as theory, as history? What does critical discourse mean to us today, at a time when audiences are fractured, reviews have been supplanted by previews, anyone can become a critic by going on-line, Balanchine is long dead, and choreographers have shifted their concerns from the formal to the cultural?

Rereading *Marmalade Me* after a number of years, I was surprised by how much less the volume said to me about dance than it did about criticism. Not the pragmatics of the critical product, which Conner and Theodores take up, but the ontology of the critical project. Beyond the book's use-value as a historical record of modern and postmodern dance from 1960 to 1968—when Jill Johnston was dance critic for the *Village Voice*—*Marmalade Me* uniquely registers the untenable, unstable, unbearable condition of the critic, who is at once invisible and at the center of attention. Johnston, whose delicate psyche crashed several times that decade, experienced an Artaudian shattering of self that was embraced by the 1960s zeitgeist, which encouraged any kind of break with reality in the revolutionary hopes of dissolving boundaries and all that they implied. Signaling through the flames, Johnston calibrated the fluctuations of her personal and professional identities.

She started out, however, as a champion of José Limón modernism (a partisan in the Martin tradition) and a conventionally formalist reviewer ("capturing movement on the page, interpreting its character, and defining the structure of its choreographic frame" [xii]). That much is confirmed by the early reviews, eighteen of which are newly included in the expanded edition. But when she switched allegiances to Merce Cunningham and then the burgeoning Judson Dance Theater, she took seriously their aesthetic credo that meaning is made by the viewer and that anyone could be a performer. That made Johnston as much a performer as a spectator, and the line in between began to bleed. Invoking Norman O. Brown, she declared (in two different articles): "The solution to the problem of identity is, get lost" (11, 148).

She began interrogating language itself, with neologisms and puns and non sequiturs. She collaged "found" sentences. In fits and starts, she discovered a writing practice that "devoured the space formerly reserved for the deeds of others" (xiii). In "Critics Critics," written as a response to an article by Clive Barnes while she was institutionalized, Johnston surveyed her turf: "I also stake out a claim to be an artist, a writer, if that's what I'm doing when I get to the typewriter and decide that I liked something well enough to say what I think it's all about" (123).

Testimony to the impossibility of the critical act is tucked into the crevices and linings and pockets of her writing, whose gaze turned from the object out there onstage back to her own self. What makes her oeuvre so important is that it is a meditation on the origins of art, self, and writing. It questions criticism—and all writing—as an inscription of the self onto the world. It wonders aloud about the nature of creation, whether of a poem or a self. In the case of the critic, the double bind is that we must know the dance so well as to impersonate it and at the same time remain in our seats. Johnston nailed the paradox by making the distinction between "seeing" and "entering," which, she writes, is "the crucial transition" (28). How can we enter, as critics must, without crossing the threshold of sameness? And is it our sameness, or that of the dance, that we are approaching? The critic's psyche is, by definition, a delicate thing.

By 1968, Johnston was writing about "the general sickness of the resigned passive spectator, rendered impotent by his own repudiation of responsibility to act, to participate, to become himself the center of his own attention" (202). She had made the move to the explicitly autobiographical writing she took up after leaving the *Voice*—even though, as she made plain, "I think I'm writing more intensively about dancing than ever before" (216). It was the formalists' insistence on erasing the line between performer and spectator that enabled Johnston, ironically, to abandon formalism. Revelation of self, including gender and sexuality, became a political and critical responsibility for Johnston when she returned to dance and art criticism eighteen years later.

Unlike Croce, Johnston has evolved with the arts community; hers is a criticism of identity politics, practiced through the lens of auto/biography.[6] But she doesn't see that contemporary dance has the critics it deserves:

> Dance criticism is not yet addressing major changes in the way dances are presented which challenge old concepts. Dance criticism continues to deal, primarily, with the formal and qualitative aspects of the medium: the way dances look, the way dancers dance, the themes of the works and so on, handled descriptively. Much good criticism is done here. But if criticism doesn't address the central and assumed values—i.e., the political underlying content of every work—it is, I believe, operating in a holding pattern, not keeping up with and contributing to the social revolutionary changes of our time.[7]

Johnston brings us full circle, back to Martin and a "reciprocal relationship" between critic and choreographer. She may have rejected formalist modern dance criticism in favor of postmodernism, but she has effectively recuperated the early 1930s model of critical advocacy. "Reviewers and choreographers should be part of a mutually cooperative community," she insists, "working together to help enlighten audiences."[8]

—*TDR: The Journal of Performance Studies*, 1999

THE INTERESTED ACT OF
DANCE CRITICISM

I admit that I am tired of Western culture. I think Western culture is tired. I think it's at a point where it's played out. Or at least this phase of it. . . . [B]allet and modern dance as we've understood it is in a fallow period.

MARCIA B. SIEGEL,
"Looking at Dance from All Sides Now"

The Present, By Way of an Introduction

A S WE NEAR the millennium, American dance critics are hungry for something to sink their teeth into. It has been more than a decade since George Balanchine's death, and the excitement stirred several years ago by the announcement of the New York City Ballet's Balanchine Retrospective Festival only served to underscore the waning of significant activity in classical ballet. In modern dance, the deaths of Martha Graham and Alvin Ailey effectively have brought to a close the era of classical modern dance. As for postmodern dance, it is a thirty-something-year-old revolution that has settled comfortably into its maturity; the younger generations' own agendas have yet to reach critical mass. As a species, critics tend to seek the fresh and the challenging; they want to engage with art that pushes the horizon line in some way, either within a certain genre or against generic boundaries altogether. It is no coincidence, I think, that against the stable—some even say stagnant—backdrop of current dance in our own high culture, critics have turned with increasing seriousness toward world dance.[1]

Such interest, no doubt informed by the current call in the United States for multicultural awareness, has become evident in recent festivals, conferences, and professional discourse. The 1990 Los Angeles Festival, for example, devoted itself to the performing arts of the Pacific Rim. Concurrent with the festival, the Dance Critics Association (DCA) held its annual conference, entitled "Looking Out: Critical Perspectives on World Dance." In her conference epilogue, critic Marcia B. Siegel summarized its underlying theme: fear of the Other, in many forms—fear that our "high art," our norms and criteria and hierarchy, and our position as standard-setters, will be questioned and de-privileged.[2] Most of the country's dance critical community gathered there in Los Angeles to attend rare performances and to explore the issues of culture, authenticity, and critical frameworks—issues that had been broached in previous DCA conferences and that continue to be raised, in articles such as critic June Vail's "World Dance: We'll Understand It When We Recognize That Bop and Ballroom Are Ethnic, Too," in which she pointedly asks: "How do we understand what we see? Should we try to figure it out, or are we allowed to sit back and enjoy the show? As outsiders how can we judge quality—by their standards or ours?"[3] Not since the early 1970s has so much attention been paid to dance criticism.

The increasingly frequent encounter between American critic and non-Western dance raises essential epistemological issues. It challenges our assumptions about the disinterestedness of the critical act, about the objectivity and universality of standards, about what constitutes "dance," and about the very status of "truth." It points to the complexity of the critical process: how observation, analysis, interpretation, and judgement are inextricably inter-mingled. And, perhaps most of all, it calls into serious question the notion of "art" as a realm disconnected from the rest of the social world.

Most recently, these questions have found their way from dance into the art world at large, through the now-landmark *New Yorker* article of Arlene Croce entitled "Discussing the Undiscussable," in which she reviewed a performance of Bill T. Jones, entitled *Still/Here,* which she had refused to attend.[4] In her non-review-cum-manifesto, Croce argues for an ideal, distanced, mimetic aesthetic, in which "the line between theatre and reality"[5] is never crossed and in which the critic's job is to judge. According to Croce, Jones's dance, which incorporates the stories of people with terminal illnesses, steps beyond the realm of art and criticism because real stories of real people cannot be evaluated as art. The article is "a plea for the critic,"[6] whom she sees as a disinterested third party to the artist and the spectator, whose job it is to perform "formal evaluation."[7] For Croce, the "art spectacle"[8] is insulated from ideology; it is about the individual rather than the group: social context is irrelevant.

The questions, raised by what I call an ethnographic approach to criticism and by Croce's canonical rebuttal, are the very questions that can be used to analyze *any* of our dance critical traditions. American dance criticism has a rich history—perhaps as rich as American dance itself. And certainly we lack a full understanding of dance history unless we understand how criticism has served to shape and institutionalize dance. As a way to initiate a systematic study of these sometimes quite disparate critical aesthetics and practices and the way they mediate our knowledge of dance and dance history, I will first articulate the fundamental questions posed by ethnographic criticism, and then use those questions to examine three other modes of dance criticism: canon, descriptive, and feminist.

Ethnographic Criticism

DEMOGRAPHICS HAVE finally caught up with the dance world. At the DCA's annual meetings over the past ten years, we heard more and more from struggling critics in cities such as Miami, San Antonio, and Los Angeles. They were struggling to cope with an increasing number of performances out of their own (largely white, middle-class) traditions, and with a similarly shifting readership. These challenges, however, are no longer unique to the border states. Critics from all over the country have begun recounting their situations and articulating an array of questions.[9] Nicole Plett, for example, a longtime New Mexico critic and sometime observer of Pueblo ritual dances, asked "persistent questions about how to look at and experience ritual dance—or whether these two concepts are perhaps mutually exclusive. How and why does one write on ritual dance? Who actually has permission to write on ritual dance?"[10]

The dance world had barely begun heeding dance ethnologist Joann Kealiinohomoku's admonishment, issued some twenty-five years ago, that terms such as "ethnic dance" are thinly veiled products of ethnocentrism, when we were faced with a true test of our understanding.[11] As long as we were writing about dancesfrom within our own tradition, the rules were clear—even if they were so embedded as to remain unspoken. But when faced with wayang wong of Central Java, or Indian kutiyattam, our professional directives seemed to come unmoored. Suddenly having become the outsider, what was the critic to do? Leave the review at the level of description? Attempt analysis? Risk interpretation? On what basis could one judge? Perhaps it was first the feeling of ignorance that bothered us. But clearly it was a matter of arrogance to attempt analysis, interpretation, or judgement without sufficient contextual knowedge.[12] As performer/critic Sal Murgiyanto, of the Jakarta Institute of the Arts, has pointed out, cross-cultural criticism is a matter of power:

> Seeing and writing are basic requirements for a dance critic. When a critic begins to judge, he [sic] must decide for whom he writes and how deep is his knowledge of the dance. Instead of acknowledging his limitations and using common dance criteria with which he is familiar, a critic might conclude that the dance is confusing—when it is he who is confused. And with the pen in one's hand, one has the power to blame. In writing about world dance, it is wise to consider the way natives look at their own dances.[13]

Considering the way insiders look at their own dances requires a shift in the critic's position: she is no longer judge, but rather interpreter.

Interpretation was the subject of anthropologist Clifford Geertz's landmark essay entitled "Thick Description: Toward an Interpretive Theory of Culture."[14] With its insistence on culture, rather than on individuals, as the matrix of meaning, the essay had already infiltrated many of the other arts, humanities, and social sciences, before being taken up by dance critics. All behavior, Geertz pointed out, whether a Balinese cockfight or a Balanchine ballet, is cultural behavior. Thus a "thin" description, which isolates behaviors and sticks to the level of surface appearances, remains wholly insufficient to the task of deciphering meaning. "Thick" description, on the other hand, is an interpretive activity that finds the meaning of a behavior as it is nested within a stratified hierarchy of cultural structures. Rather than distracting us from the dancing, viewing dance contextually brings us closer to it. For, as Geertz wrote, "A good interpretation of anything—a poem, a person, a history, a ritual, an institution, a society—takes us into the heart of that of which it is the interpretation."[15]

Geertz's culture-centered paradigm makes sense for the changing field of dance, for, as critic Brenda Dixon-Gottschild has observed, "The issues critics now face are economic and social as well as aesthetic. More than ever we are confronted with dancers and choreographers coming from many different cultural sources, and it behooves us to understand our role as mediator between them and our readership—to be versed in criteria other than the ones we grew up with or even prefer."[16] Redefining what we do as an active process of mediation (a *critical act*), rather than as a passive and transparent medium (*criticism*), underscores the conscious, embodied, and, consequently, interested nature of the activity. If the critical act is thus an intervention, as it were, into the meaning of a dance, then it benefits us to examine what kind of intervention a particular critic is making in the dances she is reviewing. We can, and should, read between the lines for a critic's ideology, or implicit world view:

1. What does the critic see as the purpose of the critical act?
2. Which mode(s) of perception is (are) emphasized: description, analysis, interpretation, judgement?
3. Does the critic see the critical act as inclusive or exclusive?
4. Does the critic see the critical act as objective or subjective?
5. How is the critic's aesthetic related to her/his cultural context?

An ethnographic approach to the critical act aims to interpret the meaning of dance by positing dance as an expression (whether affirmatively or by negation) of cultural values, beliefs, and conventions. Spawned in an era of increasing cross-cultural awareness, it emphasizes interpretation, with the support of description and analysis—but definitely suspends judgement as inappropriate. Such an approach is inherently inclusivist, because all dance is equally, if distinctively, expressive of its culture (or subculture, as the case may be). By resituating the site of meaning-making from the individual spectator or critic to the culture, ethnographic criticism dismantles the dichotomy between the world as subjectively constructed by the critic or objectively given by the dance. Both dance-maker and dance-critic are subsumed in a larger, cultural, field of meaning.

Even though ethnographic writing has different goals and subject matter than dance criticism,[17] its principles are still adaptable, not only for world dance, but for fusion and even avant-garde forms in our own culture, which may also seem "foreign" to the uninitiated. The point is that if we recuperate the critical act into the cultural field and recognize it as both a product and producer of cultural identity, then all dances and dance forms become potentially meaningful.

Canon Criticism

WHAT I CALL "canon criticism" is an approach that centers around the ideology and practice of connoisseurship. As plainly defined by *Webster's New Collegiate Dictionary,* a connoisseur is one who "understands the details, technique, or principles of an art and is competent to act as a critical judge." Canon criticism turns on the structure of judgement, in order to articulate, defend, and (possibly) expand an established canon of masters and their masterpieces ("the great works"). Thus the act of criticism becomes the enforcement of a set of standards regarded as universal and eternal, and, hence, objective. That is to say, it is a project of exclusivity. Much canon criticism has surrounded, for example, the question of whether or not Mark Morris is worthy to be elevated into the canon alongside the likes of George Balanchine and Paul Taylor.[18] At bottom, Arlene Croce's article "Discussing the Undiscussable" is a manifesto for canon criticism.

One of the clearest statements of canon criticism has been put forth by art critic Hilton Kramer, who left the *New York Times* to found, in 1982, a quarterly arts journal called the *New Criterion.* In his first editorial, Kramer defined this "new criterion" as the "criterion of truth." He looked back longingly toward "a time when criticism was more strictly concerned to distinguish achievement from failure, to identify and uphold a standard of quality, and to speak plainly and vigorously about the problems that beset the life of the arts and the life of the mind in our society."[19] Such an approach, he continued, seeks to maintain "independent high culture" unsullied by pop or commercial culture (a theme resuscitated this year by Croce), to counteract the left's "ideological impulse," and to support capitalism and democracy. Eschewing the notion that art embodies politics, Kramer advocated a criticism that strives for objectivity in the application of select aesthetic standards.

In our own field, André Levinson, Lincoln Kirstein, and, of course, Croce have been eloquent canon critics. In each case, as in others, it is no coincidence that this approach accompanies the embrace of ballet classicism. Canon criticism is well-suited to the classical ideology, which prizes tradition over the avant-garde. This is true even in the case of innovative classicists such as Balanchine, who are, despite their innovations, still maneuvering within what he called the "morality" of classicism.[20] The morality, or ideology, of classicism, as perpetuated in canon criticism, eschews self-expression (the realm of modern dance). Rather, its defining ethos is self-sacrifice to tradition: to a vocabulary and technique whose controlled manipulation through line, form, and structure—if judged favorably—functions as an aesthetic and social pedigree. In other words, the connoisseur's discerning judgement demonstrates her/his "taste."

But taste is not disembodied; it is a historical act. As French sociologist Pierre Bourdieu has convincingly demonstrated, "Taste classifies, and it classi-fies the classifier." [21] The classical attention to form over content attempts to dis-connect the critic's eye from its social basis, assuming the existence of a "pure gaze" that discerns quality apart from any historical (social, political, economic) circum-stances. But taste is a product of education and of social origin: a mark of class distinction. And, thus, the established hierarchy of aesthetics corresponds to a social hierarchy. The magical boundaries between high and low art and between legitimate and illegitimate art that are patrolled by canon criticism results in what Bourdieu calls "cultural consecration," which "does indeed confer on the objects, persons and situations it touches, a sort of ontological promotion akin to a transubstantiation." [22] This division in art—conscious or not—fulfills "a social function of legitimating social differences." [23]

This is one of the very points that choreographer Jawole Willa Jo Zollar made when she addressed the 1990 DCA conference: What is "classic"? What is the difference between a classic and a cliché? Does race have something to do with it? Zollar asked why "the words chassé, pas de bourrée, pirouette, and 32 fou-ettés (not 31 or 33) were never considered trite or cliché, but considered classic. So if in fact, a language had been developed from this [Alvin] Ailey influence, if I did [here Zollar demonstrates a movement], why was this not considered classic?" [24]

The relationship between the aesthetic and the social/political came to a boil in the dance field in a 1992 *Village Voice* dance supplement called "Something Borrowed." In an extended defense of Doug Elkins's persistent pastiche, critic Joan Acocella asserted that there is no difference between white choreographers borrowing from black aesthetics and black choreographers borrowing from white aesthetics. [25] In his own article, titled "Black Like Who?", critic, dancer, and choreog-rapher Gus Solomons Jr. stated that he has "moved beyond racial issues to explore movement as expression in itself, not as sociological or political theater." [26] As much as Solomons, I would like to believe in the possibility of "universal" art that "transcends" difference. But, given the state of the world and even the state of the dance world, I can only see that the disavowal of difference has served to legitimate some aesthetics (white ones) over all others. Furthermore, by cutting off dance from the life of the world within which it circulates, in the name of "abstraction" or "beauty," dance ghettoizes, and thus disempowers, itself.

I think that Solomons makes a dangerous distinction when he equates the intellect with "dance as a nonobjective discourse in the medium of motion" and the emotional with social/political awareness.[27] A progeny of Merce Cunningham (himself a classicist), Solomons seems to have inherited the early Cagean view that art must be untethered from worldly conditions. Choreographer-turned-filmmaker Yvonne Rainer, herself deeply influenced by Cage, nevertheless has pointed out the arrogance of an aesthetic that assumes a stance of indifference. If Cage extolled art as "a way of waking up to the very life we're living which is so excellent once one gets one's mind and one's desires out of its way and lets it act of its own accord,"[28] Rainer responded insistently:

> Let's not come down too heavily on the goofy naivete of such an utterance, on its invocation of J. J. Rousseau, on Cage's adherence to the messianic ideas of Bucky Fuller some years back, with their total ignoring of worldwide struggles for libera-tion and the realities of imperialist politics, on the suppression of the question, "*Whose* life is so excellent and at what cost to others?"[29]

Cage may have endeavored to defuse the tyranny of the Artist-as-God, Rainer argued, but his "refusal of meaning is an abandonment, an appeal to a Higher authority."[30] His gift to artists is a method to be used selectively rather than blindly, "not, however, so we may awaken to this excellent life; on the contrary, so we may the more readily awaken to the ways in which we have been led to believe that this life is so excellent, just, and right."[31]

Anyway, as *New York Times* critic Jack Anderson has pointed out, even the most rigorously formalist (classical) dances, such as Cunningham's, are not without meaning. "Works like Balanchine's magisterial 'Concerto Barocco' or the lyrical creations of Merce Cunningham, Erick Hawkins and Paul Taylor deserve to be treasured as visions of social harmony, and Alwin Nikolais's multimedia spectacles can be interpreted as studies of the intricate ways in which people respond to their environment. Some dances can assume a multitude of political shadings." Thus, he concluded, "the outside world—in all its complexity and contrariness and its possibilities for despair and glory—keeps bursting into dances."[32] I would go even further, to argue that any dance aesthetic—including the avowedly nonpo-litical—contains deeply embedded political and social assumptions. An aesthetic, however "abstract," is also an ideology that embraces the social and the political as well as the cultural. "Style," theater historian Joseph Roach has shown, "is social order as lived in the body."[33]

Descriptive Criticism

IN 1966, Susan Sontag published what turned out to be a manifesto of 1960s minimalism, from whose vehemently anti-expressive formalism she had taken her lead. "Against Interpretation" pleaded the case of form in art; in it Sontag aimed to free art from critics who insisted on wrenching content from every work they encountered. By defining the function of criticism as showing "how it is what it is" rather than "what it means," [34] Sontag insisted on a criticism of description and analysis. Interpretation—the "revenge of the intellect upon art" [35] —was to be eliminated, since it only succeeds in stifling the sensuous, immediate experience of art. A new kind of criticism, she argued, would appropriately serve—rather than usurp—the work of art.

In 1974, Michael Kirby, another avowed formalist and then-editor of the *Drama Review*, published another landmark essay, "Criticism: Four Faults." Arguing that criticism, as it is commonly practiced—that is, as an act of judgement—is primitive, naive, arrogant, and immoral, he suggested a new model of criticism, with intrinsic historical importance, that he dubbed "performance analysis" or "performance documentation." Positing perception and value judgement as fundamentally inextricable and subjective activities, Kirby then went on to suggest that the value judgement component of criticism should be eliminated, leaving the objective, analytic component: "Each value judgment is based upon some empirical observation, but an assertion of value is not the same as a description of what it was that gave rise to the feeling of value. Yet many critics objectify their taste, confuse description and evaluation, and substitute subjective feeling for objective detail. This prevents analysis by both the critic and the auditor/reader, who is left with insufficient data." [36] Kirby argued that the traditional functions of evaluative criticism—as an indication of the reader's potential enjoyment, the creation and standardization of taste, and the maintenance of a historical record—are either unnecessary or unfulfilled. But performance documentation, he further reasoned, serves a vital historical function. "[H]istory does not care whether its data is liked or disliked; it is built only upon the quality and accuracy of the data itself." [37]

Neither Sontag nor Kirby directly addressed dance criticism, but their similar calls for "a really accurate, sharp, loving description" [38] and analysis over interpretation and judgement found compatibility with the emerging generation of descriptive dance critics. Taking their cue from the dance they were writing about, these critics privileged a descriptive mode of criticism, supported by analysis and sometimes even interpretation. Given a dance interested more in the investigation of performance itself (such as many were at the time) rather than in the production of virtuosic technique, any metaphorical intervention or critical distinction between good and bad technique, for example, was rendered irrelevant. "Back then," Siegel has recalled, "it seemed a noble and exciting task to try and describe dance in its own terms—to find language that could speed movement along on the page, picture the shapes and actions we observed, and identify what it was that stirred us." [39] In 1974, Nancy Moore wrote in *Dance Magazine* that

What becomes increasingly apparent is that experimental choreographers, and their critics, are prodding the perceptual boundaries which define our experience of life, even eliminating them—as Jill Johnston tends to do.... People are looking closely at their work to see where, and how, it changes shape. To see where exactly the boundary line is when daily events become performances, art criticism becomes art, when what one sees outside becomes indistinguishable from oneself.[40]

The emphasis on description encouraged an observational rigor that was largely lacking in the work of earlier dance critics, who, with exceptions such as Edwin Denby, usually jumped over the movement directly to interpretation or judgement.

Despite Kirby's insistence that critics must overcome their own subjectivity in order to supply their readers with documentation as objective as possible, a reading of Siegel's and Deborah Jowitt's dance criticism suggests that while striving to be as "objective" as possible in terms of clear seeing, they hardly denied their own subjectivity as observers. As Siegel has written, "there is no way to describe anything without bringing subjective powers into play."[41] The literary necessity to select and order is already an interpretive act. And, as Dixon-Gottschild has pointed out, Kirby's notion of an "objective" performance documentation cannot escape its own ideological assumptions:

He [Kirby] states, "If I say that there are three performers on stage, that one of them is a black girl, that none of them is speaking, and so forth, these statements are both value-free and objective." In using the term "black girl," he has used the language of disempowerment in referring to an African-American female, since the only other females referred to, all Europeans, were referred to as women. His inconsistency shows that even the most innocent, supposedly simple and straightforward language is, in fact, subjective and value laden.[42]

In direct counterdistinction to Kirby's objectivist approach, Jill Johnston's work in the 1960s, as she registered the rise of the avant-garde, was the embodiment of a radically subjectivist approach to criticism.[43] Probably the most significant experiment in American dance criticism, Johnston's writing became a processual, stream-of-consciousness style in which all events were filtered through her own sensibilities. Dance was not something "out there" that she captured and recorded from a distance. Instead, dance came into existence only at the moment when and at the place where she experienced it.

But that was then. Today, at a time when young choreographers increas-ingly are incorporating social and political commentary into highly polished choreography, Johnston finds an exclusively descriptive approach inappropriate, because it inevitably depoliticizes political work. In today's context, she has argued, a descriptive approach assumes critical criteria that inherently support the status quo, when, in fact, many choreographers are challenging not only the formal but political assumptions of their predecessors. "Dance criticism continues to deal, primarily, with the formal and qualitative aspects of the medium: the way dances look, the way dancers dance, the themes of the works and so on, handled descriptively," she wrote. "Much good criticism is done here. But if criticism doesn't address the central and assumed values . . . i.e. the political underlying content of every work . . . it is, I believe, operating in a holding pattern, not keeping up with and contributing to the social revolutionary changes of our time."[44] Significant work, thus, is left "unseen," in the largest sense of the word, because of an incompatible framework for looking.

Despite the opposition between Johnston's early subjectivism and Kirby's objectivism, descriptive criticism—unlike canon criticism—does indeed at least problematize the relationship between critic (subject) and dance (object). Ethnographic criticism, however, goes so far as to reformulate the issue: it is no longer an either-or choice of locating the humanistic "truth" of the dance in the choreography or in the critic. While the descriptive approach posits the *individual,* in the persons of the critic and artist, as the necessary and sufficient actors in the production of meaning, the ethnographic approach emphasizes the primacy of the *cultural field* in the making of meaning. Vail has explained this distinction:

> The descriptive approach that has dominated American journalistic dance criticism for nearly twenty years assumes the critic's autonomy and art's integrity. This familiar method often separates a dance's "objective reality" from the critic's "subjective reaction"—the individual response and judgement of "only one human being." In contrast, recent anthropological perspectives suggest that to "do more in our describing and our guessing," dance critics must accept, and even celebrate, the partial, temporary, relative, and (most important) culturally shaped nature of all critical interpretation.[45]

Both world dance and the work of younger, politically savvy American choreographers call into question the appropriateness of a purely descriptive approach to contemporary dance criticism; nevertheless, in an art form that disappears as soon as it is created, description still serves today—even in an ethnographically modeled form of criticism—a strong supporting role in the critical act.

Feminist Criticism

IN THE 1980s, with the return of narrative, thematic motifs, and imagery, an exclusively descriptive approach to dance, in the strict Sontagian fashion, no longer seemed appropriate. Even dancers were complaining that criticism contained "too much description."[46] Along with this reemergence of content came a growing awareness, on the parts of both choreographer and critic, of gender politics. A feminist approach, which had already established itself in art and theater, began to question the standards by which choreographers, and especially women choreographers, were deemed good or bad. The "objectivity" of these standards was interrogated, in an effort to dismantle the canon, which was seen to have operated, in large measure, as a mechanism of female exclusion.

Feminism is a pluralistic phenomenon. There is no single "feminist" criticism (just as there is no monolithic "canon" or "descriptive" or "ethnographic" criticism), but there is one fundamental ideal shared by feminists across the board. Whether using celebratory or deconstructive strategies, feminist critics aim to improve the lives of women.[47]

Art criticism initiated a feminist critical practice in the late 1960s and the 1970s with a celebratory impulse to validate what were seen as the essential characteristics of Woman and to recover "lost" women artists. Today, however, most feminist critics in art, dance, theater, and music tend toward a strategy of deconstruction. The deconstructive paradigm (echoing the ethnographic) assumes that gender, in all its manifestations, including dance, is culturally constructed: that art is political insofar as it is both a product and producer of ideology. Deconstructive feminist criticism seeks to analyze, interpret, and ultimately to change how women have been represented, in order to empower real live women. It is not judgement of the art that is primary, but rather an ideological critique of its underlying assumptions. Inclusive in its purpose, this kind of feminist criticism seeks to expose the structures and processes by which women traditionally have been excluded from both the aesthetic canon and from the social hierarchy.[48]

In an era of growing feminist consciousness, in an art form long populated by women and focused on the image of Woman, dance provided an inevitable focal point for feminist criticism. Since the 1960s, works by Yvonne Rainer, Senta Driver, Anna de Keersmaeker, Pina Bausch, and many, many others have required a shift in critical approach. By the end of the 1980s, a younger generation of critics, in journals such as *Women & Performance: A Journal of Feminist Theory*, were exploring a specifically feminist dance critical practice. Important in articulating the terrain of this exploration was choreographer/critic Marianne Goldberg's special issue of *Women & Performance* titled "The Body as Discourse." In her preface, she explained:

> Much writing on dance has assumed that "masculine"/"feminine" differences are the cornerstones of aesthetic pleasure or that dance is beyond the need of feminist critique because so many of the great choreographers of the twentieth century have been women—Isadora Duncan, Bronislava Nijinska, Martha Graham and so goes the list of foremothers. The core questions about gender and the body are often left unasked: What kinds of images of the female body does a choreographer present, whether that choreographer is male or female; how are those images

interpreted within the power systems of a particular culture; how does the frame of the stage create conventions for viewing the gendered body; how is it possible for a woman to make the image of her own body when the range of movement for the female is delimited from the day of birth by cultural sanctions that define ideal images of male and female physicality as opposites of one another; how can a choreographer's physical imagination be activated to assert a fuller range of motion/action/interaction for the female body?[49]

In short, how does dance—past and present—produce a patriarchal ideology and how can a dance of the future subvert that ideology?

Jill Johnston, too, has argued for a dance criticism that recognizes the inherent gender politics of the art form, whether they are implicitly accepted or explicitly critiqued:

> If choreographers are promoting gender ideals, the critics should report this. If choreographers are challenging gender ideals, the critics should report this too. There is no such thing as a dance that isn't committed to either approach, whether conscious or not. The formal properties of a dance, the movements, gestures, themes, set, lighting, *everything* serves the interests of one approach or the other: the traditional which reinforces assumed gender identity, and revolutionary which challenges it.[50]

In arguing that all dance has a gender politics, whether or not it is acknowledged, Johnston also was suggesting that all dance is political. The development of a feminist critical practice not only exposed the inherent gender politics of dance; by implication, it laid the groundwork for other critiques—most importantly, of race, class, and sexuality. The whiteness of classical ballet, or the heterosexuality of most any duet, can no longer be assumed as "natural." They are man-made conventions, with cultural and historical origins. They are expressions of an ideology, with real-life implications.

The Future, By Way of a Conclusion

To summarize:

For *ethnographic* criticism, which developed out of the explosion of world dance in America at the end of the 1980s, the main goal is to show how dance is an embodiment of culture (or subculture, as the case may be): it emphasizes interpretation; operates on the basis of inclusivism; situates the critical act in the cultural, rather than interpersonal, field, which effectively negates any subjective-objective dualism; and participates in a relativist, multicultural ideology.

For *canon* criticism, whose roots lay deep in classicism, the main purpose is to uphold aesthetic standards and protect the canon: it emphasizes judgement, operates on the basis of exclusivism, situates the critical act as objective, and participates in an elitist ideology of connoisseurship.

For *descriptive* criticism, rooted in 1960s formalism, the main purpose is "to show how it is what it is": it emphasizes description and analysis, operates on the basis of inclusivism, situates the critical act as somewhere between objective and subjective, and participates in a humanistic, egalitarian ideology.

For *feminist* criticism, which emerged later in dance, in the 1980s, than in the other arts, the main purpose is to show how gender is created in representation and to encourage change in those representations: it emphasizes interpretation, operates on the basis of inclusivism, situates the critical act as a negotiation between the subjective and the objective in the realm of the cultural, and participates in a feminist ideology.

That schema presented, I want to stress that this four-part paradigm is hardly exhaustive and that individual critics rarely fit neatly into any one category. Edwin Denby, for example, fell into several of them. He has, perhaps, no equal in his ability to produce a loving description of dance, in Sontag's formalist tradition, but he also interpreted what he saw and was not shy about judging it, either. He was equally a sensualist and a connoisseur:

> I should like him [*sic*, the critic] to place a choreography or a dancer with his individual derivations and innovations in the perspective of the tradition of theater dancing. I am far more interested though if a writer is able, in describing dancing in its own terms, to suggest how the flavor or the spell of it is related to aspects of the fantasy world we live in, to our daily experience of culture and of custom; if he can give my imagination a steer about the scope of the meaning it communicates. But as I read I want to see too the sensual brilliance of young girls and boys.[51]

What must be considered, then, in any analysis of a particular dance critical practice is the critic's primary goal. In the case of Denby (especially his extensive work on Balanchine), I would argue that description and interpretation supplement the classicist's overarching obligation to measure the success of the dance within its tradition. Denby blended both the elitism of classicism with the democratic impulse to delight in all kinds of movement. A study of how his particular way of seeing shaped late-twentieth-century dance and dance criticism is yet to be written.

The work of Johnston, too, illustrates the range of positions even within the model of descriptive criticism. Certainly she rejected the canon critic's emphasis on judgement, and she hardly aimed for objective documentation. Enmeshed in the experimental arts of the early 1960s, she largely described and, to a lesser degree, analyzed and even interpreted dances, events, and happenings. At her most iconoclastic, during her stream-of-consciousness writing, what set her apart from mainstream descriptive critics and from Sontag was her radical subjectivity. The dance did not unfold *in front of,* that is to say, apart from, Johnston, in an objective reality such as Sontag described; rather, the dance unfolded *within* her. This was a politics of extreme individualism, or humanism, with the self as the point of all reference. But more recently, Johnston's critical practice has re-situated the site of meaning-making from the self into the cultural field, where significance is constructed in a larger context.

I offer this grid of analysis not as an end in itself, but as a means for future study. It is a heuristic device, through which the aesthetic of any critic, and her/his ideology, can be more clearly and precisely excavated. To conduct such an investigation is not to diminish the importance of dance criticism as an intellectual or artistic pursuit; rather, it is only by recognizing the complexities and implications of the dance critical act that its importance can be fully established.

The fact is, dance is constituted by words as much as by movement. Why, for example, has Rainer's *Trio A* (1966) become the paradigm of postmodern dance? For two main reasons, I think. First, because there is a film available for viewing. But why was this film made, almost a decade later, by the historian-critic Sally Banes? For the second reason, I would infer, that the importance of *Trio A* already had been established by the essay that Rainer had written about it.[52] *Trio A,* I daresay, is important because of what Rainer wrote about rather it than because of its choreography per se.

Unlike *Trio A,* dances created before—and even since—the advent of film and video are only accessible to us by way of clues: of traces in visual images and written or notated texts. What Théophile Gautier, André Levinson, and John Martin wrote about the dances of their day in large part constitutes our reality of those dances. Only by understanding the critics' aesthetic practice and ideological project can we gain a more balanced view of the dances that they literally inscribed into history.

The increasing presence of world dance in America and the increasing interest of our own choreographers in socially and politically aware dance, and the attendant crisis this has stirred in the field of dance criticism, offers us at least two opportunities. First, as Vail has written, "presented and viewed perceptively, world dance can be an antidote to arrogance and ethnocentrism. Vitally conveying the essence of other cultures, it prompts healthy reflection on our own ethnicity."[53] Second, it prompts similar "healthy reflection" on the interested act of dance criticism, past and present, as it has constructed and continues to construct the art of dance.

– 1995 (unpublished)

CRITICAL GESTURES
WRITINGS ON DANCE AND CULTURE

The articles in this collection have not been revised. ~~from their original publication.~~ I want them to remain as they originally ~~appeared just~~ as I want to refuse any

This collection, spanning 1986 to 2001, tells several tales. The most obvious is the one about my adventures (and rare misadventures) with dance. But ~~it is~~ is also an *assorted encounters (...) constitute* autobiography of sorts, of a writer, ~~that exposes her~~ fondnesses and ~~weaknesses, the~~ *memoir* *vulnerabilities* struggle for voice and the missteps and pratfalls of style. These reviews and articles and interviews and essays recount how choreographers expanded their attention from formal to social concerns. And then, too, they plot the transformation of dance studies in the academy from historical documentation to cultural criticism. ~~More specifically,~~ *is* ~~there is~~ my fabled love affair with feminist critical theory, chronicled from its first flush to second thoughts.

distinction b/t scholarship — journalism because their value, not secret, resides in the larger conversation in which we participate. As a whole, they tell several tales.

is
The book, ~~without any distinction between scholarship and journalism, is~~ organized as a triptych: "Writing Dance," "Making History," and "Theorizing Gender." "Writing Dance" includes pieces that directly engage ~~dance,~~ in the forms of a *concert, book or* performance, images, and exhibits, ~~books, seasons, and other occasions~~. In "Making *is* *research* History" ~~are~~ collected my ~~works~~ on Isadora Duncan. "Theorizing Gender" charts the *engagement* trajectory of my ~~work~~ with feminist theory. Insofar as this boundary-making fails (there *an essay* *analysis* is ~~a piece~~ on Duncan in the gender theory section; feminist ~~theory~~ shows up regularly in *work is informed by* the reviews; and both the historical and theoretical ~~analyses are based on~~ critical *when* observation, even ~~if~~ reconstructed in the mind's eye), I make my point that the project *The categories of* of criticism exceeds ~~its specific~~ *any* disciplinary and methodological allegiances. "Criticism," *enactments* *entities* *manifestations* are but three ~~modes~~ of the same quest for meaning.

plate 1

8 original manuscript pages

+ 3 sample croppings

assortment

www.cuddledown.com
Manufacturers & Retailer of Fine Home Fashions Since 1973

WRITING DANCE

CHOREOGRAPHERS

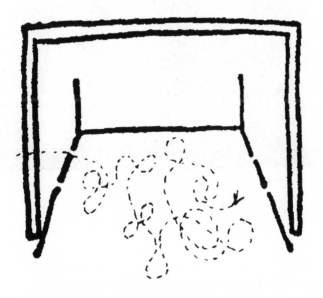

From the libretto of *Lamb at the Altar* by Deborah Hay. Used by permission.

Nur Du (Only You), a piece by Pina Bausch. Photo by Uwe Stratmann. Used by permission.

PINA BAUSCH

Tanztheater

The Thrill of the Lynch Mob or the Rage of a Woman?

Ed. Note: Goethe House New York and the Brooklyn Academy of Music co-sponsored a symposium, "German and American Dance: Yesterday and Today," on 8 November 1985. This transcript, edited and abridged by TDR Managing Editor Ann Daly, is the second half of the symposium concerned with current dance trends. Anna Kisselgoff, dance critic of the *New York Times*, was moderator. Participants were West German dance critic Jochen Schmidt; Reinhild Hoffmann, artistic director of Tanztheater Bremen; American choreographer Nina Wiener; and dance critic Nancy Goldner of the *Philadelphia Inquirer*.

Tanztheater in Historical Perspective

SCHMIDT: We lost a big part of our past, of our history, in the '30s, '40s, and '50s. I'm not quite sure if we lost more of it during the Nazi Third Reich and World War II or during the period of reconstruction in the Adenauer era. As a matter of fact, we lost more buildings and houses in the '50s than during World War II. To me, it looks as if we lost our dance tradition in the '20s not during the world war, not during the Nazi time, but during the '50s.

It was really dead in the '60s. All the German dancers, all the public, wanted to dance ballet and see ballet. There was a big, big boom of classical ballet in Germany with John Cranko [artistic director of the Stuttgart Ballet] and others. In 1967, Dore Hoyer, one of the great personalities of the '20s and the ausdruckstanz, committed suicide. Nobody knows exactly why she did, but we all supposed it was because her dance was dead.

At that time we had a lot of influences from American modern dance. It came over with the Dutch companies, mainly from the Netherlands Dance Theater, which was at that time led by Glen Tetley and Hans van Manen. So we saw a lot of our own past transformed by Americans coming back. At that time, we didn't want to do it ourselves.

I think that there was a new life for German dance for the tradition of the '20s. It has to do with the student revolution at the end of the '60s. It's no accident that most choreographers of the first generation (Reinhild is somewhat from the second generation already)—Hans Kresnik, Pina Bausch, Gerhard Bohner—were in a way connected with that social debate.

The break really came in 1973. In that year, Mary Wigman and John Cranko died. We all thought Cranko's death was just an accident that wouldn't disturb the flourishing of the ballet, but for German ballet it was something like an end. At the same time, Pina was appointed director of the Wuppertal Ballet, not tanztheater at that time. That was really the break. It was she who made tanztheater. Without her success, which was not an easy success, there would not have been tanztheater.

Now we have about ten companies in our stadtheater system which are seen as tanztheater companies—not ballet companies—and about thirty ballet companies. All the big companies, of course, are ballet companies. I think the Stuttgart is doing good work, but it is just doing traditional things.

In a way, Pina and the tanztheater have influenced even the classical ballet. William Forsythe, who is an American working now in Frankfurt, is a ballet choreographer. But I think he is much, much closer to Pina and Reinhild and Susanne Linke than he is to John Neumeier or George Balanchine or other classical choreographers. So at this moment, of a hundred performances in Germany, 70 percent are ballet, and 30 percent are tanztheater. The fame of Pina Bausch created a climate for tanztheater, so we are speaking about it, but the public likes *Giselle* and *Swan Lake*.

Is Content Taboo in American Experimental Dance?

KISSELGOFF: I'm going to read something that Jochen Schmidt wrote in *Ballett International*: "And the Germans? How are they distinguished, if at all, from the American New Dance choreographers?" He says there's a certain similarity to Meredith Monk and Kei Takei.

But there is a decisive difference to the most recent generation of New Dancers which can best be described in a statement by Pina Bausch. The New Dance choreographers, as we have seen, are interested above all in movement. Pina Bausch, however, has expressly determined that she is less interested in how people move as in what moves them—and that applies, by and large, to her German colleagues Reinhild Hoffmann and Susanne Linke. Whereas the young Americans—inasmuch as they are descendants of the Cunningham-Nikolais generation which defined dance as "motion, not emotion"—are fascinated by dance in itself, their German dance colleagues want to learn something and transmit something about their surroundings, about people's daily lives, their cares, fears, problems and joys. Dance serves them as a means for release and humanizing. They therefore have a more realistic, earthy and heavy—but also more concrete, social and political effect than their American counterparts.

Is the "German nature" in dance again to be described as primarily "deep"? Without a doubt, but for once that is no drawback. And if I interpret the reactions to this German dance rightly—especially in Italy and France—this "depth" and gravity are not considered even abroad to be a drawback, but rather as a necessary corrective to the American art of lightness, which all too quickly becomes an art of insignificance.

Elsewhere you write that content is basically taboo in the American experimental dance. Do you not feel that content can be expressed as form, that form and content can be one, that you can have abstraction which also deals with life around us?

SCHMIDT: I am sure one can, but I can't do anything with that "experimental dance." I think every art has to find out new things, things that haven't been said before. If not, it's not art. I think the new German tanztheater is trying to find out new things with movement. Sometimes with words, too, and with singing and film and other things. They are trying to find out new things about people, I think.

KISSELGOFF: We rarely see pure dance coming out of West Germany. There must be some reason why there are directions that are being taken in America and Germany which are so opposite. Do you feel that formal concerns are of no interest to German choreographers?

SCHMIDT: I think there is a lot of form in all the works of Pina Bausch.

KISSELGOFF: But not in themselves. Used for another reason.

HOFFMANN: I think it's just a question of emphasis. I think in everything is form and in everything is motion. Sometimes you put more accent on this or more accent on that. It's a choice, that's all. Maybe we in Europe are much more connected to the theater tradition. In each town there is an opera house, which has all the traditional theater pieces. Maybe that is a reason why we're still dealing with telling stories, showing characters, saying something about human beings beyond just presenting form or movement.

Each person must find his/her own movement. If that is new or not, I cannot say. It's just that we try to find our own language. I think we are full of things we have learned from our teachers, from the tradition, and also we react personally to what we have learned and what we experience daily. Through that comes a new construction. We maybe have tried to separate ourselves from movements we feel are too decorative. We try to speak as directly as possible or to find a translation which the stage allows. The stage is a world, a platform for translations, a place to say something about daily life.

KISSELGOFF: Reinhild, dance theater often discards a dance vocabulary in favor of other kinds of movement.

HOFFMANN: Sometimes I just think it's not necessary. If there is a person over there and I am here, I just go to this person. Why should I [undulates arms forward]? [Applause]

LUTZ FÖRSTER (member of Wuppertal Tanztheater and associate artistic director of the José Limón Dance Company): When we started doing *Arien,* it looked like a dance piece. There were about ten movement phrases Pina gave us that we did for a long time over and over again. In the finished piece, they all concentrated into these two big dancing scenes, which I think are some of the most beautiful things we've choreographed in terms of movement. In these scenes, the dancers form couples. One person is screaming at and chasing the other one, who is dancing different versions of those original phrases. The second such scene eventually dissolves into solo dancing. But the other things we worked on—the children's games, the women in a row being made up by the men—were much stronger than all these other movement things, so we just cut them out. Pina always starts with a lot of movement, and during the process she finds out things that are much stronger. She always tries. It's not a conscious effort not to move.

GOLDNER: Very generally speaking, I think that the chief characteristic of American dance is that choreographers are interested in movement values. Every gesture and every step has an inherent validity, beauty, and expressiveness. It's all there, all you have to do is use it.

These American ideas come from two men in the warring camps of ballet and modern dance: George Balanchine and Merce Cunningham. I think it's extremely fortunate for younger choreographers that they have these two very, very large influences from different areas of dance.

I think younger choreographers—and some of them aren't so young anymore—have always used the idea, first, that movement is interesting in itself. That we dance not so that we can express something but first of all we dance so we can move. The idea is to move—how are you going to move, how many interesting ways can you do it.

The second idea is that movements have in themselves an expressive quality, and I want to use that term "expressive" in a very loose and ambiguous way. All you can say maybe is movement has a quality about it. Even Merce Cunningham, who has been very adamant about his dances not having content, has written that we jump and we also jump for joy, and there's no way to get around the second idea that we do jump for joy.

WIENER: I came out of the Cunningham postmodern tradition, which was trying to break away from some old concepts of moving. The exploration of new vocabularies came out of trying to break away from those old concepts, and people got very preoccupied with that.

What's happening now, and I can only speak for myself, is that I'm starting to move into exploring emotional expression in a more public arena. In my early work my private concerns were my emotions, which I wasn't willing or interested in sharing; my public concerns were my form and my structure, which came out of the postmodern tradition and were interlinked through different kinds of material manipulations—which goes back to "We can move a box, and that's O.K."

Now I feel so secure in my structural and formal concerns that they are becoming very private for me. Today I don't care if the audience sees these concerns or that they are recognized. I am currently more into sharing my emotional concerns.

KISSELGOFF: Emotion is the new word among American choreographers. I can tell you that American choreographers of the '30s and '40s are laughing their heads off. I would just like to ask Miss Hoffmann if she in fact began with plotless, pure movement work.

HOFFMANN: Well, I did one early piece of choreography—more like an exercise—which was pure movement. It was like splitting two or three people like a mirror picture or like a wave movement. But I am not able to separate a personal feeling or a personal movement from a form. It always comes together. That's the impulse.

KISSELGOFF: American dance has tended to go in the direction of formalism, and the German dance as we see it is a form of neo-expressionism. These are labels, and they're too pat, but they are general categories. Do you accept them, Jochen?

SCHMIDT: Not that of neo-expressionism, because it's much more than that.

I think there have been two lines in American modern dance. One is more realistic—Martha Graham, Doris Humphrey, José Limón, and Anna Sokolow. But it was lost after Graham. I see a lot of younger American choreographers now doing things which classical ballet can do better. They are always trying to become brilliant and fast. I ask: why don't they do ballet?

For me, some of those dancers and choreographers are like hamsters. These little beasts in a wheel go around and around and around but always remain in the same spot.

KISSELGOFF: You feel Graham and Humphrey were realistic. I feel they are totally not realistic. Realism is a word that you and your fellow critics use very often in writing about dance theater.

That's very interesting to me, because I don't find tanztheater realistic. Bausch's work is expressionistic in that there is a very strong distillation of a prime emotion in every episode and every character. It's personal experience as expressed in a form of distortion, which is very common to expressionistic art, especially expressionism in Germany.

GOLDNER: It seems to me the action in Bausch alternates between large mass things and small things, where the action breaks down and there is a lot of small individual gesture. There is a lot of individuality. I think in that sense, it's quite realistic.

SCHMIDT: I know that realism can't be naturalism. We all know that. I am sure Bausch is not naturalistic, but German dance theater is closer to daily life than the dances of Nina Wiener or Douglas Dunn or Laura Dean.

KISSELGOFF: Why is Dean separate from daily life? To me she is very in tune with her generation. That's what I see—Laura Deans all around me in the street.

SCHMIDT: Just spinning?

KISSELGOFF: The symbol is spinning, but the sensibility is what her generation expresses.

SCHMIDT: Spinning is all I see.

WIENER: I think what Bausch does is extremely simple. The emotions presented are not the whole range of the emotion you could look at.

In all her dances I see the conflict or confrontation between men and women. Each time it's the same thing. That kind of angst emotion is not something that I want to participate in. That has nothing to do with whether I think she's brilliant, which I do. That angst emotion goes on for too long for me to want to participate in it.

I also have a difficult time with the sense of editing. I think the sense of time in European work and American work is very different. It may have to do with this sense of speed—in New York we go fast.

I think one of the reasons why American dance got so focused on the abstraction of pure movement has to do with the fact that we underwent the same kind of revolution that the original modern dancers underwent when they found that the ballet was very limiting for them and they had other, more earthy concerns. Modern dance became completely connected to this emotional thing, and in order to make that break, the postmoderns switched to the other side.

Postmodern dance was about establishing individual vocabularies. There was a tremendous pressure for new patterns of expression, which has just started to let up. American dance has been extremely diffuse, pushing out in all directions.

People are now trying to work more in the framework of sharing how they feel and sharing things that are more common on a personal level. It doesn't happen to be taking the form of dance theater, but it is taking another form.

GOLDNER: I think there are certain emotions which Americans think are the proper emotions to show on the stage, and they are very different from what the Germans think.

There's a common American sensibility now that says: the heavier you get, the more trivial you are, and the lighter you stay, the more intelligent it will be. I think this also comes from the Balanchine/Cunningham tradition. Americans have trouble with the heaviness of German emotion or expression, because we find the heaviness rather "lightweight." You might feel the same way about the lightness of American dance. You find us trivial because of that lightness.

HOFFMANN: Really, I think Merce Cunningham's work is very interesting and very intelligent. I enjoy it immensely. But I also think that it isn't good to say you will not deal with the problems you have. I often hear that what you see in our pieces is only about man-woman relationships. It's not meant to be so narrow. It stands for problems that human beings have, nations have, the world has. It stands for more than just man-woman.

From what I hear and see when I walk through the streets in New York, there are a lot of problems here. When young choreographers living here choose *mainly* just to move and not to relate strongly to what they see daily, then I ask: why?

SCHMIDT: Balanchine's type of choreography was in a certain sense finished because he never could make any ballet last more than one act. If you want to tell things and to make longer ballets, you need a new form. The German dance theater found a new form. It wasn't really new in the arts, because it was in painting and film. It was the form of collage and montage. The works of Pina Bausch are much closer to an Eisenstein movie than to classical or narrative ballet. The Bausch pieces are narrative. They tell things, but they don't tell stories. They tell: then it was this, then that, and that. There are always things going on, and you have to put it together in your head. She knows very well what she is doing and all the things she does are very, very formed.

Maybe some of you remember a scene in *Café Müller* with three people—man, woman, and one who helps them. They do it again and again. They become faster and faster and faster. It's a very sad scene in the beginning, and in the end when it's very fast it's very humorous. For me, she's not doing things ten times in the same way. There's always really a difference. If not, she knows why not.

KISSELGOFF: Could I ask George Jackson, do you feel the Living Theatre played a role in German dance theater?

JACKSON (contributing critic, *Washington DanceView*): Perhaps by way of Pina Bausch. I know she was over here. I do not think she saw any of the early Judson experiments. At least she said she hadn't. But I do believe she went to the Living Theatre.

Certainly the sprawling structures of most of Pina Bausch's works and what I saw in Hoffmann's *Callas* last night remind me very much of the Living Theatre. I fail to see form. That's the weakness. The material is interesting, the methods are interesting, but ultimately most of these pieces repeat themselves because they lack a competent form—compact and significant. The works go on and on, and everything that has been created is destroyed at the end.

Form means significant change. An organic structure that makes emotional sense. Emotion not as the expression of a literal, realistic feeling but a formal implementation or diminution. I would say Balanchine did succeed in creating a ballet that is more than one act and that has formal unity and formal emotion. That is his *Don Quixote,* probably his greatest ballet, I'd say. I don't see this mastery of form in the Living Theatre and the current German dance theater. I don't see that as it goes on it becomes more meaningful. I just don't see it.

Violence

KISSELGOFF: What really disturbs American audiences and dancers—especially about Bausch's work—is the violence depicted. Some say Bausch may be condemning violence but that she revels in depicting it; they say she works up the audience so they are thrilled, and it's the thrill of the lynch mob in watching people bang their heads against the wall or hit each other. Is that a characteristic of German dance?

SCHMIDT: I'll answer with a question. Would you think that way about cinema, television, drama, and literature—or only dance? I think Bausch is doing what all other artists are doing. She is not attracted by violence. I'm sure she's not. She hates it, but she shows it and she shows it in a very comic form. You really have to see the pieces more than one time, and you will find them more comical every time.

GOLDNER: It's not only the violence. It's also certain sexual aspects of the work. In *Callas,* there was much humor in the men's costumes and in the way they held themselves in the dresses and in the bathing suits. There is also something very disturbing about that. I think that's also a part of the violence you're talking about. It's not just men and women fighting each other but a certain depiction of men as women.

HOFFMANN: I want to come back to my question. I felt I didn't get an answer. Why do so many people here in America try not to be confronted in their

13

art with human problems? For example, violence, you have it daily. I hear the sound of sirens every day. I always hear it—it never goes away. It's like a fear of dealing with it, questioning it. Isn't it important to confront it?

FÖRSTER: I'm surprised when people talk so much about violence in Pina's pieces. I'm always surprised, because I see in so many American companies a lack of tenderness. In all Pina's pieces people are tender to each other.

American critics are really obsessed with violence. I am appalled to see the news in America. They really dig into everybody who's lying there on the ground. That would never happen on German television.

GOLDNER: In tribute to Bausch, what we see on the stage—and also in *Callas*—is much more powerful than what we see on television. To Americans, when we're seeing people shoot-'em-up, it's an age-old convention. It's stylized. We're eating our cereal and ironing our clothes. This is background music. We're not taking it seriously. But when we see this on the stage, it has a truth, it has an immediacy, and a power.

KISSELGOFF: In *Gebirge,* many people told me they left because they could not take the image of Josephine Ann Endicott lying down repeatedly and having her back slashed with red. I saw it as a statement of a Pavlovian response in which the victim can be taught to submit. People accused me of being overly cerebral about something that was extremely disturbing to them. I would like to deal with that image. What is comic or tender about it?

SPECTATOR: I think what we see a lot in Pina Bausch, which is the antithesis of American television, is the rage of a woman.

KISSELGOFF: Wait a minute. Don't go "ah." I didn't hear any female voices going "ah."

SPECTATOR: We would not see Maria Tallchief dancing with hairy armpits. The level of reality of violence and of sex all wed together in Bausch makes it very exciting and revolutionary for an American audience. And, I think, very hard for people to take. I thought the scene from *Gebirge* which you talked about was very powerful. We hear repeatedly about women who are beaten, tormented by their husbands and then sent to jail for killing them. That doesn't seem so real to us or upsetting, but when Pina Bausch distills it through art onstage, people get up and leave.

I don't think these dances are realistic in the way Émile Zola's novels are, but the dancers running across the stage in wet, dripping satin evening gowns destroy a certain kind of dramatic illusion that we're used to staying behind on the American stage.

SPECTATOR: The fetishism of women's clothes is nowhere better revealed than in Bausch and also in *Callas,* when you see men stripped of their gender, all coming out wearing red evening downs. In *The Seven Deadly Sins* the men come out in women's underwear. On the women we think it looks just sexy and dynamite, baby, but on the men they look jerky. I noticed in *Callas* that the dancers were used as dancers irrespective of gender. To me, that's very, very thrilling. To my friend who was there with me, it was terrifying.

I think the people who don't like the violence are really responding to some deep-seated horror. Is it possible that there is no difference between men and women—it's just clothes? Is it possible that the clothes we wear are nothing but convention that we can throw out? I think that's frightening, and not simply because of the violence.

JACKSON: One objection that people here have voiced about tanztheater is that it looks too practiced. When William Dunas threw himself against the wall in the '60s, he was doing an experiment. In the Bausch work, it looked too rehearsed, and hence the moral ambiguity.

JOAN ROSS ACOCELLA (senior editor, *Dance Magazine*): Sometimes the violence looks simply like theatrical kilowatts rather than a human problem we are seriously exploring. Also, I do think it should be considered that it's not just banging people into walls that feels violent. For instance, the opening image in *Gebirge* when Jan Minarik takes the balloons out of his swimsuit and blows them up. There's surely some relation to genitals and his nose is cramped down, and then they pop. There is a large amount of sexual humiliation that takes place in a soft, comic way—someone brought up comedy supposedly offsetting the violence in these things.

I think the problem is not so much with the subject matter—though I certainly also feel my nerves screech with that gashing in *Gebirge*—as with the way it's dealt with artistically. It's the episodic character, the fact that we can count on it. That every four minutes you're going to be hit over the head with a hammer, whether it be somebody being banged into the wall or some terrible business of a man's pants being pulled down, which eventually looks more violent to me.

It's not repetition that bothers me. It's repetition without development, variation, exploration. Development is something that we in America associate with intelligence. It starts to look after a while like something that is cheap—just a theatrical firecracker.

SCHMIDT: Can you imagine that you and the American critics are using the wrong criteria for those pieces?

ACOCELLA: It's possible that you come from one culture and we from another.

SCHMIDT: It has nothing to do with culture. We had the same problems in the beginning, because this is a new form. What you are saying about development does not concern these pieces. It's not the point.

Please remember what the public thought about Cunningham when he worked first in New York City and then when he came to Europe. Remember that people thought Nijinsky was a very bad choreographer. Now, seventy years later, we are beginning to think maybe he was fifty years ahead of his time. I think it's something that happens to all great artists at the beginning. They set a new border.

Postscript

The initial refusal of the Goethe House audience to deal with the "rage of a woman" in Pina Bausch's work is not atypical for the New York dance community. I have seen similar concerns with the way women are represented in dance dismissed at another dance critics' symposium. The dominant male/ submissive female stereotype is mutely upheld in practically all American dance criticism.

But the real subject is not the rage of a woman; it is the *unheard* rage of a woman.

In Bausch's pieces, violence comes in bursts of dense repetition. These acts of violence are neither conventional nor naturalistic; rather, they exist on the plane of metaphor. They deal with the violation of women's bodies but, more so, of women's autonomy.

In *Kontakthof,* a group of men surround a woman; their initial caresses turn into tweaks and pulls and tugs. She offers no protest. They literally pick at her for what seems a very long time. In *Gebirge,* a madman makes his way through a line of women, making each one say "Uncle" with whatever amount of force is necessary to overcome her resistance (or lack thereof).

The way Bausch uses repetition both intensifies and anesthetizes the response to the violence. At the same time that her repetitions accumulate emo-tional force, they also undercut emotional impact with the overtly theatrical (repeat-able, therefore acted and "make-believe") behavior. That's why some spectators sweat through these sequences while others laugh.

The effect varies from spectator to spectator. I was horrified by that passage in *Gebirge* in which a woman repeatedly gets down on all fours, pulls up her dress to bare her back, and gets slashed by a man with a red lipstick or crayon. The animalis-tic position of the woman, the slashing movement, the thickening red marks on her back—all signal to me quite plainly a violent encounter made doubly despicable by the complicity of the victim. Kisselgoff, viewing this scene as a model of Pavlovian response, ignores its full and strident political-social-sexual content.

There is in the dance community a resistance to Bausch's use of repetition. It's chauvinistic to dismiss such a fundamental formalist technique as formless and bor-ing just because it serves expressionist ends. The same holds true of Bausch's collage structure, which is neither as formless as the Americans say nor as unique in dance as the Germans would have us believe: the works of Yoshiko Chuma and The School of Hard Knocks and Stephanie Skura's *Travelog,* for instance, are collages.

While some American critics seem unable to read the formal and structural properties of Bausch's work, German critics seem unable to read the expressive qualities (and not necessarily emotional expression) of postmodern American dance. The symposium concretized the very different ways two cultures have of reading movement.

And yet the anti-formalists at the symposium were arguing against a straw man. American formalism today is not the rigorous formalism of the Judson days. Even the Judson Church choreographers—Lucinda Childs, Trisha Brown, most notably—are now making overtly theatrical dances. And rarely do you find a young, experimental choreographer dealing with "pure form" (if there can be such a thing). Bebe Miller, for example, gives full rein to the expressiveness of her dances. *Trapped in Queens* is a high-energy, limb-flinging dance, but it also suggests a community of generous relationships: if these people are trapped in Queens, they are doing their darnedest to help each other get out.

Bausch's work brilliantly embeds powerful dramatic imagery in formal repetition. In sequences when I realized that something would happen again and again and again, I experienced a very unsettling but at the same time pleasurable suspension of time. Instead of going forward, time expanded in another dimension. The spatial metaphor is apt, because the experience has to do with a sense of a totally enveloping, absorbing space. What's out there onstage becomes very internalized: inside/outside, before/next become one.

But what is out there on Bausch's stage is women's acquiescent powerlessness. (A psychologically unsatisfying strategy for survival: "Don't resist your rapist, and you may live through the attack.") Nearly without exception, the violence is done by men to women. Nearly without exception, the women remain passive. And it's crucial to remember that the content of the repetitions are verbatim. There is no register of change, of the woman's movement toward freedom. She remains utterly powerless, without any recourse or prospects of enfranchisement. Frustration, desperation—they're the emotions of Bausch's nihilist imagery, which bespeaks not just the physical but emotional, social, political, and economic oppression of women.

This repeated imagery can tease the spectator's heightened sense of anticipation and expectation into dread. In *Gebirge,* every time a balloon blew up in the face of that man in swimming trunks—and he must have burst at least four in his face—I jumped a foot, even though I consciously prepared myself for it. *Every time the madman in Gebirge made another woman cry "Uncle," I winced*—not just because of what was in front of my eyes but because I dreaded the thought of going through it again. Only in *The Seven Deadly Sins,* perhaps because it was the last production of the run or because it is unselectively shrill, was I disengaged. Such a flood of emotion onstage—*Sins* didn't have the power that the stark repetitions lent the other pieces. Or maybe familiarity makes Bausch's violence just as numbing as it has the 6 o'clock news.

Bausch apologists charge that American critics shouldn't be so supersensitive to the violence in her pieces when there is so much violence on American television. They overlook, however, the essential difference between the violence in these two genres.

On American television, violence is undeniably a main attraction. But the violence is always presented within a mediating ideology that espouses that "violence is immoral and illegal. Violators must be caught and punished." Most cop and adventure shows (*A-Team*, for example) are virtual morality plays. Good guys win; bad guys lose.

In Bausch, what's the mediating ideology? There is none.

Though I admire Bausch's formal techniques, what they express is repugnant. Early in her season, I felt it unfair to require that an artist go beyond depicting provocative images to providing the spectator with ways of processing them. But the more I saw, the more the violence began to undercut its own impact and the more the "unheard rage of a woman" became debilitating and even insulting. To state the obvious—that women collaborate with their victimizers—over and over again without exploring the reasons for their passivity or the ways in which they do/can/will fight back makes violence, oppression, and passivity look inevitable and "natural." Bausch may be displaying violence, she may even be confronting it, but she certainly isn't questioning it. It's as if she's built violence and oppression into a massive wall without allowing us any cracks to break it open and see what's supporting it.

She scrupulously avoids inscribing her pieces with anything that would guide her spectators toward a resolution of their emotional response by structuring each piece as a string of discrete scenes or bits. What holds each of her works together is not any point of view but rather the mise-en-scène and the heightened theatricality of it all. (Ironically, Bausch's works could be construed as even more theatrically hermetic and self-referring than the American formalist works, whose lack of overt reference to the "real world" the tanztheater proponents disdain).

Without a framework that helps us resolve the stew of emotions she provokes, we're left to deal with them through our own prior assumptions. If Bausch is aiming to foreground the horror of men's violence against women, she doesn't succeed in changing the mind of anyone who doesn't already agree with her.

—*TDR: The Journal of Performance Studies*, 1986

Pina Bausch Goes West to Prospect for Imagery

IT DOESN'T happen too often, but Pina Bausch managed to name her newest work, her first American commission, before its premiere in Germany last May. With a nod to the production's origins, the artistic director of the Pina Bausch Tanztheater Wuppertal dubbed the work *Nur Du,* the German translation for the title of the Platters' 1955 hit "Only You."

Ms. Bausch's title refers to the number that closes the first act. As the Platters croon their familiar love song, Jan Minarik, outfitted in a fox loincloth and matching stole, accessorized with heels and drop earrings, systematically gives a cookie-cutter makeover to a line of seated women, their skirts held aloft to reveal bare legs. One by one, he parts each woman's hair on the side and combs it back.

So much for the romantic notion of being his one and only.

Nur Du is the fifth of Ms. Bausch's site-specific works. In the last decade, the fifty-six-year-old German choreographer has collaborated, as it were, with four European cities (Vienna, Rome, Palermo, and Madrid), where extended residencies provided the company with its creative context. In 1996, Ms. Bausch is adding the American West, or at least Los Angeles, to her dance-theater Baedeker.

Early this year, accompanied by her longtime stage-design collaborator, Peter Pabst, she went in search of America, in Austin, Texas; Berkeley, California; and Los Angeles. (The $1.2 million work was commissioned by arts and educational organizations in those three cities and Tempe, Arizona.) After making its American debut at the University of California at Berkeley on 3 October, *Nur Du* will travel to Los Angeles, Tempe, and Austin.

Austin and Berkeley were quick trips for Ms. Bausch and Mr. Pabst. But in Los Angeles, nearly the full company—dancers, designers, prop master, technical director, general manager—spent three weeks in February doing research.

Absorbing a Diffuse City

Ms. Bausch arrives in Los Angeles without an agenda. "We'll move around with open eyes, open ears, and our feelings," she explains at a news conference on 31 January. But moving around proves none too easy, and she is dismayed by the lack of urban street life. The natives, insulated in their automobiles, are not so readily observable.

The dancers depend on two vans, which shuttle them each workday morning from the Hollywood Roosevelt Hotel to the UCLA dance building. They begin with ballet class from Alfredo Corvino, who taught Ms. Bausch at the Juilliard School in the 1960s. (What was she like? "Young, quiet, focused," he says. "I didn't know about her talent. I don't think she knew.")

After class, the dancers spend the rest of the day answering questions.

This has been Ms. Bausch's modus operandi since the late 1970s, when she shifted from a traditional choreographic method to a more collective process in which dancers generate raw materials, prompted by hundreds of questions, or ideas, posed by her. A random sampling from *Nur Du:* "Why is it called 'LA'?" "Something kitschy." "Do something leading with your elbow." "Spell Los Angeles with your body."

The performers' responses are not improvisations per se but more like studies. While some dancers work spontaneously, others spend quite a bit of time on preparation. Some create in their mind's eye; others rehearse extensively. Still others take their questions home overnight.

In rehearsal, the performers are no longer dressed in practice clothes; they get right into the tanztheater uniform. It's vintage wear: silky slip dresses and high heels for the women, shirts and trousers for the men, the same fetishistic costumes worn onstage. The performers are getting into character, literally taking on the bodies of the "man" who buttons up and buckles tight and the "woman" whose walk is narrow and hippy.

Ms. Bausch is seated at a central table, which is decorated with a vase of flowers, equipped with a smoke-eating ashtray, and littered with books (about American Indians, the Los Angeles riots, and women on the frontier).

There's no apparent format, but despite the mess of people and stuff, the space feels focused. Dancers take the stage to show their studies when they choose. Ms. Bausch watches, drags on a cigarette, and takes copious notes. Somehow it's agreed upon when a study will be repeated in front of a video camera.

During one afternoon rehearsal, the choreographer is presented with: a human fly who crawls across the wall, supported by three other dancers; a holdup scene, in which a water bottle is the victim's defense, thrust into the mugger's mouth; a disturbing portrayal of a seated woman who obsessively counts as she turns her head side to side, laughing; and a man tickling the feet of an implacable woman. Here is Ms. Bausch's wellspring: drama, idiosyncrasy, the absurd.

She looks for material that belongs deeply, and uniquely, to each individual. "She wants us," says Dominique Mercy, one of the dancers, "to be as sincere and simple as possible."

What's different about *Nur Du* is that the material is being generated completely by the performers. Ms. Bausch is not suggesting to them any movement with which to work. Instead, she is eliciting the movements from them, with more movement-oriented prompts than usual. Like: "a small phrase about the feeling of comfort," "a shape that encloses," "a pause in space."

After rehearsals, Ms. Bausch explores the city until the wee hours, with Mr. Pabst and the company's costume designer, Marion Cito. Mr. Pabst says that they are out to find the "reality" of the place, not art or other filtered information. At first it sounds misguided, to go looking for the reality of Los Angeles, city of the simulacrum. But then again, what more suitable lens is there for a company in which it's the performer's task to play herself in stiletto heels and strapless gown?

The whole company visits a wild variety of restaurants, clubs, attractions, and landmarks: from a Buddhist temple in Little Tokyo to East Los Angeles; from Venice Beach to the First African Methodist Episcopal Church in the South-Central section of the city; from a whale-watching spot to Paramount Studios. Jazz, salsa, drag, karate, boxing, performance, art, basketball.

The dancers arrive and leave with strong impressions: of spiritual impoverishment, of vacant streets, of distances, of people unable to show themselves, of glamour and illusion. America, says Daphnis Kokkinos, one of the dancers, is "too big, too easy."

Cutting the Collage

Three months later in Wuppertal, a few days before the premiere, Mr. Kokkinos reports that the piece is coming together. Ms. Bausch has worked her usual eleventh-hour alchemy, transforming hundreds of hours' worth of raw material into about 170 scenes, which she now splices together.

The lighting and the musical collage are taking final shape. The shop is scrambling to finish Mr. Pabst's design: a grove of mammoth redwoods and an airborne whale. "Nine tons of set and two tons of other stuff in fourteen containers," says the company's general manager, Matthias Schmiegelt. "It's the biggest set ever."

On the Schauspielhaus stage, the company runs through the work, a chunk at a time. Ms. Bausch's instructions: "If you make a mistake, don't get depressed. If something is wrong, it's O.K., don't worry about it. Just show me something happening, the feeling."

Nur Du has its premiere on 11 May, as scheduled, but everyone understands that, as with any Tanztheater Wuppertal premiere, it remains a work in progress. Some nips and tucks have been made since dress rehearsal, but the performance still runs three and a half hours.

Just as the dance has yet to gel, so the dancers continue to develop their parts. At least six of the company's thirty-five performers are new, and their appealing freshness does not always fit the company's performance style, which layers personal vulnerability and ironic role-playing.

Eddie Martinez, an American from Kansas who joined the company in August 1995, has broken through his diffidence. His baseball monologue and his leap-and-kiss routine (borrowed from Pilobolus) are full of committed, boundless energy. Ruth Amarante plays a somnambulistic hysteric, the flip side of Julie Shanahan, who plays a screaming hysteric. Stephan Brinkmann is irresistibly gangly-limbed, with tousled hair and a dimpled grin. Mr. Minarik, who looked puffy and pasty in Los Angeles, has lost thirty pounds.

Mr. Minarik and Mr. Mercy, longtime company members, anchor the ensemble, the former tall and stalwart, the latter lanky and expressive. Mr. Minarik is master of the deadpan. Unflappable, never speaking (in *Nur Du*, only through a ventriloquist's doll), he strides across the stage with relentless dignity, whether he's wearing a chest plate filled with live mice or a fur bikini. While Mr. Minarik's effect is one of energy gathered inward, Mr. Mercy's is one of energy scattered outward. He is a doleful dancer, an existential clown in his trademark oversize shirt, beautiful in drag, capable of suggesting the subtlest feeling in a chest that is sunken or expanded or in a head that reaches high or hangs low.

The next day Ms. Bausch gives notes in the Lichtburg, an old movie house that is now the troupe's rehearsal studio. Her corrections deal with the timing and spacing of the action, not motivation or style, because at this point what the dancers describe as the "color" or "mood" of each scene is not a matter of its apparent emotional authenticity but the result of precise choreography.

Julie Stanzak's cheerleading bit, for example, has grown too long, so its focus has shifted, from the memories of her cheerleading days in the United States to the cheers themselves. "Doing and remembering—very different," Ms. Bausch muses aloud. "For me it's not about making a great number. Not about screaming, but that we *see* Julie." The choreographer is firm: "Nobody change anything without asking me."

Window on the World

Watching *Nur Du* becomes a parlor game. Amid all the familiar Bausch shtick and obsessions, what is recognizable from the Los Angeles residency? What is American about it? The human fly, and some gestures from the dancers' movement studies. The legless dancer and the skaters from Venice Beach, as well as images of boxing and karate. There's Mr. Martinez's baseball speech, Ms. Stanzak's cheerleader, and a monologue of Hollywood one-liners.

But, as Mr. Mercy cautions, this American commission should not be taken as literal or descriptive. The point is much larger than the occasional "flash" of American imagery. There is also, he says, something behind those specific experiences that speak to larger issues of human relations.

Ms. Bausch once told an interviewer: "Yearning for home or for foreign shores —that's probably all the same thing. And sometimes you just have to look through a window." Los Angeles provided that window for *Nur Du,* as a place, among other things, where a self-consciously international company could investigate the implications of "home."

Images of home are laced throughout *Nur Du.* There are the obvious ones, such as Andrei Berezine's miniature paper-cutout house, set ablaze, or the subliminal ones, such as Mr. Brinkmann's bit with a welcome mat, his way of answering the problem of "how to be at home everywhere." The set itself is the product of an extended inquiry into the making of home, in Wuppertal and on the American frontier.

For Regina Advento, from Brazil, her passive role as "the black one" in *Nur Du* connects with her biracial experiences at home and her sorrow about the race relations she observed in Los Angeles. In the production's first week after the premiere, there is prominent blackface; by the second week, it has been cut.

Nevertheless, race is at issue in *Nur Du,* and class even more so. The sprawl of the production is overwhelming, and the connections between its different scenes uneasy—a structural metaphor, perhaps, for the multicultural metropolis itself.

But the meaning of her works, Ms. Bausch has always insisted, remains open.

So, what did two young men from Wuppertal, big Bausch fans, think of *Nur Du?*

"Funny."

"Slow."

Was it "American"?

One says no. The other says yes.

Why? Because of the music, and the cheerleader.

— *New York Times,* 1996

Love Mysterious and Familiar

Pina Bausch Brings Her Visceral Non Sequiturs to Austin

IT WAS MAGICAL, the night that the Pina Bausch Tanztheater Wuppertal came to town. The 22 October performance in the Bass Concert Hall at the University of Texas, the last of four stops on the company's first full-fledged American tour, was a UT coup several years in the making. The co-production (with institutions in Berkeley, Los Angeles, and Tempe) was an enormous project, involving students and faculty from the UT College of Fine Arts and funding from private and nonprofit sources.

Afterward, the audience applauded heartily, the patrons sipped punch, and the Performing Arts Center staff beamed. And Bausch's face looked just the way Federico Fellini had described it, in close-up: "an aristocratic, delicate and cruel, mysterious and familiar face, frozen in puzzling stasis."

And now I am left to write a review of *Nur Du* (Only You), a sprawling, three-and-a-half-hour montage whose intense imagery refuses any logic except that of a dream, or memory. Dance criticism is always a knowing act of failure, a futile effort to suggest with words what the body utters. But in the case of Bausch's work, the failure is lifted to the level of trauma. I am not optimistic. But I am persistent.

It's not that the work is "beyond criticism." I don't believe there is such a thing. And it's not just that the work is nonnarrative. Most postmodern dance is nonnarrative, and much more congenial to verbal language. With Bausch's tanztheater—literally, "dance theater"—there is something about the monumental scale, in time, space, and imagination, that confounds the linear parade of words. It is dense and complex, both in form and content. It is what semiotician/novelist Umberto Eco calls an "open text," which operates without closure, preferring to emphasize gaps and ruptures rather than transitions and conclusions. Paradoxically, this is a theater of non sequiturs that makes sense—but it makes sense in the viscera, rather than in the head.

Since 1973, Bausch has been artistic director of the city opera house dance company in Wuppertal, an industrial city in Germany's Ruhr Valley. Although not the only practitioner of tanztheater, she has become the most visible on the world touring circuit. In 1984, the company made its American debut at the Olympic Arts Festival in Los Angeles. Next stop, New York City, and the ensuing outcry of indignant dance critics ensured many more returns. Accustomed to the formalism of George Balanchine in ballet and Merce Cunningham in modern dance, American critics had trouble accepting Bausch's rampant expressionism.

They didn't know what to do with her stark, frank images of everyday life, especially the gender wars, which featured repeated acts of violence. Indeed, the message was bleak, the style jarring, and the dancing minimal. But that was more than a decade ago, and Bausch wannabes have sprung up everywhere. As an established genre, tanztheater has become, in less inventive hands, comfortably readable and even predictable.

Bausch's newest production (titled after the Platters' 1955 hit, "Only You") is the same, only different. It is a nonnarrative montage, yet it has more structure. It takes up the problems of male-female relationships, yet its vision is much less brutal. It repeats many of the same images, props, and bits, and yet they add up to something unique. Bausch is an auteur; her artistic preoccupations and symbolic repertoire may remain the same, but her angle of vision keeps shifting as she attempts to sift and sort out the vagaries and delights of the basic human need to connect.

Nur Du opens and ends quietly, with an empty stage. Unlike other of Bausch's trademark works, whose floors are covered with dirt, or salt, or water, the floor is bare. Standing at the back of the stage is a grove of mammoth redwood trees. One has been chopped, left a pathetic, gargantuan stump; another has been nicked by a giant's hatchet, left with a niche in which, later in the piece, Jan Minarik will sit and smoke and clink champagne glasses. He spends quite a bit of time lurking about the trees, climbing them in different ways, once with a pair of wings on his back.

The stage has become an ominous forest that dwarfs its visitors, intensifying the sense of isolation that the piece comes to describe. The setting (by Peter Pabst) suggests a fairy-tale forest, especially in a scene in which Julie Shanahan and Daphnis Kokkinos draw on their black clothing with chalk, marking their bodies as male and female, and proceed to search the now leaf-scattered floor with a basket in hand. They are Hansel and Gretel in the forest primeval. Or Adam and Eve in a paradise lost.

The piece, characteristically, is structured like a revue, and its numbers include expressive, gestural solo dances; stories; monologues; songs; theatrical skits; ensemble dancing; and eccentric partnering. *Nur Du* features every dancer in a solo, each one obliquely, and powerfully, emotional. The soloists sometimes share the stage with other activities, and, in the case of Kyomi Ichida, with an airborne whale.

THERE IS a recurring motif of support, both emotional and physical. Bodies function as supporting objects: to stand, recline, or sit on. In the most beautiful moment of the dance, Eddie Martinez, who has already dived headlong through the air, fearlessly, for a kiss with Ruth Amarante, is now a scared child, calling out for Andrei Berezine. Martinez just up and leaps into those sturdy arms, which cradle and carry his curled-up body offstage.

Music is used for ironic commentary: "Only You" accompanies Minarik as he transforms a row of women into cookie-cutter images of each other. Fernando Suels repeatedly hangs Aida Vainieri by her hair, as Harry Connick Jr. croons a heartbreaking love song.

But it is the production's beginning, middle, and ending images that seem to distinguish *Nur Du*. These are moments—quiet, and stripped bare—which seem to stand outside the work, looking in. As Regina Advento opens the piece, singing a mournful tune of love lost, so Dominique Mercy ends the piece, this time with a dance, a virtuoso solo of spiritual exhaustion. And just as, early in the piece, Shanahan has comically pointed out that everyone is naked underneath their clothing, so she begins the second act with a moment of naked truth, of confession, of anti-tanztheater. Her back to the audience, she speaks to the stage: I come without makeup, or hairdo, or costume, or high heels. I have no ideas. But I come anyway.

Workshopped in Los Angeles, with supplementary visits by the production team to Austin and Berkeley, *Nur Du* was billed as Bausch's site-inspired take on the Southwest. The question remains: What does it say about America, if anything?

The answer took time to find. When *Nur Du* made its American premiere 3–5 October in Berkeley, it felt much more cohesive than during its several-week run in Wuppertal, in May. By the end of the tour, here in Austin, the production hit its stride. The obvious, surface Americana is still there: the cheerleading bit, the baseball monologue, the Hollywood one-liners, the 911 scene, the mimicry of Venice Beach characters, the costume tailored from the straws, cups, and napkins of fast-food restaurants.

But a deeper sense of American energy has emerged. The music, for one, had been substantially shaped since Wuppertal, where the brilliantly chosen mix of hallmark American pop love songs, mixed with passionate tangos and sambas and blues, and punctuated with Native American music and gentle guitar music, was just mostly loud. Now, the overall rhythm of the piece shifts dramatically between the quiet and the chaotic, and is visibly produced by the music as well as the stage action. As musical collaborator Andreas Eisenschneider put it, it has a sense of swing.

There is something about the display of tricks (turning somersaults on a bar and floating a feather) and inventions (high heels fashioned from cigarette boxes and a cup hand-made from paper) that delights in good old American ingenuity.

And there is something of the American West in the sense of open but bounded space, with its undercurrent of alienation and even danger. The solos, which serve as the underlying mechanism of continuity, also suggest an American view of life, as existing primarily at the level of the individual and only uneasily at the level of the community.

But for Bausch, the human condition ignores national borders. Despite the exhaustion and despite the high risk to heart and soul, each of us still searches for connection. That search is occasionally cruel, more often difficult, sometimes delightful, and always heartrending. But we are like the performer without her costume, and without ideas: we come to the theater anyway. In the very act of arrival, there is something hopeful and noble and beautiful. That's how Bausch answers her own musical question, "Why do fools fall in love?"

—*Texas Observer*, 1996

Remembered Gesture

P INA BAUSCH sits in the midst of another post-performance dinner in Wuppertal, fawning over a beatific-faced dancer recently arrived from the Paris Opera, seated at her right. She offers the long table three toasts, the first to her longtime companion, the second to her newest dancer, who debuted in *Café Müller* this evening, and the third to life and love.

Bausch is happy, and it's because of the dancing. Tonight she performed her signature role, as the fitful somnambulist in *Café Müller*.

On these infrequent occasions when the choreographer takes the stage before curtain call, she escapes her relentlessly hectic life. Dancing, she focuses simply on the music, and her own feelings. It's like a holiday in the head, she says.

Bausch composed her first dances thirty-one years ago, not so much because she had something to say, although it is clear now that she did, as to give herself something to dance. Compared to the eclectic and iconoclastic work she had done as a student in New York City, creating new roles for Antony Tudor and Paul Taylor alike, her subsequent career as a soloist with Kurt Jooss's Folkwang Ballet eventually frustrated her preternaturally doleful expressiveness.

At Juilliard she was quiet and serious and committed, and quite successful. She was favored by Tudor, a twentieth-century master of the lyric-dramatic ballet, who admired her up on pointe, looking even skinnier than usual, her expression turned sorrowful. She even won the approval of Louis Horst, Martha Graham's early mentor and a notoriously uncompromising composition teacher.

When Tudor created a recital role for Philippine in high heels and flamboyant hat, he made a comedienne of her. As artistic director of the Metropolitan Opera Ballet, he cast her as one of the three graces in *Tannhäuser* and in act two of *Alcestis*. Several years later, back in Germany, she appeared as Caroline, the desperately unfulfilled bride-to-be, in *Jardin aux lilas,* when Tudor staged it for the Folkwang Ballet.

Paul Taylor, a Juilliard classmate, loved to watch Bausch. She was able to streak across the floor sharply, if unevenly, like calipers across paper, he says, and also to move slower than a clogged-up bicycle pump. He eagerly turned her into a praying mantis for a 1960 duet, called *Tablet,* which he choreographed for her and Dan Wagoner.

By the time she reappeared on the American summer festival circuit in the early 1970s, shortly before making her career-defining move to Wuppertal, Bausch was a discernible original. According to *Dance Magazine* critic Judy Kahn, she was the highlight of a Paul Sanasardo concert in August 1972, although her peculiar vocabulary, so well suited to her own superlimber and specially trained body, proved a challenge for the other dancers: "She releases her back in a knee-bent 'S' and flexes her foot hard, peering at the audience with a poignant sense of humor and foreboding. Her creaturesque humanoid forms hover in an abstract yet basic realm of human experience, devoid of direct intellectual association, functioning on a paradoxically distant yet intimate level, communicating in images tucked away in the subconscious, in private dreams and public mythologies. With looming pliés, elbow-led arms, chicken-claw hands, her body tensions employ opposition and each move follows from a natural gravitational path often motivated internally by breath impulses."

Bausch and Sanasardo must have felt like twin souls. He, too, was intense, gaunt, and absorbed with existential issues: "The fact is, we are all of us alone. We can never be totally in contact with another human being. But we can all embrace our loneliness in some marvelous way." Most likely she met him through Tudor, with whom Sanasardo had studied for eight years. Sanasardo had also danced for ten years with Anna Sokolow, whose angst-ridden dance dramas, most notably *Rooms*, foreshadowed Bausch's tanztheater. His dances, described with the same kind of critical skepticism ("idiosyncratic," "strange," "bizarre") that would greet Bausch's own productions years later, dealt with the underside of human relations. They starkly depicted the fiercely fearful and anxious need for love. "Paul Sanasardo whacked Donya Feuer on the head," Doris Hering began one review, "and . . . she sank away from the impact, only to crawl back doggedly."

Although Bausch probably did not realize it at the time, she was apprenticing as a choreographer. By his example, Sanasardo legitimized the exploration of disquieting subject matter, and he demonstrated how to heighten human emotion and behavior using poetic imagery, irony, and theatricality. He and Tudor served as models of the choreographer as an acute observer of human behavior. From Tudor, Bausch had the opportunity to learn about the psychological implications of gesture, the engagement of dancers as individuals rather than instruments, the creation of character, the evocative value of nostalgia (especially in costuming), the metaphorical power of the male-female relationship, and the importance of formal specificity, especially in the delineation of emotion. Jooss's technical training, which integrated classical and modern dance, produced the precision and expansiveness of her dancing; his choreography suggested the integral connection between dance and drama, the usefulness of the montage structure, and the effectiveness of vernacular dance as a social metaphor. Each mentor, in his own way, defined dance as an expression of primal human experience.

Bausch worked longest with Jooss (who coined the term "tanztheater"), first as a teenager in the Folkwang school and then as a soloist in the Folkwang Ballet. What impressed her the most in all those years with him, perhaps, was dancing the part of the old woman in his 1932 expressionist masterpiece, *The Green Table*. When the old woman is confronted by the figure of Death, her response is alternately apprehensive and accepting. She listens; his head lifts. A stand-off, then retreat. She approaches him with a stiff-legged walk on tip-toe. A bow, and they commence an intimate duet. She turns away but returns into his arms, and when she finally bends backward in surrender, he lifts her and carries her off. The duet structure, even a similarly halting walk, but mostly the same abject attraction, appears at the climax of Bausch's own *Rite of Spring,* when a series of virgins confront their fate in the form of a male priest or elder who will choose one of them as a ritual sacrifice. Here is Bausch's proto-male/female dynamic. He is a tempting as well as a menacing figure, and the Chosen One is driven as much by fear as by desire.

Bausch astonished audiences in 1995 when she appeared onstage for a solo in *Danzón*. It was her first new role in the repertory since *Café Müller* premiered seventeen years earlier. Accompanied by the plaintive soul-scrapings of a Latin American singer-guitarist and partnered by an enormous fish swimming in projection behind her, Bausch stands rather diffidently, continuously stretching her long, longing arms outward and then recalling them back into and around herself again. This study in rhythmic flow—the spatial tension, the interchange of opposing forces, the organic cycling of outward and inward, the alternation between self and other, the dueling desires to reach out and to withdraw—is as explicit a manifesto as Bausch is likely ever to offer.

Her lyrical, even romantic, movement style persists from her Juilliard days, when the subtle interplay among arms, neck, head, and chest was already richly suggestive. Hers has always been an elegant and vulnerable neck, and her chest a sensitive register of emotion. Bausch arcs her arms with such concise intention that it looks like a narrative gesture; she requires only minimal vocabulary to explain herself.

Bausch's aura is alluring, because she is present, even sensuously engaged, and yet still remote. Her figure is frail and her eyes veiled as she strokes her skin and waves her arms as if slipping through a summer pond. She is a creature both detached and deeply empathic—the sleepwalker in *Café Müller,* or the blind princess in Fellini's *And the Ship Sails On.* Each one sees, but with eyes closed. And what she envisions is meta/physical.

Bausch's inward gaze is replicated in her dances. Composed, as they often are, of the performers' reenacted memories, fantasies, and dreams, there is something charged behind the actions, something felt but not quite visible, that compels us. Onstage, the performers are Bausch's doppelgängers, bright and dark, real and projected. Dominique Mercy, for example, carries her sense of existential isolation, and humor; the large, implacable Jan Minarik plays the bogeyman.

Early-twentieth-century dance theorist Rudolf von Laban (who taught Jooss, who taught Bausch) had a beautiful phrase for it, the way that dance inhabits a larger social and psychic space than its own impulse. Remembered gesture is what he called those lingering, inexorable, imprinted shadows that haunt Bausch's dancing body.

— *BAMazine*, 1999

Mellower Now, A Resolute Romantic Keeps Trying

THE REPORTS from Germany confirm it: Pina Bausch has mellowed.

"Gone are the days of the all-too-ugly battle of the sexes," announced one critic. Another wrote that the artistic director of the Pina Bausch Tanztheater Wuppertal "has become gentle," displaying a "new and almost old-fashioned tenderness." Kissing couples abound, as do scenic projections of erotically bursting petals and shivering stamens. Last year's *Masurca Fogo* was described as "an often funny, cheerfully melancholic piece." This summer, *O Dido* turned out to be more sensual than spectacular.

This "kinder, gentler Pina" was glimpsed by New Yorkers as early as 1994, when the company performed *Two Cigarettes in the Dark* at the Brooklyn Academy of Music. When the troupe returned with *Der Fensterputzer* (The Window Washer) in 1997, the New York dance press, which had largely dismissed Ms. Bausch's initial appearances in the mid-1980s as Euro-trash, was quick to note the production's lighter touch—its lyrical music, delightful humor, and joyful dancing.

This romantic impulse should come as no surprise, really. The perpetual yearning, the sublime terror, the mysterious symbolism—the belief in the possibility of love in the face of incontrovertible evidence to the contrary—have always underpinned the Wuppertal productions, albeit with a postmodern edge. The very fact that Ms. Bausch continues to probe the human condition, after having explored its foulest, most malignant territories, bespeaks the romantic's refusal to surrender to rational argument. What Ms. Bausch once explained about her dancers applies most of all to herself: she is not repeating herself; she is trying again.

The Pina Bausch Tanztheater Wuppertal returns to the Brooklyn Academy for its seventh appearance this week (Tuesday and Thursday through next Sunday), after a month-long tour in California, Arizona, and Texas. This time, the company brings the 1995 production, *Danzón,* one of only two dances in the repertory that feature Ms. Bausch onstage. She performs her pensive solo partnered by enormous and splendidly colored fish swimming in projection behind her. There's a certain innocence to *Danzón,* and Keatsian melancholy. It ends with a recollection of mortality by the elderly Goethe, who, after revisiting one of his youthful poems, concludes, "Now we can leave."

The company's cultlike appeal to audiences began in New York during its debut at the Brooklyn Academy fifteen years ago. The critical response was just as strong, but hardly devotional. The formalists accused Ms. Bausch of being a feminist, and the feminists (myself included) accused her of being a nihilist.

Coming to grips with Ms. Bausch's twenty-five-year oeuvre at such a remove from Wuppertal is difficult. We see only a small selection from the thirty-three-work repertory every few years, out of sequence and out of sync with her current work. The density and protraction of each piece demand repeated viewings, but if you want to study videotapes, a small monitor in a cramped theater basement in Wuppertal is your only option.

It was *Nur Du* (Only You), Ms. Bausch's 1996 co-production with several American universities in the Southwest and California, that laid bare the fundamental romanticism of her vision.

Act II opens with a despondent dancer, Julie Shanahan, approaching the edge of a redwood forest as if she were arriving at the rehearsal studio—dressed in her civies, dance bag slung over her shoulder. Standing with her back to the audience, she is the lonely figure out of a Caspar David Friedrich landscape, humbled by the exalted vista spread out before her. Ms. Shanahan confides to the trees that she doesn't have any ideas. Or any costume. She's not wearing high heels. But still, she came anyway. "I don't have a hairdo," she continues. "I'm not wearing makeup. I'm sorry. Anyway, I still came." And then she screams.

Sometimes, just showing up is an act of faith.

Like her mentor, Kurt Jooss, who is best known for his prescient 1932 antiwar masterpiece, *The Green Table,* Ms. Bausch connects most powerfully not with any aesthetic tradition or artistic style, but with her life and times, especially its proliferating anxieties. *Café Müller, Blaubart* (Bluebeard), and *Kontakthof* (Contact Courtyard) were created during the worst years of West German terrorist kidnapping, hijacking, and murder. *Blaubart,* the choreographer later recalled, dealt with her fear of violence, and dealt with it in an extreme manner befitting that particular moment in her life. When these dances were presented in New York, Ms. Bausch was roundly denounced for her bleak and brutal vision of humanity. Perhaps only now, after the accumulated horrors of the Columbine High School shootings, a Texas lynching, and a homophobic murder, can we appreciate the wonder, even the triumph, of "going on"—in life or in theater. For Ms. Bausch, the fact of the theater as a communal space where feelings can be shared and meaning generated constitutes its source of strength and beauty.

"I marvel not why someone dies outside his lover's tent," says the actress Mechthild Grossmann in the 1989 film, *Die Klage der Kaiserin* (The Plaint of the Empress). "I marvel though when someone loves and still goes on with life." Ms. Bausch's works have always addressed the abyss between desire and reality in one form or another, most often in the crucible of male-female relationships. We long for love or autonomy or perfection. We rarely, if ever, get it, but we'll die trying. And in the meantime, we'll make theater out of its shadows. But instead of smoothing over that desperate chasm, Hollywood-style, Ms. Bausch adapts its structure—incompletion, fragmentation, disruption, and interruption—as a way to inhabit and inspect it more fully.

WHAT DIVERTED our attention from Ms. Bausch's romantic disposition was the veneer of gritty hyperrealism in her work. The dancers share their own memories and stories, manhandle each other, and plow their way across dirt, grass, and water. The scenery looks so real that it's obviously fake. By playing conspicuously with the open secret of theatrical illusion, Ms. Bausch overturns the usual presumption that art mirrors life. Acting becomes the primal behavior and our own performance anxieties just so many variants on the actor's almost unbearable vulnerability: the desire to be loved and the fear of rejection, the desire to be seen and the fear of humiliation, the desire to show off and the fear of failure.

Ms. Bausch's art aspires to the condition of poetry in order to express the inexpressible. Choreography then becomes a search for the external form—images and pictures, mostly—of what she already knows but cannot yet articulate. There is an exact knowledge somewhere, she said, circling her hands around her body and her head during a recent lecture in Austin, "but I don't know where it is."

Not unlike the sightless but insightful princess she portrayed in Fellini's film *E la nave va* (And the ship sails on), Ms. Bausch gropes toward form and clarity by asking her dancers questions. When choreographing site-specific commissions, she begins with several weeks of "research" on location. Her entire career (even she admits that the repertory feels like one long dance) has been a sustained inquiry into human behavior, onstage and off. "It always starts with life," Ms. Bausch says. "Why are we together? Why are people dancing? What does it mean? Why does it mean?" Her answers, each one provisional, are necessarily but not explicitly political.

What few artist-philosophers we have left in this country are writers or artists, and certainly not choreographers. Bill T. Jones is the exception who proves the rule. According to high modernist decorum, choreographers are supposed to confine their attention to matters of form and style and leave the muck of human relations to politicians and popular culture. (In other words, stay barefoot and in the studio.) But hasn't modern dance always been responsible for rooting out the telling gesture?

Surely Ms. Bausch learned about that when she studied with Antony Tudor, a twentieth-century master of the dramatic ballet. With an auteur's radically subjective eye, Ms. Bausch has pursued to its logical extreme Martha Graham's dictum that "movement never lies."

In the early 1960s Ms. Bausch was a favored student of Graham's mentor, Louis Horst, at the Juilliard School in New York. Horst was a notoriously rigorous composition teacher, and the German exchange student apparently learned her lessons well. Her tanztheater is crammed with telling gestures, arresting images, and intense emotions. But "in the end," she once remarked to an interviewer, "it's composition."

In his book *Study of Modern Dance Forms* (1961), Horst included dances of "introspection," "expressionism," and "impressionism," which sound remarkably like tanztheater. "The Impressionist dance," for example, "has a romantic tone but still achieves the dissonance that belongs to our time. It arouses an intensity of attention by its very failure to complete, which is hauntingly affecting. The style has been used by contemporary choreographers to create a poetic mood with a modern texture, removed from any specific development of a plot." He offered as an example Tudor's *Lilac Garden,* whose leading role, the unfulfilled bride-to-be, Ms. Bausch herself danced under the choreographer's direction.

It may well turn out, in hindsight, that Ms. Bausch was a romantic postmodernist after all. (The film director Rainer Werner Fassbinder called himself a "romantic anarchist.") What looked at first to be clotted angst appears, with some distance, to contain at least the fantasy of some human solace. Despite the anomie and exhaustion, the Wuppertal productions have never trafficked in anger, and maybe that's why they've been able to outpace the despair.

But then again, maybe age is nature's palliative. "Perhaps the older we get," Ms. Bausch wondered aloud, while still in her early forties, "the more we fight for love?" Now facing sixty, she has renewed her pursuit of the beautiful. Next year she will direct a Wuppertal production of *Kontakthof*—her most riveting confrontation between the sexes—with senior citizens. "In old age, too, there is beauty," she says.

—*New York Times*, 1999

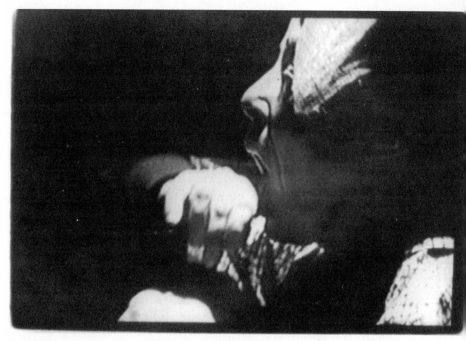

Voilà by Deborah Hay. Photo © Todd V. Wolfson. Used by permission.

DEBORAH HAY

Review: *The Man Who Grew Common in Wisdom*

AMONG THE pioneers of postmodern dance, Deborah Hay is one of the most
persistently reflexive. After about thirty years as a dancer, she is still concerned with the basics of performance. Dissatisfied with the presentational "look"
she had cultivated after so many years of dance training, Hay in 1970 headed in
the opposite direction. Her continuing quest is for a performance of pure presence, in which the process of doing some rather mundane actions can become
thrilling for the spectator, not just to watch, but to share.

At a time when most dance audiences are encouraged to sit back, relax, and
be entertained, Hay is determined to bridge what she sees as the huge gap between performer and spectator in those conventional presentational situations.
She wants, she says, to "invite being seen"—to make the interaction between
herself as a soloist and the audience members a two-way street. She is trying, in
effect, to develop a performance practice that empowers spectators to be more
than just passive observers.

"The Navigator" (1987), Part I of her new trilogy, *The Man Who Grew Common in Wisdom*, is a statement of Hay's intention to "invite being seen." In a

strikingly outsized and linearly designed white linen suit and dark skullcap, Hay goes through a series of quite prosaic movements, accompanied by composer Ellen Fullman humming New Age tones. (Fullman composed for all three pieces.) Hay's utter sense of calm penetrates the stage space, echoed by the wispy clouds projected on the backdrop. She proceeds unhurriedly from one thing to the next. The dance is made up of a series of actions, not of choreographed phrases that draw upon a character or a set vocabulary or even everyday activities. She stretches out on the floor, for instance, or ripples her spine while on all fours, or waves her arm as she sinks deep into the ground.

It is not the "what" that counts; it is the "how." Because this is not "choreography" with a beginning, middle, and end, Hay is not bound to maintain connections with the past and anticipate the future. Her absolute focus on what she is doing at the moment allows the audience to perceive the smallest shifts in her attention. Although the dance is by no means improvisational, it seems to be. Hay appears to be actively "listening," as it were, with her entire body, to both the space around her and the space inside her. The final, poignant moment of "The Navigator" comes as she bends over from the waist and extends her arms, like a bird in the moment before it takes flight, when the movement has already begun, vibrating within the stillness.

The intensity of Hay's presence at moments is exhilarating. I think the pleasure is not so different, in a perverse way, from the thrill of watching a great ballet dancer: both kinds of dancers reach the outer limits of human capacity. Unlike ballet, however, Hay's performance has a radiance that is without a content beyond itself—it is the performance of becoming.

"The Gardener" (1988) and "The Aviator" (1989), Parts II and III, respectively, are very different from "The Navigator"—they are funny, theatrical, and energetic. In these pieces Hay deals more explicitly with the amusing limitations of the physical body and the deadly seduction of the stage.

"The Gardener" begins in complete darkness, onstage and in the house. All the audience hears is feet slapping the floor. Gradually, a sharp sidelight comes up and Hay is seen in tights and leotard covered by a striped top and an elaborate, pointed cap. She travels around the stage, but her movements are unsure—twitching, stuttering, broken, her lips wiggling and her shoulders rotating. In a very playful way, the movement centers on how her body negotiates its weight on the floor. Hay grows more mischievous, coming to the edge of the stage and making a bit of a soft-shoe joke. She continues these jokes on performance traditions—doing a play on port de bras, on bourrées, on grand battements. You can see her asking herself: "How high can I kick my leg? To my hand?" Much of this she does downstage, playing to the audience not only with her bodily feats but also with her face. She narrows her eyes and vaguely puckers her mouth, silently cooing to the spectators.

To begin "The Aviator" Hay comes flying in from the wings, broadly circling the stage with a limp and a fool's grin. She wears a clownish outfit—a jumpsuit with ruffled cuffs at wrists and ankles. Her short, dense hair is loose and she wears dangling earrings. At irregular intervals she exits the stage, the first time for an unexpectedly lengthy period. Hay's grin never disappears, whether she is shuffling her feet and circling her arms à la Shirley Temple or patting her extended rear in mock coquettishness. Finally, she bourrées across the stage on her toes, her poetically curved arms folded across each other on her breast—an archetypal ballerina image. She gives in to the pleasures of her own movement, succumbing to the deadly seduction of "performing." The death throes are ugly and protracted.

—Theatre Journal, 1990

The Play of Dance

An Introduction to *Lamb, Lamb, Lamb, Lamb, Lamb, . . .*

It took me twenty-two years to learn how to dance, and it took me twenty-two years to unlearn how to dance.

—DEBORAH HAY, 1989

AT FIFTY, Deborah Hay is one of the few original postmodern choreographers still actively exploring an antitechnical aesthetic. While the likes of Trisha Brown, David Gordon, and Twyla Tharp have turned to increasingly virtuosic dancers and movement styles, Hay is still interested in the aesthetics of the lived —rather than the mastered—body. She still exists (both literally—in Austin, Texas—as well as metaphorically) at the margins of the art, refusing to buy into the conventional standards of beauty that have reentered the field in the last decade. She simply has eliminated that kind of hierarchy from her vocabulary.

"By calling dance 'dance' we are then making a judgement about stuff we are not calling 'dance.' I have an unquenchable thirst to present that area of movement not recognized as dance—to pull it back into the world of dance."[1] The choreographer's model remains John Cage, whose insistence that anything —including noise and silence—could be music, revolutionized the fate of late-twentieth-century art.

Hay grew up in Brooklyn, feeding on the Roxy corps and the New York City Ballet. She did indeed learn to dance well enough to join the Merce Cunningham Dance Company in 1964, but soon quit that in favor of the avant-garde community of the Judson Dance Theater. She discovered in its fondness for non-trained performers a whole new world of possibilities. She never took another dance class (it felt limiting); instead, she explored tai chi chuan, whose centered, grounded, smooth way of moving is still recognizable in her thick and gentle, honey-textured movement style. Onstage and off, Hay commands an aura that is very focused and very calming. Her voice is mellow and deep—luxurious space runs among her words.

In 1971 Hay left New York for a commune in Vermont. There, with only a tiny room to dance in, she had to rethink the very basis of her work. Since then, she explains, "my practice and resources as a dancer and choreographer have shifted from physical to perceptual challenges."[2] In 1976 Hay moved to Austin, where she has conducted twelve large group workshops, each one lasting from three to five months and culminating in public performances. The Deborah Hay Dance Company was formed in 1980. Until 1985 it was a four-member company; since 1986, Hay has worked primarily as a solo performer.

Hay does not warm up, and she does not rehearse. She is not interested in mastery—she is interested in process. She calls this process a "practice," emphasizing the getting there, not the arriving. "I practice the performance of movement. I practice being awake and whole and in relationship to you."[3]

The work is about what is traditionally called "presence." Why, even when all else (e.g., technique, experience) is equal, is one performer more compelling than another? It has, I think, to do with a saturated quality and intensity of focus, with the simultaneous, connected attention between the performer's inner and outer life.

Hay describes this state of being as one of *wholeness* (emerging out of what she terms "cellular consciousness") and *change*. "It's attractive to see wholeness," she points out, using sports—the baseball pitcher and hitter, or the martial arts practitioner—as a prime example.[4] No matter what a person is doing, onstage or off, if she is concentrating on it purely, with all her being (Hay calls it "pure intelligence"), we are attracted. We all know the person who, upon entering a room, exudes a palpable energy. "Somebody walks into a party, and that person has command of themselves. Everybody at the party stops talking and notices that person. You notice that kind of sense of oneself. It's really present. You know what it is. Somebody is present. That is what I am practicing: that attention elicits attention."[5] It is, then, the act of performance rather than the object of performance that matters to Hay. "We don't have to *do* anything startling, we just have to *be here*."[6]

It is precisely "the whole person in relation to the rest of the world," Hay argues, that is missing from life today. That relationship is what we are longing to see. So the point of performance is not self-centeredness, but to embrace the audience, as well as fellow performers. "My generation spent a lot of time looking inward, being sensitive and articulating that. But to survive as a planet, we must start relating to each other. It's about the self and the self in relationship."[7] In her annual large group workshops, Hay emphasizes the consciousness of others—not necessarily seeing them, but sensing them. And in performance, she has experimented with dissolving the boundaries between performer and spectator: by using her home as a performance space, by raising the lights in the theater, by speaking to the audience before a performance, and by directly looking at her spectators while performing.

Hay thinks of her work as play. Play is a form of performance neither goal-oriented nor script-generated; within a set of given parameters, it focuses on the present, on activity, and on the possibility of discovery within those parameters. Beyond the structure of play, however, Hay's performances are becoming more overtly playful in their content. When she literally played the fool in *The Aviator* (1989), she wore a clown's outfit and perpetual grin. At a recent benefit performance, she did her turn as an elf of sorts, exploring various parts of the stage space, trying to elicit applause without actually making the obvious mime gestures, and racing up and down the aisles. Certainly the "Mary Had a Little Lamb" material used in *Lamb, lamb, lamb, lamb, lamb, ...* (1991) suggests less (or more) than a self-conscious seriousness about the making of art.

What follows is the movement libretto for *Lamb, lamb, lamb, lamb, lamb, ...,* the production that capped her 1991 large group workshop. (The title *Lamb, lamb, lamb, lamb, lamb, ...,* by the way, is always accompanied by a gesture: one or two hands scooping the air back up into the mouth.) Hay uses her annual workshops as an opportunity to see how other dancers fulfill a specific set of movement directives. Her solos, then, become a distillation of the work begun in the large group. "My large group workshops are really an opportunity for me to choreograph for myself," Hay explains. "Because then, if I'm watching twenty-six people practice performing a movement I'm thinking about I get incredible feedback about the infinite possibilities."[8]

Lamb, lamb, lamb, lamb, lamb, ..., was fun. It was not too unlike a three-ring circus, with several different areas often offering a variety of activities from which to choose. There was no obviously linear structure to hold onto, and the things the performers (professionals and nonprofessionals alike) did—moving about, as well as pulling sounds out from within themselves—could look and sound very odd. Why they were hopping or "popping" or reconfiguring the moveable flats was inscrutable, but also irrelevant. Even after the entire group assembled for a chorus of "Mary Had a Little Lamb" at the performance's end, it was never obvious to me that the sounds being produced throughout the piece were deconstructed from the nursery rhyme. Hay's performances are not built on the conventional structure of theme and variation, which requires logical thinking. Instead, they require something certainly more difficult for today's audiences: openness and attentiveness. Part of the pleasure, for me, at least, is in the experience of going with the flow. I find it restorative and invigorating.

The following libretto is rather startling documentation, for it reveals what is not apparent in the performance itself: the score. You don't *see* the instructions behind the behavior ("freeze without freezing") or *hear* "Mary had a little lamb" in the vocalizations. But you *experience* people being, focusing, vibrating. Despite the improvisatory feel of much of Hay's work, the performance is clearly structured and the movements clearly delineated, if not traditionally "choreographed."

If Cunningham used chance to step away from his ego and his habits, Hay has her "tricks," or movement koans. These tricks, different for each dance, keep the performer centered in the movement. And they prevent the performer from becoming fixed, either in the movement or in his ideas about what performance is or looks like. Some of the koans are unachievable: "freeze without freezing," or "come to a fake stop." Others are strangely vague: "fingertips willed through the tops of the feet," or "make rain with the feet." All of them require dancing with both body and mind: "imagining the head where the shins are."

"I don't *get* them," emphasizes Hay. "I *play* with them."[9]

The choreography—these sets of "tricks"—are like monkey bars. "My real interest is in the unknown of going from that one [bar] to the other, and it's in that space. But the choreography is there so that I do have something to grasp onto." She conceives of choreography as "a sequence of tricks that maintain my attention from the beginning to the end." The tricks are ways to keep the performer excited "about every moment that's coming up. You know, how to take your arms from here to over there and not *be* anything. Really, just be everything and nothing at the same time."[10]

The trick, Hay says, is finding a way to get the dancer to not be a character but to be her own self: to walk the tightrope. Thus the koans are not about steps or poses; rather, they elicit an attitude toward movement. They divert self-absorption. They supply Hay's need for movement that is "unafraid, unembarrassed, undiluted." She devises these ridiculous, illogical, contradictory tasks in order to eliminate the "rules" of movement. The point is not representation (Hay never demonstrates movement for her dancers), but how to get beyond representation, to "the body's infinite capacity to inform."[11]

Every movement, she insists, "is potentially a revelation, if you don't get caught, trapped, stuck, attached to line and form, and feeling."[12]

The work, then, is about the body's visibility: about our mysterious abilities to see and be seen.

—*TDR: The Journal of Performance Studies*, 1992

No Exit

Deborah Hay's Latest Work a Meditation and Celebration in Space and Time

LIKE MOST everything in our culture, with the conspicuous exception of politics, dance is identified with the energy of youth. And solo dancing, in particular, has been reduced to the balletic star-turn, presided over by tender-aged virtuosos of strength, speed, and precision.

Deborah Hay gives the lie to that limited vision. At fifty-three, after two decades of solo dancing in Austin, Hay achieves a transparency of expression rarely offered by those young, sleek dancing machines. Hay's dancing is not about the body's surface and trajectory; nor it is about mastery. It's about depth and focus: the inner impulse made manifest only through practiced surrender. In Hay's solos, energy is not measured in outward accomplishments but experienced through inner intensity. Hers is a body that is older, wiser, and more comfortable, but definitely not complacent. She has none of that vainglorious need to prove something—a need that obscures young dancers as delicately but as surely as a fine-net veil.

Hay appears the naïf, a quality she shares with two others in the soloist peerage, seventy-six-year-old Merce Cunningham and eighty-nine-year-old Kazuo Ohno. It is this playful attitude, this utter devil-may-care abandonment to self-exposure (the arthritic Cunningham hobbles across the same stage as his company's young beauties; Ohno bares his aging flesh or wears women's clothes) that affords these master soloists their compelling presence. And it is this public vulnerability, what Hay has called "inviting being seen," that often embraces the erotic. (The link between vulnerability, eroticism, and performance presence was made clear to me by choreographer Senta Driver, who once explained a company exercise in which she asked her dancers to move as if the one they loved were watching them.)

Hay's two-week run (2–12 November), of two solo premieres at the Public Domain theater, was her first solo appearance in Austin since 1992. Over the years, Hay has presented herself in a range of conventional and alternative spaces around town, some more compatible to her work than others, but in the loft-style space of Public Domain, she has discovered an ideally intimate setting. After climbing the hollow wooden stairs and gathering in the anteroom, we were invited to enter the theater all together and were introduced to the nature of Hay's project by a friend of hers.

And at the short evening's end, in that transitional time between the extraordinary space of performance and the reentry into everyday life, we were provided with catered food and a festive moment in which to extend the time with Hay and with each other. There was also an opportunity to inspect the historical panorama of posters and reviews lining the walls: Hay's hairstyle may run the gamut (bushy, coifed, capped), but the ease, the vibrance, and the plenitude—as well as that wide smile of unfettered exuberance—persist without interruption.

The performance proper lasted only forty minutes: the brief, concentrated *Exit*, followed by the more expansive *Voilà*. Providing a segue between the two was a recorded text, written by Hay, ostensibly describing a dance performance in the year 2075. This is the choreographer's sly way of inserting a "viewer's manual" right into the performance. The floating voice describes the joy of attending a performance without knowing where or what it is. "I am terribly happy," she says, "to be going where I'm not expecting to be." Eventually, she finds herself in the middle of the performance as she's walking down the street, and all perceptual means are ignited: she begins to expand her field of vision, noticing "the space between things," "the edges," "density," and how "everything seems so fragile in terms of time." The dance-goer becomes the dance and recognizes her own "potential for the history I embody." And that's the essence of Hay, in a nutshell.

Voilà, characteristically, was choreographed using material from her annual large group workshop and performance, this year entitled *my heart*. She literally gallops, prances, processes, and hops her way through the half hour. The material is a radical, absurd pastiche: not just eccentric, even awkward movements (those confused, darting arms sometimes look just like Merce Cunningham's), but also storytelling, vocalizations, and assorted emotional outbursts. She is, in quick succession, fierce, tentative, sad, amazed, earnest, exasperated, excited. She makes ugly faces, and does silly kid stuff.

Hay's vocalizations are especially poignant, sometimes gut-wrenching: guttural, incipient rumblings that never quite reach full release; odd, isolated sounds; and child's oral games, such as mouth farts and a clucking tongue. Here, as usual, Hay plumbs the tragic in the humorous, and vice versa, keeping us emotionally mobile and receptive. The condition of watching, and of being, becomes perpetually transformational, without continuity or closure. It's an experience of constant deferment. (After all, her body is, she says, "a Buddhist body, a rippling of appearances.") Sometimes the feeling is productive, and sometimes it feels choked off, aborted. To be constantly in the moment can produce joyful expansiveness, but it can also result in existential isolation.

Exit is another story, however. A departure of landmark significance for Hay, who helped pioneer the iconoclastic postmodern movement in dance in the 1960s, *Exit* is a classically abstract dance, whose coherent form suggests a rich metaphor for leaving/arriving (again, a phenomenon of the in-between, or, perhaps more accurately, the simultaneous). The first professional dance Hay has choreographed to music (the hauntingly bittersweet adagio from Samuel Barber's string quartet), it is one slow exit on the diagonal, punctuated by a succession of turns backward to her starting point. With a compasslike right arm outstretched toward her distant goal, Hay is compelled to reconsider, or honor, or let go of her past, even as she progresses forward. She accomplishes all this with the most pristine minimal means, without resorting to anything resembling conventional acting. The gesture of her hand, the drawing in of her arms, the focus of her eyes and body are what tell the story.

Like Isadora Duncan, who, eighty years ago, approaching fifty and having developed her aesthetic into a kind of living sculpture—what she envisioned as pulsating movement-in-stillness—Deborah Hay, too, has exited into the mythic realm of the tragic actress.

—*Texas Observer,* 1995

An Experimentalist in Soul and Body

DEBORAH HAY, a pioneer of postmodern dance whose explorations started in the Judson Dance Theater movement in the early 1960s and have yet to slacken, cannot recall how she happened upon the title for her latest solo. So she utters it aloud—*Voilà*—attempting to retrieve its history. Her right hand punctuates the sound with a sudden upward flourish. "It feels so appropriate," she decides, "because it describes the work that I do. 'Here it is.' It just appears, and then it's gone. This momentariness is part of the spirit of the dance."

As with all of Ms. Hay's recent work, the spirit of *Voilà,* which she will perform Thursday through next Sunday at the Kitchen, is playful. She literally gallops and prances through the forty-minute solo, enacting a radical non sequitur of material: not just eccentric, even awkward movements, but also storytelling, vocalizations (tongue clucks and guttural rumblings that never quite reach full release) and various other sorts of emotional outburst. She is, in quick succession, fierce, tentative, sorrowful, amazed, earnest, exasperated. She makes ugly faces and does silly kid's stuff. Ms. Hay is plumbing the tragic in the comic, and vice versa.

True to her roots in the Judson Dance Theater, an informal collective of experimentalists who rejected traditional choreography and technique in favor of open-ended scores and ordinary movement, Ms. Hay defines dance expansively.

"Dance is the place where I practice attention," she says. "It's a kind of alertness in my body that I have at no other time. So dance for me is about playing awake."

Ms. Hay has lived in Austin, Texas, since 1976, after moving there from a commune in northern Vermont. At fifty-five, she is concerned about the fate of her solo repertory and about her reputation as an idiosyncratic performer. These concerns have led her back into territory from which she exiled herself more than three decades ago: choreography, trained performers, even dance preservation. "Whereas before I thought of choreography as what you did in order to perform," she explained, "the idea of choreography as a separate art form has suddenly become very interesting to me."

Over the years, the format of Ms. Hay's work has changed from folklike communal dances to company concerts to solos, but her deeply philosophical, even spiritual, interest in the presence of the body has never waned. Proceeding from question to question about the nature of performance, she has extended into the 1990s a rigorous experimental agenda, with provocative results.

From 1980 to 1995, she conducted an annual four-month workshop for trained and untrained performers, as a means of developing her own solos. Each workshop explored a specific "meditation" formulated by Ms. Hay. For 1995, for example, the meditation was this: "Imagining every cell in my body at once has the potential to dialogue with all that there is." That workshop culminated in the large group dance *my heart,* which inspired *Voilà.*

Because she wants to delve deeper into the possibilities of choreography, Ms. Hay has temporarily suspended the annual workshop to work with trained performers. Now she generates new pieces by quoting her previous ones, in increasingly complex ways. After *Voilà* had its premiere in Austin in November 1995, she wrote its sixteen-page libretto, an intricate layering of description, memoir, commentary, and stage direction that slides between first- and third-person perspectives. Then she performed the libretto as a monologue, entitled "a performance of a performance." For its newest incarnation, at the Kitchen, Ms. Hay has invited two other dancers to remake *Voilà* from the libretto, which now doubles as a score, and to perform with her.

"I am resourceful," explains Ms. Hay, who last appeared in New York three years ago. "I like taking material apart. Rather than go on to another dance, let's see what else I can learn about this material from another perspective."

AT THE KITCHEN, Ms. Hay hopes to learn more about her work as it exists independent of her own body. "For those people who see Deborah Hay's work as something only Deborah Hay can do," she says, "then what is my work as performed by other people?"

"I like these dances," she adds. "I want to see them go on. I like the idea of a dance student being able to reconstruct them from a score without our spending billions of dollars on technology."

Ms. Hay was once told that her dances were impossible to score in Labanotation, the field's generally accepted notation system. "I got very excited, because I didn't like the way it looked on the page," she says. "It really bothered me to think that my dance would be limited to these shaded rectangular boxes."

Any transmission of her dances needs to be an open process, because Ms. Hay does not want to close off the dancer's creative space.

"What I'm looking at with this process is: Can you pass on dance without telling anybody how to move, but instead by giving them a whole other set of parameters or conditions for recreating the dance? And is it still that same dance?"

To perform her experiment with *Voilà*, Ms. Hay chose Grace Mi-He Lee, twenty-nine, and Scott Heron, thirty-four, two former workshop participants. They received the libretto and meditation last year, but the choreographer will not see the results until this week. The three solos will be done separately, beginning with Ms. Hay's.

Mr. Heron, who is based in New York, recently performed his evening-length dance *The Goat Story* at P.S. 122. Ms. Lee, who presented an evening of her solo dances at P.S. 122 last year, lives in Philadelphia. "They make me laugh and cry more than any other performers," says Ms. Hay. "There is nothing those two won't do."

Ms. Lee, who saw a run-through of *Voilà* and a performance of *my heart,* sees the libretto as a screenplay. "I make sense of it as a whole," she explains, "by seeing it as an epic western, in which I play all of the outlandish characters playing out all of their individual dramas: protagonists, antagonists, and cameos."

"I love the humor in the score, and I play it out fully," she says. "Deborah's work must be done with total involvement. You can't mark it or reduce it to a vocabulary. This may sound serious, but her work actually frequents the realm of absurdity."

Mr. Heron, too, remarks on the appealing absurdity of the project. His challenge, he says, was "to take what first appears to be complete nonsense and find the logic, mystery, and beauty of the dance."

Ms. Hay's libretto-based monologue *a performance of a performance* will follow the three solos at 10 P.M. on Saturday only. Speaking the writing of the movement, Ms. Hay explains, has given new dimension to the original solo.

"The last few words in the libretto," she explains, "were simply a direction for what I was doing on stage: 'She began galloping in circles. Horse rider woman playing dancing. A human being galloping off.' But when I write that down, it goes so many places. It's not me on the dance floor doing movement. Suddenly it has a fullness and poetry to it as an event. The words become embodiments. When you're speaking it, the picture just gets bigger.

"And so now when I go back to dance *Voilà,* I'm not just galloping in circles and exiting off. I really feel so much bigger than the act you're looking at on stage."

—*New York Times,* 1997

Horse Rider Woman Playing Dancing
Ann Daly Interviews Deborah Hay

THE LANDSCAPE of American experimental dance is parched and desolate. Even the youngest generation, once presumed our best bet for innovation, now emerges from college dance departments where once revolutionary ideas have calcified into tepid technique and bad choreography. How ironic that some of today's most radical dance is being made by a fifty-six-year-old, Deborah Hay.[1]

But maybe not so ironic. The last two decades have demonstrated that youth is not by definition radical, or even resistant. My dance history students struggle less to identify with Louis XIV's court than they do with the Judson Dance Theater. "I'm so glad," one student grumbled during a class about the 1960s, "that I didn't live then." Experimentation as an ideal has been supplanted by marketability; the avant-garde had a long run, but it is over.

The Judson community, which included Hay, was unprecedented, and is irreplicable. Except for Douglas Dunn, Hay remains the only choreographer fully living out its experimental ethos. (Yvonne Rainer moved out of dance, into film, in the 1970s.) More so than Merce Cunningham, Hay has followed the lead of John Cage, and herself became an artist-philosopher. Since 1970, she has committed to the daily practice of "playing awake"—a perpetual perception exercise, a constant state of inquiry.

It was after her 1964 world tour with Cunningham that Hay renounced her formal training and set out to "un-learn" a lifetime of dance, which she began as a pupil of her mother, who had danced in the ballet corps at the Roxy Theater. The adult Hay began making dances for untrained performers, consisting of stripped-down movement set within highly organized structures. In the 1970s she created a series of Circle Dances, recorded in her book *Moving through the Universe in Bare Feet* (Swallow Press, 1975), that adapted the energy flow of tai chi for a folk dance format. In 1976 she moved to Austin, Texas, and performed her first solo dance concert. In 1980 she created a small dance company (disbanded five years later) and taught the first of fifteen annual large group workshops, each of which provided the ground for her solo repertoire, including *The Man Who Grew Common in Wisdom* (1989) and *Lamb at the Altar* (1992), which she documented in *Lamb at the Altar: The Story of a Dance* (Duke University Press, 1994).

The solo *Voilà* was inspired by Hay's last large group workshop, held in 1995. Shortly after its premiere, she wrote a sixteen-page libretto, an intricate layering of description, memoir, commentary, and stage direction that slides between first-and third-person perspectives. Then she performed the libretto as a monologue, entitled *a performance of a performance* (1996). For its final incarnation, Hay invited two former students, Scott Heron and Grace Mi-He Lee, to reconstruct *Voilà* from the libretto and perform their versions with her at the Kitchen in New York City in April 1997. The complex genealogy of *Voilà* is testament to Hay's fundamental inquisitiveness, resourcefulness, devotion to process, and fondness for play. For Hay, dance is a way of knowing, one that our culture obstinately ignores. It's her job to tease out what the body knows, and dancing is the "trick" she deploys to do so.

Hay refuses the dancer's posture of mastery. Instead, she relishes playing the fool. In *Voilà,* she surprises us with her mouth farts, so shockingly childish a pastime to see so earnestly performed on stage. As are the strange faces and stranger costume, in which she is emperor, horse, and jester. As in most play, Hay's is serious. With *Voilà,* in its myriad manifestations, she posed an ambitious range of aesthetic and spiritual questions: What is the identity of a dance? How does it exist beyond the moment of performance? How can choreography be transmitted without proscribing the performer's creativity? How is self and other simultaneously embraced and denied in performance? Is borrowing ethical? How can writing become choreography? What is prayer?

Like a physicist, Hay first proffers propositions about the unknown in order to discover what may be knowable. She speaks a language similar to the physicist's, too—at once mathematical and allusive, precise and mystical. But as conceptual as her dances are ("My perception," she explains, "is the creative act"), they remain utterly theatrical. Not just because of her stunning dramatic presence as a performer, but because she relies on make-believe to conduct her experiments: If I behave *as if* "I am the impermanence I see," then what would my dancing look like? And what would it tell us about our potential for seeing, and being seen? Hay's universe is always expanding.

ANN DALY: How do you define dance?

DEBORAH HAY: The closest analogy is that dance is where I practice attention, alertness, an awakeness in my body that I have at no other time. It is playing awake, like a dog to its master devotedly, unabashedly. Whatever it takes, I will take it on, to experience that awakeness in my body. That's where I am touched when I am looking at dance. It awakens me.

DALY: Awakens you to what?

HAY: It awakens me to . . . It's a very sensual, boundless experience, like being agog. Agogedness.

DALY: Are you more present to yourself or to the world?

HAY: It's an intimate experience, and at the same time it parallels a primal alertness, like a hunter.

DALY: Alertness implies an object. What are you hunting?

HAY: I don't think there is an object. I say "hunter" in terms of the kind of listening hunters do. It's not a nothingness. It's a feeling of congruency. Until recently I imagined only the fifty-three trillion cells and now I include in that imagining the whole body at once. There's a congruency. I'm also seeing myself seeing myself awake. There are layers upon layers of perspective I have of myself as a performer in relationship to the audience. So, presence is intimate, it's multiple, and it is local.

DALY: The solo *Voilà* was created out of the group work, *my heart,* which culminated in your large group workshop in Spring 1995. Underneath each of your dances is what you call a "meditation." What was the meditation for that one?

HAY: It was "imagining every cell in my body has the potential to dialogue with all that there is." Which translates down to the practice of prayer. I was looking at prayer. What does it mean to me? How do I relate to this, as a cynic, without much religious background, and who has no relationship to prayer at all in a conscious way? What does prayer mean? When I prayed as a child I was having a talk with a great unknown that I firmly believed heard me. In this exploration I used my whole body to dialogue with all that there is. I didn't look for the dialogue, and I didn't create the dialogue, and I didn't wait for it. I simply imagined, presumed, that dialogue exists with all that there is and that this is prayer. I'm not determining that this is true or not true. I simply play it out and notice the kind of feedback I get when I imagine every cell in my body has the potential to be in dialogue with all that there is.

DALY: Your bodily practice—your dance—is not just about the physical body, but about the physical/spiritual body.

HAY: This is crucial. In dance I do not divide the body into physical, spiritual, mental, emotional, psychological parts. I am adamant about this. The whole body is the perceiver of everything imagined, created, invented, not imagined, guessed, faked.

DALY: How do you get from the meditation to *my heart*?

HAY: On the best days, if you walked into the studio to see this group practicing "the whole body at once has the potential to be in dialogue with everything there is at every moment," you would see total chaos. It would look closer to a madhouse than it would to a dance workshop. And that's because part of the practice is that there is no one way that the meditation looks. Plus we're challenging each other to see the practice being applied, no matter how it might appear on the surface, within the context of that opening part of the workshop every morning. There is no one way it looks.

DALY: How do you communicate this to the performers?

HAY: I introduce the same meditation every day for four months, reminding them that there is no way it looks, reminding them that it's every cell in the body that's practicing it. I do this throughout the hour and a half. I keep coaching them to return to playing the meditation and not go off on their own thing. And crucial to the meditation is seeing in it other people, so you're reminded of the meditation by seeing others practicing it. The assumption is that nobody can do it all of the time, so that doesn't matter. The assumption is that we're all playing. It's like setting up the rules for a basketball game. These are the rules, and we're all collaborating at playing it. It's exactly the same, except there's no basket. There's no achieving the meditation.

DALY: How long is each workshop day?

HAY: Three hours, two parts. The first part is the meditation without the shape. The second part is the meditation with the shape. That's the choreography.

DALY: Tell me about the second part.

HAY: *my heart* was a very different experience from the other large group workshops.

DALY: How so?

HAY: The very first day I asked everyone to perform a three-minute solo, thinking that this would get the horror of performing over with immediately. Ninety-five percent of the people in that workshop were not trained performers. The directions for the three-minute solo were: one, not to feel you have to be creative; two, not to perform out of the rush of adrenaline; three, the solo could happen anywhere in the space. I took notes on all the solos to get an idea of the people. I was amazed that in every single solo there were moments that were incredibly beautiful and strange and wonderful. Before I knew it, the material that I saw during those solos became the structure of *my heart*. I just took each one of the things I wrote down that struck me and developed and expanded it into the material for the piece. For instance, the farting sequences were done by a fifty-five-year-old man who had been dealing with AIDS for years. Just a clear, bright, gorgeous man who sat on the floor and expelled lots of air from his mouth, like a bad boy, an imp, a baby, a child, a tramp, an ingrate, an idiot.

All of this found its way into the composition. I pasted the material together. There were certainly choices being made—where things would happen, embellishments, new material—but a lot of it came from those solos. It was so easy. It was the only time I choreographed a group dance that was literally structured in six weeks. I felt so guilty. There was a part of me, and I was suppressing it, that felt guilty about taking other people's material and using it as source material for a piece I was supposed to be choreographing. And that's when I had this dream about looting: "A man dressed in medieval hunting clothes grabs a small bird by its tail feathers. He presses the tip of its tail onto a table. As the bird frees itself, some of its feathers remain on the table and scatter. The man turns to me and says, 'This means looting.'" When the man said "looting," I thought he meant that to hold on to anything, like the material my students had performed, was looting. So I put the dream in *my heart*. Beverly [Bajema] and Sylvie [Senecal] both told the story. Twice a day, for four months, I listened to it. Because "looting" was so difficult to say and be understood, they had to emphasize its pronunciation.

I was in a dream group at the time. While I was working on my solo *Voilà* the following fall, I went to my dream group to talk about this dream for the first time, and I was encouraged to describe the man who spoke to me in the dream. He was beautiful, an alchemist. When he says "this is looting," it was gentle and loving. He implied that the feathers were a form of looting, and that it was positive experience. That art is looting. That the transformation of a bird into feathers is like the transformation of paint into painting or movement into dancing. That all art is a form of looting. It is about adaptation and transformation. So that understanding was built into the solo work.

DALY: *my heart* was performed at the conclusion of the four-month workshop, in April 1995, at the Helms Fine Arts Center at St. Stephen School in Austin. As usual, then, you turned the group piece into a solo. How does that happen?

HAY: On 1 May I went back into the studio and started practicing the material that most interested me in the group piece.

DALY: When other dancers use the word "practice," they mean to rehearse a series of steps until they get really good at it. What do you mean by the word "practice"?

HAY: To give you an example of practice, I'll talk about the gallop. I would play out every gallop that I had looked at for four months, over and over and over again, with seventeen different people galloping differently every single day. I just let all those visions of gallop run through me and allowed myself to take on everything that I had been watching in practice for four months. Simultaneously I would exercise the meditation to free me from the stylistic patterns assumed by my body in its vast capacity to mimic the others.

DALY: At what point did the practice begin to take a shape for the solo?

HAY: By July I had the overall shape of it, but because the material originally came from other people, I had to rid my body of playing characters. One of the things I love about performing *Voilà* is that I had to play the character and let go of that character simultaneously. To be the person who so influenced me while watching *my heart* and surrender that person's attributes as they were physically manifested was a very rich experience. I had to keep doing it so that it was me performing the movement and not me performing them performing the movement.

DALY: Vocalizations—these eruptions of sound from inside the body—are an important element of *Voilà*. This is new territory for you. Where is it coming from?

HAY: I think it started with the "Aviator" section from *The Man Who Grew Common in Wisdom* [1991]. It was the first time I was able to laugh at myself. I was able to just laugh at the whole history of being a dancer and how absurd it is. And, as a dancer who's growing older, a part of it was also to be able to laugh at the insanity of gesture, the insanity of the historic role of the dancer, how the dancer appears. In my workshops I had always asked people not to speak and not to use their voices, because I felt that it was a distraction. I think my breakthrough came through laughing. I spent one year's workshop [1992] with a combination of people, and we laughed constantly for four months. I laughed more in that four months than in my entire lifetime. That was the beginning, to be able to laugh at myself and what I was perceiving. Yes, it's like an eruption, as you say, of the voice, to hear the voice, then to use the voice and bring the laughter into other sounds. Why limit the meditation to the movement of the body when you could be projecting sound into space? You can then play with the sound as part of the meditation. It takes on space. It has dimension to it. It was using the voice and language and including that with the body. It's not accompaniment. It is an extension of what I can do with my body.

DALY: Has the vocalization revealed to you new things about movement?

HAY: It adds to the boundarylessness of movement. In using my voice and really hearing it moving out there, I see how big the dance is. I can use my eyes in relation to the audience to see how big the dance is, but then to color the space with voice makes me aware of what a great tool it is in dance-making.

DALY: How did you get the title for *Voilà*?

HAY: I don't know. It just came. It describes my work. "Voilà," here it is, and then it's gone. Here and gone. Momentariness is the spirit of the piece.

DALY: When did you start the version of *Voilà* that you'll be performing with Grace Mi-He Lee and Scott Heron at the Kitchen?

HAY: In December 1995, I came back from Mexico, where I had written the libretto. I sent it to Scott and to Grace and said, "Look at this and tell me if you're interested in learning the piece from the score." They both said they wanted to. I didn't have a performance date or anything like that. My original idea was to give it to them as a kind of gift, to learn it and some time come together to do it. Scott met Neil Greenberg, the dance curator at the Kitchen, and Neil said he was interested in producing it there. So they went to work on it. They've had it almost a year.

DALY: The score is itself an abridgement at the same time that it is a documentation of the solo. I'm wondering about how the notion of a "score" resonates with the experimentation of the '60s, in which scores were frequently used. But you call it a libretto.

HAY: It was originally written in a prose form, and I thought, isn't that how librettos are written, in a prose form?

DALY: But now, for the performance at the Kitchen, you're using it as a score, which is part of the complication. It's not a pure score. It's a description from memory—indicative and suggestive. It's not directive, like a score. Which is part of the complexity of the transmission.

HAY: The scores of the '60s were simply from the point of view of the dancer who was dancing it, whereas with the libretto, which I also think of as a score, you get the view of how the observer sees it. You have more than one perspective into the dancing of the dance. A score is written for a dancer to take to read the movement to be the dance. A score is directed solely toward the person who is taking the material and putting it on their body. But this text is also from the perspective of the observer. And it's also from the view of the choreographer—

DALY:—who's recalling the dance as well as the writing of the libretto of the dance. It's mostly told in the third person, and that's a lovely slippage when you're performing it. You've worked with librettos before. You wrote a libretto for the group piece *Lamb, lamb, lamb, . . .* [1991] and then expanded it into a book, *Lamb at the Altar: The Story of a Dance.* Had you done this before *Lamb*?

HAY: I wrote a score for *Snakeskin's Girl* [1986], an erotic duet with Michael Arnold. It was published in *Contact Quarterly.* I wrote it afterward because I wanted to see if I could write erotic text. When I choreographed my first Austin-based group dances in the 1980s, I made lists of images for program notes. And then when I stopped working with images, I had to find a way to remember the dances, so I wrote descriptions of the movement, because I always refused to learn dance notation.

DALY: So this was your choreographic notation.

HAY: Yes.

DALY: So writing began out of notation. How did it become more than notation?

HAY: I noticed how much I learned from writing it.

DALY: What kinds of things did you learn?

HAY: I learned about other dimensions of the dance that I did not know were there until I wrote them down.

DALY: Is that mind-boggling for someone who's chosen to work in movement, that there is more to learn about the movement by describing it in words, apart from doing the movement?

HAY: It was a fantastic revelation.

DALY: When were you making this realization?

HAY: Around 1990, during *The Man Who Grew Common in Wisdom*. I was teaching the "Gardener" section to a group of people at Wesleyan University. One of them said she was going to try to score it through Labanotation. And she came back to me and said it was absolutely impossible. The dance did not fit that language. I got very excited about that, because I didn't like the way Labanotation looked on the page. I didn't like those little boxes. It really bothered me to think that my dance would be limited to these shaded rectangular boxes. And I began to develop an interest in writing it. I did a score for "Aviator" that was a combination of drawings and descriptions.

DALY: How would you define the word "writing" here? You are recording, exploring, even producing movement by writing.

HAY: The last few words in the *Voilà* libretto, which were originally simply a direction for what I was doing on stage, are: "She began galloping in circles. Horse rider woman playing dancing. A human being galloping off." That's how I'm describing the exit. A human being galloping off. Then I read, "She began galloping in circles," it goes so many places. It's not me on the dance floor doing movement traveling through space. Suddenly it has a fullness and poetry to it. It's an event; it isn't an action. It becomes something else. The words "horse rider woman playing dancing" become embodiments. When you're speaking it, the picture gets bigger. And so now when I go back to dance it, I'm not just galloping in circles and exiting off. I'm in the whole shape of the stars in heaven. I'm the whole universe. I feel so much bigger than the act you're looking at on stage.

DALY: I've counted five incarnations of *Voilà*: the workshop group piece, the solo, the libretto, the performance of the libretto, and now the trio with Grace and Scott. Why?

HAY: Why? I am resourceful. I like taking material apart and taking it apart some more and taking it apart some more. I like that uncovering, finding out what's in there, rather than going on to another dance. Let's see what else we have with what we have. What else can I learn about this material from another perspective? There's another thing, too. What is my work? Some people see my work as idiosyncratic. By Scott and by Grace performing this libretto, the question becomes: What is my work? What is the idiosyncrasy that some people see as my work? What is my work as performed by other people? Who is the choreographer? What is choreography?

DALY: This is the perennial aesthetic distinction between the dancer and the dance. How much of the performance is just "personal style" and "presence"? This distinction has been made for a long time. Soloists from Isadora Duncan on down through the century have been acknowledged as talented performers, but not necessarily recognized as choreographers—as creators—because the criterion for what constitutes "choreography" as a serious art appears to be work that can be replicated and performed by someone else.

HAY: I'm calling this choreography. And this is how I can see passing choreography on.

DALY: That's a new concern for you.

HAY: I like these dances. I want to see them go on. I can't see performing *The Man Who Grew Common in Wisdom* again, for example. Maybe I could learn it from the video, but it would be a huge undertaking. I like the idea of other dancers being able to get the score and re-create that material from the score. I am concerned about the transmission and the preservation of dance without having to spend billions of dollars for technology to be able to find ways to record and keep dance alive. If I could find a way to preserve dance, using language and not complex technology, I'd like to do it. I think it can work. Typically, when you see a piece that's carried on, a Balanchine piece, for instance, that's carried on year after year after year, you know what you're going to see. It has very specific parameters to it. And the same thing with Martha Graham and Paul Taylor. You know you're going to see the same thing. The transmission of dance has been about training the body to move in a certain way. It's been crucial to the passing on of dance.

DALY: To be repeated exactly, using the body as an instrument.

HAY: Yes. But what I'm looking at with this process is: Can you pass dance on without telling anybody how to move, but by giving them a whole other set of parameters? Can you provide conditions for re-creating the dance that are not about telling the body how to move? And is it still that dance? I think that this experiment that we're going to be doing at the Kitchen will let me know that. Then a whole world could open up. Handing people bodies of material to work with that's not simply about the manipulation of the physical body but involves the whole person in translating this material. That could be very exciting.

DALY: Another major shift for you is the desire to work with trained performers. Is this related to your concern with transmission?

HAY: It has to do with going deeper into choreography. Before I thought of choreography as what you did in order to perform. I now think that choreography by itself is interesting as a fine art.

DALY: What do you mean, "as a fine art"?

HAY: I've always appreciated Merce [Cunningham]. I'm finally getting a taste for time and space. I think it's there in my last two solos, but it's only beginning. The opening of *Voilà* is: "She remembered prancing sideways clipped and poised." I would like to choreograph each one of those prances down to the millisecond, without losing the freedom I have found in performing. Is that possible? I can't do that with people who are not trained performers. They have to have many perspectives on themselves at a given moment, so that they can really play all their options. I don't think they have to be trained dancers. They just have to be performers who can be in more than one place at a time at a given moment.

—PAJ: A Journal of Performance and Art, 1999

BILL T. JONES AND ARNIE ZANE

Dance at Prospect Park

High Art, Lowbrow Spectacle

BILL T. JONES and Arnie Zane can play both sides like nobody since George Balanchine. High art and lowbrow spectacle come together in their dances in a slick, infectiously exuberant way.

If Balanchine, the greatest ballet choreographer of the century, chose to do pop spectacles such as *Union Jack, Who Cares?,* and *Stars and Stripes,* why shouldn't this dynamic duo? When halftime shows are considered appropriate commemoration for supposedly august occasions such as the Statue of Liberty centenary, it's no wonder Jones and Zane are hot properties. After all, this is the aerobics generation.

The overflow audience at the Bill T. Jones/Arnie Zane & Company concert at the Prospect Park Bandshell 28 June didn't miss an opportunity to applaud the company's pyrotechnics. The seven dancers (Zane didn't perform) were each strong and swift, crystal clear in their attack and seductively buoyant. With their punkish hairdos, they exhibited just the right dose of petulant avant-gardism.

Technical daredevil Sean Curran did it best. He's sharper-edged and more aloof than Jones, whose leonine virtuosity set the tone for the whole company.

Curran entered late in Part Three of *Freedom of Information* (1984). His solo encapsulated the escalating frenzy of the entire ensemble. He kept crossing the stage, exiting and crossing the stage again, each time pirouetting or jabbing the air with a karate leap. Then he spiraled and sputtered out of control into the wings.

For their movement material, Jones and Zane have raided their artistic heritage and pop culture as well. Their choreography gets its brocade texture from the variety of movement and imagery it embraces: ballet, sports, contact improvisation, jazz, gymnastics, social dance. But the choreography is never crowded or messy. There is an elegant spareness to the string of gestures, as in *Fever Swamp* (1983).

Fever Swamp started out as a line dance, with six dancers in synchrony to Peter Gordon's bouncy, snappy sax melody. A shoulder roll would be followed by a raising of two fingers, which would be followed by a head cock. These unlikely sequences were performed so crisply, though, that the increasingly complex pattern of movement never got blurred.

Flouting Convention and Stereotype

WITH TONGUE firmly in check, Jones performed a solo, *Dance With Brahms* (1983). Contrasting the Jones/Zane brand of angular, semaphore-style arm gestures with the soft, curvaceous style of ballet, he parodied the ecstatic outpouring of emotion that was once the style. He even quoted Nijinsky in *Le Spectre de la rose,* his arms expressively arranged above his head; later, he gushed over a bust of Brahms. And in the midst of all this balletic propriety, he defiantly ground his pelvis and picked his nose.

Shared Distance (1981, revised) was a portrait of a partnership at first harmonious and then growing dissonant from self-preoccupation. Heywood McGriff is a tall, black leading-man type, and Karen Pearlman is a powerful, compact white dancer with Shirley Temple pep. They are opposites in size, race, and gender, but they negotiated their partnership with equal strength and determination. Pearlman may be a small woman, but she lifted and supported McGriff without missing a beat. Jones and Zane, themselves opposite in size and race, have cultivated a gender egalitarianism in their repertoire that far outreaches the stereotypes still perpetuated by most ballet and contemporary dance.

It might be easy to write off Jones and Zane as crowd-pleasers, but I think it's a mistake. Sure, their stuff is all surface—pure style, as shiny and impenetrable as instant shoe shine—but it's also rich with ideas about movement and structure, politics and artistic convention. That they can accomplish all that and appeal to lots of people at the same time is a considerable feat.

— *Prospect Press*, 1986

Review: *Body against Body,* edited by Elizabeth Zimmer and Susan Quasha

I FIRST MET Bill T. Jones and Arnie Zane in 1981, in Pittsburgh, where they were collaborating on a site-specific dance for the Three Rivers Arts Festival. Jones was charming, and Zane's enthusiasm for organization and order was endearing: both were kind to a novitiate dance critic.

Dance for the Origin of the Ohio, a combination of semaphore-like arm gestures and gymnastic partnering for local dancers, turned out to be of incidental importance to the duo's oeuvre, meriting only a mention in the chronology of the recently published *Body against Body: The Dance and Other Collaborations of Bill T. Jones & Arnie Zane.* Edited by dance critic Elizabeth Zimmer and designer Susan Quasha, the slim black-and-white volume is an impressionistic glimpse of contemporary dance's most important choreographic team through the words of Jones, critics, and collaborators, and through images by Zane and others.

Zane, who died in 1988 of AIDS-related lymphoma, and Jones were a classic example of opposites attracting: the former small, white, and angular, the latter large, black, and fluid. They built their stage relationship on difference. They cultivated it and found their strength in it. They provided spectators, as well as photographers such as Robert Mapplethorpe, Lois Greenfield, Paula Court, and Frank Ockenfels, with an iconography of difference that questioned the inevitability of the larger lifting the smaller or of a man partnering a woman. Questions of distinction among races, creeds, classes, genders, sexualities, and genres of dance permeated the work they made for their company, Bill T. Jones/Arnie Zane & Company.

At first Jones and Zane made an issue of bodily difference by regarding it as a nonissue. It was nonetheless a painfully difficult one, forcing them to confront the social and political questions of identity and power. One of the reasons that I admire Jones and Zane as artists so much is that, by framing their work as "body against body," they set themselves up to have to deal with these questions every day of their lives together, both personally and professionally. And as far as I can tell, they never flinched.

They never remained static, either. Their views on the body evolved over their seventeen years together, and Jones's views are still evolving. In 1979 he told an interviewer from the *Kent News:*

> I really don't believe that I am just my body. The body suggests to me much that society has put on the body. You have been defined as not only a social security number, but defined as a black person, and in another context you have been defined as a male, and in another context you have been defined as an American, and so on. So the body represents a definition; it represents an identity which I think on some levels is fallacious. As the Hindus would tell us, it is maya. It is illusion.

But in Michael Blackwood's 1988 documentary *Retracing Steps: American Dance Since Postmodernism,* Jones reveals a change in thinking:

> When I began to blossom as a dancer, I was rebelling against everything. I was rebelling against being considered my body. I was involved in transcendental eastern religion for just that same reason—that I was not my body, I was not my gender, I was not my past. And, therefore, I set off to find a society that was going to accept me on those terms, and I thought that's what I found in the dance world. Now I don't feel that way so much anymore. I think I am a black man, and I think that's different than him [Zane] being a white man. He's also a Jewish man, of Jewish and Italian parents. I think all these things are very important now. I don't know exactly how to articulate them as well. That's what I really want to find out more about.

The most significant difference between Jones and Zane, embedded in their body images and ways of moving, was aesthetic. During the 1970s, the initial years of their collaboration, Jones was primarily interested in emotion, while Zane, who came out of the visual arts, was a structuralist. Jones's solos were a visceral, confrontational manipulation of his and the audience's emotional responses to explosive social issues. The prose and poetry published in *Body against Body,* accompanied by Zane's extraordinary photographs, reveal the depth and texture of Jones's felt life, layered with childhood memories and adult longings. Zane's visual images, among them a series of torsos of the aged and the ill, are severely cropped, with lots of ponderously still, empty space. They are stark and objective, and yet they are no less affecting than Jones's overtly poetic meditations.

The collaboration between Jones and Zane was largely characterized by this tension between form and content, and the recognition that one did not necessarily exclude or invalidate the other. This thorny issue—how to revive content without forsaking formalism—threads its way through *Body against Body.* At nearly every turn it becomes an issue with Jones and Zane taking a variety of approaches.

Jones's early solos originated almost exclusively in personal experiences. The collaborative *Blauvelt Mountain* (1980) signaled a move toward structuralism, though still layered with Jones's personal, poetic texts. *Social Intercourse: Pilgrim's Progress* (1981) was an attempt by Jones to make something with a black voice, in a way that foreshadowed the duo's later interest in spectacle and pop culture. "We want to make works that deeply affect people," he said, "and yet are cool and distant enough so that they can be observed as a presence, appreciated for themselves and what they represent."

Just as with Zane's portraits, audiences tended to read metaphors and symbolism into formalist works such as *Blauvelt Mountain* and *Social Intercourse,* even without their being consciously inserted. More recent works, such as Jones's *Red Room* (1987) and Zane's *The Gift/No God Logic* (1987), similarly testify to the dramatic power of form.

With *How to Walk an Elephant* (1986), the pair made a work as "abstract as Mondrian sitting and playing with his grids," Jones explained. "Right now I'm not even so concerned with the totality of structure because I actually believe in ways similar to Merce Cunningham that in performance you really only go from moment to moment." That kind of fluidity, without the severe overarching logic of structuralism, manifested itself in their last collaboration, *The History of Collage* (1988).

Through Jones and Zane we can see in a microcosm contemporary American dance negotiating its way from the 1960s to the 1980s. They both were healing the split between form and content, yet they did not return to a transparent fusion of the two. Their work developed into an exemplary postmodernism: the willful and skillful collision of genres, vocabularies, and aesthetic approaches, stylistically unified by their embrace of popular culture. To my mind, *Secret Pastures,* their 1984 extravaganza at the Brooklyn Academy of Music, was their most successful reimagining of the form/content dilemma. Hyped as a narrative work at a time when narrative dance was not quite yet cachet and with its implications of content driving form, *Secret Pastures* was actually a deconstructed narrative, using a slim story as the pretext for a lot of dancing for the sake of dancing. It worked brilliantly on both levels.

Despite Zane's death, their collaboration is not yet over. At the Brooklyn Academy of Music this November, Bill T. Jones/Arnie Zane & Company will premiere *The Last Supper at Uncle Tom's Cabin.*

The idea began as something of a joke between the two men several months before Zane's death. The dance will feature a found-photo essay of Zane's called "Negroes for Sale," as well as *Lament,* a work Zane conceived to feature himself, standing on an oversized table and chair shouting a Japanese lesson instructed by choreographer Ruby Shang.

"After Arnie died," Jones told the *New York Times,* "I began to look more closely at the idea. There is so much about people being torn from each other and people in pursuit of each other and with the kind of robust, athletic partnering that we do, I think we'll produce something quite evocative."

—*High Performance,* 1990

Dancing the Unsayable

Bill T. Jones's *Still/Here* Becomes a Meditation on the Possibilities of Postmodernist Art

Still/Here is no longer a dance. It has become something much more, or much less, depending upon your point of view.

Choreographed by Bill T. Jones for the New York-based Bill T. Jones/Arnie Zane Dance Company, *Still/Here* was an HIV-positive gay man's attempt to "transcend ... difference," but it became, for a while, at least, fodder for neoconservative reactionism, thanks to *New Yorker* dance critic Arlene Croce. Her "review" entitled "Discussing the Undiscussable," which denounced the choreographer's evening-length meditation on death and living (without benefit of actually having seen it), launched an intense public debate among critics, intellectuals, and artists, the likes of which is usually reserved for literature and the visual arts. The silver lining in the whole debacle was that dance suddenly had been inserted into the realm of cultural politics.

And the cause célèbre, no doubt, has boosted the company's visibility and box office. *Still/Here* has been touring this country since its premiere in September 1994 in Lyons, France. In February, it was presented in Dallas (16 and 17 February, by the International Theatrical Arts Society), San Antonio (20 February, by the Carver Community Cultural Center, in association with Dance Umbrella, JumpStart Performance Company, and Esperanza Peace and Justice Center), and Houston (23 and 24 February, by the Society for the Performing Arts).

The two-part *Still/Here* is a multimedia piece—although dancing is never displaced from its center—exploring the twin issues of mortality (*Still*) and survival (*Here*), through the stories of real-life people facing life-threatening illnesses. Their "stories," expressed to Jones in a nationwide Survival Workshops series that he began facilitating in November 1992 here in Austin, are not just verbal, but visual and gestural as well. Their words are heard in the lyrics of the music ("Still" by Kenneth Frazelle, "Here" by Vernon Reid); their faces are projected onto the large video screens that dominate the media environment, designed by Gretchen Bender; their gestures serve as the basis for Jones's choreography.

I had intended to ignore Croce's tantrum when writing about *Still/Here* but soon faced the impossibility of that approach. No work of art is bounded and defined by its cover, or its frame, its score, or its final curtain. A work of art is as much constituted by what is said and written about it as by its internal physical form.

For example, there is a climactic moment in George Balanchine's masterwork, *Concerto Barocco* (1940), that will always be seen (despite how it's actually performed) in the way that poet-critic Edwin Denby wrote about it: as a "deliberate and powerful plunge into a wound." For another example, Yvonne Rainer's *Trio A* (1966) has become the Ur-postmodern dance (amidst all the possible candidates) because she wrote an influential manifesto about it and, furthermore, because a film was made of it. Extended in verbal and visual discourse, *Trio A* took on a larger life, as a cultural icon.

So it has happened with *Still/Here,* which has become only the most recent pre-text for a rallying cry of neoconservatives against avant-garde artists, who see art as a site for social and political dialogue, if not change. But unlike the case of the NEA Four, against whom political and religious leaders led the fight in the name of "family values," this offensive was launched by a dance critic in the name of "art."

Croce, as the field's acknowledged standard-bearer of the classical aesthetic, has made a career of enforcing her formalist agenda, separating the "good" from the "bad" from a position of confident omniscience. (And, it must be said, within that circumscribed world of classical ballet, she does possess the connoisseur's impeccable eye.) Croce never found any reason for postmodern dance or a postmodern world, and after a while she just stopped writing about anything but classicism, supplanting her bitter words with dismissive silence.

But clearly the world had shifted too far for her to remain mute any longer. For Croce, *Still/Here*—or rather, her fantasy of *Still/Here,* since she refused to see it, on the grounds that, as "victim art," it placed itself beyond art, beyond criticism—stands for all that is wrong with the contemporary arts: the focus on content over form; the emphasis on the group's "political clout" over "individual spirit"; the tolerance for theatrical bodies that "present themselves as dissed blacks, abused women, or disfranchised homosexuals." As such, "victim art defies criticism," because it resituates dance from a platonic aesthetic sphere squarely into the social/political sphere.

By attempting to police the boundary between art and non-art, Croce was making a none-too-subtle effort to wrest back her foundering critical author-ity over both audience and artist. Her manifesto reconstructed the vanishing object of her critical desire: virtuosic, musical, hermetically sealed dances that deal with life only from the safe distance of metaphor and that require for their completion the critic's formal evaluation.

CROCE'S ARTICLE generated a media frenzy and an expectation of *Still/Here* as the exemplar of "these AIDS epics, these performance-art shockers." Her fantasy about this dance is, in fact, a repetition of our entire cultural imaginary about AIDS and, hence, gay culture: as disease, death, and victimhood.

It was this very stereotyping of gay identity that prompted Jones to create *Still/Here* in the first place. Although in her fantasy Croce describes Jones as someone who "declared himself HIV-positive and began making AIDS-focused pieces for himself and members of his company," his HIV-positive status actually was leaked by a gay magazine. (Jones's status was not a complete surprise: his longtime partner and collaborator, Arnie Zane, had died of complications due to AIDS in 1988.) Jones devotes the final extended chapter of his recent autobiography, *Last Night on Earth* (Pantheon, 1995), to an exegesis of the production.

After being outed, he recalls, he was alarmed. Jones—who for so long was identified as the tall black partner to short white Zane—bristled at being redefined as "Bill T. Jones, tall, black, HIV-positive." "Most of us, with or without HIV," he writes, "are burdened with the perception, justified or not, that being HIV-positive equals death. Once again, I found myself an outsider. This I refused to accept."

It is here, in the struggle to acknowledge difference (as an HIV-positive gay man) while refusing to be *othered* (as "Jones the AIDS victim," Croce's moniker), where things get complicated—for Jones and all the other many artists and art theorists who work with identity politics.

Although Croce marked *Still/Here* as an "AIDS epic" about "dying," Jones—in his autobiographical countertext, which will forever, with Croce's *New Yorker* essay, constitute the dance—rejects such a label of difference. Instead, he chooses to universalize AIDS as one of a number of life-threatening illnesses. In the dance, breast and ovarian cancer are given as prominent a place as AIDS.

In the process of creating *Still/Here* "around the ideal of commonality," however, does Jones further marginalize gay identity, by not only rejecting otherness but also erasing its difference as well? Does he, therefore, implicitly maintain, along with Croce, that AIDS is a disease that needs to be rendered, in his terms, "a commonality," and, in her terms, "undiscussable"—in other words, invisible?

Is there some kind of perverse resonance between Croce's insistence on "disinterested art" and Jones's belief in "commonality"? Both notions under-estimate the limiting power of the social, the former in favor of individual free will and the latter in favor of the "natural."

Both Croce and Jones write about "transcendence," but while Jones intended to "shape a work that transcended difference," Croce wants art to transcend (and "sublimate") the social world altogether. For her, any acknowledgment of a "group" rather than "one man, one death, one art" threatens contamination. "The end of twentieth-century collectivism is the AIDS quilt," she writes. "The wistful desire to commemorate is converted into a pathetic lumping together, the individual absorbed by the group, the group by the disease." This is the logic (a handy revival of the Cold War's theory of the "domino effect") of AIDS phobia, which explains why, for Croce, inserting AIDS into a dance about human mortality automatically diseases everyone.

By ignoring the specifically homophobic way that mainstream culture constructs mortality as "victimhood" for people with AIDS, does *Still/Here* cover over their ensuing struggle for individual dignity?

The irony is that Croce's fantasy of *Still/Here* gives it far too much credit as a work of radical identity politics.

In fact, the dance has a formalist patina (pace Croce) that I find problematic, because as a "well-made dance" with all the necessary unity and continuity, it glosses over some disruptive tensions that need to be addressed. First, there is the tension between art (the dancers) and life (the Survival Workshop participants). The fit is too tidy to be affecting. Second, there is the deeply ironic tension between the abundant health of the dancers and the physically ailing workshop participants whose bodies they are representing. Third, there is the tension between the voices of the workshop participants and the appropriating voice of choreographer Jones.

Still/Here is a work of performance ethnography, not unlike the work of theater artist Anna Deavere Smith, who interviews subjects involved in major cultural conflicts, such as the Los Angeles riots, and transforms them, seemingly transparently, into theater. The problem is, the transformation is never transparent. As I think about *Still/Here,* I wonder if it would have been more effective if performed by the workshop participants themselves.

But, as Jones writes, and as his long, rich, and provocative career illustrates, "grand summations only result in more questions." Jones has been dealing head-on with the politics and aesthetics of difference throughout his whole career, and what I so admire is that his position and strategy have always kept evolving, never gotten stuck. Jones and Zane's work has been a dialogue with, reflection of, tirade against, and love affair with American life. As a record of late-twentieth-century cultural politics, the significance of their oeuvre has yet to be articulated.

—*Texas Observer,* 1996

When Dancers Move On to Making Dances

IN THE BEGINNING of modern dance was Ruth St. Denis. She begat Martha Graham, who begat Merce Cunningham, who begat Douglas Dunn, Neil Greenberg, and Steve Paxton. According to the laws of apostolic succession, a choreographer is born only after lengthy service to an established company, not just as a dancer but also, in effect, as a choreographic apprentice.

"Any dancer-choreographer relationship can potentially be an apprenticeship," says Janet Lilly, a choreographer who danced for eight years with the Bill T. Jones/Arnie Zane Dance Company.

Epitomizing the stylish rigor and energy of second-generation postmodernism in the 1980s, Jones/Zane took an eclectic, experimental, sometimes irreverent approach to dance. Their partnership was an exercise in artistic ingenuity: Mr. Zane, who died of AIDS in 1988, was a photographer with a formalist's eye; Mr. Jones, a charismatic performer, created movement with deeply personal resonance. Given their inclusive aesthetic, it is no surprise that so many of their company members have felt equipped to move from dancer to choreographer.

A cluster of concerts in the next six weeks will attest to the fifteen-year-old company's track record for producing new choreographic talent. Lawrence Goldhuber and Heidi Latsky will perform "Do We Dare," a program of their duets, Thursday through next Sunday at P.S. 122; Sean Curran Company will be at the Danspace Project at St. Mark's Church 24–27 April; Amy Pivar Dances will perform 24–27 April at the Clark Studio Theater at Lincoln Center; and Arthur Aviles's Typical Theater will appear 10–11 May and 17–18 May at the Point Community Center in the Hunts Point section of the Bronx. The work represented ranges from witty partnering to pop-culture extravaganza to feminist commentary.

"The reason why so many choreographers have come out of Bill and Arnie's company," explains Ms. Lilly, thirty-nine, who lives in Milwaukee and teaches at the University of Wisconsin there, "is that they encouraged the dancers to participate in the making of the work."

Ms. Lilly recalls how she learned about composing dances by observing the two choreographers in their gamelike rehearsals. Dancers were asked to learn a phrase or to generate their own material, which would be refined and shaped on the spot by Mr. Jones or Mr. Zane, with directives such as these: Do it again, very slowly. What does it look like if we turn it inside out? Try making it into a duet.

The forty-five-year-old Mr. Jones, who describes the company that he founded with Mr. Zane as "a place for self-confrontation and empowerment," confirms her memories. "From both me and Arnie," he says, "a young dancer would hear: What do you think? How can we solve this problem? Can you make something here? I believe these three questions act as a compass in the development of any artist."

Ironically, Mr. Jones and Mr. Zane themselves ignored the laws of apostolic succession. In love and fresh out of school, they blazed their own path in the freewheeling downtown scene of the 1970s. What does Mr. Jones know now that he wishes he had known back then? "Take your time," he says. "Ask hard questions, look and ask again. Are you willing to try something and fail? Know that you are, and are not, your work. Do you have a life?"

Mr. Jones and Mr. Zane hired dancers as iconoclastic as their own partner-ship (the former is tall, lyrical, and black; the latter was small, percussive, and white). They chose performers who had fire and who were independent thinkers. Many of them were already choreographing. So for these Jones/Zane alumni, the transition from dancer to choreographer was logical, if not always apparent.

Lawrence Goldhuber's break with the company, in December 1995, was prompt-ed by a serious injury, but for him a shift to choreography was almost as unlikely as his entry into the company had been. A professional actor, he joined in March 1987. "At that point I was 360 pounds," recalls Mr. Goldhuber, thirty-six. "I couldn't point my feet. I had a good sense of rhythm and of spatial relations and a good stage presence. But Bill saw something else. In life, you say yes instead of saying no. And here I am eleven years later, making my own choreography."

Ms. LATSKY, his thirty-eight-year-old collaborator, describes her career change as "organic." A small but fiercely energetic dancer, she left the company in De-cember 1993, "because of the touring, because I was older and because I wanted to spend more time at home."

"I tried dancing with other people," she continues, "but it didn't work. It be-came clear to me that what I wanted to do was choreograph."

As passionately as Ms. Latsky and her former colleagues talk about their choreography, there remains some nostalgia for the dancer's life—being sup-ported by a community, for example, and being challenged by a director. Not to mention the paychecks and guaranteed performance dates.

"What I miss most is doing the work," says the fast-footed Mr. Curran, thirty-five, who spent a decade with the company until 1993. "One of the hardest things after leaving was knowing that someone else was doing my part in *D-Man in the Waters,*" he says, referring to a 1989 work by Mr. Jones. "In a lot of ways, *Where I End and We Begin,* which we'll do at St. Mark's, is my version of that dance—lush, romantic music and physical dancing that's about connectedness and community."

Dancing and choreographing are not so different, Ms. Lilly points out. Both are about making choices. But beyond craft, a choreographer needs something to say.

"I have a great love of formalism from Arnie, and my love of invention in a way comes from Bill," explains Mr. Curran, who, in addition to choreographing for companies as far afield as Houston and Copenhagen, dances in *Stomp,* the off-Broadway show.

He describes his dances as poetic, theatrical collages, with themes of "health and well-being." "Now it's all my own ideas," he adds. "When you're the chore-ographer, it's your agenda, your vision."

In her early twenties, Ms. Latsky was frustrated by her first attempts at choreography, because, she says, "I had no idea what I was saying." But in her final year with the company, she returned to choreography with a strong and clear voice. "Bill had challenged me," she says, "and I learned so much about my own politics and what I believed in. So now I had a lot to say, and I wanted to say it."

In the studio, Mr. Goldhuber and Ms. Latsky—an odd union of physical opposites, much like Mr. Jones and Mr. Zane—are still working out the mechanics of collaboration. That requires productive disagreement and compromise. (Mr. Goldhuber looks up the word collaboration in the dictionary. "I like the second definition better," he says with a laugh. "Cooperating with an enemy.") Along with the ubiquitous video camera, each serves as the other's director, or external eye. A notebook holds a record of their ideas, the timed structure of a work in progress and even a list of words used to generate movement material.

The legacy of the Jones/Zane partnership, distinguished as much by its sociopolitical content as by its aesthetic innovation, is easy to locate in the next generation's concerns: Mr. Aviles, thirty-three, explores his identity as a gay man negotiating a place between Puerto Rican and American cultures; Andrea E. Woods, thirty-two, who made the move from company member to choreographer in December 1995 after being injured, documents her family history, speaking as "a black woman in America"; and Ms. Pivar, thirty-eight, tackles women's issues.

"In a way," Ms. Pivar explains, "I chose to do the thing that was hardest for me. I should have been a math teacher. I was that kind of person. I wasn't the artist."

Looking back now, she realizes that after a few years with the company, she wanted to be more than just a dancer. "I was jealous of Bill and Arnie's power and their lifestyle," she says. "They were the artists. They knew how to make choreography, and that's the highest place in dance."

After five years of on-the-edge dancing, a knee injury sidelined her in 1987. She went into the studio and made a breakthrough. "For some reason, I started talking, which was really unlike me," she says. "People had always told me as a dancer, 'You have so much energy.' And I thought, 'That's not all I have.' I decided I wanted more of a response from people. The only way I could do that was to talk."

In 1990, Ms. Pivar and her companion, the writer and therapist Freda Rosen, founded Amy Pivar Dances, a company devoted to creating environments that promote artistic and social dialogue. This month, the company will present the premiere of *These Women,* studies of six people whose struggles have inspired Ms. Pivar. "I didn't think the world needed another choreographer to make another dance," she explains. "If you're not going to take up your concerns as a human being, why bother?"

As much as these emerging artists gleaned from their years with Mr. Jones and Mr. Zane, choreography still requires on-the-job training. The false steps, sour notes, and miscues are all obligatory points on the learning curve. "One of the things I learned from watching Arnie," says Ms. Lilly, whose own choreography features dark humor and strong characterizations, "was that there was nothing more he loved than a good mistake."

Mr. Curran, who discovered choreography in high school, has been making dances professionally since 1988. His lessons have been many: the importance of being a good editor, that there is "great beauty in simplicity," that a sense of invention is "extremely important but extremely difficult," that "work as an artist will nourish you but it won't sustain you." And that making dances can be a form of healing.

Considering the long shadow cast by their artistic parentage, these Jones/Zane progeny exhibit little need to act out their independence. For Ms. Latsky, it was more a matter of claiming for herself the power that she had given to the men she most respected: "You see in them what you really want for yourself."

Mr. Aviles is emphatic: "I have no problem being someone who came after Bill." But then, for him, the issue of originality is moot. He has taken the postmodern principle of appropriation to its extreme: he openly copies, everything from Disney movies to whole dances by Martha Graham, José Limón, and even Mr. Jones. "If I see something I like, why shouldn't I use it, especially if it inspired me?" he reasons. "Originality is dead, but inspiration is alive. I put myself into that artwork and see what it does for me." Next month, in the premiere of *Maéva de Oz*, he will recreate *The Wizard of Oz* as an intercultural identity crisis.

The best of apprentices always move on, having learned to integrate old lessons with new goals. "As I get better at this," Ms. Pivar reflects, "I realize more and more about what Bill and Arnie did. My first five years, it was always Bill and Arnie. But I don't have them with me in the studio anymore. I've gotten beyond that."

—New York Times, 1997

The Long Day's Journey of Bill T. Jones

COMING FROM A family of migrant farm workers, Bill T. Jones knows in his bones what it means to make a journey. Nearly a quarter of a century ago, the young choreographer signed a pact with himself, agreeing, as he recalls in his autobiography, "to go on a long journey equipped with nothing more than my body and this hunger." Since then, Jones has spent his artistic life investigating the formal and expressive possibilities of people moving from here to there. And with the Kennedy Center world premiere of *We Set Out Early . . . Visibility Was Poor*, Jones addresses dance and life as mutually metaphorical journeys.

The relationship between art and life has preoccupied twentieth-century artists since Marcel Duchamp, whose ready-made sculptures revealed the conventional boundary between art and life as a line drawn only in sand. Jones, inspired by Duchamp, as well as by postmodern choreographers, structuralist filmmakers, performance artists, African-American music and literature, and his early family life, has traversed one of the most challenging transitions of this century from 1970s postmodernism to 1990s identity politics. Is it enough, today, to continue making art randomly generated by appropriation and juxtaposition? Or should artists assert a social agenda? Are these two positions mutually exclusive?

Unlike his modernist forebears, who steadfastly developed their early discoveries (Martha Graham's expressionism, Merce Cunningham's chance aesthetic, George Balanchine's formalism), Jones has never settled upon a single technique or credo. Throughout his odyssey, from a bohemian counterculture existence in upstate New York in the 1970s to the hip spectacle of downtown Manhattan in the 1980s, to an international touring schedule in the 1990s, Jones has remained alive to new ways of approaching fundamental questions about movement, art, identity, and culture.

Jones's early experiments with his late partner and collaborator, Arnie Zane, emphasized pure movement over story or expression, but the couple soon discovered that, despite their rigorous formal concerns, audiences perceived in the work powerful meanings both personal and political. "Resonant abstraction," as Jones calls it, eventually gave way, when Zane died of AIDS in 1988, to Jones's desire "to take a stand." The evening-length *Last Supper at Uncle Tom's Cabin/The Promised Land* (1990), for example, moved from a deconstruction of the eponymous slave narrative to a utopian landscape of social harmony.

Over the years, Jones has embraced both anger and faith, seduction and alienation, the cool distance of the virtuoso and the impassioned plea of the preacher. He has been led sometimes by movement, and at other times by politics; he has both emphasized and erased social difference. The impetus has been personal, or conceptual, or political, or hyperphysical, or all of the above. In his current quest for the meaning of art and community in the face of death, each question, provisionally answered, produces another. Jones's unflinching willingness to adjust his course, in response to shifts in internal desire and external circumstances, makes for work that is uncommonly wise, if not infallible.

For *Still/Here* (1993), an evening-length dance based on material gathered from workshops with survivors of life-threatening illnesses, Jones had considered disbanding his company in favor of HIV-positive individuals from around the country. In the end, however, video portraits and voice-overs of the real-life survivors shared the stage with the professional performers. With *We Set Out Early . . . Visibility Was Poor*, Jones comes full circle in his thinking. The dancers are not merely metaphorical stand-ins for other people, real or imagined; the dancers themselves, and their process of inhabiting the dance, are the stuff of the journey.

Once again, Jones is composing his dance according to strict formal parameters such as space, density, texture, and musicality. "The story," he explains, "is in the body performing the sequences of movement. The journey is how the movement material comes into the world, how it goes into the dancers' bodies, and what it means when it is set afire in the performance space."

The musical journey of *We Set Out Early . . . Visibility Was Poor* echoes Jones's renewed enthusiasm for the transformative potential of art, despite the loss of faith he senses around him. The dance begins at century's curtain-raising, with Igor Stravinsky's 1917 "L'Histoire du soldat," and ends with the approaching millennium, with Peteris Vasks's "Stimmen" (Voices). For Jones, this contrast between the early modernist's exuberant self-confidence—in the midst of world war—and the contemporary Latvian composer's heartrending plea for healing maps a significant change.

"I don't think that artists today believe that art can change the world or tell the truth. How did we get from Stravinsky's youthful idealism to this spiritual fatigue? For me, as a man in his mid-forties, whose generation has been decimated by AIDS, there are a lot of parallels and questions in this journey."

In the age of AIDS—and Jones himself is HIV-positive—the very notion of a "journey," by nature a forward-pressing movement, becomes an existential challenge: How to prevent the journey from narrowing into an exodus? How to embark without the illusion of boundless time—in other words, with such poor visibility?

We Set Out Early . . . Visibility Was Poor has returned Jones to his formalist roots ("It's old, but it's fresh"), a radical departure from the rhetorically motivated *Last Supper at Uncle Tom's Cabin/The Promised Land* and *Still/Here*. "Once you've named names, once you've pointed to something and expressed how you feel about it," Jones explains, "you either leave the poetic world or dive back into the mystery." He chose to dive.

"I have recommitted to dance. It's not anthropology. It's not literature. It's not sign language. If we let it, dance can surprise us again and again. Just when I thought I had lost interest in everything, some movement shocks me and intrigues me. It leads me to 'what if . . .' That's where I'm at right now."

—*America Dancing: The Revolution Goes
Worldwide,* season program, John F. Kennedy
Center for the Performing Arts, 1997

Bill T. Jones in Conversation with Ann Daly

ANN DALY: You've always been a great interview. This bothers you?

BILL T. JONES: I have the uncomfortable sense that speaking about my work could historically overshadow the work itself. I look at a hero of mine, Merce Cunningham, and I wonder, having read almost everything that I can of his, if I did not know the work as well as I do know it, would I be interested in the man speaking and would he hold my interest on the page? I doubt it. I think in some ways that is what he has been trying to say to us all these years about the primacy and importance of dance as an art form. It doesn't need any exterior explanation. I think he's very proud and protective of the idea that dance is a domain, a country unto itself. It does not need literary references, art-historical references, philosophy. In fact, it can be subjected to all of those categories, but dance itself is something primary and pure.

And the word "pure" has been a concern of mine ever since I knew there was such a thing as "purity" in art. I think of pure as a child. Pure was when you rinsed the clothes until the water ran clear, or pure. Or the sheets that my mother pulled out of the washer that were white, white, white, meaning that they were clean, they were pure. That one's heart was pure and that God knew what hid in the recesses of it.

Then I became acquainted with art, and they were suddenly talking about abstraction as the pursuit of a pure aesthetic. Pure form, pure sound, pure beauty.

DALY: Pure movement.

JONES: This question of purity, I think, is in opposition to another question that I have been dealing with my whole life. That is the question of honesty and truth, I suppose. And here is where I always find myself falling into a pattern in an interview, wherein I suddenly say, how can I—a person who was a child of slaves, a person who was abducted, brought here, force-fed religion, culture, values, denied education, denied my "true heritage" as an African person—how can I ever expect to take part in this quest for purity, because the question arises: whose definition of purity? There we have taken what was basically an aesthetic discussion into the realm of politics and the kind of emotionalism that follows. This has been the dance that I have been dancing a great deal of my creative life.

Arnie Zane and I would make our formalist duets that were really about movement, signs, and gestures that had a musical and sculpturally constructivist slant. We would always find ourselves interjecting words, a little dialogue. The words could have been Dada words, completely opaque. And I guess opaque becomes transparent. I would choose words that were loaded with political, social, sexual, emotional connotations, and he and I would have it out in performance.

DALY: At that point, were you considering the interjection of text as a sullying of this "purity" of movement?

JONES: I guess I introduced the metaphor of dirty and clean, so "sully" is a fair term. But I thought what I was doing was making it real, bringing it into a more challenging arena, which was the arena that I thought united us outside of the aesthetic. That is, cultural and historical problems that we were having as a nation, as a country, as a people.

DALY: So you mean "we" in the largest sense, not just you and me.

JONES: That is very important, because there was a lot of criticism at that time of a lot of performance work that I was doing and that others were doing that was confessional. It was called self-indulgent. But I felt that the more personal it was, the more it invited a larger discourse. Suddenly the audience couldn't feign consensus. We couldn't feign anonymity. We resonded. *We* had to respond to the fact that I was a black man who used the word "nigger" in the context of a work that had been a moment ago—we thought—purely about form, time, repetition, maybe the personalities of the dancers, but even that was not really prized at the time. So, I thought that the formalist palette was being expanded.

DALY: So, you didn't see it as a "sullying" of pure movement.

JONES: I thought it was the other question, the search for truth. My truth was not everyone's truth, witnessed by the way I looked, the way they looked, the way Arnie looked. I thought that the truth was in the ambiguity. Therefore, pile on more and more logs, more and more contradictions, more and more painful references that are unresolved and *cannot* be resolved in dance.

When Arnie and I were working, he never wanted autobiographical materials in his work. He had a very clear idea of what he wanted his art to be. I think he was striving for rough elegance. He was looking for the rebellious that could be cloaked in seductive form. I think that is what he wanted in his photographs and in the way he and I cavorted onstage. He knew he was dancing with a big black man. He knew he was a short, "funny-looking," Jewish-Italian man.[1] He was convinced that form could make everything seductive and elevated. And I went with him. I believed it, too.

At that time the whole Paris of the 1920s—Stein and Picasso and Matisse and Cocteau—they were our heroes. We wanted that sophistication and yet that boldness and rebellion that those artists represented. We wanted to do bold things that talked about form but also talked about sex and love and death. I went with Arnie, but I would insist on the interjection of a word game or a story. It was me trying to make some sort of bridge between those two questions: what is formal purity, and how does that fit into what I understood to be the truth as I had been taught it, being who I was, born who I was, looking as I looked, feeling how I felt. How could I make them fit together? Let's face it, most of the artists we admired were white Europeans. Or an American aristocrat Jewish woman. And we didn't see a conflict in that. I just thought they had laid down the ground rules—you can do anything you like, you can be anything you like, but you must do it well, and you must develop a style to do it.

DALY: Can you discuss how you worked out these dueling concerns, with form on the one hand and with "truth" on the other hand, in the choreography?

JONES: The best example was the trilogy, which was *Monkey Run Road* (1979),[2] *Blauvelt Mountain* (1980), and *Valley Cottage* (1981). Those were intensely formalistic works in terms of the way the space was delineated and the way material was introduced and manipulated. The overall impression was of watching a puzzle being worked out. And yet it was studded with evocative, provocative gestures. Some things suggested coupling, some things suggested forbidden, homoerotic touching. But just *suggested* those things, because a gesture could be easily slanted one way or another, and we played with that a great deal. And, of course, there were the texts, which would be sotto voce, or word games. Sometimes they were dialogues we had written that were cryptic but that, when you listened to them in performance, seemed to be talking directly about the two men onstage, and the two men onstage reflected an even larger set of concerns.

In Arnie's and my duet from *Secret Pastures* (1984), we were still thinking about contact improvisation.[3] A lot of movement was grounded, with the notion of leverage, counterpull, flux, and flow in space. However, there was a theatrical image that we were trying to develop as we were doing this formal exercise. I was a large, lumpen golem, if you will, and he a small, darting man, the professor, with a shock of white hair, who was trying to bring to life, or teach, me. So it was expressionistic. It was very theatrical, but it was not really pantomime. It was really about the values in my big body and his body trying to make something that was well-crafted, clever, and winning.

DALY: *Secret Pastures* was quite a landmark, because it took on narrative on such a large scale, and so conspicuously. And in such a postmodern way. The narrative was just a pretext for dancing. I remember a post-performance talk that you and Arnie did at BAM. You said that, for you, the dance held larger implications about the Third World and racial politics. And Arnie waved away that comment. You added that, of course, you hadn't mentioned this to Arnie as the work was being made. Right there was a wonderful enactment of that tension between Arnie's structuralist sensibility and your insistence that the work had metaphorical resonances in the realm of the political.

JONES: Exactly. The question might be, "Why Bill, do you think that it is important to bring the metaphorically political into the art world?" And that is what we are talking about, the fact that I thought that was somehow or another more true. It would add a level of relevance. That is a strange word to use, "relevance." And maybe only relevant to me. Maybe I truly did believe that there were certain things that I had to continue to pursue in everything I did. Now, is that what it means, "up from slavery"? I go back always to these basic tenets. Who is talking? This is a child of people who were potato pickers who wept at the Civil Rights Act of 1964, because they knew what it meant. They knew what had been denied them before. I never had a clean slate where I could feel that I owned anything, so everything had to be fought for. Therefore, everything you made somehow had to bear witness to the struggle. Now, not to say that I was at all a polemicist . . .

DALY: The personal was the political. On a very basic level that is what you were feeling and doing and knowing.

JONES: Right, which I think is true. At that time I had a great deal of pain and some ire at the sanctimoniousness of people in this world who would say, "Oh, you have management? Oh, you have sold out, you have management." Or, "Haircuts, they all have haircuts by a designer?" Unfortunately, his name was not in the program, so there was an insert. As people opened the program, the insert fell out, and "Oh, hair design by Marcel Fieve, Oh, who do these guys think they are? This piece is just a fashion show. Willi Smith, what-have-you." We truly felt that you could speak of the highest aesthetic values and you could do it with fun. You could do it with color, you could do it with character, you could do it with decoration and makeup. We didn't have to deny ourselves. By doing *Secret Pastures,* we ran the risk of being considered not serious, of being dismissed as glib and facile. But the freedom, the color, the light that was at stake was worth the risk. That's what we set out to do.

DALY: *Secret Pastures* transgressed the rules of the avant-garde.

JONES: Right, exactly.

DALY: It risked the taboo against narrative, a very serious taboo at the time.

JONES: It seems so silly now, narrative as a taboo. *Secret Pastures* was placing a gloss on the taboo. We were trying to wink at the avant-garde.

DALY: In a very sly way. And it prefigured the intellectual, theoretical context that surrounds art now, identity politics.

JONES: Right. That duet from *Secret Pastures.* Think of what we were doing there: the big dumb black savage at the hands of the small mercurial white professor, who the savage ends up killing in the end.

DALY: You've talked about the trilogy and about *Secret Pastures* as two key works in which you dealt with this tension between formalist and personal concerns. Would you point to *Still/Here* (1994) as a third one?

JONES: Or *Last Supper at Uncle Tom's Cabin/The Promised Land* (1990).[4] All those are big works, and I feel remiss here in not thinking about smaller works like *Freedom of Information* (1984), which was our version of an endurance dance.

When I looked at us doing those leaps and that unison work, with lots and lots of repetition, and I looked at Amy Pivar and Janet Lilly and Poonie Dodson and Heywood "Woody" McGriff Jr., and Arnie Zane in his jodhpurs, I saw that we were speaking loads just by who we were together. And it was subversive, even. And our intensity and sensuality, our sexuality, and the violence that was in us—all of this stuff was coming to the fore. I thought that the tension between the formal and the emotive, or the formal and the evocative, was just there in us. Which is my belief now. The work that I am making now, *We Set Out Early ... Visibility Was Poor* (1997), was pulled way back on polemic.

DALY: Is this new dance less content-driven than *Uncle Tom's Cabin* and *Still/Here*?

JONES: Well, let's talk about that. In *Uncle Tom's Cabin,* when my mother is praying in a very traditional way—which was taught to her by her mother and her mother's mother—and then I'm standing next to her on the opera house stage and I'm shuddering, doing isolations in the joints, the back, the shoulders, the hips, it is not *interpreting* her words at all.[5] I'm responding to the cadences, the rise and fall of her voice, her breath, the rhythm which is there. I'm trying to underline: do you see what a poet she is? Do you see what an orator she is? And this is a completely unschooled, uneducated, older black woman. By the way in which I was able to ride her rhythms, her meter, I was talking in a way about form, inside of something which is overwhelmingly expressionistic. It's worship, even. So I was trying to have it both ways, and I thought it was a growth on my part. It was at once taking a bigger risk with political statements but also more clearly delineating what is form. Or at least debating what is form.

DALY: I think you're critiquing the assumption that form and content are separate. You're saying, here's a moment where they weren't separate. That you came to the point where you didn't have to make a choice between form and content anymore.

JONES: A friend of mine, Robert Longo, used to say, "You guys aren't interested in collaboration, you're interested in collision." In this sense with my mother I'm not sure I had gotten to the point where I could say I didn't have to make a choice, but I said to hell with choice-making. That's why that piece was so big, so rambling, so jumbled, because I was forcing—just jamming—things together, and trusting, almost like action painting. We throw it together and there is a result. It will send off sparks. It will do something. That's what I was doing at that time. Was it good craftsmanship? Probably not, but was it good art-making? I think so, because it was take your materials, and then all the skill you have, and all the courage you have, and your sense of timing, and throw it in.

That's what I was doing in that whole piece, telling the story of *Uncle Tom's Cabin* in the way I did—deconstructing one episode from it, "Eliza on the Ice." The whole ramification of Uncle Tom as the black martyr Christian and his subsequent fate at the hands of the brute Simon Legree informed the whole latter half of the piece—"The Supper" and "The Promised Land." I interjected LeRoi Jones's *Dutchman* into this piece, which we think is about the coming together of races but at the most crucial point is an ugly, ugly public display of a fight between a white woman and a black man in which she ends up killing him. Already retro at that time in the early 1990s, it harked back to a time that many people would like to forget, of real anger in the '60. Black rage was allowed then. In the '90s, black rage is not allowed anymore, because supposedly we all have moved on past it.

DALY: In your autobiography, you recall your mother praying as your first experience with theater. So there you were together onstage in *Uncle Tom's Cabin*, you making theater out of the cadences of her ritual.

JONES: And asking the audience to put quotations around quotations. There is the tender prayer that I'm sharing with you, my family heirloom, the thing that inspired me as a five-year-old boy. There is the thing that I am experiencing at that moment with my mother. Then there is the formal thing of her speech in and of itself, and then there is my formal take on the formalism of her speech. So I was assuming that the audience was smart and that they were able to look at layers and layers and layers, of deconstruction or reconstruction. That's what the whole piece is trying to do. And you had to be quick on your feet and you had to be culturally pretty sophisticated to know, for instance, that, no, in a black church you don't dance to the preacher. We weren't doing church. This was a hybrid and, what's more, she was in a room full of many people who were disbelievers. And she was praying as if they all believed. Was there any irony in that? And what anthropological distance did they have to take on in order to be able to hear and see all these layers that I'm talking about? It was a very active thing I demanded.

DALY: Your work has always acknowledged the space of the spectator.

JONES: Yes. Somebody who wants something.

DALY: How do you conceptualize the role of the spectator in your work, and what responsibility, if any, do you feel toward the spectator?

JONES: The spectator is, number one, a person, a member of society, and they probably come there with a need that many of us have, and that the ancient Greeks had. I as the spectator would love a transformative experience, even if I don't think I do. I would love to go into the theater and have something happen that would shed light on my predicament, being alive.

In a lot of the work that I was doing in the past, I would attempt to undercut this transcendent experience by bringing in what I took to be the nuts and bolts of modern life, something mundane and painful that maybe was divisive, when we were all trying to have a cathartic experience.

DALY: Are you referring to your early solos, when you were short-circuiting the spectator's desire to be seduced?

JONES: Well, yes. And once again, I used text to do that. Language was one way it was easy to do that, particularly when people come to dance with the idea that it is a mute and transcendent experience and I'd say, "Oh no, it isn't." Just at this moment when I have you here, this gesture is so tender, and you're loving it so much, then I will say this. Why do I do that? Why do I distance you like that? I distance you so that you and I have to work to come back together, because I believe that this is the metaphor for what all human intercourse is really about. Falling apart and fighting back together.

DALY: You had to trust that your audience was willing and invested enough to fight to come back to you within the context of a dance concert, in which the attitude usually is, "If you lose me, I'm out the door."

JONES: Yes, and sometimes I lost. But sometimes I didn't. Sometimes I was able, through the winningness of personality, maybe the interest of the movement, maybe the vulnerability that was shown, maybe some other sleight of hand, or theatrical thing, to bring people back again.

DALY: So you were using the notion of transcendence and playing off it.

JONES: And subverting it.

DALY: But in more recent dances, like *Uncle Tom's Cabin* and *Still/Here,* you seem to aim for transcendence by emphasizing commonalities instead of differences.

JONES: Well, this aesthetic struggle that goes on between the expectations of an audience and the performer who subverts them becomes the means by which the spectator can actually understand how he or she lives. This is really what it takes to live. The same process. You come into the world as a child full of hopefulness. Hopefully you have been loved, you've been taught that things are good and bad, and what have you, and then the world throws you the most vicious ambiguities. You're torn to shreds in love, and in nationalist beliefs, and in all sorts of things. But we keep going. Why? We find out that there are some enduring values: beauty, the love of a parent for a child. There is this space in our heart that I call a spiritual space that implies that I'm a part of a huge immensity which, even though it appears to be disparate and broken and torn up, is *one* thing. A thing made of such an amazing consistency that it can be good and it can be bad, it can be pain, it can be pleasure, it can be all these things. I'm saying when the work of art is good, and that experience has dragged you through it, as great art does, you're bruised but you somehow feel a rightness. I say there's something uplifting in just the struggle of having deal with this thing. And "uplift" is a bad word these days.

DALY: But when you pair "uplift" with "struggle," it seems to go beyond the cliché.

JONES: It asks, "Do you dare live?"

—Art Performs Life, exhibit catalogue,
Walker Art Center, 1998

Voice Lessons

WHEN I THINK of Bill T. Jones, it's not just his gleaming face and spring-loaded dancing that I see. His voice appears too—deep, sonorous, and cadenced, each sentence a gift, shaped neatly with a ribbon. Sometimes hushed, sometimes pointed, his voice rolls along like the weather, intensifying and dissipating with seductive force.

In dance, Jones (featured in *Time,* profiled by Henry Louis Gates Jr. in the *New Yorker*) has become the voice of our era. It's a time, since the mid-1980s, when artists have grappled with the diminished capacity of modernism; when African-Americans and other marginalized populations have claimed unprecedented visibility in the mainstream of arts and culture; when gay rights gained ground, and AIDS became a household word. The line between art and politics smudged and faded.

A dubious distinction, no doubt, for an artist to be considered a spokesman on all these points. In good measure, Jones was an unwitting candidate, in the right place at the right (or wrong) time. Early on, there was his artistic and personal partnership with Arnie Zane, which was seized upon eagerly as an emblem of the politics of difference. Then a few years ago there was *New Yorker* critic Arlene Croce's formalist manifesto against "victim art," which used Jones's *Still/ Here* (1994), sight unseen, for target practice. But his position as our exemplary agent provocateur also follows from the fact that he dares to speak beyond the cloistered conversation of "Art."

Jones knows full well that he's mouthy. (Would he be considered less harshly if he weren't a dancer, an African-American, a gay man—all categories traditionally consigned to silence?) And he has managed to stick his foot in it on more than one occasion. Perhaps that's the risk of promiscuous eloquence.

The reach of his life's work remains extraordinary. For Jones, art is about social relations, whether or not it is about social issues. His structuralist duets with Zane, for instance, commented on race relations without ever addressing the subject. By choosing a motley group of dancers for his company, he

77

told us something about how different bodies can find a way to work and play together.

Yet he spoke explicitly as a descendant of slaves in *Last Supper at Uncle Tom's Cabin/The Promised Land* (1990), and he recuperated from his "outing" as an HIV-positive man by creating *Still/Here*. In both cases, Jones attempted to redeem the brutish violence of mortals and mortality by making room for faith. In *How to Walk an Elephant* (1986), he and Zane played with the conventions of classical ballet, and made a gender-bending critique in the process. Even an entertaining romp such as *Secret Pastures* (1985) remarked on the oppressive Third World implications of conspicuous consumption. But, of course, the body has its own language. *We Set Out Early . . . Visibility Was Poor* (1997) evoked a sense of communal journey, using what's long been a metaphor for "the poetry of motion."

A voice can resound and echo. It lifts up. Rings out. Gets thrown. It is not easy to find, and too infrequently claimed. Ambrose Pierce defined fallibility as being "mistaken at the top of one's voice."

Jones's voice is not a voice of reason. It's more the emotional prosody of the preacher man, who, as a child, he was predicted to become. With each dance, Jones calls out, hoping to hear back an "Amen." An approving response, an act of community.

When the soul takes flight, speech becomes song. Increasingly, Jones is turning to song to invoke spirit and community. He has been preparing a solo program for himself in which he sings as well as dances. (It's a time-honored profession, the song-and-dance man—James Brown, Bojangles, Sammy Davis Jr.) In one solo, Jones dances an angular, side-sidling Suzie Q as he sings an old Texas prison song:

"Where have you been, Billy Boy, Billy Boy?
Where have you been, John Billy?
I've taken me a wife.
She's the jolly of my life.
She's a young girl who cannot leave her mother."

The blues, these old folk tunes are instruments of ancestral memory. They deliver him comfort. Singing them, Jones is a griot—the tribal storyteller—giving voice to the voiceless of history. Each one, he says, is like "a little window that opens up in time and space. I'm able to go through the air to people who are long dead."

Jones generates movement by improvising to music, but also in silence, because there's music in those joints and muscles. His dance vocabulary is highly gestural. And isn't gesture another way of giving voice to the body's memory? In *Still/Here*, Jones collected material by asking survivors of terminal illness to tell their stories in gestures as well as in words, which in the final work invoke the presence of those individuals who have since passed on.

Use of the speaking voice goes back to the beginning of Jones's career, when he and Zane added dialogue to their duets, such as *Rotary Action* (1982):

"A: Make a speech.

B: Make a statement.

A: OK, it's my turn to begin.

B: Let me introduce you.

A: Waiting . . ."

In Jones's solos during those early years, he seduced and confronted his spectators, at once verbally wooing and accusing them. Since then, Jones has refined his coloratura: he's been angry, ecstatic, defiant, hopeful, outraged, and mournful. But never timid or tentative.

I asked Jones: As an artist, what have you learned about developing your voice? He broke out into song and fell silent just as abruptly, cocking his head and softening his eyes. "I sing, and then I listen. I sing again, and listen a little more."

> —*America Dancing: From Revolution to Evolution,*
> season program, John F. Kennedy Center for
> the Performing Arts, 1999

Geography by Ralph Lemon. Photo © T. Charles Erickson. Used by permission.

RALPH LEMON

Review: Ralph Lemon Repertory Concert

O N THE SURFACE Ralph Lemon's dances, with their flowing lines and enigmatic gestures, look like throwbacks to a naive romanticism. He chooses seemingly romantic settings: a wedding in the tradition of Bronislava Nijinska's *Les Noces,* a country 'n' western bar (*Happy Trails*), and an idyllic encounter between the sexes (*Boundary Water*). But these situations, as Lemon choreographs them, only hold the promise of love. What they actually deliver, despite the patina of grace and lyricism, is violence, alienation, and resignation. This is neoromanticism for the postmodern age.

Lemon's anti-utopian vision (and a few of his choreographic devices, too) is strongly reminiscent of Pina Bausch's dance theater. What she did for the German dance hall in *Kontakthof* Lemon has done for the American country 'n' western bar in *Happy Trails*. In the large vacant space of the bare stage a cast of desolate characters ventures center stage from their stools to enact their woeful lives. At one point the wracked characters stretch their arms upward, turning out their wrists, as if they had just slit them.

While Bausch uses anecdotal imagery as her basic material, Lemon uses style. He has taken a gestural, ornamental look long banished from postmodern (and even modern) dance and turned it inside out. At the same time that he uses romanticism as a choreographic conceit, he subverts the very ideal of heterosexual love that it stands for. For he manipulates romanticism as a surface style within whose fissures he makes subtle and powerful comment on the difficulties—really, on the illusion—of making intimate contact with the opposite sex.

In *Boundary Water*, for example, men and women amuse themselves separately in Eden-like tranquility, but their partnering is marked by a pattern of aggression and withdrawal. Women suddenly go limp when they are picked up and dragged across the floor. A woman flings a man away from her, then embraces him. Lemon's own solo, *Wanda in the Awkward Age*, portrays the emotional and physical contradictions and frustrations of adolescence by embedding passages of gracefulness, feet-stomping, and body spasms within each other.

Les Noces seems an emblematic vehicle for Lemon, since it is a dance ritual about the reluctant bride and groom in an arranged, communal wedding. In Lemon's version, everybody holds roses—the giving and withholding of which symbolize their shifting affections. These people never stay together lovingly. A woman repeatedly embraces a man. He initially responds by going limp, but at last remains physically stalwart against her intrusion. Violence is never deep under the surface of things; at best, the male-female couples are disinterested in each other. When a woman literally hangs upside down from her partner, her legs a garland around his neck, he remains oblivious. At end, the couples manage to resign themselves to their fate.

—*High Performance*, 1988

Conversations about Race in the Language of Dance

R ALPH LEMON emerged as a major choreographic talent in the late 1980s. With an unerring instinct for the perfectly pitched gesture, he revealed an unsuspected sensuousness within the formal rigor of postmodern dance. Critical acclaim, plum commissions, and prestigious awards followed him into the 1990s.

But when it came to conferences, festivals, and articles on "black dance," Mr. Lemon was rarely included. He saw one African-American luminary walk out on his work. Another said she forbade her dancers to attend his concerts. Implicitly and explicitly, this African-American choreographer from a white suburb of Minneapolis was accused of betraying his race.

Looking back, Mr. Lemon acknowledges that his work was, as he put it, "Eurocentric." For a decade, the Ralph Lemon Company was the prototypical downtown dance troupe: abstract, formalist, and technical. Except for the choreographer, and the occasional dancer, his company, which he disbanded in 1995, was exclusively white.

Now things are different. In his new work, *Geography,* which begins three performances at the Brooklyn Academy of Music's Majestic Theater on Wednesday, Mr. Lemon's dancers and drummers are all black: six are from performance ensembles in Abidjan, the Ivory Coast; one is a Guinean griot who lives in the Greenpoint section of Brooklyn; and one is an African-American "house" dancer (a blend of forms from hip-hop to modern) from Richmond.

To Mr. Lemon, forty-five, these performers represent a range of locations on the diasporic route between Africa and America, and they have provided him with the means to undertake a full-scale inquiry into his own racial identity. "Mirrors of my black self," he calls them. Their ambitious collaboration charts the labyrinthine map, or "geography," of Mr. Lemon's long-denied and still ambivalent relationship to African and African-American cultures. "This dance," he said, "is my *Revelations.*"

That work, choreographed by Alvin Ailey in 1960, endures as the touchstone of the African-American repertory. (*Revelations* will be on the program at City Center, where the Ailey company just opened its winter season.) As Ailey recalled in his autobiography, it was part of a plan to develop a black folk-dance company and embodied his interest in "projecting the black image properly" and establishing dance as "a popular form, wrenched from the hands of the elite."

Almost forty years later, African-American choreographers continue to explore the same question, one that predates Ailey and even the modern-dance pioneer Katherine Dunham. It was first posed publicly in 1933 as the topic of a forum at the 135th Street YWCA in Harlem: "What Shall the Negro Dance About?"

That question is not as readily answered by Mr. Lemon as it was by Ailey. At the same time that *Revelations* was winning audiences with its theatricalization of slave spirituals, an artistic revolution was under way that produced a new generation of African-American choreographers. The term "black" yielded to the more culturally specific "African-American," and the expressionist genre of modern dance gave way to the formalist vision of postmodern dance.

Choreographers such as Mr. Lemon, Blondell Cummings, Garth Fagan, Bill T. Jones, Bebe Miller, and Gus Solomons Jr. did not follow in the footsteps of Ailey, who focused on vernacular African-American themes. Nor did they emulate Arthur Mitchell, whose Dance Theater of Harlem inserted black bodies into the traditionally Euro-American genre of ballet, or Chuck Davis, who restaged African dances.

In the 1990s, the question of black identity in dance has been further complicated by a shift from the paradigm of art for art's sake to one of identity politics, which adapts formalist techniques in order to critique the exclusivity of mainstream culture.

The sold-out house at last year's Town Hall debate between the African-American playwright August Wilson and the Euro-American critic Robert Brustein demonstrated that artists were as essential to the national conversation on race, culture, and politics as were the pundits and policy makers. African-American choreographers such as Ronald K. Brown, Donald Byrd, David Rousseve, and Jawole Willa Jo Zollar, co-founder of Urban Bush Women, are making inroads into the investigation of the role of race in America, now formally institutionalized by President Clinton's Initiative on Race and Reconciliation.

Choreographers are increasingly exploring the limits and possibilities of existing dance forms to address African-American issues, as Mr. Lemon is doing with postmodern dance in *Geography*. They are reconsidering the premise that an African-American aesthetic even exists. "Personally," Mr. Solomons, a former Merce Cunningham dancer, once wrote, "I can't accept racial separation either as a social or artistic proposition." They are also analyzing how racism operates. In his work *The Minstrel Show,* for example, Mr. Byrd invited audience members to contribute racist jokes to the performance.

Some choreographers are articulating the complex ways racial identification is affected by class, religion, sexuality, and gender. Mr. Rousseve has probed the connections between being black and being gay, and Ms. Zollar has looked at the interplay between sexism and racism. With the epic *Last Supper at Uncle Tom's Cabin/The Promised Land,* Bill T. Jones sought to acknowledge and move beyond the apparent schisms among his African-American history, his mother's Christian faith, and his 1960s counterculture utopianism. And in *Bring in 'Da Noise, Bring in 'Da Funk* on Broadway, as in much contemporary African-American choreography, personal narrative rekindles racial memory.

WITH *Geography,* everything is at stake for Mr. Lemon—his identity, his politics, his art, his very way of moving. He has put postmodern dance on trial, and race is the grand inquisitor. "This cross-cultural collaboration," he said, "has challenged every aspect of dance as I know it."

All along, Mr. Lemon has referred to the project as "research." Recalling the

83

methods of Dunham and Pearl Primus, whose choreography was generated through anthropological study of dance in the Caribbean and West Africa, respectively, Mr. Lemon has undertaken his own performance ethnography. But instead of conducting his fieldwork on site, he took it inside American dance studios, where he directed a cultural, personal, and aesthetic encounter between himself and a handpicked group of West African performers, brokered by an Algerian French-English translator.

After dissolving his dance company to pursue related projects, including a book and a film, Mr. Lemon wondered if his color-blind aesthetic was as choiceless as he had thought. "Nancy Hauser, a Mary Wigman-trained white woman, was my first mentor, my heritage," he said. "What does that have to do with Ralph Lemon as an African-American?"

"I wasn't that attracted to the ghosts my parents had in the house," he added. "The stories I was told were not happy, comforting stories. It was freeing for me to find dance, a world where I could deal with different issues that others were saying were very important and that weren't about slavery and segregation and murder."

Through *Geography,* Mr. Lemon has wrestled with the contradictions between his artistic and personal selves, between his Zen-inflected humanism and his newfound sense of racial difference, and between his passion for dance and his desire to "include some black in my life."

Mr. Lemon made his first visit to West Africa in August 1996 and spent the next sixteen months feeling both fearless and fearful. Overwhelmed by the foreignness of the Ivory Coast, awed by the beauty of the performers he found there, exhausted by a hyperawareness of being black, resistant to change but desperately desiring it, he was ready in March to begin what he called the "breakdown" process. As he reluctantly stepped onto a concrete slab to perform for the Ivory Coast village of Ki-Yi, all familiar ground disappeared from under his feet. By the time *Geography* opened at Yale's University Theatre on 28 October, the start of a nationwide tour, Mr. Lemon had so incorporated the eruptive energy of his collaborators that he actually managed to implode—without destroying—his loping, looping movement.

Geography, which is loosely structured after Aeschylus's *Oresteia,* sketches the journey of a central figure, who is described by Mr. Lemon as a kind of "James Brown meets Orestes." It begins with an introductory section called "Map," continues with "Crime" and "Trial," and then culminates in "Divination." Mr. Lemon portrays the exiled son of his mother Africa. Dancing is his crime, a stoning his trial, and an ancestral chorus his threshold to the future.

"The 'Crime,'" Mr. Lemon explains, "is what we think of each other's dancing, and what my dancing is supposed to be as an African-American." He and the West Africans dance next to, toward, and against each other, while the young

African-American Carlos Funn shuttles between those two worlds. They eventually transform each other.

At every juncture, the collaboration posed difficult questions about representing African dance and culture within the context of America's slave heritage. Mr. Lemon decided not to present dancers with bare chests, even though their movement is best seen that way, because he did not want them to be perceived stereotypically. Instead, they will be dressed in linen suits and gauze gowns.

"It was important to me that they were not wearing kente cloth, or fabric with obvious African marks," Mr. Lemon said. "And then it got scary. The question became 'What's theirs?' Or 'What am I leaving them?' I thought maybe they'd wear shoes. 'Be careful,' I thought, 'because you can go too far with this. You could completely strip them, so they're your dolls.' It's a struggle."

The set, by the installation artist Nari Ward, creates an environment of urban detritus but with a "mythical, almost sacred" patina, explained the choreographer. "Almost everything that comes from this world is either organic or old, because I think the last time I was a black person was in the '60s."

Filling this deliberately retro, low-tech space is a highly textured soundscape: West African singing and drumming, poetic text by Tracie Morris, electro-acoustic music by Francisco López, and a sensor-triggered sampling of urban and natural sounds by Paul D. Miller.

Ms. Morris and Mr. Miller, both African-American, approached the choreographer's quest through their own concerns. Ms. Morris wanted to balance references to the transatlantic slave trade with acknowledgment of the Africanisms that were retained in the New World rather than destroyed.

For Mr. Miller, the matter of "origins" is irrelevant. Everything—whether music or identity—is constantly being remixed. "Identity," he said, "is an arbitrary choice, conditioned by our consumer environment." Nevertheless, he admired what he called the choreographer's idealistic "willingness to create dialogue between the two communities."

Of the *Geography* cast members, six are from Abidjan. Four of them, the dancers Djédjé Djédjé and Nai Zou and the drummers Goulei Tchépoho and Zaoli Mabo Tapé, are members of the Ki-Yi M'bock ensemble. The others, Akpa (James) Yves Didier and Kouakou Yao, dance with the Ensemble Koteba. Another member, Djeli Moussa Diabate, a Guinean griot now based in Brooklyn, travels around the world to perform and teach. They consider themselves ambassadors or messengers who have been given an opportunity to help African-Americans in search of their roots.

"We are teaching Ralph about the past, and about living now in Africa," Mr. Djédjé said. "Maybe as Africans and African-Americans together, we might find another solution for the future."

Here is the fundamental work of *Geography*: to generate a dialogue between two dance traditions and the world that each one carries. Something as seemingly perfunctory as the dancers' gaze, for example, can provoke a long and serious exchange. As director, Mr. Lemon had to negotiate the differences without either erasing or cementing them.

He tried to inhabit the Africans' way of moving while recognizing that goal as an impossibility. "You can never really give up your own culture," said Mr. Lemon, who recalled being labeled "white" in Ghana because he is not from Africa, "but you have to surrender to the situation."

Refusing simply to blend the two vocabularies or compose an obvious turn-taking structure, Mr. Lemon chose instead to use as his material the very tensions, contradictions, and disruptions that arose during his intercultural experiment. "When all is said and done, we'll be looking at those grand discrepancies."

Mr. Lemon's style is individual, silent, light, supple, free-flowing, and internally focused. The West Africans' style is communal, theatrical, strong, grounded, rhythmic, structured, and externally directed. Mr. Lemon's sense of space is geometric, and theirs is organic. He dances secular energy; they dance religious spirit. His knees give out after sixteen counts of their dancing, and their hips resist opening out for his. Where his feet point, theirs flex.

To MAKE THE creative process as mutual as possible, Mr. Lemon devised a procedure that began with the dancers' movement material and cycled it through a series of improvisations. In short: the dancers responded to videotapes of themselves responding to Mr. Lemon responding to them. To further the fracturing, he asked them to manipulate their own movement—to reverse it, for example, or perform a sequence without using the arms. The drummers and dancers worked out the counts for the final phrase, which Mr. Lemon continued to tweak. At the end of these extended exchanges, the dancers remained themselves, only turned inside out.

Some observers have accused Mr. Lemon of naive dilettantism or arrogant colonialism: another Picasso raiding the African continent for his own artistic gain. In response, Mr. Lemon insisted on his right to express ambivalence about these personal issues. And he reiterated his obligation to proceed responsibly, always cautioning himself against cultural projection and romanticizing. "I can only approach all this as an artist, not as a sociologist," he said. "At the end of the day, it's going to be about our moving."

In the midst of daily rehearsals, race receded. Mr. Lemon described the final weeks as "being completely inside of race."

"It's completely inside of black and therefore colorless again," he added. "I stopped seeing African. I stopped seeing black. I stopped seeing men. It just becomes people in a communal experience."

Making *Geography*, he said, was like being a griot sent out into the bush to learn about spirit. "At the end of this, I will be in a different home."

—*New York Times*, 1997

Afterword

(of)

a book

a journey

a dance

I begin at the end

THE DANCE entitled *Geography* was conceived, choreographed, and directed by New York-based postmodern choreographer Ralph Lemon. *Geography* premiered 28 October 1997, at the Yale Repertory Theatre, then made a national tour until closing in December at the Brooklyn Academy of Music in New York.

The dance ends with a story. There is other spoken and sung text in *Geography*, but it is never narrative. Like the whole of the dance, the spoken text, when in English, is poetically abstract and nonlinear. When in dialects from the Côte d'Ivoire, the spoken text presumably reads as melody and rhythm to its English-speaking audience.

So when we are told a story in English at the end of an hour and a half, it stands out as an event of clarity and drama. The story is told by Moussa Diabate, a griot from Guinea who now lives in Brooklyn. He stands very still and glowing in a pitch-black void, speaking to what appears as an empty stage space, and then circles it in a series of careening jumps. The story he tells is metaphorical, about the moment of diaspora, the kidnapping of a man such as this West African for the slave trade.

This illicit journey is described as blurry, black, and confusing. With something to see.

The theater is a place to see. *Geography*, by way of the fact and the trope of diaspora, is an attempt to remap the theater and what it makes visible. *Geography* takes its place alongside other great texts about late-twentieth-century African-American culture, such as Alvin Ailey's *Revelations* and Bill T. Jones's *Last Supper at Uncle Tom's Cabin/The Promised Land*. Lemon's project, however, goes beyond either celebrating or deconstructing the African slave experience. *Geography*, in the end, is about space, just as its title announces. It's about the space that marks identity and that is marked by journeys, and in particular by the African diaspora. And it's about ritually transforming stage space from the secular to the sacred.

I.

The fundamental irony of dance history is that
the dances that get inscribed—
on celluloid, on magnetic tape, on paper—
are the ones that become real.

Geography is as much a book as it is a dance.
Really, Geography is an autobiography.

Note quite the melodrama of Duncan's My life
Or the soap opera of Gelsey Kirkland's Dancing on My Grave.
A tragedy instead, Greek.
Who is the hero, and what of his fatal flaw?
Who will be stoned in the town square?

What hubris does the artist assume when he decides to tell his/story?
Powerful posture, confused gait.

I.

For Lemon, *Geography* is a trip into unknown territory. Acclaimed as a formal-ist, downtown choreographer, he was uninterested in any content, let alone racial content, for most of the decade he spent directing his company. He acknowledges that his past work has been "Eurocentric." Only a few members of his company over the years were African American.

With *Geography,* the cast is all black. He chose to work with four dancers and two drummers from Côte d'Ivoire, one Guinean griot, and an African-American "house" dancer from Richmond, Virginia.

For Lemon, these performers represented a range of locations on the diaspor-ic route between Africa and America, and they provided him with the means to undertake a full-scale inquiry into his own racial identity. "Mirrors of my black self," he called them. Their ambitious collaboration charted the labyrinthine geography of Lemon's long denied and still ambivalent relationship to African and African-American cultures.

For a year and a half, Lemon undertook what amounts to a performance ethnography. He conducted his fieldwork in the American dance studio, where he staged a cultural, personal, and aesthetic encounter between himself and a handpicked group of West African performers. It is this encounter, this space in between two cultures, that *Geography* addresses.

Geography was loosely structured after the *Oresteia.* It obliquely sketches the journey of a figure Lemon conceived of as "James Brown-meets-Orestes." It begins with an introductory section called "Map," continues with "Crime" and "Trial," and then culminates in "Divination." Lemon portrays the exiled son of his mother Africa. Dancing is his crime, a stoning his trial, and an ancestral chorus his threshold to the future.

While this story provided the conceptual framework for the piece, in performance *Geography* is a dense work that defies such causal logic. I've heard the dance criticized for needing editing, and for needing better cues as to when spectators should or should not applaud, given the very different role of the audience in American and African dance practices.

II.

Djédjé stands magnificently atop a tall ladder—
calling out, calling forth from the mountaintop—
as a tinkling glass-bottle curtain lowers behind him, a setting sun, a veil of tears.
He is so solid, and rooted so deeply.

That's what they all are. Each a tree.

When the Africans dance, I hear their feet
padding and pounding the floor.
Ralph slips by soundlessly.

Ralph is fascinated with trance.
Initially, he fumbles in his effort to elicit the altered state.
Too dangerous, he is told. But they could fake it.

In the end, he achieves his own kind of rapture.
Divination
Benediction
Consecration

II.

To require that *Geography* conform to existing laws of genre and culture is to exert exactly that pressure the dance is resisting. *Geography* literally lays bare the space of the stage, revealing the fire wall and the wings. We see the performers who stroll around the edges of the stage when not in action. As soon as they finish their phrases, they resume their offstage manner. They enter and exit and position props with everyday matter-of-factness. The boundary between onstage and offstage is emphasized so as to be questioned.

But at the same time, the space is highly theatricalized and filled with symbolic references. Rumpled linen suits, straw hats, and a lazily turning ceiling fan, mottled shadows of moonlight through the trees and the gentle cries of crickets (did I just imagine them?) suggest a sweltering evening. Everything is converted into space—lighting, movement, even singing is manipulated for its ability to describe the space between here and there, the space between call and response, and the space between inside the body and out. Silence, too, affects the size and density of the stage.

Space is the medium of exchange between dancers, between cultures, between performer and audience, between secular and sacred.

III.

Who does Ralph want to be?
Emerson or Ellison.
James Brown. A Temptation.
A griot. A god. An underworld informant.
Or, rather. Where does Ralph want to be?
Have body, will travel.
The question is no longer: what is dance.
The question is: what does dance do.
When these African dancers look into your face,
You may fall out of your seat.

III.

The dance begins with a ritual exchange between two spectral figures dressed in ancestral gauze gowns, who will reappear toward the end of the piece when an apotheosis restores us to the moment of origin, the story of diaspora. The ritual exchange that begins it all is the discovery of rhythm, in the form of a rock banged against the earth. When another man approaches the first, the gift of rhythm is bestowed upon him, and the rock 'n' roll chant of James Brown cues the dancers, who burst onto the stage and as quickly depart. Such eruptions, disruptions, interruptions, disappearances that produce rather than erase new appearances, dispersals, and displacements are the condition of this dance, which embodies the condition of diasporic culture.

Exchange, or dialogue, was the material project of *Geography*. How do two sets of bodies, constructed and practiced so differently, create a single dance?

Lemon tried to inhabit the Africans' way of moving while recognizing that goal as an impossibility. As he explained it, "You can never really give up your own culture, but you have to surrender to the situation." He recalled being labeled "white" in Ghana, because he is not from Africa.

Refusing simply to blend the two vocabularies or compose an obvious turn-taking structure, Lemon chose instead to use as his material the very contradictions, tensions, and discrepancies that arose during his intercultural experiment.

Lemon's postmodern movement style is individual, silent, light, supple, free-flowing, and internally focused. The West Africans' style is communal, theatrical, strong, grounded, rhythmic, structured, and externally directed. Lemon's sense of space is geometric, and theirs is organic. He dances secular energy; they dance religious spirit. His knees give out after sixteen counts of their dancing, and their hips resist opening out for his. Where his feet stretch, theirs flex.

To make the creative process as mutual as possible, Lemon devised a workshop method that began with the dancers' own movement material, itself an amalgam of their pan-African performance troupes at home, and cycled it through a series of improvisations. In short: the dancers responded to videotapes of themselves responding to Lemon responding to them. To further the fracturing, he asked them to manipulate their movement—to retrograde it, for example, or perform it without using the arms. The drummers and dancers worked out the counts for the final phrase, which Lemon continued to tweak. At the end of these extended exchanges, the dancers remained themselves, only turned inside out. And Lemon had so incorporated the eruptive energy of his collaborators that in his central solo he actually managed to implode—without destroying—his own loping, looping movement.

IV.

I've never observed someone so fearful and fearless at the same time.
(Ralph realized immediately the price of passage.)

Geography plots a disorienting route,
not because it traverses such distance
as fatigues the limbs
but because it fathoms such depth
as unhinges the equilibrium.

IV.

As important as the movement is the mise-en-scène. The set, by installation artist Nari Ward, is an environment of urban detritus but with a mythical patina. And its shadows limn a shifting landscape. Filling this deliberately low-tech space is a highly textured soundscape: West African singing and drumming, poetic text by Tracie Morris, electro-acoustic music by Francisco López, a sensor-triggered contrast of chirping birds and blasting alarms by Paul D. Miller, and always the sound of feet, which patter as expressively as the tongue.

And the spoken text situates the real and mythical place as well, referring to heaven and hell and to the womb, and to a dead garden.

Lemon choreographed not so much a dance as an environment that hosts an interlocking series of interactions. *Geography* is structured like its front curtain of embroidered mattress springs, which functions as screen and frame and fence and cage. It is like the backdrop of glass bottles. The bottle and mattress-spring curtains are fragile quilts of everyday objects made sparkling and beautiful. They are artifactual shards of a life unseen, which fit together like the drums onstage, each contributing its own to the fabric of the whole.

And violence is a part of that fabric. What starts out as the minuet transforms into hand-to-hand combat. The veneer of civilization reveals its violent underbelly.

The rocks reappear, this time for use in a ritual stoning.

But the ancestral figures reappear, too, and the stage is then transfigured. Very slowly the curtain of glinting, tinkling, jewel-like bottles lowers to the floor. And as it lowers, one dancer's voice rings out, reverberates, blesses this place that now fills with white-gowned figures, whose popping, intensifying energy is matched by a howling, hollow sound that grows to engulf them. The movement and sound seem to expand the stage. There are no edges, no boundaries, no borders.

And then Moussa tells his story.

And like the story he tells, *Geography* is blurry, black, and confusing. And it is something to see.

But what's seen is not simply another dance in Lemon's repertoire. He has transfigured the very ground of his practice. *Geography* is, in a sense, a project of recovery and a ritual marking of the stage as a sacred place. By inquiring into the nature of the diasporic journey and his own racial identity, Lemon has asked: How does the body circulate? Sound travels, light travels, energy travels, the body certainly travels. And so does identity. Lemon has reinvented the theater as a place to see more than just the changing shapes and patterns of arms and legs. The stage that the griot addresses may appear to be a pitch-black void, but it is not. The space is filled with ancestors telling their stories.

—"Afterword" to Ralph Lemon,
Geography: art/race/exile, 2000

PERFORMANCES

ction Heroes by Elizabeth Streb. Photography by Rose Eichenbaum. Used by permission.

Review: Kei Takei's *Light, Part 20 & 21 (Diary of the Dream)* and *Tetsu Maeda's Evocations*

KEI TAKEI told an interviewer not too long ago that if she weren't a choreographer, she would be a farmer. That's very easy to see in her dances, which have a distinctly earthy weightiness about them. In *Light, Part 20 and 21 (Diary of the Dream)*, dancers' feet pounded and caressed the ground in changing rhythms. They carried bundles on their backs. In simple, peasant's clothes, they attended to their repeating and gradually evolving motions with devotional concentration.

This Zen-like calmness, the sense of extended time and the movement's resemblance to martial arts reflect Takei's Japanese heritage.

In this latest installment of her continuing epic called *Light*, she made overt reference to Takei the choreographer. Dancers stepped out of their silent, dancing personae to vent their frustrations about working with her. Their complaints called attention to the use of space in the piece, the ambiguity of "Part 20" being intertwined with "Part 21," and to the choreographer's impish sense of humor.

In *Light, Part 20 and 21 (Diary of the Dream)*, instead of the natural stones, sheaves of wheat, and radishes that have been featured in other parts of *Light*, the fetishes here were plastic garbage bags each filled with an empty cardboard box. As these artifacts of synthetic culture were tossed onstage like manna from heaven (or at least from the wings), their bulky shapes suggested a thudding massiveness that was immediately dispelled by their easy landings.

The dancers tumbled, hurtled themselves through the air, embraced, attacked, rolled, collapsed, and climbed onto each other in a human chain like disaster victims hoisting themselves onto the safety of a lifeboat. Three dancers, traveling like immigrants with their possessions packed on their backs, stomped back and forth as other lost-looking souls walked in meandering, unfocused paths. Takei's own solos had her scuttering across the floor like a feral child.

Also on the program was *Tetsu Maeda's Evocations*, a vehicle for the stunning set design of Tetsu Maeda. He made the stage twinkle and vibrate and sparkle and shine with gleaming white strings and ropes, powder, and plastic and blinking colored lights.

The most beautiful moment came when lighting and thick white ropes hanging from the rafters created a kind of twilight arcade—a simple but majestic temple. Dancers stood wondering at these pillars, focusing on them but barely touching them. Then, in an instant, the lights died and the ropes fell, their sturdy agelessness disappearing into formless puddles on the floor.

—High Performance, 1985

Review: Fred Holland's *Harbor/Cement*

FRED HOLLAND brought a sculptor's sensibility to *Harbor/Cement,* presented 6–9 June at the Danspace Project at St. Mark's Church. Although the piece featured a sequence of emotionally charged monologues, dances, and visual imagery, what really resonated were the spaces in between.

Harbor/Cement was tied together by poetic rather than linear logic. Dedicated "to the memory of the eleven members of the Move Organization killed in Philadelphia, May '85," the piece quickly changed from a serene, meditative environment into a caustic, alienating one.

Holland spread out his metaphoric cityscape from the theater entrance, where a large, black wheel confronted the arriving audience, to the tiny sailboats bobbing in a pool of water at the far end of the theater to the shadows of violent combat thrown high against the front walls of the church balconies.

Each part of the environment was positioned and spotlighted in isolation —here a nude man lying face down on a patch of dirt and there a tiny colony of miniature houses. Likewise, the activities discretely spread out over the hour-long performance rarely overlapped. They benignly ignored each other like commuters in a crowded subway.

Intimacy was thwarted all the way through *Harbor/Cement.* Intensifying this frustration were electronic music and lighting that could be as unnerving as they were soothing.

During the course of the evening, an old man, felled by a stroke, talked about being terrorized by youth gangs in his changing neighborhood. A man at a school desk read newspapers, recited vital statistics of victims of violence, and then made little sailboats.

A group of big-boned women at first sprawled out on a platform. Then they tore around en masse, coming down heavy on the floor with their work boots. Two of them slow-danced together, while the others wandered aimlessly.

A man inside a closed tent—with only his shadow against the canvas visible to the audience—talked about frustrated love, the inability to communicate.

Harbor/Cement indulged in the expansive space of this two-story church, but it was about the critical lack of urban space. The piece seemed to suspend time but warned in one monologue that our time may be running out.

When a lashed-together ark suspended over the center of the performance space slowly ascended in a dim twilight, it seemed as if this were the only escape from such a dismal existence, such anomie.

Holland pulled together the work of musician David Linton; lighting designer Carol Mullins; choreographers Lucy Sexton, Ann Iobst, and Kaja Gam; and a host of writers. The visual and theatrical beauty of the production more than made up for the occasional platitudes.

— High Performance, 1985

Review: Jane Comfort's *TV Love*

IN *TV LOVE*, rock singer Fortuna Desire worries her way onto a television talk show, passes off her recent two-city junket as a world tour, joins in an impromptu aerobic dance number, and is abandoned by the host, guests, and crew during a commercial break. In the dim, silent studio, she pulls up a camera and performs a flowing sequence of abstracted sign-language gestures. Focusing on the camera lens, she makes a steady backward progression upstage, grounding the sometimes sweeping, sometimes minute gestures in the metronomic sway of her hips, shifting from one leg to the other.

Is this the private Fortuna, no longer obsessing about showing her good side, fluffing her hair, or leaning into her questions? Or is it just a dancer (Jane Comfort) dancing a dance? As a story, Fortuna's talk show appearance raises more questions than it answers, but, alas, the story's not the thing. Comfort is only flirting with narrative; it's one of the TV conventions she's parodying.

In the Fortuna segments Comfort makes fun of the empty pitter-patter of talk show storytelling by substituting all forms of the word "talk" for the bulk of their vocabulary. In other segments she plays up the artifice of soap opera plots and the orgasmic enticement of commercials.

Early on, four dancers (Karen Callaghan, Bradley Lake, Ann Papoulis, David Thomson) play out a soap opera scenario in which Feona finds her lover in a ménage à trois and then tries to shoot him. He explains away the indiscretion by telling her it's not real—they're all actors, and this is a television studio. "It's all pretend. You too can be an actor.... Darling, it didn't happen." And then, in a brilliant stroke, Comfort has the dancers "rewind" the scene, its words taking on interesting patterns of skewed meaning as they're spoken in reverse order. Television, she reminds us, though it appears to present reality, is just an illusion.

TV Love parodies the way television creates desire—for money, for fame, for sex, for beauty, for love. When the talk show guests' alter egos—who stand behind them onstage—want attention, they urge the host to "love *me*, love *me*." And later, when Mr. Wonderful struts out of their lives, the myth of "happily ever after" explodes in his panting lovers' faces.

Mr. Wonderful, in tux, shades, and slicked-back hair, first appears posed at the top of the upstage steps, with head tossed back and pelvis seductively tilted forward. One arm is draped against a pillar and the other is tucked casually into his pocket. He takes a drag on his cigarette. He pops open a bottle of champagne, letting it run down his face and over his chest. He rips off his clothes, and his four spectators are driven into a fit of passion. This is each of their "dreams come true." They follow him, reach for him, all rhythmically chanting "fifty," "forty," "fuck" faster and more feverishly until it climaxes with the thrusting of his G-string. Another drag on the skinny brown cigarette, a quick retrieval of his scattered clothes, and Mr. Wonderful is gone. That's the end of the dance.

What opens the dance, though, and reappears between the brash TV scenarios, are passages of soothing, introspective dancing that seem a further abstraction of Comfort's sign-language solo. During the course of *TV Love*, the dancers' gestures become familiar, like when they extend their spread-fingered hands forward and then pull them back past the sides of their heads, almost as if they're miming wind rushing through their hair.

The gestures take on a hypnotic, meditative power when four dancers perform them in unison right before the talk-talk-talk show. They cup a hand to one ear. They extend their right hands to arm's length and then draw them into their faces. They stand there still, wiping their hands across their lips as if they are rubbing off lipstick. They gently stroke their upper chests, smooth back their hairlines, pat their shoulders. The dancers, with eyes closed, seem in deep reverie, and their quiet ritual culminates in an embrace.

—*High Performance*, 1985

Review: Kazuo Ohno's *Admiring La Argentina* and Kuniko Kisanuki's *Tefu Tefu*

B UTOH, the Japanese modern dance form, is a very expressionistic style. It deals with the universals of birth and death and the sometimes unbearable, sometimes ecstatic limbo in between. Yet butoh, as practiced by both originator Kazuo Ohno and the young choreographer Kuniko Kisanuki, has also its very formal elements.

The originators of butoh were influenced by teachers with strong ties to Mary Wigman, a pioneer in early German modern dance. Though Ohno and Kisanuki share this heritage with the current German choreographers such as Pina Bausch and Reinhild Hoffmann, the Japanese focus more on movement than the Germans, who focus on action.

Hoffmann, arguing against American formalism at a symposium at the Goethe House in November, asked: "If I want to get from here to there, why shouldn't I just walk there? Why do I have to do this?" At which point she rippled her arms forward.

Hoffmann and her counterparts attend to what the body does in terms of getting somewhere. The Japanese are not interested in getting somewhere or doing something but rather in *being* something. To them, the body's own properties are expressive and emotional. While the contemporary Germans manipulate gestures of the everyday world to make their statements, Ohno and Kisanuki concentrate on the transformative possibilities of their bodies.

Images and emotions flicker through Ohno's body. It's not just his facial expression but his wandering arms, his ever shortening and lengthening neck, and his changing sense of weight that achieve the panorama.

The evening-length solo, *Admiring La Argentina,* refers to a famous Spanish dancer of the 1930s and 1940s. In it, Ohno spends most of his time in fabulously flamboyant, old-fashioned woman's clothes, complete with heels and hat. His painfully thin figure and wrinkled, powdered, sexless face make the gender switch less political than poignant. Appearing first in a seat in the audience, he adjusts his hat, dabs his face, lowers his eyes, and flutters his eyelids. With mincing arms, he becomes the grotesque shadow of a young coquette. He drapes himself across the edge of the stage in the serpentine curves of traditional femininity and then kicks up his foot like a young lover.

I don't think the image is meant to degrade or criticize women's vanity. I think that like the rest of the dance, it's meant to display the poignant vulnerability of performing, whether it's an old woman performing a young woman or Ohno performing La Argentina or Ohno just plain performing.

The dance progresses onstage, and Ohno advances and retreats from an invisible force. The force takes the form of a light, toward which Ohno makes a slow progression. At the end, he runs away, back over his diagonal path in little, light tiptoe steps.

Ohno also deliberates between heaven and earth—between the bright light overhead and the floor. His weight settles somewhere in between, though occasionally he sinks to the earth or stretches skyward.

Ohno often bends his knees inward, as if he's sagging under his own weight. At one point, when his legs are weakened under him, he stretches his arms up imploringly toward the light, suggesting a crucifixion image.

He often keeps his arms close to his body. When they do spread and lift, they're almost weightless and totally without goal; many times, they're contorted in angles. He has a pathetic way of shrugging up one shoulder and settling his chin into it like a scared and puzzled child. At other moments, he nobly lifts his chin and lengthens his neck.

His approach is indirect and his presence remote. He is so fragile, except in one scene in which he wears a heavy, black priestlike robe. Briefly, he becomes powerful and direct, lunging from side to side in a wide stance, kicking his legs and flinging his arms.

The connection with La Argentina is strongest during the two songs that feature her playing the castanets. Ohno does fleetingly suggest her performance; for example, he ripples his body to suggest her rhythm.

There is always a tension—an interesting, not a distracting one—between the images he suggests and his artistry. Perhaps because his work is highly improvisatory, he can maintain a dual focus that is at once inward but never loses touch with the audience.

Kisanuki is less generous with her attention to the audience. Sometimes her ballet-derived technique seems to require all her concentration.

Like Ohno, she begins *Tefu Tefu* in the audience, where she also ends. Single-mindedly approaching the stage down the aisle steps, slowly, unflinching, almost unblinking, she seems to be preparing for a ritual. The dance is like a ritual, ridding her of bad spirits.

Once onstage, she begins upright, in flat-footed arabesques that fall over into somersaults and back bends that test the limits of gravity.

Stretched across the back wall are expanses of cloth, like tattered and discolored ship sails. They have endured destruction, and so has the dancer, whose now-distorted limbs tell of violence, disfigurement, pain.

Now squatting, she floats over the stage in a womblike position. She hops up and down and away from an invisible attacker. Repeatedly she falls from her squat onto her right thigh. Lying on her back, she raises her pointed toes in a V and then cringes them into a crippled profile.

Eventually she stands again, running and jumping high, then landing in a crouch. In mid-crouch, she sways her arms. She slowly brings her toe to her ear like a prima ballerina. She flutters her legs like the wings of the butterfly (*Tefu*

Tefu means "butterfly"), skips along and then spins in ecstasy. Having emerged from this rite, she exits back into the audience.

—High Performance, 1986

Review: Molissa Fenley Repertory Concert

M OLISSA FENLEY's works at the Joyce reminded me more of Laura Dean's choreography than did Dean's latest dances. The ritual power of repeating and kaleidoscoping motions—once the mainstay of Dean's spinning dances—was as strongly present in Fenley's solo and group work as it was absent in Dean's newest, arabesque and pas de deux choreography.

Fenley, Jill Diamond, Silvia Martins, and Scottie Mirviss moved nearly non-stop (Elizabeth Benjamin was out with an injury at the performance I saw). Once a dancer was onstage, she didn't exit until the dance was over. There were no entrances and exits to mark off the dance, and there were no clear-cut floor patterns, either. Dancers flowed around the space. Few sharp-edged units of anything kept the motion from spilling forward.

Not that there was a big push toward climax—on the contrary, the repeating, gently permutating figures were equally mesmerizing at every moment, like a long train passing by, each car following the next in a thrillingly predictable manner.

The dancers' arms—held away from the torso—constantly curved, circled, and arched all around them as they stepped, turned, sometimes skipped around stage. Each dancer was a single whirling body; the ensemble's changing profiles provided the works' color and texture. The dancers bent low from the waist, stretched high with arms curved heavenward, held arms straight out to the side with hands flexed, or pushed arms high with hands curved forward like bunny ears. Fenley's arms became almost disembodied, because all their impetus came from the outside of her upper arm rather than from the hand or forearm. This gave her dancing a distorted and ecstatic look sometimes, as if she could not control its exuberance.

Her solo, *Second Sight,* was very much an ecstatic ritual—both intimate and incantatory. She looped her arms, whipped her hands around her circling head, and picked up a bent leg with flexed foot like a statue of an Asian god. Though she danced around the stage, she kept returning to the straight path down center stage as if it were magic territory. This piece, with its grounded, open-chested body posture and polyrhythmic score by Peter Gordon, harkened back to Fenley's Nigerian upbringing.

Cenotaph incorporated a more Western dance vocabulary—arabesques, pliés, attitudes—though there were still references to Shiva's angled, upraised arms. The piece subtly progressed from a duet to a trio to a quartet.

The program opener, *Cenotaph* was of particularly high energy. It featured whipping turns, legs flung back in attitude, high extensions. In a poignant moment at the end of their duet, Fenley and Mirviss, facing the audience side by side, held hands as they each raised a leg backward in arabesque. Then they leaned away from each other in deep plié. The trio dancers were at first quite independent but then wove themselves into a more communal space in loose configurations, sometimes moving in unison or canon.

Esperanto was calmer, even romantic. The lighting alternated between gently colored backdrops and flashes of bright white, when the dancing became faster and more feverish. The women's athletic bodies were partially covered with skirts that reminded me of the early modern dancers. There was an acute sense of direction in the dancers' bodies; there was little jumping or upward thrust, and heads often dipped forward. The arms, though, were very curvaceous, softer, with a lot more lightness and suspension. The piece ended with a coda, which was rather an odd-man-out. In it, Fenley, Martins, and Mirviss were stripped back to leotards, leaving the audience with the image of sleek, powerful female bodies.

I see a lot to admire about this ensemble of strong, resilient, self-possessing women. And I find appealing the contrast between the primal and space-age impulses in Fenley's choreography. Its organic feeling and repetitive structure appears ascetic and all-absorbing, and yet its thirst for speed and precision is thoroughly modern.

—High Performance, 1986

Review: Gwall's *Exit*

AT THE BEGINNING of *Exit*, two men and three women are all wearing the same Barbarella black tops whose low, low neckline runs under and up between exposed breasts. They look great on the guys—smooth, firm pectorals and all—but the ill-fit does nothing for the women, except probably pinch and squeeze them.

The rest of the dance is just as unflattering to the women, portraying them as useless, masochistic bores in a male-run universe. A male couple, in futuristic black warrior boots, with thumbs hooked in their black leather pants, prefer to throw around their shared woman partner until she leaves, and then slow-dance with each other. Later, the couple returns, waiting motionless against a wall while three seated women desperately seeking their attention finally give up their preening and posing and leave in a huff.

The press release says all this is "bursting with irony," but absolutely nothing of the ironic comes through. These men are so self-involved, so into being defiant-chic that there's nothing to smile a wry smile at. When a man and woman, both wearing pink knit dresses and thick black gloves, grab the other by the mouth and yank her/him around the stage, the dread and savageness of Parisian choreographer Yannick Kergreis's world looks beyond redemption.

The only funny-approaching-ironic moment, I thought, was when a tall rail of a man with large flat hands and clunky boots—a Giacometti sculpture in black leather pants and teeny bolero—imitates the long, loose, limping run of his partner-in-pathology. She's a petite woman whose attraction to this goon indulges his violent responses. He throws her to the ground and grabs her by the hair, glaring at her (and us) the whole time. This Lurch nary lifts a foot, instead shuffling or sliding heavy across the floor, so when he does his lumbering version of his partner's jetés, the joke is a welcome relief.

This couple's continuing saga is interspersed throughout the piece, serving as serial entr'actes between the larger sections. Most of what seems to interest Kergreis in these other sections is legs. Legs are always doing most of the work, turning in-and-out, pounding with flat feet, shuffling, but mostly stepping side-to-side. The dancers shift weight from side-to-side with the sway of loose, lusty hips.

In the opening section, five dancers in a V-formation spend fifteen minutes repeating the sinuous side-stepping to the insistent beat of the music. The stepping from side-to-side becomes a slide to the side, then a jarringly balletic bourrée to the side, and even a passé to the side.

Later, they come onstage in bathing suits and goggles. With their backs to the audience, they wag their bums back and forth and back and forth and back and forth. They've wrapped their arms around themselves so it looks to the audience as if some unseen, anonymous person is caressing them.

The final scene, with the dour dancers twitching their suddenly palsied arms, is as enigmatic as the earlier violence is gratuitous. Why had that man in a black trench coat dragged around a rope-tied woman so viciously? Why did he, at end, draw her up into his arms?

A lot of current dance in New York features physical violence linked with sex/love, and much of it is violence done to women by men. That this reeks of trendiness is frightening. At least Pina Bausch ritualizes her violence; though it wrenches your guts, there is an aesthetic distance there that says, "Yes, I know this is a despicable state of affairs." In *Exit*, women are portrayed as if they deserve the abuse: they are primping bores, picking their nails, bending over to show off their tightly clad asses, and too stupid to know that they're unwanted.

—*High Performance*, 1986

Review: Lucinda Childs Repertory Concert

THERE ARE some who believe that the purpose of art is to connect with an underlying unifying spark of life: the aesthetic. No better case could be made for that argument than the choreography of Lucinda Childs. Watching her precision-patterned dances, swathed in lighting so alive you could almost touch it, was like levitating, like human hydroplaning.

I've always associated Childs with the geometric notations she makes of her dances. She is, by and large, considered the most austere and cerebral of the American formalists to come out of the Judson Church days. She's a kind of litmus test for the German dance theater apologists who accuse American formalism of being "lightweight."

In *Dance #1,* dancers burst unpredictably across the stage one at a time. Opening and closing their arms as they turned, then doing a few traveling steps before repeating the sequence, they went straight from wing to wing, in neat lanes. The effect was like the strobe light pulses you get when you stare at the intersecting black lines in a Mondrian painting. The stage, bare between the dancers' crossings, was electrified.

As the light eased from blue dimness into clear brightness into a golden glow, the dance took on its own subtle variations. Some treks were faster, or more dancers filled the space at once. Dancers dipped off-center, skipped, and scissored their limbs.

The dancers started coming on in couples, at first on cue together, and then staggered. Couples turned into a group, doing more progressively complicated steps. They mixed up their entrances from either wing. The rhythm was bouncy, and the feeling was fleet, like wind. The side-to-side, tennis court rhythm was finally broken by diagonal formations, as the dancers broke into jetés, faster and faster until the climax. At the end, there was an empty stage, black and silent.

From Robert Wilson's *Einstein on the Beach* came Child's *Field Dance #1,* full of seamless turns, and *Field Dance #2,* more of an ensemble piece with hopscotch steps and arabesques. *Dance #1* and the two Field Dances were jam-packed into one program, all to Philip Glass's kaleidoscoping minimalist music. The other program, *Portraits in Reflection,* was a full-length dance premiere.

All the recent disparaging talk about American formalism must have gone to Childs's head. In *Portraits,* although the balletic vocabulary, the patterned format, and the delicious lighting (by Gregory Meeh) are the same as in her earlier pieces, the tank tops and chinos are gone. The bare stage is gone. The spark is nearly gone.

Instead, we get Robert Mapplethorpe's photographs of flowers and emaciated hands flashing on a cameo-shaped screen above the dancers; Grahamesque ritual, and part baroque/part space age costuming (by Ronaldus Shamask). There seemed to be a real effort at content, but what this "dramatic" piece was all about, I haven't the foggiest.

Childs appeared in the second part, arms angled like an ancient icon. It was her image, complete with matriarchal headdress, that was flashed onstage at the very end, as white dust fell briefly from the rafters.

The ritual centering on Childs in part two seemed to be the dividing point from a climaxless, regularized style of dancing to a larger, more lyrical and joyful style. In the final section, the dancers wore wide skirts of fabric panels, a kind of cross between historical dress and Loie Fuller. Manipulating the fabric, they worked their way from diffident half-turns and flutters to a tumultuous diagonal crossfire.

Unmuddled by messy, everyday emotions, Childs's best dances provoked a pure aesthetic emotion, what I imagine is akin to the aesthetic of higher mathematics. Far from being "cool" or distant, Childs's dances, when they worked, resonate deeply.

— *High Performance,* 1986

Review: Merce Cunningham's *Roaratorio: An Irish Circus on Finnegans Wake*

THE Brooklyn Academy of Music's (BAM) 1986 Next Wave festival opened with the premiere of Merce Cunningham and John Cage's *Roaratorio,* subtitled *An Irish Circus on Finnegans Wake.* In the BAM tradition, the work was billed as a "collaboration," but, of course, in the Cunningham/Cage tradition, *Roaratorio* was really music and dance just sharing some time together.

It was one of Cunningham's more thematic dances, a takeoff on the quickstepping of Irish dance. Like his *Grange Eve,* which premiered earlier in 1986, *Roaratorio* was full of playful camaraderie and extraordinary little movement anecdotes. In one movement, for instance, Kristy Santimyer spun quickly across the long diagonal of the stage, her yellow cheerleader's skirt floating around her hips. At the end of her path was a small circle of dancers, and when she neared, two men pivoted outward, opening the circle like a pair of swinging doors that then enclosed her safely inside.

The mood was relaxed. Dancers literally "sat out" their time onstage, watching the action from high metal stools. They exited and reentered a lot, often returning in different articles of clothing—sweatshirts, skirts, and leggings in bright, mix-and-match colors. They also tied bits of clothing on the stools, which were periodically moved around. But *Roaratorio* was largely a partnering dance —friendly duets of pattered-out rhythms of the feet; measured, elegant duets; awkward, clomping duets; la-dee-da stroll-in-the-park duets.

Roaratorio was met with more than the usual excitement for a Cunningham/ Cage premiere because it was so long in the making for its first American appearance. The score was composed in 1978; Cunningham's dance was added in 1983. While it has been produced twice in Europe, *Roaratorio* hasn't been scheduled during Cunningham's annual seasons at City Center because the piece requires an unusually large space for both dancers and musicians. At BAM, the fifteen dancers used the opera house stage, while the six musicians were located in lighted loges above both sides of the stage.

The score consisted of Cage reciting his text *Writing for the Second Time through Finnegans Wake;* five Irish musicians playing traditional Irish music on fiddle, drums, uileann pipes, and flute; and a tape filled with sounds from Joyce's novel—street noises, people noises, animal noises. It was a nonstop collage, except for one pause when a curative silence briefly leaked in, and another a few moments before the end when I could finally hear the dancer's own rhythms being pounded out by their hard-working legs.

Both the music and the choreography for *Roaratorio* were intensely rhythmic, with the patterns constantly shifting. Like the 1980 *Fielding Sixes,* which also used scraps of Irish jig music, there was a constant push-and-pull between the rhythms of the score and the rarely coinciding rhythms of the choreography. Often, sight and sound seemed only a split second out of sync, which was especially disconcerting.

Roaratorio reminded me of how radical Cage and Cunningham's aesthetic is, even after more than thirty years. Dance is far easier to watch when music carries it along, in terms of rhythm, phrasing, and mood. But when the dance and music come at us in separate shapes and colors, looking becomes a chore—a teasing, uncomfortable, delightful chore. Which is just the way these artists want it.

—*High Performance,* 1986

New York (USA): Experimental Dance

B Y MID-October, the downtown venues for experimental dance were operating at full tilt. The Danspace Project at St. Mark's Church opened its season with a solo by Eva Karczag. P.S. 122, which has been chock full of performance events since its "New Stuff" program in September, offered an evening of works by Charles Dennis. Dance Theater Workshop began the new performance year with Kinematic's *The Snow Queen*. And at Movement Research's opening production at the Ethnic Folk Arts Center, Simone Forti and protege David Zambrano shared the bill.

Karczag's *Opening the Launch Window* (3 and 4 October) was an hour or so of incredible beauty. In the midst of so much current dancing that makes a strident spectacle of itself, Karczag's performance reaffirmed a very "old-fashioned" idea: that of the eloquence and transportative qualities of the moving body.

Having worked with Trisha Brown for six years, Karczag still possesses that loose, through-the-joints kind of movement in her basic style. She moves in complicated but easygoing counterpoint of head, torso, arms, and legs, creating gentle in/out, up/down, left/right rhythms and always keeping the seamless motion going through her hips. Her clear, pink face, with its narrow chin and thin lips, echoes the calmness in the rest of her body.

In *Opening the Launch Window*, Karczag moved with a keen sense of awareness of the sensual flow of her body, and yet she could at the same time appear very remote. I felt in these shifts or splits of focus that I was following her from the here-and-now activity of dancing to very faraway places she was remembering or imagining.

The work was a series of brief sections, beginning with Karczag cross-legged on floor, an earthen jug by her side and a kerchief over her head and face. Her chest filled and emptied with each breath. Eventually, she pinched the kerchief off her head and into it she poured sand from the jug. Tying up the kerchief into a small sand bag, she repeatedly rolled it bit by bit down her back, from shoulder blade to knee. The forward thrust of her body, the controlled tension of her back, the jug, the kerchief, all suggested a sense of burden and of the earth.

In one section, Karczag flung her arms against a wall. In others, she worked on the floor or slowly stepped backward as she emptied all the sand from the jug. In still another, she clenched her floating doughy hands until her neck and head strained backward from the tension, and when she released the contorted hands, they seemed even softer and lighter.

In between these sequences, Karczag would stand at either sidewall for a breather. She rubbed her nose, pushed back her hair, wiped the sweat from her upper lip. At one point, standing with hands on hips, she focused on something in the center of the stage space, seemingly waiting. She looked as if she were in the wings of a proscenium stage, monitoring the action onstage for her next cue—just as she must have done hundreds of times in Brown's company.

Kinematic's *The Snow Queen* (9–12 October) was a TV fantasy gone awry—Hans Christian Andersen's fairy tale broken apart and reassembled in a nougat of unlikely people and unlikely circumstances. The tale emanated from a television set, which smoked and glowed as if it were alive. And the dancing—lots of enigmatic gesturing and high-spirited romping—that accompanied this "story" was just as much of a non sequitur.

The dancers (Tamar Kotoske, Maria Lakis, Mary Richter, Thom Fogarty, and Carlos Arevalo—each one of them wonderful) kept shifting perspectives: one moment they played out the action as if they were in it, and the next they reacted to it as if they were listeners ("horror," "surprise"). Sometimes the movement seemed to have a vague, perverse correlation to the words, and it was in this fuzzy space between logic and nonsense that *The Snow Queen* played its witty games.

City Animal, the solo on Charles Dennis's three-part program at P.S. 122 (3–5 October), had its hyperrealistic moments—like when he gnawed on a meat bone or nosed into a bag of slimy garbage or lapped up a bowl of water on all fours. As he narrated the life of the city animal, he periodically jumped high with his knees bent under him, pounding back into the floor in a martial arts stance and yelling, "Huh!" Urban aggression and base physical needs were what this dance was clearly all about: that familiar stranger at the loft party who lives "on the edge of danger, for the thrill of blood" (roughly).

Simone Forti's improvisational *Roadcut* (18–20 October) sounded intriguing: a group dance developed through immersion in the Manhattan environment. But in performance it seemed thinner than I had expected. David Zambrano's three improvisational pieces showed him to be an extraordinarily supple and sensual dancer with a sly sense of humor.

—*Ballett International,* 1987

Review: John Kelly's *Ode to a Cube*

JOHN KELLY is fascinated with the powers and vulnerabilities of the artist. In *Pass the Blutwurst, Bitte* he focused on painter Egon Schiele, and in *Find My Way Home* he reset the myth of Orpheus and Eurydice in the speakeasy 1930s. With *Ode to a Cube,* a one-man concert, he literally enacted the performer in the theater, from the backstage perspective, behind the footlights and in the dressing room. The climactic moment came as the unnamed performer pried open one of the set's black cubes. As it turned out, this "ode" of a performance was about a seemingly impenetrable cube that secrets within itself makeup mirror lights, a metonym for all that is transformational about the theater.

Kelly started off the hour-long performance in a downstage "dressing room," smudging on makeup and pulling on wig and costume. A gorgeous countertenor, doing songs and arias from Bizet to Saint-Saëns, Kelly repeatedly made his way to the "stage," in front of the footlights that lined the side edge of the small La MaMa space. With an adjustment in costume and gesture, he was crooner and ballet dancer, diva and rock star. The tour de force of the evening was Kelly as the ultimate artist's muse, the Mona Lisa. A swift, deft handling of his dressing room paraphernalia, and the transformation was remarkably apt. "I don't understand the artist. He's crazy," the artist's model complained during her lip-synched monologue.

Kelly's work asks what role, after the modernist notion of the artist-hero has disintegrated, the postmodern artist plays in today's culture. Is the artist much different than the child who plays with the toy kit providing naked female doll, wig, and wardrobe? (There is one of these kits nestled within the clutter of the dressing room table.) Is artistic transformation a transcendent state of being or a superficial effect that television and film do better anyway? Is the act of creation just an illusion? Even so, can we endure without that illusion?

It is hardly incidental that much of *Ode to a Cube* was in drag. And though I don't question Kelly's good intentions, it makes me uncomfortable that women's roles are still so easily—and to our great entertainment—appropriated, and thus defined, by men.

Kelly is a singular talent. The pathos and the theatricality with which he enacts the displacement of the artist is unabashedly romantic. He is a poet in a decidedly unpoetic world. Kelly will, perhaps, suggest to us where and how such an artist can insinuate herself/himself into the 1990s.

—*High Performance*, 1989

Review: Ralf Ralf's *The Summit*

IT SEEMS appropriate that, during the presidential election season, DTW brought back London-based Ralf Ralf's *The Summit* for a repeat performance, after its successful run there in the summer. *The Summit* is a two-man confrontation, á la Reagan and Gorbachev, complete with lecterns and negotiation table. Using verbal patter (made up of nonsense languages) and gesture, performers Jonathan Stone and Lars Goran Persson enacted opposite styles of rhetoric—one dogmatic and the other anecdotal. The piece developed in vaudeville-like "bits": the political speech, the politician's initial encounter-turned-inspection, the mutual invitation to the table, and the negotiation itself.

The stylization of these familiar televised rituals was telling, and often funny. Stone and Persson managed to turn these strategic maneuvers into rhythmic clogging, the verbal patter into music. At one point, one of them literally turned a cartwheel to cajole the other into sitting down at the negotiation table first. A simple flourish of the hand would not do—paranoia suspects etiquette as much as it does compromise. Their negotiation proceeded in a proposal-and-refusal kind of counterpoint. In a brief dream sequence, their hostilities transformed them into tongue-splitting gargoyles.

The politicians' defenses eventually wore down, however, as they commiserated about the bright lights they were under, literally and metaphorically. Sitting side by side, their legs dangling from the negotiation table, they awkwardly tried to break through the language barrier, like children, naming the parts of their clothes, playing hand games, and sharing toy trinkets.

They were soon interrupted. Each leader was recalled by his political machine, represented by a blinding light shining in from opposite wings that each man greeted with his photo-opportunity persona. The men resisted, preferring to teach each other a folk dance; they harmonized and played on the floor with pebbles. But, in the end, they resumed their head-of-state exhortations.

Sparked by the tenure of Reagan, the "great communicator," there is endless talk these days about contemporary politics being a matter of television image rather than of substance, but no one ever goes further than the observation. *The Summit* did go further; its outlook was mixed.

I found the men-behind-the-image section quite endearing—it was hopeful: on a direct, person-to-person level, these men could reach out toward each other. But at the same time, the work's ending admitted pessimism. Despite their personal frustrations and aims, they were puppets of their ideological machines. *The Summit* turned inside out the old saw that leaders who declare war should fight it themselves; in this case, Ralf Ralf was saying that direct human communication, without the baggage of national rhetoric and myth, would be our utopian salvation.

—*High Performance*, 1989

Molissa Fenley's State of Darkness

Vaslav Nijinsky's *Le Sacre du printemps* premiered in 1913 to legendary scandal, and has long served as a touchstone of twentieth-century modernism. The fact that it soon became a "lost" dance contributed to its powerful mystique, until Millicent Hodson's painstaking reconstruction for the Joffrey Ballet in 1987 catapulted it to even greater stature. The reincarnated dance left nary a spectator or critic unmoved—even postmodern iconoclast Yvonne Rainer was impressed.

Molissa Fenley was also inspired to choreograph her own dance to the richly emotional and polyrhythmic Stravinsky score. She called it *State of Darkness*, and it premiered in June at the American Dance Festival. A few months later at the Kitchen she made it the centerpiece of an extraordinary evening of solos. What had always felt ritualistic in her all-female ensemble works has in the solo format become palpably religious. Instead of a community careening toward its unknown but inevitable fate, Fenley alone enacts the anguish of sacrifice and the promise of redemption.

State of Darkness was not a narrative per se, but it did portray a woman—not unlike the Chosen One of the original *Sacre*—coming to grips with an unspeakable fate, her own or maybe her culture's. She struggled with her private demon, alternating between fear (sometimes bordering on hysteria) and acquiescence. The Chosen One is the sanctioned female version of Christ's passion: she was the reluctant but ultimately dutiful savior whose own death gained life for others.

For Fenley, who lost a close friend to AIDS around the time she saw Joffrey's *Sacre*, "It's time now that we need a humanist point of view, because we're living in a 'state of darkness.' It's time we have to be vulnerable and giving." Inspired by the Joffrey piece, the choreographer set out to make an overtly emotional dance. (She good-naturedly points out that, even though in her mind her dances have always been about emotion in an abstracted, "architected" way, emotion has not always been apparent to the audience.) The result, *State of Darkness*, was an incantation: a rather desperate act of faith in the future of humankind.

Fenley last danced solo in public in 1982. Soon after she came to prominence with her ensemble pieces, in which her dancers' energy streamed steadily forward, without any overt form that you could comfortably trace through time or space. These communal rites were very powerful—they seemed to hold unspoken secrets and unbroken beliefs. In *Geologic Moments* during the Brooklyn Academy of Music's 1986 season, Fenley experimented—not successfully—with unaccomplished men dancers and diluted balleticisms, which did not coalesce with Fenley's inherent mannerism. (Edwin Denby wrote somewhere that style is a matter of making the best of one's imperfections. Fenley is riveting because of her short legs and hyperextended spine. What else could she have done but to focus on her upper back?) The men intruded on the bond between the women dancers, which was very much an integral part of the choreography. But, admittedly, my eyes always found themselves trained on Fenley, like a sorceress, with her placid intensity and her spindly arms constantly conjuring up the space around her.

Fenley burst on the Next Wave scene when aerobic dance was peaking in popularity, and viewers tended to focus on the company's aggressive fitness and nonstop energy. With so many bodies onstage, it was easy to get lost in the morass of momentum. Alone in the Kitchen's performance space, Fenley changed the scale of her work, both physically and emotionally. In *State of Darkness* she opened her arms, embracing the space all around her, drawing it into an intimate environment for her performance. She did not perform the concert with breakneck abandon: in *State of Darkness* she danced from a primal passion very deep within, and in *Provenance Unknown* (parts I and II) and the coda from *Esperanto* she danced from an inner calm that reached toward the sublime.

Fenley focused fully on each moment as here and now, as if there were no past or future. Her back has always been quite expressive, especially her upper back, which anchors her arms. Now, especially in *Provenance Unknown* (parts I and II), she has developed the nuances of her shoulders, as well as that zone of space between shoulder and chin that, in her dances, is constantly rearranging itself. Fenley tells us a lot by the way she inflects her head in relation to a rolling shoulder, or by the way her chin nudges toward her shoulder or maybe stretches away from it.

In *State of Darkness,* Fenley wore only tights, leaving visible her breasts and rib cage, which registered her changing emotions through varying breath rhythms, from the initial quivering nervousness to, eventually, convulsions of terror and grief. There was a mix of vulnerable back bends, flashes of robotic blankness, and large slashing arm and leg movements. Gestural images accumulated some force—fingers rubbing together as if they were sifting through red earth, a hand slicing across her torso. Fenley's toplessness also showed off her impressive back. She works out and has developed a well-defined—but not at all bulky—upper back. She moves her arms from deep in her upper torso, holding them back unusually far, almost like bird's wings. Her forearms and flexed wrists are left to seemingly float. The result is extremely exotic—angular, almost disembodied designs and shapes.

As turbulent as *State of Darkness* could be, the coda from *Esperanto* and *Provenance Unknown* (parts I and II) were exemplary visions of tranquility. Fenley danced *Esperanto* as if she were moving through honey—it looked near heavenly. *Provenance Unknown,* actually choreographed to monastic burial music, was accompanied in performance by a live piano rendition of Philip Glass's "Metamorphosis." Fenley luxuriated in the sweet, melodic music. And yet there was a hint of melancholy coming through the large, curving arms and the occasionally hidden face.

Fenley is hardly alone in her choreographic move toward what she calls "humanism." The current climate of death and alienation in America is hitting the dance community especially hard. Though postmodern dance has traditionally emphasized issues of physical form and aesthetic inquiry, it now seems to be making small steps back toward the expression of emotion. This swing has already happened in the visual arts—the importance of Anselm Kiefer, most notably. I think John Kelly is also searching for a performance world where a human being, not just a body, is at its center. Ralph Lemon, not unlike Martha Clarke with her *Miracolo d'Amore*, is using the sheen of romanticism to explore the flip side of humankind, its baser nature.

For her part, Fenley is struggling to make sense of our turn-of-the-century scourge on basic human dignity. What she seems to be suggesting is that, yes, there is some place of grace. It's just, how do we get there?

—High Performance, 1989

Review: Susan Marshall's *Interior with Seven Figures*

A T A TIME when most dancers' stock-in-trade is the height of their extension, it's refreshing to see Susan Marshall's company. They are not dancers dancing. They are simply people moving. No outstretched limbs, no "here-I-am" presentation, no fancy technique. Instead, they are persons of substance, constantly activating and reactivating their weight. As a result, in *Interior with Seven Figures*, the performers exerted an extraordinary sense of intentionality—without an overt plot or set of characters ever being explicitly developed. Made up of ten duets, trios, and quartets divided into two sections, the dance was a series of complex interactions—vignettes evocative of the human condition without portraying it literally. For me, that is when dance is at its most profound.

Marshall's vocabulary was a blend of familiar gesture and abstract movement, always soldered together within some oblique but dramatic situation. A man arched off the floor, as if ill, and a man and woman fought over him. Two men, drawing each other near, then pushed each other away. A man and woman leaned on each other, falling one atop the other. Another man and woman slipped from one awkward position immediately into another, never successfully grasping each other.

The interaction was often manipulative—helpful, and then aggressive behavior that takes at least two to produce. And repetition often brought these little scenarios into the realm of ritual. Luis Resto's score reinforced the distinct mood of each encounter.

In the final section of each half, Arthur Armijo was singled out in a corridor of light, as all the other "characters" (named Brothers, Mother, Father, Women, and Man, for no discernible reason) obliviously negotiated their way across his path. At the end of the first half, they engulfed him: for the finale, they lifted him in an apotheosis.

—High Performance, 1989

Review: Dana Reitz's *Suspect Terrain*

DANA REITZ is a soloist whose ability to transform a large, empty space into an intimate and palpably nuanced environment is simply stunning. Thus it is to her enormous credit that she spent four years spearheading an elaborate collaboration between herself, three other well-known improvisers (Steve Paxton, Polly Motley, and Laurie Booth), lighting designer extraordinaire Jennifer Tipton, and sound designer Hans Peter Kuhn, recently of Robert Wilson fame. Even if the result was barely the sum of its participants' talents, *Suspect Terrain* was a brave and worthwhile experiment in improvisation and *true* collaboration.

The tone of the evening—experiment, taking chances—was set by a program note written by Paxton, the originator of contact improvisation: "Improvisation has always been a suspect terrain on well-known maps of dance. Choreography is much more secure as a study. In performance, improvisation is seen in overview by the audience, but each performer has only a partial view of the scene. It is different to see the light than to be in it. It is different to see the space than to feel and explore it. It is different again to listen to the sound than to move to it and be moved by it."

The eighty-minute-long piece took place in an 80' × 80' cavern—a silty black space with tremendous possibilities. One of my biggest frustrations was that, but for once, when Booth loped around the area in a circle, no one really worked with the luxuriant space (not just the place, but the space) they were in. The environment was left neutralized instead of electrified—at least by the dancers. The lighting was another story. Toward the end of the piece, the shape and texture and drama of the space itself, created by Tipton's spare but brilliant lightscapes, took the lead in the production.

Kuhn's kinetic score—it literally traveled around the variously located speakers—was a collage of everyday and synthetic sounds that began with a fly buzzing at your ear and ended with dogs barking. In between it had a few theatrical climaxes, one in real 2001 Space Odyssey fashion, with dancers proceeding in slo-mo suspension across the space to a sustained tone. What surprised me was how programmatic the music seemed at times—mostly because the dancers *chose* to be led by it.

Despite the top-notch performers, the dancing was the least interesting element of the collaboration. The performers seemed ill at ease with each other. They rarely interacted. And when they did, they often looked stumped as to what to do with one another. Paxton appeared withdrawn, and Reitz timid. Booth was a delight for both his gymnastic bravura and his generous sense of humor—he was the one initiating most of the interaction. Motley seemed an odd-woman-out, without the depth in her own work that the others clearly possessed.

Nevertheless, there were memorable moments. As when Booth engaged Reitz in a little duet. She played a charmingly recalcitrant partner, her feet behaving in a quite contrary mood. Or Booth invisibly sweeping around the blackened space. Tipton's mysterious beams momentarily engulfing him, here and there, in a slice of light.

—*High Performance,* 1989

Review: Nina Martin's *Changing Face* and *Date with Fate*

NINA MARTIN doesn't fool around with minor themes. In *Date with Fate,* a raucous existential meditation created in workshop with fourteen local performers, she went straight to the heart of things: Why are we here? In her own solo, *Changing Face,* she dealt with the angst of becoming and remaining an individual. Using text and film (by Tal Yarden) as well as music and movement, Martin tends toward a heightened theatricality—*Date with Fate,* with its broad, cartoonish, TV-scale humor, and *Changing Face,* with its surrealistic nervousness.

Martin's solo opened with a home movie of her in a variety of paper-cutout costumes, like a little girl trying on different identities. When we first saw the live Martin, she was an embryo in a gauzy white cocoon, twitching and wriggling across the floor, struggling to free herself. She finally did break through, only to find herself in a world where virtue is more and more difficult to define, where change is threatening, and where you can never get an even break. Give up sugar, caffeine, alcohol, and sex, and the sun will kill you.

Revealing herself in a series of high-strung, increasingly paranoid monologues, this unnamed woman in a nearly transparent jumpsuit struggled to hang on to what little pretense of calm was left in her. She gossiped with a friend on the phone, as she edged along the rear brick wall, clutching it for dear life. She talked to herself while trying to avoid the police and the world. "I'll turn the music up loud, and stand here with my eyes closed, and nobody will find me." As the disembodied voice of her therapist interrogated her about wearing day-old underwear and paying sixty dollars for a haircut, she blurted out the only possible response: "We're all guilty of something!" At one point she donned a suit that was just a structural grid—the bones, without the flesh. It was, essentially, an illusory armor for the soul.

Changing Face is actually about *not* changing face, clinging to old fears and prejudices as a protection against the intrusion and insanity of the world. Besides, Martin said, "If I changed, I'd feel naked—my friends wouldn't recognize me."

Date with Fate, although technically a danse macabre, ended on a much happier note. It, too, began with a film, this one setting up the question, "Why the hell am *I* still here?" The ensemble piece was basically a high-energy assemblage of broadly played "bits," including a number with crutches and a stand-up tragedian, as well as extended sequences of demolition derby dancing.

Most of the performers were outfitted in large, red-stained bandages, crossed into an "X" signifying "injury" in cartoon shorthand. The scenic symbolism was just as conspicuous: a brick wall that was toted around the stage and three oversized dice that, swung round and round, were used to stop performers dead in their tracks.

—High Performance, 1990

Susan Marshall Choreography Explores Tragedy, Joy

IN THE final moment of *Fields of View,* one of choreographer Susan Marshall's two premieres presented Thursday and Friday at the University of Texas (UT), dancer Eileen Thomas stands paused, but ready, before the curtain of falling snow that separates her from life beyond, where all of her fellow travelers have already gone. Will she remain where she is, or run headlong through this beautiful, mysterious threshold?

Marshall's choreography never offers obvious, or easy, answers. For more than a decade, the New York-based choreographer has been creating brutally realistic portraits of human relationships. Intimacy, she has shown us again and again, is about falling as much as it is about embracing, about aggression as much as it is about tenderness. Life is neither pure joy nor pure tragedy: Marshall's art is forged out of the gritty stuff in between.

In fact, Marshall has become almost too good at revealing the complex drama of emotional interaction. The last time I saw Susan Marshall & Company, in 1992, the program had a distinct feeling of thematic and choreographic sameness. With this new program, however, Marshall consciously tries to choreograph against type. *Fields of View* and *Spectators at an Event,* co-commissioned by UT and the Brooklyn Academy of Music, where the pieces will make their New York debut in November, represent a deliberate attempt at abstraction and theatricality.

If *Spectators at an Event* is attracting more media attention—because it is the kind of "high concept" collaborative piece on which the Brooklyn Academy of Music has built its annual "Next Wave" festival, *Fields of View* is the more artistically satisfying of the two.

It is a lyrical "white ballet," complete with gauzy iridescent costuming (of a postmodern sort, mixed with gray spandex) literally floating in a breeze, and, of course, the falling snow, marking the right edge of an otherwise empty stage open to the wings. (Both costume and set design are by Judith Shea.)

In contrast to the sturdy structure that has traditionally cemented Marshall's compositions, *Fields of View* is elliptical, without an obvious through-line. Without the narrative that usually emerges in Marshall's works, this is a mood piece, which only fleetingly suggests character and relationships, because its very point is the perpetual shifting of experience. Set to Philip Glass's "Fourth String Quartet," the full company of eight romps through a playful opening section.

The second section, in which the falling snow is blown ever-so-gently across the stage, seems to occur in mythical space and time. The dancers are no longer directly present to each other, but are internally focused. They seem to be remembering, or maybe imagining.

Marshall here is especially brilliant in how she suggests the interior life of different individuals as they find themselves "odd-man-out" of a double line formation that sets the structure for the section. And try as she might to get past her proven strengths, Marshall still gets the most mileage out of gesture.

The sequence repeated here is a stylized phrase in which one hand widely circles up to the dancer's brow, followed by the other hand placed on the heart. With particular poignance, Thomas repeated the phrase with such a sense of vulnerable remoteness, it's as if her body is reenacting its memories from long ago.

But the best is last, in a final section that centers on a melody repeatedly introduced, moving forward without resolution and beginning again. Marshall matches the music's suggestion of constant oscillation by having the dancers proceed forward and backward through the curtain of snow at the stage's edge.

If in the second section the dancers performed as if they were in a faraway time, here they are literally gone, offstage. The time they spend offstage, before entering back through the snow, creates a powerful sense of anticipation, and loss. Without the expected resolution, the music and the dancers keep flowing across the threshold of here and there, now and then. Until Thomas's final, appropriately betwixt-and-between stance, as the theater curtain falls.

In *Fields of View* Marshall succeeds in adapting her command of gesture, structure, and space to a more abstract project, which, for all its so-called "abstraction," turns out to be just as affecting a comment on the human condition as her previous works. With *Spectators at an Event,* the transition into large-scale spectacle is not as smooth.

Spectators has a gimmick: the use of 1940 crime-scene photographs by Arthur Fellig, who was known as Weegee. Offered the use of photographs for a new work by the Brooklyn Academy of Music, Marshall was compelled less by the images of victims than by those of the bystanders.

The piece is an ambitious one in terms of theme, technology, and logistics.

Thematically, Marshall must make a tricky choreographic maneuver to connect the viewing of crime scenes with the viewing of a dance event. Technologically, she (along with lighting designer Mark Stanley and set designer Sarah Lambert) must integrate the use of a video camera, a video projector, a portable spotlight, and two screens—one aloft and one on wheels—into the action. Logistically, she must choreograph not only for her own eight dancers, but for the thirty local extras who serve as an expanded cast of bystanders.

Set to the alternately driving and melancholic second string quartet ("Quasi una Fantasia") by Henryk Gorecki, *Spectators* is a sophisticated collage of dance sequences and vignettes of crisis, some stylized and some seemingly "real." If the work has its flaws, I still admire it, because Marshall handles the large ensemble sequences so readily, and because there are several passages whose use of weight and gesture as metaphor demonstrate once again that Marshall is the closest thing to a poet American dance has seen since George Balanchine.

The stylized situations—people crowded around a prone body, for example—worked well with the powerful photographs (which were not displayed as static images, but transformed into moving pictures by video designer Christopher Kondek). But the attempts at staging "real" events in the theater, after the first one, felt hollow.

The video is used effectively, as when the camera is turned on the audience, and helps to set up the provocative connection between spectators at a crime scene and spectators at a dance concert. Marshall suggests that all spectatorship, whatever the "event," is voyeuristic: irresistible, narcissistic, and sometimes morally problematic.

But spectatorship is a form of witnessing, which can encourage community. And in a frenzied finale that harks back to the *Rite of Spring*, with its stomping folk vocabulary circle formation, Marshall returns to gesture. With the embrace, one of Marshall's most enduring motifs, she offers hope for human connection after crisis.

—Austin American-Statesman, 1994

Review: Merce Cunningham Repertory Concert and Robert Wilson's *Four Saints in Three Acts*

IN TEXAS. Austin and Houston. San Antonio too.

Merce Cunningham. Robert Wilson. Merce (a global honorific) doubling John Cage. "Waco Bob" (a local honorific) doubling Gertrude Stein.

Merce and John and Bob and Gertrude. Arguably the four horse(wo)men of this country's modernist apocalypse. Gertrude a novelist turned playwright. Bob an artist turned director. John a composer turned philosopher. Merce a dancer turning.

Emotion.

GERTRUDE: "What happens on the stage and how and how does one feel about it. That is the thing to know, to know and to tell it as so."

Moving happens.

Saints moving. Saints in hoop skirts stand sit walk kneel lay fall still. Catch butterflies. Assemble. Exit and enter. Procession.

Sets moving. Rise. Descend. Upend. Glide. Float.

Colors moving. Delicious fruity colored light.

Voices moving. Through libretto sometimes choppy sometimes musical. Stage directions as dialogue. Master and mistress of ceremonies like sideshow front (wo)men or saints in their cathedral niches.

Moving happens in spacious time in protracted space.

What emotion is. Scale. The expanse of physical landscape.

What emotion is. Play. The delight of mental landscape.

Where emotion is.

JOHN: "The emotions love mirth the heroic wonder tranquility fear anger sorrow disgust are in the audience."

Interlude.

GERTRUDE: "It is quite exciting to hear something unknown really unknown."

Sight and sound.

Disjunction perhaps but always synergy. Happy accidents.

JOHN: "The function of Art is to imitate Nature in her manner of operation."

Sight. Bare midriffs. In black and white. Turns inside-out. Leapfrogging. Rump wiggles. Stillness. Arms in backward flight. Arms upturned. Arms swimming. Frédéric Gafner the angelic exuberant daredevil. Dim haze into morning glow. Whipping turns. Backdrop sculpture. His hand on her pelvis his hand on the small of her back. Dancers as creatures with mismatched body parts. Awkward grace. Virtuosos made more human than ever more sexy more alive more young more hip.

Sound. An irresistible texture of clacking vacuuming siren blaring animal cawing growling. Trumpet fanfare heralding New Age-ish harmonics. Trombone and garden hose. Live conch blowing in surround sound.

GERTRUDE: "Is the thing seen or the thing heard the thing that makes most of its impression upon you at the theater. How much has the hearing to do with it and how little. Does the thing heard replace the thing seen. Does it help or does it interfere with it."

Yes.

The problem of time.

JOHN: "A performance is characterized by the programmed time length calculated beforehand and adhered to through the use of a stopwatch."

Merce with stopwatch seated in rehearsal. Rhythms slapped on thigh. Dancers count internally cue each other visually. Body time not clock time. Body time not story time. Music and movement meet only to depart.

My game I try to anticipate the end. I lose.

GERTRUDE: "The business of Art . . . is to live in the actual present, that is the complete actual present, and to completely express that complete actual present."

Interlude.

JOHN: "In Zen they say: If something is boring after two minutes, try it for four. If still boring, try it for eight, sixteen, thirty-two, and so on. Eventually one discovers that it's not boring at all but very interesting."

Space.

I should know better, complaining about sitting far left. Off-center the better. Like an oblique camera angle. Bursts of movement everywhere. I don't miss anything even what I can't see.

JOHN: "Each person is in the best seat."

GERTRUDE: "I made the Saints the landscape.... A landscape does not move nothing really moves in a landscape but things are there, and I put into the play the things that were there.... There were magpies in my landscape and there were scarecrows."

In Bob's landscape there were flying sheep hung moons palm trees hollow houses snow falls the hand of god giant eggs gianter llamas dipping in from the wings.

In Merce's landscape. Arms the space behind. Headarmschest the space between. Man woman the space distant or collapsed.

The curtain.

GERTRUDE: "In the first place at the theater there is the curtain and the curtain already makes one feel that one is not going to have the same tempo as the thing that is there behind the curtain. The emotion of you on one side of the curtain and what is on the other side of the curtain are not going to be going on together. One will always be behind or in front of the other."

The curtain more hurried than usual. Less well-mannered. Descends before the singers have come to a standstill. Descends before the dancers have come to a standstill.

But they don't stand still, as if in art. They keep moving, as if in life.

JOHN: "Our intention is to affirm this life, not to bring order out of chaos nor to suggest improvements in creation, but simply to wake up to the very life we're living, which is so excellent once one gets one's mind and one's desires out of its way and lets it act of its own accord."

—1995 (unpublished)

The Choreography of Crisis
Women, Machines, and Utopia Lost

MOST choreographers have to make a choice between form and content: Ultimately one precedes the other. Not so with Llory Wilson. She refuses to sacrifice either her love of motion or her need for meaning, and the resulting tension—between movement as physicality and movement as metaphor—is one of the most exciting (and at times maddening) aspects of her choreography. Her newest work for her Tallulah Dance Company, the seventy-minute *lush méchanique,* is as much a study in space and partnering as it is an anti-technology manifesto, and the way it teeters between these dueling loyalties isn't about choreographic clumsiness, but about choreographic mastery. A richly textured dance whose message is woven deep within the high-density movement/music/ mise-en-scène, *lush méchanique* does not yield its mysteries easily. It gets more interesting with each viewing.

Wilson, who divides her time between Seattle and Austin (where she is a faculty member at the University of Texas [UT]), bills herself as the "movement orchestrator" of *lush méchanique,* performed on 27 and 28 January at the Mc-Cullough Theater on the UT campus. In doing so, she effectively underscores the genuinely collaborative nature of the production, whose costuming, score, lighting, and set design are integral to its success. Shauna Frazier's retro bathing-beauty outfits and Rosie-the-Riveter work clothes suggest the historical context. Beliz Brother's lighting and set design, consisting of six huge swinging mechanical poles, or "arms," define and redefine the space and mood of the environment. Jami Sieber's expressive score layers the sounds of an amazingly versatile electric cello over a rhythmic bass—offering the nervous strains of a plucked string, melodies foreboding or plaintive or bittersweet, and the sounds of sirens and heartbeats. What the score provides for *lush méchanique* is dramaturgical scaffolding.

That is not to say that there is any "story" to the dance. Wilson works in abstraction, and the most apparent narrative of *lush méchanique* is the confrontation between nature (the lush) and technology (the méchanique) as experienced by a community of six women whose pale skin and dark lips and eyes suggest silent film heroines. At first they playfully cavort with each other—mostly in pairs—in Coney Island bloomers, but eventually their attitudes turn workmanlike when they don more practical shirts and slacks. It's not long before the sirens wail and three of them are writhing and bellying across the floor, stalked by the searchlights that hang off the ends of the now-sweeping mechanical arms. Afterward, the women appropriate the function of searchlights themselves, as they wear lights strapped to their foreheads. Utopia has been terrorized and the women now dance in isolation, with a great thick effort, in the dark. Light-in-the-darkness continues as the expressive motif, as three dancers (the same three who were fleeing the air raids?) in skeletal hoopskirts meander through the space, whirling around them beaconlike lights. This haunting image of yearning, of searching, of stubborn faith in the face of utter darkness, is one of the most poetically effective in the dance, and it provides the transformative moment that launches the women back into their bathing suits and group frolic. At dance's end (only after one final restorative duet), the mechanical arms come to rest in a single line down the middle of the stage, and under them the women arrange the kitschy fake flowers they have been moving around the stage for the past few scenes. Here is the final alignment of the "lush" with the "méchanique," as the women one by one take their frantic (still shell-shocked?) exits.

Besides the flowers and mechanical arms, the thematic opposition is echoed in other formal oppositions: angles and curves, dark and light, warm and cool, air and floor, percussiveness and lyricism.

Wilson has a prodigious talent for inventing movement vocabulary (raw kineticism, enigmatic gestures, everyday stuff); at times, it's almost too much. *lush méchanique* is marked by changes in level, use of arms, intricate partnering, and turning (the most amazing are the spiraling falls and jumps).

The dancers of Tallulah Dance Company are fearless, and beautiful: there's petite Kate Basart; the waifish yet spunky Andrea Beckham; the sure and sturdy Theodora Fogarty; Natalie Agee, who is unselfconscious and somehow still mysterious; the wide-eyed Vanessa Schoeni; and Wilson herself, who is sometimes strong, sometimes lyrical, but always intense.

Most of the dancing is done in pairs, even during ensemble sections, and the community, in both its initial and reconstituted form, is represented by an extended duet. The third duet, near the end of the dance, is the most playful. It makes sense that two other dancers look on happily, lazing amidst the flowers. This community has suffered through its catastrophe successfully, and even thrived. Its members dance not just with each other, but now for each other as well.

Wilson says that the piece had its beginning in her fears about the information superhighway. And there are references, some more oblique than others, to machines. In one case, a dancer, her body rigid and her outstretched arms and legs forming symmetrical diamonds, is passed down an ever-extending assembly line. In another, all the dancers lie in a line on the floor, rolling, turning, and twisting in sequence, each one an anonymous cog in a magnificent machine: a cooperative community, but one without individuality and without couples. And then, of course, there are the robotlike "arms" that dominate the entire stage.

But the piece is more than just a nostalgic romp through a simpler, purer era of Mack Sennett bathing beauties (an era that was neither simple nor preindustrial). *lush méchanique* is about crisis, as was Wilson's last full-length piece, the 1991 *This Cordate Carcass,* and her 1993 *TITANIC.* Physical crisis, emotional crisis, world crisis. A crisis Wilson manages to see as somehow lyrical. A crisis that is devastating but nevertheless generative, and therefore bittersweet.

—*Texas Observer,* 1995

Ballet with Attitude

(or The Ballet of the Sexes)

THERE IS a key moment in the "Sentimental Cannibalism" section of *Bristle* (1993), one of three repertory excerpts performed 17 February at the Paramount Theatre in Austin by the New York-based Donald Byrd/The Group: In an obvious nod to the final masturbatory image of Vaslav Nijinsky's 1912 *Afternoon of a Faun,* Byrd has one of his male dancers lying prone on the floor, downstage center. His head is turned away from us in the audience, toward the four women standing further upstage. As they seduce this lone man with the fast, almost contortionistic movements of their exquisite bodies, he humps the floor. Because Byrd has positioned the man—both literally and figuratively—in our spectatorial place, we are forced to identity with his sexualized response. It's an effective device that unveils the voyeuristic structure of most dance: women displaying their bodies for the satisfaction of their male-identified spectators.

The problem is that Byrd—despite his rhetoric of political and social engagement—delights in the bodies of his dancers and especially in the splayed-out legs of his female dancers. The entire evening, which featured excerpts from *Life Situations* (1995) and *Drastic Cuts* (1992) as well, consisted of men and women struggling with each other: women the willing or resistant objects of desire, men the faceless bearers of desire. Byrd certainly has mined a myriad of possibilities of partnering women's legs, but it wears thin, and worse. At the close of the evening, in the last moment we see of *Drastic Cuts,* a woman extends her leg forward, up to her face, clasps it and falls headlong into the arms of three or four men on the floor, who cheerfully proceed to fondle her. Any claim that Byrd might make to a politics of gender deconstruction is effectively discredited.

Byrd, who presented his *Minstrel Show* to Austin several years ago, has choreographed more than eighty works since 1976, including commissions for the Alvin Ailey American Dance Theater, the Lyon Ballet, and Dallas Black Dance Theater. He started Donald Byrd/The Group in Los Angeles in 1978 and moved it to New York in 1983; today it's an award winner on the contemporary dance circuit. The group's mission is "the creation and presentation of work which reaches the broadest possible segment of society while reflecting the African-American experience and exploring new artistic boundaries." That's a difficult tightrope to walk.

Much like Oliver Stone's *Natural Born Killers,* in which the violence that was being critiqued was so seductively presented that it became impervious to criticism, Byrd's repertory program ends up exploiting the most sexist conventions of classical ballet. And in this sense, he's fallen into the same trap as similarly ambitious choreographers William Forsythe and Karole Armitage (back in her punk ballerina phase), who also attempted to deconstruct ballet. You can't have it both ways: If you're going to play to the pleasures of a woman's legs—the pointe work, splits, and partnering—you can't pretend to be critiquing either the genre or its sexual politics. This particular program belies Byrd's reputation as choreographer of cultural politics.

Ostensibly, Byrd's "Sentimental Cannibalism" is about the power of both sexes, for they square off against each other in a *West Side Story*-style challenge dance. But Byrd's fondness for manipulating women's legs just gets the better of him. This penchant for duets (or trios with one woman and two men) is a self-conscious reference to George Balanchine, whose ultramodernist classical ballets such as *Agon* (1957) and *The Four Temperaments* (1946) used the ballerina, and especially her long, prehensile legs, as an implacable object of beauty to be manipulated like a piece of living sculpture. But Byrd is no Balanchine. Balanchine could do classical, romantic, modern, even kitsch. He was a master of dramatic contrast. Byrd, on the other hand, seems to know only one speed. Fast. And one costume. Black. And one score. Electronic, repetitive, and loud.

As a result, the dancers look monotonous, too. They are kamikaze hard bodies, which the audience adores, but that doesn't stay interesting for very long. Who are these dancers, I kept wondering. The tight, linear way that Byrd choreographs separate parts of the body in isolation from each other gives the dancers such an alienated, machinelike appearance. Except for the occasional pouting, strutting, and glowering, the dancers are asked mainly to endure the high-speed chase to the finish.

For *Life Situations: Daydreams on Giselle,* Byrd imports four fully pedigreed ballet dancers (two Frenchmen, a Canadian, and an American). The references to *Giselle* are slight—some vaguely recognizable stuff in the opening male solo, and the Byrd dancers, like *Giselle*'s villagers, standing around looking at the ballet dancers go at it. According to Byrd, he was exploring "abstractions of technical romantic devices, specifically pointe work and the partnering technique pointe shoes make possible." Pointe work and partnering continued to develop and evolve to higher degrees of artifice in the classical and neoclassical ballets. Onstage, the connection with *Giselle*'s Romanticism is slim: These are not the nocturnal creatures who skimmed across the stage high on half-pointe, with the gentle assistance of their partners. These are unquestionably 1990s dancers, competing for attention in the age of extreme spectacle, whose stock-in-trade is their daggerlike pointes, acrobatic flexibility, and titanium-charged attitude.

—*Texas Observer,* 1995

Margery Segal's Primal Emotions

I'VE BEEN puzzling about Margery Segal for several years now. Since I first saw her *Texas Sweat* evening at Synergy Studio in 1991, her seemingly contradictory impulses toward both lyric vulnerability and in-your-face-girl-chick attitude have held me in my seat, unblinking.

Since arriving in Austin in 1991 as an artist-in-residence with Dance Umbrella, Segal has choreographed mostly group works, from the hyperrealistic *The Home* (1991), to *The Girl Project* (1993), based on the true stories of local teens, to *Nerve* (1994), performed by the three-year-old margery segal/NERVE dance company and billed as "a dance-theater performance about smashing into what you don't want to look at." Before that, in New York, she choreographed a series of mostly solo dances, dealing with the gritty realities of women's lives.

Segal's work in dance (she also choreographs for the theater, as artistic associate from Frontera@Hyde Park Theatre) is, more often than not, about struggle: the psychic struggle against encroaching despair. Her works are filled with the dark intimations of mental illness, death, sex, violence, alienation, and rage. Even so, there's always been at least a ray of light visible in the very cracks of her women's psyches, and that light has been growing brighter lately. The stories about lurking, menacing men told by the teens in *The Girl Project* might have been chilling, for example, but the spirited, self-possessed way in which those girls handled themselves was even more powerful.

With her newest work, a solo, Segal seems to be moving through despair. "So the darkness shall be the light," she quotes T. S. Eliot in the program, "and the stillness the dancing."

untitled, reflections on an uncollected life was the anchor piece for a series, called "Personal Dances," curated by Segal, that ran 13–17 February at Hyde Park Theatre in Austin. Some of the best independent choreographer/performers in town (Andrea Ariel, Beverly Bajema, Heloise Gold, Deborah Hay, Scott Lehman, Linda Montano, Jason Phelps, Jean Fogel Zee) were invited to "explore the concepts of their lives and/or themselves as the icons of their art."

untitled (directed by Annie Suite) has Segal's hallmark edge—the black humor, the intense subjectivity, the appreciation of the absurd. She structures her pieces as collage, so that logically irreconcilable opposites can attract, and reverberate, without overwhelming or eliminating each other. There are the tender intimacies, and the glaring looks. There is assaultive music ("Oh, baby, baby, you sure like to fuck") alongside swelling romantic music (Shostakovich and Whitney Houston). There is first-person storytelling (sometimes spoken live and sometimes an interior-monologue voice-over) alongside abstract movement (structured improvisation danced to the music). There is the opening image, of a body half nude (revealed) and half cloaked (reveiled). There is the colorless, vaguely threatening trench coat and the delicate white frock. There is the movement itself, which alternates between convulsive eruptions and sensual play. The result is a strange landscape that can accommodate the sometimes dreamy, sometimes nightmarish images of memory.

untitled splays out the fractured memory (this is, after all, "an *uncollected* life") of a character simply designated as "The Woman." (I have too much respect for the art of performance to assume that the tale is either true or autobiographical. Besides, Segal herself begins the performance—which is built with words and symbols—by pointing out that "There are no true words, no true symbols.")

We piece together The Woman's life from her stories, told in no particular order, and in various tenses and voices: a politically engaged but emotionally removed father who fails to protect her from an abusive friend of the family; rape, alcohol, and heroin. A gun in the hand. Mental hospitals. And a romantically imagined immigrant heritage featuring her father as a playful but unaccepted child and a cantor grandfather who loses his children to the state.

What of women in these memories? They are remarkable only for their absence. The mother is in the hospital, having another child, when The Woman is first molested. (The only other reference to her is, perhaps, in the opening image, when The Woman pours "mother's milk" down over her half-nude body.) The grandmother dies, her white funeral shroud metaphorically inserted into the stage design running along the bottom edge of the back wall. The troubled friend Kitty (whether "she" is actually a kitty cat, or The Woman's alter ego, is hard to tell) leaves for a mental hospital.

It would be easy to label *untitled* as a "rape story," but that's not what the work is about.

It's about women claiming their own histories, and themselves. What's important is not necessarily "truth" ("There are no true words, no true symbols"), but identity. "If I tell you my story," The Woman asks the audience, "will you tell me yours? . . . Will you live in the memory of remembering yourself, will you hold hands with the moments that have most mattered to you?" Memory, Segal suggests, is embedded in how we see (and vice versa), and how we see is who we are.

But, most of all, *untitled* is a love story. Or a story about love, how it hurts, and how we long for it and rage against it all the same.

In a way, that's always been what I've unknowingly perceived in Segal's extraordinary dancing. Her style is deceptively simple, without pyrotechnics. She looks like an ordinary person—no turning out, no pulling up. Using her body as a whole piece, her vocabulary consists of mostly large arm and leg movements, with some twisting and turning of the torso. The look is kind of a cross between Isadora Duncanesque skipping and rock 'n' roll dancing, accented with an occasional silkiness reminiscent of Trisha Brown—or an occasional bout of hysteria reminiscent of St. Vitus.

Segal uses her arms like a ballerina uses her legs: as a divining rod fine-tuned for the subtlest expression. (It makes sense that in the 1988 solo *Everything That Will Be Will Never Be Again,* Segal danced with prosthetic arm extensions.) Segal's arms flail and wrench and caress and float and waver, registering a seemingly endless range of emotions.

There are several powerful movement episodes in *untitled.* Caught within the light of a film projector, Segal enacts a series of clichéd female "fright" poses from horror movies: some of our most common images of women as victims. Then there's the strung-out addict completely pressed up against the back wall, slowly feeling her way across its expanse, refusing to let go for fear of free-falling.

BUT BEYOND Segal's movement style is her distinctive presence—her ability to project both vulnerability and anger at the same time. What I finally figured out in *untitled* is that these two powerfully primal emotions—the one that opens us up and the other that closes us off—are held together in love, in the pain/pleasure of loving, being loved, and needing to be loved.

Segal makes the point brilliantly in an extended, virtuosic solo performed to a tortured Whitney Houston torch song, which turns out to be the central moment of *untitled.* The music up to this point has been nerve-grating acid/punk stuff and Segal has just come out of the acutely desperate wall-crawling sequence. She slowly rearranges her clothes, smooths her hair, and then steps into place as the music begins. In this context, the lushly romantic Top 40 sound is rendered so absurd that some viewers laugh.

But Segal is serious. She stands in place, her body still except for the arms, which erupt convulsively, twitching and jerking away from her. The image is horrific—she looks as if she is suffering death throes, except that they are clearly being phrased with the song, whose words and melody embody our treasured ideal of romantic love: I love you more than anything, don't leave me, I can't live without your love, I'm nothing—nothing—nothing if I don't have you.

The pain of longing at any cost becomes palpable as a punch in the gut. But the remarkable thing about the solo is that there are moments in which the pain transforms into pleasure, and Segal's ecstasy registers in an occasionally lilting arm and in her beatific smile. In these exquisitely unbearable moments, Segal shows us the profound and complicated human need for love, even by someone for whom it has come to mean only pain.

Segal ends the performance with mindful hopefulness. Having pulled on a white cotton dress, she places eggs one by one across the stage floor. As she carefully sets each egg in place, she speaks a simple, sensuous declarative sentence. "I touch." "I riot." "I arouse." "I feather." "I verge." "I mark."

She climbs atop her stool, amidst these shining white orbs, for one final story. If The Woman's own father was a neglectful parent, her grandfather provides the model of a devoted one. His beloved wife dead and his children removed from his care, he secretly visits them at night, watching them sleep, "the street light catching the glow of longing." That's the same glow—the ambient light seeming to come through a window, casting two large rectangles of light against the theater walls—that is used in Jason Amato's lighting design.

Segal has used egg imagery before, in *Nerve*. (In its program, Segal quotes Paul Klee's reference to the egg as the "realm of the dynamic.") She has drilled eggs onstage, she has fried eggs onstage. Now, she crushes them. And as The Woman breaks each shell with her knee, symbolizing Kitty's desperate warning that "we are soft, we are so soft," she utters another "I thrill" or "I shake" or "I tease." And as the lights dim to the bittersweet violins of Shostakovich, she chooses a different mantra: "I hope." "I hope." "I hope."

—*Texas Observer*, 1996

No Gravity No Boundary

WITH ALL the bravura it can muster, New York-based Streb/Ringside pitches itself as "part Chinese acrobats, part Olympic gymnasts, part NFL daredevils, part free-fall skydivers." You can hear the carnival barker's deep voice ringing from the press copy: "For the thrill seeker, it's a big bang experience, for the aficionado it's an adventure in spacial transformation. Oh, yes, it is definitely the demolition derby of dance and it is the highest of artistic enterprise."

Artistic director Elizabeth Streb has managed to turn what may hold her most suspect in the world of dance into a hot commodity in the world of popular entertainment. (Her work has been showcased on MTV and used in a Madonna music video.) Rejecting the obsession of modern dance with expression in favor of pure physicality, the forty-something athlete-turned-dancer seems to have hit her stride with a touring extravaganza that rekindles middle America's longstanding love for what was called "physical culture" at the end of the nineteenth century. Like the circus, vaudeville, world's fair midways, dance marathons, professional wrestling, and races, derbies, and exhibitions of all kinds,

Streb/Ringside appeals to our appetite for the fierceness and danger of extreme physical behavior, our attraction to the spectacle of bright lights and bright colors, and our childlike wonder at the human body in flight.

In a way, the same can be said of really great ballet—but ballet is protected by a veneer of the "aesthetic" that covers over what, in the elite classes, have been considered base physical impulses. There's no sweat, no grunting. But with Streb/Ringside, the work of the body is displayed openly, and even exaggerated with sound and lighting, in a way that middle- and working-class Americans traditionally have embraced.

At San Antonio's Carver Community Cultural Center (16 March), the audience was filled with kids of all ages who spent the evening gasping, squealing, and clapping with impunity. At the much larger, much more formal University of Texas Performing Arts Center in Austin (19 March), the audience was more discreet in its pleasure.

This bit of theater is slick, in the best sense of the word. Painstaking choices have been made about every aspect of the production—when to reject illusion, when to use it, and when to give the audience a laugh.

The evening features seven relatively brief acts, all involving equipment. The first half of the show features low-tech plywood equipment—a wall, a box, a sprung platform. The second half features a behemoth construction consisting of a trampoline with scaffolding on either side, bridged at the top by a pipe grid. The equipment is an integral part of the show. At the Carver, spectators watched the intermission setup with as much interest as the dancing itself and, at points, cheered for the crew, who looked like carnies assembling the rides.

It's unusual in both the dance and popular entertainment traditions, but Streb provides notes for each dance. They're pretty clinical. For example, *Wall* (1991) is described this way: "Performed on an upright red wall, five dancers throw their bodies against a vertical space attempting to occupy it. In turn, the audience observes how this wall environment affects the dancer's action. *Wall* is Ringside's method for the reinvention of the floor."

All the acts can be reduced to such simple descriptions: In *Bounce* (1994), the action centers on an eight-foot-square platform. In *Little Ease* (1985), Streb explores the movement possibilities within the claustrophobic space of a box, about six feet wide by three feet high and deep, upended on its side. In *Surface* (1993), the dancers interact with two plywood panels—it's like *Wall*, but the dancers have to keep reconstructing the walls as a moving target. In *Free Flight* (1993), dancers leap from scaffolding onto thick pads. In *Rise* (1995), two dancers, rigged in harnesses, rise and fall on a twenty-two-foot pole. In *Up* (1995), the dancers jump between a trampoline, a scaffolding platform to either side, and parallel bars above.

THE DESCRIPTIONS barely suggest what it's like to watch these hard bodies encased in blue bodysuits. If the work were just about clever feats of physical prowess, it would hardly distinguish itself. But Streb is the consummate showperson/choreographer/director all rolled into one. The idea is almost simplistic: "We're drawing shapes of action in space." It succeeds because the choreography has been so finely theatricalized that you feel—more so in an intimate space such as the Carver—like you're up there free-falling with the pros.

The work is obviously designed by a skilled choreographer, insofar as the vocabulary and structure of the dances are ingeniously sophisticated. Only a seasoned choreographer could build into the dances such required precision, in terms of both time and space. And she knows the body well enough to keep imagining new ways of supporting it with parts other than the feet. ("Unless you get both feet off the ground," she says, "you're not moving.")

Every dance is about defying gravity, and yet each one manifests a very different quality of movement. My favorite was *Up,* because of its sense of the body as suspended in a smooth, sensuous, continuous life flight, from down to side to up and down again. This is a world of ease and buoyancy; there are no edges, no obstacles. And the dancers need not prepare for their travel. It's as if they are being propelled by mental telepathy rather than physical will.

The kinesthetic buzz that the dancing elicits in the spectator has as much to do with the sound and lighting as the choreography. Not only are we privy to the grunts and groans of the dancers as well as their near desperate verbal cues to each other ("go!" "turn!"), but the amplification of the bodies slamming against the wall, thudding on the floor, or landing on the trampoline makes the physicality that much more palpable. In the same way, each act is lit in order to heighten the sense of movement. In *Bounce,* intense white light catches just the tops of the careening bodies, making them appear like sparks of pure visual energy; the box in *Little Ease* glows and seems to float several dozen feet above the stage floor.

Streb seems to erase the boundaries between "high" and "popular" art: she refuses to be limited to any one performance tradition. Sports, games, dance, comedy. They're all about taking the body to its limits, literally: to the wall, over the edge, hanging in midair.

—*Texas Observer,* 1996

The Freedom of Tradition

O N 10 OCTOBER 1994, *Time* magazine's cover trumpeted a "Black Renaissance." "African-American artists," the subhead explained, "are truly free at last." While the mainstream mouthpiece may have grossly overstated its self-congratulatory case, especially in light of its emphasis on how such choreographers as Bill T. Jones "are closer in spirit to the works of white choreographers like Mark Morris than to those of Alvin Ailey" (which raises the question: does "free" mean "white"?), it is certainly true that African-American choreographers have had a major impact on dance in the last decade.

Jawole Willa Jo Zollar, artistic director of the New York-based Urban Bush Women, has figured prominently in the postmodern dance scene since the summer of 1984, when the *New York Times* gave the company's premiere performance a favorable review. Since then, Zollar has delivered the keynote address at the 1990 Dance Critics Association annual meeting, choreographed for the Alvin Ailey American Dance Theater, been awarded a 1992 New York Dance & Performance Award and a 1994 Capezio Award, and seen her 1990 work *Praise House* adapted for film by Julie Dash.

Zollar, presented most recently by San Antonio's Carver Community Cultural Center on 2 April, along with David Rousseve, presented by the Carver last season, and the San Francisco-based Robert Henry Johnson, presented by Austin Dance Umbrella last month, are harvesting one of the richest of African-American performance traditions. Storytelling and family oral history bring to the stage a journey—a way of looking backward that can propel us forward. That's exactly how Zollar has approached her newest work, *Bones and Ash: A Gilda Story.* As one character explains, through stories, "It's as if I were seeing the world for myself."

Based on the novel *The Gilda Stories* by Jewelle Gómez, the evening-length dance/theater/music piece—part realistic, part phantasmagoric—traces the life of "GildaGirl," an escaped slave who is taken in by Gilda and Bird, the lover-proprietors of a New Orleans bordello. GildaGirl's story spans two centuries, because she has been given the gift of perpetual life by Gilda, who is part of a vampire community. The first act begins in the year 2050 and travels back to 1850 New Orleans, and the second act shifts forward from 1890 New Orleans to 1955 Boston. In the preface, one of the vampire chorus, a trio that accompanies us on this epic trek, tells us that "the past is a place I visit on my way to the next two hundred years." The shape of her life, she explains, is motion. As GildaGirl makes her way through time and space, she finds women dressed like boys, a world ruled by gold and scattered with black bodies swinging in the air. She builds community "anywhere there are two of us" and finds that a century later little has changed.

In 1955 Boston, GildaGirl encounters the past: her childhood friend, who becomes her lover, and the male vampire Fox, whose violent nature, a product of white oppression, has left a trail of battered and murdered female bodies across the centuries. In a battle of opposing forces, GildaGirl kills Fox, as she did the white man who tried to rape her in 1850 New Orleans. Women, she finds, are still struggling to find their power, which "is a frightening thing." At evening's end, we are left with an image of the female body as the repository of history, journey, and wisdom: "a tightly-bound package of everything we need to know."

The production, whose evocative set design (by Douglas D. Smith) is one of its strongest features, is not without its problems. Overall, the realism and the fantasy tend to remain discrete and the narrative rather linear, and except for a few key scenes, *Bones and Ash* never quite achieves the feeling of poetry that has characterized earlier works. And although the company's own notes describe the vampires as women who "take blood and leave whatever vision, idea, or dream the person is seeking," the dramaturgically muddy representation of lesbianism as vampirism is, unfortunately, a stereotype that works against the production's intended celebration of these women as "nurturers and healers—and warriors if need be."

Zollar's aesthetic of collaborative theater—which integrates words, music, and dance—draws upon her childhood experiences in the floor shows for black social clubs, upon her participation in reader's theater with a gospel choir, upon African-American folklore and spiritual traditions, and upon the expressive forms of the African-American community, especially those of the church. The movement derives from Zollar's early Afro-Cuban dance studies with Katherine Dunham student Joseph Stevenson and later studies in jazz improvisation with Dianne McIntyre. In the work of Blondell Cummings, Zollar recognized the usefulness of personal history and gesture, and in that of Kei Takei she saw the necessity for training people to move naturally.

For choreographers such as Zollar, Rousseve, and Johnson, the challenge has been to find a way to work with both the Euro-American forms of dance and African-American traditions. And they have succeeded, creating a genre that is betwixt and between, keeping both traditions in dialogue, without settling on either side too comfortably. In fact, this body of work supports an argument that postmodern dance and African-American movement practices are quite mutually informing. Their work is adding an emotional richness to contemporary dance that is, for the most part, elsewhere lacking.

For example, Johnson's solo with drummer, *A Nappyred Summer: Vesper,* reaches for poetry of both word and motion, telling the story of peaches and a nappy-headed stranger, a seduction of metaphors and bodies that outdoes the elder Rousseve, whose *Urban Scenes/Creole Dreams* takes up the story of his powerful, gentle, unrelenting grandmother.

When Rousseve was a keynote speaker at a conference on dance and gender, he was taken to task by a white woman for being another man appropriating a woman's story, in particular her rape memory. I found such criticism unfounded, and still do, because oral history functions so differently in the African-American community than it has in the Euro-American community. Such storytelling is a cultural legacy, and in that sense Rousseve does indeed "own" his grandmother's story. She made a gift of it to him, in the hopes that he would own and retell it.

In *Bones and Ash,* as Gilda bites the neck of the young GildaGirl, thus bestowing upon her the potential of eternity, she explains that the gift is "learning how to live": seeing people how they really are and still wanting to continue on. Urging faith and promising life everlasting, the theater becomes a church. The sacred and the secular, like flesh and blood, like Gilda and Bird, become one.

—Texas Observer, 1996

A Chronicle Faces Death and Celebrates Life

NEIL GREENBERG's newly completed trilogy, like a serial novel choreographically reimagined for the age of AIDS, chronicles four years in the life of his company, Dance by Neil Greenberg. A dancer goes to Australia. A baby is born. A choreographer falls in love. But what resonates most deeply in the work is a battering series of losses—a brother, a mother, a father, an ex-lover, a litany of dear friends.

This "immortality project," as Mr. Greenberg has described it, delves into the dueling impulses of grief: to relent and struggle, to remember and forget, to hold on and let go. Both elegy and paean, it responds to the AIDS crisis not with bitterness or fatalism but with an intelligent, recalcitrant dose of camp.

The trilogy will be performed in its entirety for the first time, on two programs, Tuesday through Sunday, as part of the 92d Street Y Harkness Dance Project, held at Playhouse 91 on East 91st Street. The title of the final installment, *Part 3 (Luck),* makes a double-edged reference to Mr. Greenberg's own confrontation with mortality.

The story began in 1994 with *Not-About-AIDS-Dance,* which later became the first part of the trilogy. In this work the choreographer informed his audience, via texts projected at the back of the stage, that not only had his brother recently died of AIDS but also that he himself was HIV-positive. In *The Disco Project* the following year, Mr. Greenberg revealed that he was still asymptomatic, mourning new losses and getting angry but determined to have some fun.

With *Part 3*, itself divided into three sections, Mr. Greenberg decided to shape a trilogy. *Part 3 (My Fair Lady)* recalled his childhood memory of Audrey Hepburn and the first movie musical he saw, as a five-year-old. *Part 3 (Judy Garland)* evoked another gay-world icon, this time an adult meditation on the tragic diva.

In *Part 3 (Luck)*, Mr. Greenberg, thirty-eight, continues his story, with happier news. "I had to make a new piece, because I had to update the audience," he said. "In *Not-About-AIDS-Dance,* I enacted my brother's death by showing what he looked like in a coma. By doing so, I implicitly asked the audience to imagine me dying of AIDS.

"Now I'm on these new drugs. My viral load is undetectable. I told my parents and the company, and I feel I have to tell the audience. If I've asked an audience to get involved with me, I have a responsibility not to just leave them dangling."

Part 3 (Luck) accelerates the trilogy's self-consciously presentational style. "There's no fourth wall," explained Mr. Greenberg. "We dancers know the audience is there and watching. And they know we know they're watching us."

The projected text, reprised from the first two parts of the trilogy, he added, provides the audience with a "door into the powers of the dancing," which, for all its baroque muscle, remains abstract. "I am putting the words in there in order to help the pure dance read more strongly, so that an audience not used to reading dance meanings can start to read them."

He first used the device in 1987 in *MacGuffin or How Meanings Get Lost,* the breakthrough work that started his investigation into the nature of meaning in postmodern dance, a form largely defined as "movement for movement's sake." The text in *MacGuffin* resulted from his dissatisfaction with his previous dance, which he concluded had failed to communicate to its audience.

"I thought I was trying to say something, in my strident, very young way," Mr. Greenberg said. "But looking at it now, I was just trying to be known, to have my full self, including the parts I thought were unacceptable, be accepted. But I was only putting little clues in the dances, subtle things that only I could read."

The second breakthrough came with *Not-About-AIDS-Dance,* when Mr. Greenberg began to reveal information about his real life and those of his four dancers. The work won a prestigious New York Dance & Performance Award.

As a former dancer with Merce Cunningham, whose choreography eschews personal meaning in favor of chance procedures, Mr. Greenberg had entered forbidden territory. Nevertheless, he explained, "It was the kind of change that most artists go through in their lives as they get more and more courage to present themselves."

Contrary to Mr. Cunningham's well-known aesthetic position, Mr. Greenberg insists that Cunningham's dances are full of meaning, even if that meaning is unconscious. "An artist has the desire to be known," he said. "That is in Merce's work, but in great code. Now it's in my work, but in less and less code."

THE TEXT FOR *Part 3 (Luck)*—part memoir, part supertitle, part stage direction—makes public the kind of information that is usually kept private. In deceptively transparent language, in a voice both vulnerable and cheeky, the choreographer comments on the dancing ("This material is from *Not-About-AIDS-Dance*"), on the audience ("Does anyone know of a large one-bedroom in Manhattan for under $1,200?"), on the choreographic process ("We lost some rehearsal time"), on his own life ("I take the pills twice a day"), and on the lives of his dancers ("Ellen is moving to LA").

As with the entire trilogy, *Part 3 (Luck)* is not limited by its brief appearance onstage. It reaches back in time, to the months when it was being made. And it extends outside the theater, into the lives of its performers. This is an "immortality project" that expands and retrieves and sometimes even freezes time into a perpetual present as a way of resisting closure, and holding off death.

"The year I made *Not-About-AIDS-Dance,* I wanted to make that moment stand still," Mr. Greenberg said. In *Part 3 (Luck),* he aims to conquer another loss, this time of a company member, Ellen Barnaby, who will leave the troupe next month. "I had to deal with the emotional trauma of not being able to hold onto the moment anymore," Mr. Greenberg said.

Without Ms. Barnaby and another original cast member, who has already departed, it is unlikely that the trilogy will be repeated.

Mr. Greenberg does finally bring his epic to an end, by saying goodbye to Ms. Barnaby and glimpsing a future of his own (which includes the premiere in May of a dance commissioned by Mikhail Baryshnikov's White Oak Dance Project). The trilogy's parting words, as usual, mean more than they say: "Good luck."

—*New York Times,* 1998

A Dancer Discovers a World of Profit and Daredevil Feats

AT A RECENT dance forum, Elizabeth Streb introduced herself with considered clarity: "Ten years ago I thought of myself as someone who had a dance company. Today I think of myself as someone who creates wild actions and movement moments in a show that I sell."

Ms. Streb, artistic director of Streb, has never been a typical choreographer. More like a daredevil, she gained recognition in the mid-1980s for her gravity-baiting feats of physicality using trampolines, gyroscopic belts, and bungee cords. But like a true postmodernist, she hated music ("too bossy") and rejected narrative. Her focus was on the abstract properties of pure movement—time, space, and the body.

For her new show, *Action Heroes,* parts of which will be performed on Friday and Saturday at Vanderbilt Hall in Grand Central Terminal, Ms. Streb has pumped up the spectacle with a music-sound score and at least the semblance of a story. During the seventy-minute show, the eight performers career through more than a dozen episodes, including crashing through a pane of glass and bouncing off walls. Ms. Streb has gone Vegas. Or, at least, that's where she's headed.

Action Heroes embeds new and familiar stunts into a music-video-style format that pays homage to Ms. Streb's early inspirations, such as Evel Knievel, the motorcycle showman; Cannonball Richards (he caught them in his gut); and Annie Edson Taylor, the first person to survive Niagara Falls in a barrel.

With *Action Heroes,* Ms. Streb leaves the dance world behind, at least in economic terms. Her technical ambitions for its ultimate development will be too costly for dance venues, so she is turning to public spaces, commercial ventures, and an earned-income business model.

The company's self-contained metal performance structure, a box truss nearly twenty feet tall, is considered an exemplar of market-driven strategies for nonprofit arts institutions by the Joyce Mertz-Gilmore Foundation, which financed the portable stage in 1998. The performance space—complete with its own lighting, moving walls, video screens, and sound—lets the company set up cost effectively in any context. No longer limited to large, traditional theaters, Streb productions can be marketed to broader audiences and potentially yield more earned income.

The line between performance and entertainment has blurred considerably in the last few years. Riverdance, Matthew Bourne's *Swan Lake,* and most notably the teaming of the experimentalist Julie Taymor with Disney to produce Broadway's *Lion King* have forged significant links between art and commerce.

Ms. Streb, herself a hybrid of working-class roots and MacArthur Foundation "genius grant" credentials, cites Ringling Brothers and Barnum & Bailey, Cirque du Soleil, Stomp, *Bring in 'Da Noise, Bring in 'Da Funk,* and Zingaro as precedents. The franchise scheme used by Blue Man Group, the sly East Village trio that has organized outposts in three other cities, she says, "is radical and very inspiring to everyone."

Ms. Streb was one of a number of downtown performance artists who approached the Blue Man operation in the early 1990s, after it had managed to break through to the mainstream media. Manuel Igrejas, the press representative for

Blue Man and now for Streb, had learned that the public was ready for exciting new work. "It was starved," he recalls, "for entertainment that moved it on a fundamental level.

"I think a lot of artists want to move out of the not-for-profit zone. I think there is a funding ceiling that can keep artists at a certain level. It takes a lot of courage to turn down the beneficence—which is arduously sought—of a kindly Uncle Funder. Blue Man Group has created the template for artists to be self-sufficient and self-producing, to make work the way they want to and make a profit."

Carol Derfner, president of C. W. Shaver & Company, Inc., a consulting firm for nonprofit organizations, agrees. She advises her clients, including the Paul Taylor Dance Company, to "start thinking their way out of the scarcity model of economics that the not-for-profit management system is based upon."

"Entrepreneurial artists and cultural executives are figuring out that they produce something with real value in the marketplace and are taking more control over their destinies," she says.

Before Grand Central, Ms. Streb was seen on MTV, at Coney Island, and under the Brooklyn Bridge. The company performed during a baseball game at the Metrodome in Minneapolis. Now, she wants to follow Blue Man, Cirque du Soleil, and the new vaudevillians Penn and Teller to what Mr. Igrejas calls the "new frontier in entertainment": Las Vegas.

"It's my next dream," says Ms. Streb, who is fifty and retired from performance. Las Vegas offers her an appealing scale: more people, more space, more equipment. "I am very interested in what I would make if money were not an issue," she says. "Well, what artist wouldn't? So right now it's 'Las Vegas or Bust.'"

She now conceives of her art as a series of events in public places, not as a repertory dance company. And public space, she adds, is not tame territory. Dur-ing the month-long residency at Grand Central Terminal, people wandering or hustling through the hall gave her instant and uncensored feedback. They told her if they didn't get it, didn't like it, or couldn't believe she got paid for doing it. The terror of receiving such uninhibited (and instructive) commentary from complete strangers enthralls her.

"I wonder if it's how we look, the unitards and all?" she says. "I try to analyze all of the private symbols and secrets we employ—choices we made way back when. They are so automatic that we don't notice them any longer."

Nevertheless, her artistic goal remains the same: to take her audiences on a ride, inducing their own physical experiences and spatial confusion. To "amaze, even shock, worry, and surprise" them, she says. But not to alienate them. So for *Action Heroes* she has integrated video projections and music as narrative devices to remind the audience that the performers are real people, not cartoon characters.

"People like music and need to be told a story," Ms. Streb says. "Me, too. It's a welcome relief from having to experience real work. It's the sherbet moment that cleanses the palate. So I am using music and story to mitigate the brutality of what we do and its eventual numbing effect on audiences."

The ostensible story—more associative than narrative—is Ms. Streb's own story. "This is the action whence I hail," she says. "The action heroes I emulated as a kid growing up. It was at the circus that I actually witnessed transgressive, outlawed, and untidy action in America."

Nick Fortunato's "video rodeo" brings Evel Knievel, pole sitters, monster trucks, Harry Houdini, and bull riders right into the ring. Using a layered mix of live cameras, pure geometric forms, and prerecorded images such as old newsreel footage or cloud formations, Mr. Fortunato, a video, installation, and performance artist, evokes the spirit of action heroes past and present.

The projections sometimes function as moving scenery, as when drifting clouds give the swan-diving dancers an expansive sense of flight. The images are sometimes referential, as in *Squirm,* a Houdini tribute, which features a clip of the escape artist wriggling out of a straitjacket. "All the while, I am controlling his movements live, in time and to the music," Mr. Fortunato says. "The result is something like Houdini break-dancing."

The music similarly ranges from the abstract to the emblematic, including the company's aural trademark: the amplified sounds of the performers' bodies colliding with floor and wall.

Ms. Streb's free-fall into music comes with an immediate caveat. "I am not actually interested in music," she says. "Music is the true enemy of dance."

The composer and sound designer, Miles Green, explains: "Often music is used to provide propulsion to dance. Elizabeth's movement has so much thrust that the music has to be carefully constructed to not get in the way. The score is more about mood than drive." He has created a palette of organic and human sounds, taking his cue from the pioneering daredevils themselves, who "dealt with really basic elements: water, air, wood, breath, and bone."

Mr. Green also uses popular songs to suggest the genealogy of Ms. Streb's action vocabulary. A vintage 1920s recording of "Happy Days Are Here Again," for example, leads into the pole-balancing sequence, but then the mood darkens, with composed music that conveys the drama of the danger-seeking desperados.

By placing the performers in historical context, Ms. Streb hopes to defuse any questions that might distract her spectators. "If someone asks, 'But why do you dive through the glass?' I have failed. If the event I construct does not take over the physicality of the person watching, then it is not an integral enough moment.

Well, perhaps now it will be clear why we do it. We are transgressive action maniacs and have no other choice but to do the move right now this second."

—*New York Times,* 2000

IMAGES AND EXHIBITS

El Jaleo by John Singer Sargent. Used by permission of the Isabella Stewart Gardner Museum, Boston.

New York (USA): Dance and Fashion

WHAT DOES dance mean in American popular culture? Judging from "Dance," this year's annual Costume Institute exhibit at the Metropolitan Museum of Art, it means glamour . . . fashion . . . image.

Judging from the stir that *Tango Argentino* and *Flamenco Puro* caused on Broadway in the last year, it means passion and sex.

Judging from a new television commercial that uses a ballet audition (inspired by the climactic scene of the movie *Flashdance*) to compare a ballerina and a ballpoint pen, it means precision.

In anticipation of the "Dance" exhibit, fashion magazines have been filled with photo spreads on a dance theme. Most of the clothes are really just fancy evening gowns, but one interesting column in *Vogue* focused on San Francisco designer Derek May, whose long, tubular designs are reminiscent of Martha Graham's "long woolens" back in the late 1920s and early 1930s.

It's no coincidence, I think, that the increasing popularity of Diana Vreeland's annual costume exhibits has coincided with the Reagan era, in which Nancy's Adolfo suits and new china were only an overture to the first couple's taste for formal entertainment. And the country followed their lead. This year's opening night gala for the Brooklyn Academy of Music's (BAM) Next Wave festival garnered more space in the *New York Times* than did the performance.

If dance once signaled the old-money glamour of masquerade galas and debutante balls, as the Met's show vividly demonstrates, dance today is more on the order of avant-garde chic. Discos and nightclubs have gone the way of Studio 54. The place to be seen in your most outrageous duds is now opening night at BAM, where art gallery owners, fashion designers, movie stars, and the corporate upper crust rub elbows with "high art." The avant-garde has been transformed from an oppositional provocateur into an emblem of social prestige.

The appearances of *Tango Argentino* and *Flamenco Puro* seem to have hit America at just the right moment. People are entranced by the colorful exoticism and the raw, earthy sexiness. Tango classes are burgeoning, ad execs are taking up the Latin dance theme, and Piaget has even named one of its new watches "The Dancer." Last year, the Council of Fashion Designers of America gave *Tango Argentino* an award for its impact on fashion.

And, of course, the aerobic dance craze has played a lead role in popular culture. Dancewear became chic with the rise of Jane Fonda's workout video; she even backed her own line of aerobic clothing. The current de rigueur streetwear in New York—leotards, bunched-up socks, and heavy sneakers—comes straight out of the aerobics studio.

One of my favorite galleries at the "Dance" exhibit is the one dedicated to the masquerade ball. There, life imitates art. Costumes on display borrow from the commedia icons of Pierrot and Columbine, or the Harlequin; Orientalia as in the Ballets Russes is plentiful, too. One costume, made for Baron Alexis de Rede's 1969 Oriental Ball, is a reproduction of a Bakst design for *Le Coq d'or.* In another gallery, there's a 1955 "kabuki coat" that was worn by Pauline de Rothschild. And, as if to demonstrate that fashion is an endless cycle, there's a large gallery devoted to the influence of flamenco: the black-and-red color scheme, the trailing ruffles, the boleros, the bare back, and the shawl. The range of adaptations is remarkable—especially the 1965 miniskirt version.

The flow of influence these days seems to be *to* dance rather than *from* it. Fashion has infiltrated the stage. The general obsession with collaboration has made costumes and sets as important as the dancing—maybe even more so. The most infamous examples that come to mind are Karole Armitage's *The Mollino Room,* with sets and costumes by David Salle, for American Ballet Theatre, and David Gordon's *Transparent Means for Travelling Light,* whose every aspect was overshadowed by the endless costumes changes. This concern with the "trappings" seems to be a gimmick that experimental choreographers, many of whose work matured in lofts and small spaces, have found to fill the opera house stage.

The Metropolitan's show is, of course, only about a certain kind of "dance." The dance of the upper classes—court dances, the debutante ball, fancy masquerade balls given by the likes of the de Rothschilds and the Vanderbilts. The only exception is the gallery devoted to the 1960s, when the "let it all hang out" attitude had just about everyone moving to the music in miniskirts and Nehru jackets.

There are interesting comparisons to be seen in the show among the many ways different eras literally shaped their body image. In the 1950s gallery, it was plain that the bodies were mere mannequins for the strapless dress designs. The Victorians' gowns, encrusted with marvelous materials, were like hourglass shells in which the body itself was hardly discernible. If the 1880s had the bustle, the late 1700s had its artifice, too—the exaggerated width of the hips. The rich brocade, the long lace sleeves falling from the elbows, the immobile hips and tender breast area all contributed to a very elegant bearing.

The antique revival of the early 1800s featured much looser skirts flowing from an empire waist and an exaggerated softness of the breast. The loose, straight flapper dresses of the 1920s disregarded women's curves. The 1960s—a decade of hippies, rock 'n' roll, and free love—emphasized the sensuality of the body and lots of leg. It was the age of the miniskirt, along with figure-clinging jumpsuits and peekaboo dresses made of transparent plastic or chain link.

—*Ballett International,* 1987

John Singer Sargent and the Dance

El Jaleo was John Singer Sargent's first undisputed masterpiece. The monumental painting, roughly 8' × 11', depicted a single Spanish dancer in front of a long wall lined with other performers, and it also established Sargent, who would become famous for his Anglo-American society portraits, as a virtuoso performer in his own right. Unveiled at the Paris Salon of 1882, *El Jaleo* showcased Sargent's bravura painterliness, his deft handling of oils and strategic use of color worked into heightened visual effect of unabashed theatricality.

The National Gallery of Art in Washington, D.C., put together a marvelous show (1 March–2 August), simply called John Singer Sargent's *El Jaleo,* that follows the creation of the recently cleaned masterwork from its beginnings in Sargent's 1879 tour of Spain and North Africa. For five months the young Italian-born American, fresh from five years as an art student in Paris, traveled throughout what was then considered a part of the exotic Orient, stopping in Seville, Madrid, and Granada. He recorded all types of dances and dancers—gypsies, Andalusian dance, flamenco, the tarantella—in his sketchbooks. The sketches progressed to studio drawings, watercolors, and then paintings, some preparatory and some, such as *Spanish Dancer* (1880–1881), seemingly ends in themselves, until the completion of *El Jaleo.* The sheer abundance of items in the show (more than fifty) evidences Sargent's fascination with the dancer as subject matter, which persisted even after the completion of *El Jaleo.* What was it about the image of the dancer that so compelled him?

Clearly, a documentary rendering of a specific dance or dancer did not interest Sargent. *El Jaleo* may have begun with on-the-spot sketches in Spain, but much of its gestation took place in Sargent's Paris studio. Models, probably French and Italian, imitated the hands and neck of the Spanish dancer, so that Sargent could refine the details. He worked through several alternate compositions: in *Spanish Dancer,* a single dancer (the main figure of *El Jaleo*) is presented in the manner of an academic portrait; in *The Spanish Dance* (ca. 1880), a mysterious nightscape, three couples slowly emerge from the darkness. But for the final Salon submission, Sargent decided upon the format he used in several early sketches, with its emphatically horizontal backdrop of seated musicians, singers, and dancers.

El Jaleo was more about art than dance, as even the ambiguous title suggests. It is not clear whether the title was meant to indicate *jaleo de jerez,* a specific dance often performed then in Seville, or (more likely) to indicate the broader meaning of the term at that time, as the ruckus of encouragement given a dancer by hand-clapping and chanting accompanists. For Sargent, such concern with authenticity seems to have been irrelevant. On the cusp of modernism, Sargent and his more forward-looking colleagues turned toward realistic images of modern life, seamy side and all. As one reviewer of *El Jaleo* wrote, "artists no longer paint angels, martyrs, and high-level people alone. The question is not nowadays so much the matter upon which you employ your art as with how much force and truth you can present it. The lower the subject, therefore, the greater the feat if you can raise it to the level of high art." The alluring Spanish dance, which allowed the Salon-goer to "slum" with impunity amidst the exotic, passionate, and, thus, by definition, vulgar Orient offered Sargent an irresistible artistic challenge: to render a low subject high. To achieve such a transformation was a mark of the shaman, the modern artist. And by invoking a specifically Spanish image, Sargent was associating himself with Diego Velázquez, whose fondness for the ordinary, and even the deformed, served as a model for the Parisian avant-garde. For an aspiring portraitist, a dancer—and especially a Spanish dancer, with her complexly twisting posture—would seem a logical choice of imagery. After all, a subject painting of a dancer, who expresses herself through her body, without benefit (or liability) of words, is not so different from a portrait of a society woman, who is certainly no less the performer. In fact, in 1882 Sargent submitted both *El Jaleo* and a portrait of Charlotte Louise Burckhardt to the Salon. If the crisp finish of *Lady with a Rose (Charlotte Louise Burckhardt)* bespoke Sargent's traditional training at the Ecole des Beaux-Arts, the rough and irregular brushwork of *El Jaleo* implied the influence of the then-controversial Impressionists. The painting was built on brush stroke rather than line, on the passion of visible action (both the artist's and the dancer's) rather than the control of concealed action. The literal sensuality of the paint strengthened the illusionistic sensuality of the dancer's movement.

The image of the dancer, with its inherent sense of movement, was an ideal way for Sargent to experiment with looser, bolder brush strokes. Critics, who were not yet convinced of the merit of the Impressionist aesthetic, might understand the use of such sketchiness in the service of rendering the dancer in motion. The dancing body provided Sargent a crucible for the rendering of light, space, and texture as they come together to suggest movement on the flat canvas.

And, in fact, some of Sargent's boldest technique was used to create the painting's most conspicuous signs of motion. The shawl, for instance, which is sent flying into space, was painted with a feathery stroke. The skirt, whose manipulation serves as a frame for the dancer's footwork, was heavily layered with paint in order to suggest a different sense of motion—one less airy and more emphatic—that was further intensified by its deep shadows. The dancer also gains a sense of movement through the cloud of shadow that envelops her.

The hazy shades of indistinct color create not just a spatial dimension, but also a sense of time, in which we can imagine her leaning backward from the pelvis as she turns her head into her rising arm, then snapping her head and furiously stamping her feet.

In *El Jaleo* Sargent achieved the drama of visual contrast less through color, which was used with effective restraint, than through chiaroscuro, the pronounced arrangement of light and dark. Through careful orchestration of the type of light and its source and direction, Sargent created an atmospheric environment without distinct edges that would seem to grow and shrink as the dancer moves. Harsh light projects theatrically into the space from the front, floor level, as if from footlights. It highlights the face, arms, and skirt of the main dancer, glints off the guitars and the other dancers, leaves most of the floor engulfed in darkness, and throws deep shadows on the wall. All this happens with an environment sharply circumscribed by the imposing back wall, which stretches out to the horizon so relentlessly. The flatness of the wall, reinforced by the guitars hanging on it, only serves to emphasize the three-dimensionality of the dancer's body.

This, the spatial complexity of her posture, was what most attracted Sargent to the image of the dancer. His formal challenge was to capture the three-dimensional form of the figure and the volume it created around her. The National Gallery exhibit makes this quite clear: Sargent returned again and again to the spatial dynamics of the dancer's body. The studies show the artist exploring the figure in space, her own immediate space, or kinesphere, and its interpenetration with the surrounding architectural space.

Sargent began timidly, with the simple sideways tilt of a male flamenco dancer, his arms lying lifeless on the paper. But it is plain that, from the very beginning, the artist was interested in body attitude rather than detail. He then took up the intertwining figures of couples, in deep tangolike bends from the waist. As he settled then on the image of the single female dancer, he started playing with frontal poses. But it was an oblique pose—the more dynamic one that he pursued, and then settled on, for *El Jaleo*.

In the three years between his trip to Spain and the finished painting, Sargent learned more and more about the structure of the dancer's body: the relationship of chin to shoulder, upper to lower body, and pelvis to chest. It was an asymmetrical body he drew, broken at the pelvis, with the weight shifted forward below, and the torso above sliding backward. The expressive linchpin, however, was the volumetric relationship among chin, chest, and arms. Sargent experimented with various configurations, some more linear, others more open.

He had to work at the drastically foreshortened arms, the angle of the elbow, the break of the wrist. The arms he drew did not reach outward; they were always kept in dialogue with the torso, mainly because of a strong connection maintained from arm to arm, through the shoulders and across the chest. Sargent was particularly sensitive to the relation of the arms to the torso, especially to how an arm can pull the shoulder forward or upward, changing the size, shape, and emotion of the chest. Supported by a deep sway in the lower back, the chest was held high, its strength extending upward through an elongated neck. The angle of the head, and particularly the relation between the dancer's chin and the upper torso (whether it juts up and outward, or in toward the shoulder, for example) gave his images varying shades of emotion.

Sargent worked out the connection between body and space: the way the pelvis was subtly thrust forward, the way the neck stretched backward or inflected sideways, and the way the arms met their surroundings. He sketched arms in a variety of configurations: intertwining with a partner's, bowing outward onto the hip, sweeping downward, extending forward or upward. In one sketch, of a couple, the woman and her arms are draped backward over the man's outstretched arms. It was broadly sketched, with an interest only in the overall line of the figures, and especially the outstretched arms, whose length is exaggerated. What is most significant, however, is the placement of the image in the lower right-hand corner of the blank page. Despite this isolation, the dancers' arms seem to reach across, and even occupy, the expanse.

After years of rehearsal, Sargent was able to execute *El Jaleo* with extraordinary quickness and assurance. He captured the complex inflections of the body in space, thus enlivening the dancer with a sense of motion rather than surrendering her in a static pose. It was, no doubt, a formative experience for a young man headed toward virtuoso portraiture.

—*DanceView,* 1992

Lois Greenfield, the Frames That Bind, and the Metaphysics of Dance

PHOTOGRAPHER Lois Greenfield started making images of dance twenty years ago. Since then, her pictures—of companies from Feld Ballets/NY to Bill T. Jones/Arnie Zane & Company—have been published in leading national magazines and newspapers. She is identified most closely with the *Village Voice,* where her work has been seen regularly, running alongside dance reviews, since 1973. Despite her long-established specialty, Greenfield doesn't like to be labeled a "dance photographer." And after living for a while with her new book, *Breaking Bounds* (Chronicle Books, 1992), I understand perfectly her unease with the label. Indeed, the eighty-seven black-and-white plates in the book, released simultaneously with an exhibit of her work this fall at New York's International Center of Photography, are really less about dance than they are about photography. Greenfield is a photographer first—one who just happens to take dance as her subject matter. (It's her "landscape," she explains.) As a formalist concerned with exploring the fundamentals of her art form, Greenfield finds in dance a congenial subject matter, one whose content is its form. "Photographing dance freed me from the responsibility of conveying information," she tells William A. Ewing in the end-of-book interview. "My editors would always select the photo with the correct 'content,' rather than the one with the best lighting and composition. I didn't have to worry about that in dance photography."

If Greenfield's first allegiance is to the photographic image rather than the dance, her practice still shares the same underlying paradox as that of her subject matter. Just as dance exhausts itself, disappearing, at its moment of fulfillment, so does the viewfinder of Greenfield's Hasselblad camera go blank at the instant she clicks the shutter.

The Hasselblad format is Greenfield's signature. It produces a 2¼" square, rather than the usual rectangular, image, and the photographer often purposefully leaves intact the thin black line surrounding the image. Not an even line but rather an uneven, notched and hence textured one, it serves as a self-conscious frame for the composition within. And composition is what distinguishes Greenfield's art. Witness Daniel Ezralow, who seems to be the fulcrum balancing Ashley Roland and Jamey Hampton on the tips of his palms; or the members of Iso, in a tight mass of suspended bodies exploding outward with a terrific centripetal force; or Elizabeth Streb's Ringside company, which is arranged, Mondrian-style, along the horizontals and verticals of a monkey bar structure. Everything is subsumed to the way that lines and curves interact with each other, and with that stalwartly square frame. Of course, those lines and curves are dancers' torsos and limbs, and Greenfield captures their configurations not in held poses (which she abhors) or at their climactic moments, but in the midst of transition. Greenfield chooses to freeze, in a photograph, the moment that is not usually perceived as singular by the human eye in the course of watching dance flow by. That's what gives her crisp, spare images such a strange, it-looks-familiar-but-it's-not feeling. (Sculptor Auguste Rodin, who himself was concerned with rendering movement, chose to take the opposite route, integrating different moments of a motion into a single sculptural gestalt, so as not to confuse the eyes.)

Greenfield says she isn't interested in the "thin slice of the split second" per se; rather, she wants "to play with the elastic notion of the stretched moment." Quite frankly, the images don't suggest movement to me at all, in the conventional sense of the word. More ambitiously, Greenfield manages to express something of the metaphysics of dance. To me, the isolated images, because they are con-figurations not usually "visible" in everyday perception—the pointe shoes hang-ing in the air, the body in the midst of falling, leaping, turning—leave linear time, entering the realm of myth, where time, sucked into a black hole, converts from distance to depth. This effect is most pronounced in the images without a ground line, where the dancers—looking always serene and godlike—are suspended in bleached-white space without horizon or shadow, bounded only by the stubborn black border of the negative.

It is in physical relation to that border that the shape of the dancers' bodies creates the tension, the dynamism, the "movement" of the photographic image. Greenfield has an impeccable eye, which, in this situation, means great timing. I had always just assumed (naively) that her incredibly precise compositions of multiple bodies flinging themselves into space must be the product of motor drive, cropping, and lots of wasted film. But contact sheets provided in the book reveal that Greenfield composes—or, if you will, choreographs—her image quite fully beforehand and has an uncanny ability to gauge the moment to shoot. (The Hasselblad, which she can sync at a shutter speed of 1/500th of a second, also helps.) These are, as the photographer herself points out, literally snapshots. Severely cropped images are created that way in the original image, not in the printing process.

These severely cropped images, ones in which bodies are in physical contact with the border, and sometimes partially left "offstage," as it were, beyond the frame, underline the physical materiality of the bodies—and of the photograph. "I'm asking you to take my square *literally* as a boundary, not just an arbitrary window on infinity," Greenfield says. "So now you've got the dancers butting their heads and brushing limbs against it, or hanging onto it, or being pulled off it. There's a force, as it were, that surrounds the frame that's affecting them, and it's something other than the usual conception of gravity."

What is that force? Metaphorically, I take it as any of the forces (psychological, social, political) that bind, or limit, or box in the body. But, it should be added quickly, those very forces that bind, or limit, or box in the body are the very same ones that make it visible in the first place. That's what a frame—whether the negative border or the proscenium arch—does. It sets off what's inside for focused attention.

In one particularly compelling photograph, Greenfield captures Daniel Ezralow at the left of the frame, in the middle distance, and David Parsons as he is escaping the viewfinder, in the foreground, only his trailing back leg and arm literally visible. Where, I cannot avoid asking, is he going? Greenfield clearly implies a body in a space—a possibility of "breaking bounds"—beyond the frame. Similarly, she experiments with the use of mirrors within the mise-en-scène, implying a kind of cubist space that splays apart the human figure into more dimensions than the flat surface of the photograph or the frame of experience can accommodate.

In 1990 Greenfield literalized her concept of the frame by asking Parsons to dance with a real black frame, $6' \times 6'$, which takes the place of the camera frame. In the four final images of the book, he dances around and through the floating frame, which, since it is always positioned obliquely, becomes elastically rhomboid instead of square. It does not confine Parsons, who plays with it, or ignores it, in either case exceeding it. Sometimes, when Parsons's body crosses over the threshold of the frame, it is the frame that is erased, rather than the body. Greenfield seems to be suggesting that the body can affect—as much as it is affected by—its frame.

Recently, Greenfield has become interested in expression: "I have been moving away from strict formalism and pure movement and working for an emotional and dramatic context for the figures." (That is not to say that the rest of her photographs are unexpressive. Their spare compositions are very dramatic.) Inspired by dance photographer Max Waldman, who often alluded to classical themes, she was, at the time of the book's production (1990), working on a series entitled "Explorations on a Theme: Expulsion from Paradise," after Masaccio's fresco. The images are all of a central man (David Parsons) and woman (Gail Gilbert) distanced from the frame by the vast void of undifferentiated white, empty space. In contrast, Greenfield has lit the bodies themselves with deep chiaroscuro, rendering them very sculptural, massive, and poignant. In some images they are midflight; in some, they are supported by gravity, but in all of them this loinclothed Adam and Eve are somehow entangled, their arms and legs pressing hard around each other. Echoing Masaccio's shamed and lamenting figures, there's a faint but present suggestion of writhing here, of the desire to exorcize internal demons.

That Lois Greenfield tells us so much about the dancing body with mere photographs is a tribute to her visual and poetic intelligence. I am eager to see where she'll go from here. Rather than wait for her next published collection, I'll have to mail in that subscription to the *Village Voice*.

—*DanceView*, 1993

Becoming Artaud
Solo Performances at Drawing Center Expand MOMA Exhibit

Antonin Artaud: Works on Paper," at the Museum of Modern Art through January 7, marks the one hundredth anniversary of the Frenchman's birth. More importantly, it signals the expansion of Artaud territory in America. He was first claimed as a performance theorist soon after M. C. Richards's 1958 translation of *The Theater and Its Double*. Thanks largely to Susan Sontag's 1976 anthology of selected writings, Artaud was drafted into the literary canon. Now, with MOMA's premier presentation of his drawings in this country, he gets annexed into the annals of art history.

But these portraits, hallucinatory drawings, and incantatory letters situate Artaud back squarely in the realm of performance: what he does here is stage the Theater of Cruelty on paper. Its surface, a kind of skin, becomes the space of his shattered body's surfeit knowledge. Artaud's graphic excesses—intimately linked to the pain of his mental illness, drug addiction, and electroshock treatments—transgress the limits of language, culture, and genre. Each work is an action, a gesture whose hieroglyphic trajectory sears the spectator as well as the paper, despite—or because of—the insufficiency of verbal language.

It's only fitting, then, that the series of Artaud events at the Drawing Center (35 Wooster Street) concludes 22 November with an evening of solo performances, featuring Penny Arcade, Jeffrey Jullich, John Kelly, Deb Margolin, and DJ Spooky.

"These are not performances about Artaud or Artaudism," explains series organizer Sylvère Lotringer, who teaches French at Columbia University. "It's going to be an evening of good performance, keeping Artaud in mind." Lotringer circulated ideas, texts, and audiotapes. To Kelly, for example, he offered "Doctors and Patients"; to Arcade, "Van Gogh, the Man Suicided by Society."

"I've been compared to Artaud my whole life," exclaims Arcade, who calls herself the Antidiva, "and I just started reading him last week." What resonates? "Like me, Artaud believed that one goes to the theater to experience what one is unable or unwilling to experience in life. We want a visceral, transformative experience. Otherwise, why go out?"

The evening, Lotringer says, "is not about honoring Artaud. That would be like a funeral." He cites visual artist Nancy Spero, who related to Artaud's rage from a feminist position, as the "perfect metaphor" for how new connections might still be made.

A newcomer to Artaud, Margolin is attracted by how he was "grossed out by permanence and posterity" and how "psychosis and addiction were the wind beneath his wings." The monologuist will perform two scenes from *Of Mice, Bugs and Women*—both involving a moment from the suspended life of a female character who has been deleted from a novel—that investigate the tension between the present tense and posterity and blur the line between the real and the imagined.

Becoming Artaud rather than just imitating him, says Lotringer, requires imagination. "It puts pressure on you to invent yourself. In performance, you get that chance."

Kelly, who has read Artaud extensively, plans to deliver a live rendition of "Doctors and Patients" in French, alongside an English translation recited via computer. "It's about me and my version of what I imagine he was like. I want to inhabit him visually, verbally, and dramatically."

"Artaud interrogated the notion of what it means to be someone. He was so bereft of it," says Lotringer. "He was a huge question mark raised to culture, and to the self. He asked, What does it mean to be a writer, to be a performer?"

—*Village Voice*, 1996

Body of Evidence
Schneemann Retrospective Exposes Subversive Gestures

PERFORMANCE art pioneer Carolee Schneemann is one of those artists history leaves behind, with a wheezing sigh of relief, because she just won't acquiesce to the available categories. In the 1960s, Schneemann refused to serve as a "cunt mascot" for her male counterparts, but also refused to toe the feminist party line in the 1970s. She made her reputation with landmark performances such as *Meat Joy* (1964) and films such as *Fuses* (1964–1967), and yet she identifies herself as a painter. She was a riot grrrl before they became the rage, auto-biographical before that became fashionable, and sexually explicit before such images became passé.

So another "difficult" woman languishes in legend, the art world limbo that reduces an artist to cliché, usually in the form of a photograph, and to rumor. Is it true, someone asked me the other day, that Schneemann fucked her cat? No, I replied, they just French-kissed, for a photo series, *Infinity Kisses* (1982–1986). Her cliché image is *Interior Scroll* (1975): a nude, paint-covered woman, standing in a slight squat, removing a long piece of accordion-pleated paper—a feminist tract—from her vagina.

Schneemann continues making art, commuting weekly between New York and New Paltz. And now a remarkable retrospective at the New Museum of Contemporary Art (through 26 January) promises to restore her to the realm of history. Senior curator Dan Cameron's show, "Carolee Schneemann: Up To And Including Her Limits" (titled after a 1973 performance), gathers a collection of rarely seen materials dating from 1959 to 1995. There's a student landscape that had been forgotten in a shed; a prototype for the infamous scroll, mounted like a totem under Plexiglas; the performance score for *Snows* (1967); and hours of performances, interviews, and films (transferred to video) screened in rotation.

The exhibit charts Schneemann's trajectory from painting to performance to installations, giving concrete support to her insistence that, despite her reputation as a performance maker, she remains a painter. Although she's been well known for extreme actions either erotic (*Meat Joy*) or angry (*Interior Scroll*), the retrospective reveals the emotional depth, sensuous richness, and theoretical complexity of her oeuvre. The New Museum's intimately scaled galleries—crowded with paintings, drawings, constructions, photographs, collages, video monitor, and installations—are saturated with the tensions between presence and absence, joy and grief, sex and death.

Grief, and its yearning for resurrection, permeates the space most palpably in works that invoke lost lovers, friends, pets, even cultural heroines. The entire project of painting, says Schneemann, "is 'in memoriam.'" It goes back "to the notion of not wanting to die. Of not wanting to lose everything. Everything is so remarkable and amazing and vivid and vital: how do you capture it? Painters are capturers."

As abundantly fleshy and messy and wet as her work could be (*Meat Joy* featured bikini-clad performers cavorting with chickens, fish, and paint), Schneemann never confuses the physicality of representation with reality. The painter's eye, which she calls "body-full," remains at a remove from the body, its only blind spot. The body in performance, she emphasizes, is not the self. "It's about obliterating the literal self in order to discover a residual mark or act."

Schneemann sees herself as a "witness," in the production of "fossils," "relics," "souvenirs," and "artifacts." Somehow, the body is rendered more powerful by its apparent loss and attempted recovery. Her body has made its mark on canvas, film, and paper. The rocks in *Video Rocks* bear the faint impressions of her hands and feet; in *Up To and Including Her Limits,* Schneemann hangs in a tree surgeon's harness and, crayon in hand, marks the passage of time on papered walls. Then she shadows that body by transforming the performance into a video installation. "I am using the body," she explains, "to reformulate its evidence."

In her most recent tour de force, the 1994 installation *Mortal Coils,* Schneemann pushes the transformative possibilities of the body's evidence so far as to raise the dead. The painter/performer/cultural critic has spent her career harnessing the inscriptive power of the body as brush/gesture/pencil. Her "pleasurable weapon," the body is her means of writing into representation what culture has censored out of lived experience. She brings to the foreground the ultimate taboo that has been pulsing beneath all her work: death.

A transparent yet piercing memorial to fifteen recently deceased friends, *Mortal Coils* deals with (dis)appearance. Sidewalls are papered with columns of newspaper "In Memoriam" notices and punctuated by homemade binders of photos and texts honoring her subjects. Through a grove of suspended, turning ropes whose ends coil on the floor, leaving mandala-like traces in white dust, we watch a subtle layering of ghostly images of the dead, intercut with startlingly realistic close-ups of a vulva or an ass, as well as wintry landscapes.

"When I see the works in the retrospective I'm immediately involved in the way I was when I was working on them," says the fifty-seven-year-old Schneemann, gracious and forthright though soft-spoken, her self-possessed bearing exceeding her actual height. *Mortal Coils,* she says, shares the same Cézanne-esque problem as her 1959 landscape, that of "simultaneity in space."

Schneemann's corpus from 1959 to 1994 demonstrates that the body's physicality is both material and immaterial. The body implied in the early paintings, assemblages, and constructions (*Native Beauties,* 1962–1964) becomes a body materialized in performances (*Snows,* 1967) and then rendered virtual in video installations (*Video Rocks,* 1989).

Films such as *Fuses, Plumb Line* (1968–1971), and *Viet-Flakes* (1965) operate across all three bodily domains. If the acute physicality of her multimedia performances is impossible to recover, it remains alive in the films, where celluloid becomes skin: *Fuses,* a self-shot film of her and her partner making love, was "baked, stamped, stained, painted, chopped, and reassembled," explains Schneemann. "And I wanted to put into that materiality of film the energies of the body, so that the film itself dissolves and recombines and is transparent and dense—like how one feels during lovemaking."

Judson Dance Theater choreographer Yvonne Rainer made the memorable claim that "the mind is a muscle," and Schneemann did the same for the eye, which, she wrote in an early notebook, "benefits by exercise, stretch, and expansion." She aimed to cultivate the audience's "projective" (rather than passive) vision, which included the kinesthetic faculty. "The body," she wrote, "is in the eye."

"Before I would paint," she recalls, "I would put on Bach and work out, stretching and dancing, getting into a little frenzy of energy. And then I knew that I was clear, because I was completely in my body and I could see better." Conversely, before she performed *Interior Scroll,* the artist painted her body. "It's very calming. I stroked myself with mud and got very concentrated."

After dealing with the dilemma of how to extend the space of the canvas, she had to "accept that I might actually have to give up my privacy and stand up and move myself to realize these images. That was torture, because then I couldn't see it. I'd say, 'What happened? What did it look like?' I was falling through time. It went so fast. It was gone."

As a performer, Schneemann may have gained her body at the expense of her painter's eye, but she was able to locate in this blind spot the gap between subject and object, representation and experience, mind and body. She captures the feeling of distance and disjunction in *Video Rocks,* whose intercut multimonitor images of walking feet are interrupted midstride, like an eruptive hiccup.

But *Video Rocks* sat, unseen, in Schneemann's studio for several years. "It's enormously important to have the work go out into the world," she says. "The retrospective is a wonderful confluence, where the history and the actual work can be examined, appreciated, and judged."

—*Village Voice,* 1997

An Inspiration Compounded of Hands and Feet

IMOGEN CUNNINGHAM photographed Martha Graham in the summer of 1931, in Santa Barbara, California. They worked outside, in front of the barn at Graham's mother's home. The afternoon was hot, the smell unpleasant, and the flies bothersome, but together they managed to produce a collection of nearly ninety images, an extraordinary double-portrait of both photographer and choreographer.

The new acquaintances were well matched. Graham, thirty-seven, stood at the forefront of the modern dance movement back in New York. Cunningham, forty-eight, one of the most important experimental photographers on the West

Coast, was given her first retrospective exhibition later that year, at the M. H. de Young Memorial Museum in San Francisco. The work of both artists was marked by clarity and simplicity and the afterglow of a youthful lyricism. What Graham had to say about modern dance applied as well to Cunningham's photography: "It is not 'pretty,' but it is much more real."

By the time she met Graham, Cunningham had shifted her focus from plants to body parts, especially artists' and musicians' hands. Both vegetation and human form were rendered so literally as to become abstract, and poetic. Her portraits of Graham's hands and feet retain a palpable sense of the organic, even though they are severely cropped and composed. The picture frame functions for its interior space much as Graham's masklike face heightened the expressiveness of her body. There is something quite poignant in the way these hands and feet converse, echoing each other in lines and triangles. Shape, Cunningham observed, is the photographer's only means of empathy. And to animate those shapes, she often used natural light. Graham's skin is touchable, and her toes graspable.

For Graham, the feet and hands were neither to be ignored nor wasted on decoration. They were an integral component of the tensile body structure that she was in the process of building: flexed feet that pressed the ground and cupped hands that pressed the air. "Think of what a wonderful thing the hand is," she said, "and what vast potentialities of movement it has as a hand and not as a poor imitation of something else."

The feet were to function as sensitively as hands, able to apprehend all the minute adjustments made throughout the body during even the simplest shift of weight when walking. *Primitive Mysteries,* immediately acknowledged as a masterpiece after its premiere in February 1931, was based on a walk. Graham's group had investigated this fundamental movement for months and even visited Jones Beach on Long Island to press their feet into the surf. Graham's technique required a complete articulation of the foot; all of its bones must move, she said. Cunningham understood the preternatural strength and flexibility of those feet and made monuments of them.

In those early years, Graham's now-famous contraction and release was not confined to the torso. The hands and feet, she insisted, must respond as well. This relationship was activated in the warm-up to her technique class, which had been largely codified by 1929–1930. Cunningham's photos suggest this first sitting position.

Graham made little use of these photographs, which are held by the Cunningham Trust in Berkeley, California, and can be seen by appointment at Photography: The Platinum Gallery in New York. Today, we identify Graham with the later repertory pictures by Barbara Morgan. Cunningham suspected the choreographer's disapproval, and, most likely, she was correct. Graham spent six more decades cultivating a portraiture as theatricalized and archetypal as the characters she danced. In contrast, Cunningham's images feel far too sensuous and intimate. In them, the dancer regains her human flesh and sinew.

—*New York Times*, 1999

Turning a Photographer's Vision into Choreography

HISTORY HAS neglected Arnie Zane, co-founder of Bill T. Jones/Arnie Zane Dance Company. His partnership with Mr. Jones produced the paradigmatic postmodern repertory of the 1980s, but after his death from AIDS in 1988 and the notoriety of Mr. Jones's subsequent career, Mr. Zane faded into a shadow legend, invoked less as artistic innovator than tragic hero.

Paradoxically, it is an exhibition of Mr. Zane's photography—a solo pursuit predating his entry into dance via Mr. Jones—that promises to revive Zane the choreographer. "Continuous Replay: The Photographs of Arnie Zane," on view through 8 August at the UCR/California Museum of Photography in Riverside, outside Los Angeles, traces his oeuvre from 1971, the year he met Mr. Jones, to the early 1980s, when he let his photography lapse in favor of a dance career. The multimedia exhibit features about a hundred original prints as well as slide projections, an interactive Webcam installation, and video footage (some newly discovered). Selections from the show and catalogue are accessible on-line, at the museum web site: www.cmp.ucr.edu.

The show and catalogue, organized and edited by the museum's director, Jonathan Green, comprise an extraordinary recovery project that fundamentally changes the way we understand "the other half" of the Jones-Zane collaboration. Mr. Zane was a dancer neither by nature nor formal education, but he contributed more to the company's aesthetic than may have been previously apparent.

Side by side, Mr. Jones and Mr. Zane cut a dramatic chiaroscuro, and critics were eager to cast the couple as a pair of "opposites attracting." Mr. Jones was tall, fluid, and black; Mr. Zane was short, percussive, and white. The former verbal, the latter visual. Mr. Zane was the cool structuralist foil to Mr. Jones's emotional personal politics.

"Continuous Replay" tells a more complex story.

Mr. Zane's genre was portraiture; he even named his earliest dance solo *First Portrait* in 1973. Like himself, his images stood small and square, with a powerful center. Eclectically inspired by Jacques-Henri Lartigue's concept of timeless photographs, the glamour of Richard Avedon, and the series of workmen by August Sanders, he aimed for what he and Mr. Jones called "rough elegance."

If Mr. Zane had started out by searching the surface of the human body in the retro-chic portraits of his bohemian circle of friends, by the time (around 1975) he turned his attention to Pearl Pease, a wizened eccentric in his Binghamton, New York, community, he was looking deeper into the fissures of the body's collapsed, creased, and cracked flesh. Ambivalent about exposing his own body onstage, Mr. Zane identified with her vulnerability—and her self-possession—as an outsider. Tightly cropped and frontally composed, the images were as provocative as any of Mr. Jones's explicitly combative solos. Asking "What is beauty?" was a political as well as an artistic question.

Mr. Zane expanded into a series of widely varying nude torsos (including those of Mr. Jones, young tough guys from the neighborhood, fellow go-go dancers, and other acquaintances), whose gestures and attitudes he used (as had the founders of modern dance) to reveal a person's inner life. With infrared photography, he hoped to plumb the body even further.

Becoming ever more the choreographer, Mr. Zane launched the photographs into time (by serializing them) and space (by projecting them). An image repeating itself in a progressively tighter frame gains a momentum akin to gestures accumulating into a dance. By integrating slides into his performances, he explored, both literally and metaphorically, what it meant to "project" a performative presence.

Mr. Zane disliked talking about art; instead, he channeled his theoretical rigor directly into the work, which can be recognized, two decades later, as a sustained investigation of the body: the production and location of identity (particularly gender, sexuality, and race), the rhetoric of difference, the expressive value of gesture, and the relationship between sight and knowledge. He was already engaged with a very postmodern set of concerns, yet he approached them with a utopian spirit that the art world left behind in the 1970s. Zane hoped to find a body both physical and "transcendent."

In his catalogue essay, Mr. Green makes a convincing argument that the results were more performative than photographic. Mr. Zane's pictures were staged events—costumed, directed, and repeated. Indeed, his visual experiments prefigured his choreographic vision, which persists in the company still bearing his name. There is the emphasis on diverse body types, on gesture and structural precision. The use of multimedia. (Mr. Zane played with found images, Polaroid and Xerox copies of photographs, photo-booth sequences, video, and magic-lantern slides.) And the intimate relationship between art and life.

But the most obvious connection is the vocabulary of the pose.

Early on, Mr. Zane modeled for art classes and studied film, processes that both depend on the illusion of movement produced by stillness. He often left the frame lines strategically visible in his photos and would also serialize a single image by incrementally cropping it, as if to remind the viewer that in order to exist, an image requires its limits—that an image, and by implication the viewer as well, is constituted by its frame.

As a choreographer, Mr. Zane favored a similar accumulation of discrete gestures, which were effectively "framed" by the poselike moments of stillness in between. These hairline fractures stood outside the flow of movement, and yet at the same time they constituted the flow of movement.

Therein lay Mr. Zane's radical critique of the dancing body.

The body, he was suggesting, is indeed the site of knowledge, but that knowledge is not the continuing, seamless, coherent experience that the conventional dancing body would have us believe. Rather, our body-knowledge halts and falters. Lurches along in fits and starts. Doubles back on itself, only to begin again. It is, as Mr. Zane titled a dance in 1982, a "Continuous Replay."

—*New York Times*, 1999

What Dance Has to Say about Beauty

IT'S PROBABLY not surprising that, at the start of a new millennium, artists are reviving old issues with new points of view. Since the advent of modernism, beauty had been questioned as a sufficient, or even necessary, requirement for art. Most recently, it had been dismissed as irrelevant to the avant-garde's concerns with identity and culture.

But the Hirshhorn Museum's exhibition "Regarding Beauty: A View of the Late 20th Century," which ran in Washington last winter, demonstrated that beauty is still a force to be reckoned with. For a decade, visual artists, like the thirty-six represented in the show, have been grappling with the concept and tradition of formal harmony, the sublime, and visual pleasure. Who defines the body beautiful, and how has this definition been affected by feminism, multiculturalism, mass media, and new technologies? If beauty is in the eye of the beholder, what kinds of images still have the power to produce such sensory experience?

What are the implications of these questions for dance, which by and large rejected the burden of beautiful bodies and pleasing stage pictures in the 1960s?

Bill Bissell, director of the Pew Charitable Trusts' Dance Advance grant program in Philadelphia, organized a trip for this year's grantees to view the Hirshhorn exhibit in mid-January. Afterward, the fourteen attending choreographers, artistic directors, and presenters gathered to discuss their responses.

Ann Daly, who teaches performance studies at the University of Texas at Austin, moderated the conversation, which for an hour and a half ranged from issues of craftsmanship to audience to education. The discussion, like the exhibition, raised more compelling questions than it could answer.

ANN DALY: Do you believe in beauty?

MANFRED FISCHBECK (artistic director, Group Motion Company): For me there's no question about beauty in life, beauty in art, beauty in existence. When I experience something that is fully what it is—when it doesn't present itself as *being* something but just *is*—then I feel I'm witnessing beauty. Galloping horses are beautiful, but the horses are not galloping and thinking, "Oh, we are so graceful." If they were thinking this, then they might not be beautiful.

MICHAEL A. CARSON (choreographer): I come to dance from a nontraditional background. I had Mary Wigman-based training. I'd always been taught that traditional beauty was something that you didn't really strive for. The first piece in the Hirshhorn show, which is a deconstruction of a statue, is the thing you went for immediately. Somehow this graceful line, if it was distorted, was much more interesting, much more artistic, and much more important. If it was just a little bit too beautiful, it was somehow frivolous. For it to truly be postmodern dance, it had to be atonal—pulled and pushed around a bit.

MICHAEL ROSE (managing director, Annenberg Center/University of Pennsylvania Presents): I think you may also want to ask the converse—what is *not* beauty? Within the context of dance, is it something that is imperfectly put together, or something that doesn't have structure, or that is crassly commercial? I think you have to address this question to understand the aesthetics of dance.

MYRA BAZELL (choreographer): I don't think "beauty" is the right word for this whole thing, because the word "beau" or "beauty" for me means "not ugly." It's not the right word because what we're striving for is to accept what's honest, what's nature, what's sometimes organic to an extreme, or sometimes inorganic to such an extreme that it moves us. But what I find beautiful are things that are ugly as well as beautiful. We have to invent a new word. Maybe "creamy," as in "cream of the crop."

EVA GHOLSON (choreographer): Instead of being so preoccupied with what's beautiful or what's not beautiful, I'd like to talk about what is good art and what is craftsmanship. Unlike Michael, I was trained (by Bessie Schöenberg) to create well-developed compositions. I think that good art is autobiographical. This is about perception. It's personal. There is a way that both the ugly and the beautiful can coexist. But the pendulum keeps swinging back and forth—you've got to look like this, now you've got to look like that. Well, let's talk about what is good art, how do you make good art, and what is integrity in craftsmanship.

TERRY FOX (dance curator, the Painted Bride Art Center): I think that the dance field is actually much wider open than the art field. You can still have a ballet, and a ballet can also be modern.

JOAN MYERS BROWN (executive/artistic director, Philadanco): There is so much more that dance can bring that is beautiful. I can go to a ballet and hate it, but I can still see beauty in it. Then I can go to a modern dance concert and see great beauty in what other people don't think is beautiful.

ERIC SCHOEFER (choreographer): I am drawn to the concept of beauty as an experience—beatific, to beam, to emanate—versus the concept of beauty as an object—form, space, and time. The strongest flash of beauty for me recently in experiencing dance was working with a party of hip-hop kids in North Philly in a warehouse space with a lot of graffiti. These boys were dynamos. It will never be caught again. It was an embodiment of energy and motion.

BAZELL: What does the audience want, and what are we creating? We lose the audience when things slow down and become a little more like nature. This is connected to the state of the world now, and the destruction of nature. It's impatience with things that take time. I feel subjected a little bit, as an artist, to the pressure of what viewers feel is beautiful or what they need from beauty. There's a void socially and politically at so many levels now that can't be filled, and I see it manifested in the art and the commentary in the art. What you're getting from the art is not the breath inside the experience but the constant commenting of the artists on art. This is a sign of the times. There is something missing about what is natural and what is beautiful.

FISCHBECK: It's not that audiences have no more channels or no more ability to perceive and experience beauty. They are ready, in the same way that we are, to experience what is real, or what is captivating, or what is engaging. When my company on occasion went out on the street to dance, people would gather and watch. Most of them had no idea what they were watching. We were not trying to do something to them; we were just there. Opening up the organic and expressive side of a particular dance to the audiences is what I'm concerned with. People actually can experience the beauty, the realness, the truth of the nature of movement in whatever form it comes.

BAZELL: Is beauty our responsibility? That's a big question for me.

DALY: How do you deal with the audience expectations that you know or imagine are there?

FISCHBECK: Well, we need to go on and do what we're doing. But there is another side to our work. People grow up with music, they grow up with art, they grow up with literature. They do not grow up with dance, for the most part. The dance experience has to be made available on a much larger scale. Dancers, choreographers, or teachers, all of us, need to keep that in mind. The teaching of dance, bringing that into the school or into the everyday experiences of people in whatever way you can think of, should be part of our concern.

CARSON: I'm working in a humorous vein, and I find that I can say almost anything as long as I make people laugh. Making them laugh gives me license to talk about something that's very uncomfortable. In terms of beauty, you've got to give a little beauty if you want to give a little ugly and keep people in their seats.

DALY: What does dance know about beauty that visual art hasn't grasped?

ANN VACHON (choreographer): When Manfred was talking before, I kept getting an image of his daughter. I had the experience of watching her in a performance in which she was so incredibly focused on what she was doing that I almost was worried that she had lost touch with herself. That kind of total focus of the performer in the moment is beautiful.

SCHOEFER: The concept of beauty in dance has something to do with presence. It's just a moment, really. Not only, in a traditional sense, is it this human form making this ideal form *right now.* It is also right now that this human being is alive and breathing and making an action.

FISCHBECK: When you look at somebody dancing, you see who that person is. You can talk to them for three hours. You can know all of their stuff, but when they start dancing, you see them. It's only in dance where you can have that.

—*New York Times,* 2000

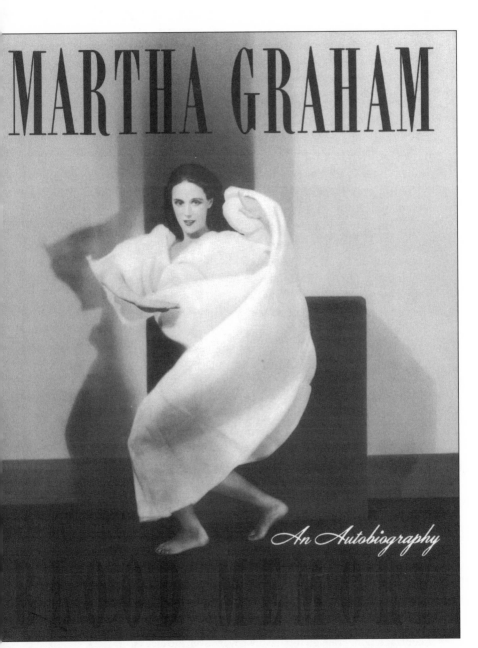

Cover of *Blood Memory* by Martha Graham. Used by permission of Doubleday, a division of Random House, Inc.

Review: Sondra Horton Fraleigh's *Dance and the Lived Body*

DANCE TRADITIONALLY has not attracted philosophical consideration, primarily because of the suspect nature of the body in distinction to the mind or soul. Dance is not a verbal or necessarily linear phenomenon, and it operates in its own systems of logic. It resists analysis in any terms but its own, and not until relatively recently have those terms been sufficiently articulated. As an art form of the body, however, dance is quite consonant with twentieth-century philosophy's concerns with self and agency. Sondra Horton Fraleigh, herself a choreographer, argues for the compatibility of dance with existentialism and phenomenology and sets forth a descriptive aesthetics of dance. As she makes her way through her aesthetic analysis, Fraleigh is often provocative, if not always persuasive.

In *Dance and the Lived Body: A Descriptive Aesthetics,* Fraleigh begins with the concept of the lived body, which emphasizes the experience of the self in the world as both subject and object. The dancer's body, she explains, is not an instrument of the mind; rather, it is a "minded body" (9). Body and mind together give rise to movement, self, and agency. Based on this premise, Fraleigh aims to posit an ideal of the dancing self that unifies body and mind and undercuts the subject/object split.

Although Fraleigh begins with a critique of dualism between mind and body, she explores dance strictly in terms of oppositions, which she calls mythic polarities. When Fraleigh talks about modern dance as the return of the Great Goddess, for example, she reiterates all the conventional rhetoric about gender dualism (male/female, culture/nature, heaven/earth, Apollo/Dionysus). This insistence on the transparent structure of opposites (despite the hazy distinction between "dualism" and "polarities") is responsible for the very mind/body split that Fraleigh wants to eradicate.

Fraleigh allows for "a dialectical and lived dualism but not a dualism of body-soul or body-mind" (4). This paradox is not unlike that in some current feminist theory: on the one hand, social and political advocacy for women as distinct from men is recognized as a concrete necessity; on the other hand, the metaphysical difference between men and women is denied. Fraleigh's aesthetics exhibits the same paradox, but while feminists recognize and deconstruct this contradiction, Fraleigh too hastily covers over the cracks.

Fraleigh is not a pure phenomenologist, for she believes that all movement takes us beyond itself. Neither is she a strict existentialist, for she considers that outlook too bleak. After Arturo Fallico, she combines these philosophies—adding a curious dose of myth, Zen, and Jung along the way—and puts her own cheery spin on them. For her, "dance is most basically an aesthetic affirmation of the body and of life" (56). It must be universalizing and vitalizing—these are the qualities that are important to the health of a culture. (Biology is literally linked to art.) Her preferences are for high art over low art, modern dance over postmodern dance, and humanism over nihilism or deconstruction. Fraleigh's humanism has roots in early modern dance, which, she says, had an existential context because it started from ground zero: each choreographer founded a vocabulary and technique based, not on an inherited tradition, but on her/his own body.

Like the early modern dancers, Fraleigh vehemently argues against the misinterpretation of dance as self-expression. When the movement is invested with just the right effort, the performer and spectator are dissolved into the dance itself. The goal is

> union with the larger aesthetic purpose of the dance and . . . communion with others. The magic here is that self is surpassed toward the dance and toward others. This is the aesthetically constituted, universalized (impersonalized) self. (29)

The dancer sacrifices the self to that higher good called the dance; without a self, there can be no self-expression. Within this aesthetics, the dancer is a sacred vessel for truth, goodness, and beauty. Dancing becomes transcendent. Although ballet is far from Fraleigh's frame of analysis, what she unwittingly outlines is George Balanchine's aesthetic. He believed that when dancers "just do the movement," without imposing their own persona on it, dancing becomes a moral act.

The process by which spectators merge with the dance is unclear, beyond Fraleigh's assumption that, since we all have a body, we live the dance along with the performer. (This, too, has precedent in early modern dance, in John Martin's theory of metakinesis.) The problem is, most people no longer experience their bodies in this way. Despite the romantic assertion about the body's "disposition toward communion" (60), our bodies by and large are commodified as private domains to be conquered by diet and exercise, then to be displayed for sexual consumption.

The process of communion that Fraleigh describes does not occur in all dance. On the contrary, much contemporary dance, once again obsessed with spectacle, keeps the audience at a distance and emphasizes a subject/object split. What makes the difference between dances that invite us in and dances that keep us out? A rigorous phenomenological inquiry into how dance is framed by the body, by choreography, by the stage space, and by cultural codes would go quite far in answering that question.

—*Theatre Journal*, 1989

"What Revolution?"

The New Dance Scholarship in America

SELMA JEANNE COHEN, the matriarch of American dance scholarship, is fond of telling a brief anecdote. She recalls reading in a manuscript that "During the revolution, there was a new production of *Giselle*." In her most exasperated voice, she delivers the immediate punch line: "*What* revolution?"

Dance, as we are all acutely aware, is a relatively young field of study. Quite out of necessity, dance traditionally has been approached at the level of factual narrative and aesthetic analysis. In the 1980s, however, there emerged a new attitude, exemplified by Cohen's (literally) revolutionary anecdote. What has long been called "dance history" has been expanded in its approach, subject matter, and methodology, into "dance studies." The model of objective history has been succeeded by that of interpretive history, for writers both inside and outside the dance field proper are realizing the richness of dance and other types of performance as an embodiment of cultural identity and change. Given the direction of the field and the interests of its most lively practitioners, I suspect that in the next few years some of the best scholarship will be focused on dance as social and cultural history.

Basically, two factors have facilitated this changing dancescape: first, the pioneer scholars who successfully laid the groundwork for an accurate dance history, and second, the current interest of the humanities and social sciences in issues of culture and representation.

At its worst, traditional dance history has been anecdotal, uncritical, and narrow. At its best, it has established the basic factual framework necessary for the development of the field. As much as I am sometimes frustrated by its undeniable stargazing, I am also impressed by its dedication and perseverance. For example, Ivor Guest's *Adventures of a Ballet Historian* still functions as a source of inspiration, and the monographic series "Dance Perspectives," edited by Cohen, remains an unrivaled collection of first-rate research. Unlike art history, whose artifacts tend to remain intact, most dance is but an irretrievable object of desire for us today. We do not have the luxury of film reproductions before the twentieth century (and even here the record is sketchy, until videotaping became standard practice in the 1970s); we often are required to reconstruct the "original" in our mind's eye. The present thrust toward interpreting the larger significance of dance to its time and place could never have developed without the basic historical groundwork established by earlier generations. Of course, the surface remains to be scratched in many areas, but that is part of the appeal of dance studies: the territory is wide open.

Dance studies is not singular in its turn toward cultural analysis. This kind of thinking—and the doggedness of its detractors—is peaking across the country: in universities, in museums, in funding offices, in books, in journals, and even in daily newspapers. An amazing convergence of discourses—from fields as diverse as anthropology, literary theory, feminism, history, and African-American studies—has vitalized current scholarship across the disciplines. What they share is the belief that all artifacts and processes of life, including the arts, are embedded in culture. Scholarship, then, becomes a search for the meanings of culture, and, in some cases, a critique of cultural values and standards. The arts, insofar as they produce as well as reflect culture, are fundamental to cultural identity and change.

That is not to say that all new dance scholarship is or should be done toward the end of cultural change. It does mean, however, that dance scholarship can no longer be done in a vacuum, as if the black hole of the theatrical stage is a world unto itself. Only by placing dancing of every sort—theatrical, ritual, social, Western, non-Western—in its current context (what anthropologist Clifford Geertz termed "thick description") can the full meaning of that dancing become apparent. This concept is not so new to dance, anyway. Joann Kealiinohomoku and Adrienne Kaeppler have for almost two decades been clearing ground for this practice in the anthropology of dance.

The best of the new scholarship is informed by cultural theory and practices thick description at the same time that it utilizes the most time-honored scholarly techniques, including exhaustive research of primary sources and solid formal analysis. Lynn Garafola's *Diaghilev's Ballets Russes* (Oxford, 1989) is exemplary. In her preface, Garafola eloquently illustrates both the debt owed to early dance scholars and the departure from that record prompted by newer interpretive paradigms. It is worth quoting here at length: "The era of the Ballets Russes is probably the most chronicled in dance history. Yet this book is the first to look at the company as a totality—its art, enterprise, and audience. The task has led me to ask new questions of familiar sources and has taken me to archives in Paris, Monte Carlo, New York, Berkeley, Syracuse, and Princeton previously unexamined by Diaghilev scholars. This is also the first book to challenge the premises of what might be called the British school of Ballets Russes history, which came into being in the 1930s. Its writings, above all those of Cyril W. Beaumont and Arnold Haskell, created the basis for modern Diaghilev scholarship, providing first-hand accounts that remain indispensable sources. Over the years, however, little has changed in the school's interpretative framework. In the many works of Richard Buckle, today England's leading Diaghilev expert, the company appears either as the link in an apostolic succession leading from Russia's Imperial Ballet to England's Royal Ballet or as a maverick untouched by the arts and ideas of its era. Buckle has unearthed new facts, but has failed to rethink their significance. And he has assiduously avoided the newer methods of social history, dance criticism, and feminism that have vitalized American dance scholarship, and to which this book is indebted." [1]

The book, last year's winner of the de la Torre Bueno Prize, has broken new ground not only with the depth and breadth of its cultural and aesthetic analysis, but also with its detailed economic analysis. By giving serious attention to money matters, Garafola opens up the matter of patronage to serious scholarship. As she notes, "without money, chances are there would be no ballet. . . . Almost always, money—how we get it, how we spend it—bears the imprint of social reality. In the case of the Ballets Russes, this reality necessarily intruded on artistic concerns and had artistic consequences." [2]

The 524 pages of *Diaghilev's Ballets Russes* make dance germane to the larger questions of history and culture: and for a field that has been marginalized for so long, this is no small feat.

This shift toward the cultural analysis of dance can be traced back to Suzanne Shelton's *Divine Dancer: A Biography of Ruth St. Denis* (Doubleday, 1981). Shelton's deftness in handling the broad range of subject matter essential to the telling of this tale of Americana was unprecedented. It set the standard. Seven years later, in 1988, both Deborah Jowitt's *Time and the Dancing Image* (University of California Press) and Judith Chazin-Bennahum's *Dance in the Shadow of the Guillotine* (Southern Illinois University Press) were published.

Jowitt, longtime dance critic for the *Village Voice,* used her experience as a regular dance-goer to investigate the history of Western dance since Romanticism:

"Some years ago, no doubt influenced by a longstanding addiction to *National Geographic,* I began to find it useful, on occasion, to blot out all expectations based on knowledge of styles or techniques. Instead I imagined myself an anthropologist skulking in ambush, observing the activities of members of a hitherto undiscovered tribe—trying to discern their customs and social hierarchy before I stepped out of the bushes and made myself known to them." [3]

The result was a survey book unlike any of its many predecessors. As Jowitt explained it, she was "questioning how the social and cultural climate, discoveries in science, and developments in philosophy and the other arts may have influenced the domains created onstage and the character of those who inhabit them."[4]

Similarly, *Dance in the Shadow of the Guillotine* excavated the significance of dancing during the French Revolution. This period is usually overlooked in favor of its predecessor, the *ballet d'action,* and its successor, Romanticism. Chazim-Bennahum's analysis, linking fundamental changes in costume and subject matter with the social and political upheaval of the day, has successfully retrieved the revolution period from a dance historical no-man's-land.

And most recently, Cynthia J. Novack's *Sharing the Dance: Contact Improvisation and American Culture* (1990) became the newest in the University of Wisconsin Press series, "New Directions in Anthropological Writing." Authoring a rich account of the contact community since its inception twenty years ago, Novack sought to "understand contact improvisation as part of culture, to see the changes in it as revealing and commenting on transitional moments in recent American history."[5]

The book series is edited by George E. Marcus and James Clifford, writers preeminent in their field. Their co-authored book *Writing Culture: The Poetics and the Politics of Ethnography* (University of California Press, 1986) has helped to shape major issues of the day. Anthropology constitutes a lively portion of the recent debates over culture and representation, for ethnographers have become sensitive to the power relations implicit in their undertaking. The question of who "owns" the story—the anthropologist or the culture under study—cuts to the heart of poststructuralist theory. How can ethnographic accounts adequately describe social reality? And, in turn, how do these representations create their own reality? Writing, the act of representing the other, has become problematic.

Not only writing, but reading, too. The new generation of scholars is interested not only in *what* dance means but *how* it communicates that meaning. Susan Leigh Foster's *Reading Dancing: Bodies and Subjects in Contemporary American Dance* (University of California Press, 1986) drew upon semiotic and poststructuralist theory to analyze dance as a representational system, both theoretically and historically. Foster posits a paradigm of contemporary dance, which she calls reflexive dance. This kind of dance involves viewers in the task of sorting through and synthesizing a variety of possible interpretations. In other words, the viewer not only passively "reads" the dance but actively helps to "write" it.

The broadened scope of dance studies is not only evidenced in books such as these, but also in journal articles, conference papers, and the upcoming *International Encyclopedia of Dance,* edited by Cohen. Due for publication by the University of California Press in Fall 1991, the five-volume set will encompass a wider cross-section of dancing than in any single previous dance encyclopedia: theatrical, ritual, and social; historic and contemporary; African, Asian, and Western.

171

Conferences, hothouses for new ideas, are clearly moving toward interdisciplinary and multicultural themes. Last year's annual Dance Critics Association conference focused on non-Western dance; this year's meeting of the Society of Dance History Scholars was devoted to dance in Hispanic cultures. In 1992 the Dance History Scholars conference will focus on the influence of a multicultural U.S. experience on the world of dance. And immediately following that conference, the University of California Humanities Research Institute and the University of California Multicampus Dance History Research Group will sponsor a two-day conference called "History Making Dance Making History Dance," involving an interdisciplinary and international group of scholars working in dance, musicology, art history, the history of the body, and the history of sexuality. They will join to discuss the unique contribution that dance history can make to the current debates on: (1) what is history? (2) how is it written?

The dance studies community is expanding internationally—witness the success of recent gatherings in Essen, West Germany, and in Hong Kong. While traditional dance scholarship was mostly the domain of journalists or "gentleman scholars," pursuing their research while remaining lawyers or booksellers or the like, the younger generation is more often emerging from academic ranks. More and more scholars participating in conferences both here and abroad are Ph.D.s or well on their way to becoming one. Universities are proving a more viable means of livelihood than the shrinking freelance writing market.

The new American dance scholarship, as I see it, is a healthy development. The shift in approach is opening up new ways of seeing; it is provoking new sets of questions, new areas of inquiry. It has the potential to contribute even richer insights into what we already know of dance as an aesthetic, cultural, and political phenomenon, and it has the potential to lead dance into a more prominent place in the humanities and social sciences.

Of course, the "revolution" is not universal. There is a strong anti-intellectual, anti-theoretical, anti-academic element in mainstream dance criticism. It could be true, as alleged, that interdisciplinary thinking may potentially do damage to the field, but *only* if the specificity of dance is lost at the expense of theory. The misuse of methodology is an inherent danger in any paradigm, even the most traditional. The richness and depth of understanding that the new American dance scholarship is bringing to our field, however, is well worth the risk.

—*Ballett International*, 1991

Review: Martha Graham's *Blood Memory* and Agnes de Mille's *Martha*

DANCE HISTORY is a young discipline. Until too recently, it read more like public relations than scholarship, emphasizing anecdote and personal devotion over research and critical perspective. But all that has changed in the last decade, as a spate of books on topics ranging from the Ballets Russes to contact improvisation have offered powerful arguments for the aesthetic, economic, and political significance of dance as a cultural practice. The best of the new dance history displays scrupulous research, a broadening reach in methodology, a longer perspective on the place of dance in culture, and a fresh set of questions.

Twentieth-century American dance, in particular, is a mother lode for historians. George Balanchine, although born a Russian, created a distinctly American form of classical ballet—fast, sleek, and large-scaled. Isadora Duncan and Ruth St. Denis transformed nineteenth-century skirt-dancing and Delsartism into a completely new genre of dance. (Distinct from her peers, Duncan led a racy personal life that gained her entry into the pantheon of American popular mythology.) Doris Humphrey and Martha Graham, leaders of the next generation of modern dance, pumped into their work all the aesthetic modernism and social utopianism of their era. The reputation of Graham, with her emphasis on gesture and theatricality, has outpaced that of Humphrey, whose dances depended on the more subtle and abstract manipulations of line and structure. Humphrey never manufactured a school and an empire, as did Graham, who has become almost as large a cultural icon as Duncan.

Clearly, Graham (1894–1991) is a huge historical subject. Her life spanned nearly a century and her art reached around the globe. She choreographed more than her share of recognized masterpieces, established a technique still considered one of the field's standards, and ran the country's most enduring dance company. Two recent books on Graham leave plenty of unexplored territory for future scholars. One is her autobiography, with the characteristically fraught title *Blood Memory*. The other, entitled *Martha: The Life and Work of Martha Graham*, is a biography by fellow choreographer (*Oklahoma!, Rodeo*) and sometime dance historian Agnes de Mille.

Both books are easy reads, clearly aimed toward a lay audience. Except for some familiar opening pronouncements on the art of dance and some fascinating asides, Graham largely charts the surface terrain of her life. She manages to reveal as little as possible about the depths and complexities of her private and professional self. For de Mille's part, she admits that her perspective, as a longtime friend ("mainly as an adoring younger sister") and colleague of Graham's, is a personal and impressionistic one. De Mille's book contains some obvious

173

errors, and that suggests it may contain other unreliable information. Much of the story is based on oral history, which gives us rare access to the accounts of many important eyewitnesses but also requires further corroboration. And although the volume is subtitled *The Life and Work of Martha Graham*, it concentrates primarily on the dancer's life rather than on her work. The art is considered only as psychobiographical data.

Nevertheless, within each book lie the seeds of new ideas to be explored, new connections to be forged, new interpretations to be considered. Given Graham's willful destruction of documentary materials and the tight control over those that survive, the significance of these volumes is not in any conclusions they assert but rather in the leads they suggest.

The best part of Graham's autobiography—besides the photographs—is her account of her family life (beginning in Pittsburgh and moving on to Santa Barbara, California) and her early years, spanning an apprenticeship with Ruth St. Denis and Ted Shawn, her several years with the Greenwich Village Follies, her year of teaching at the Eastman School of Dance (in Rochester, New York), and the beginnings of her own company. Before the book descends into a patter of name-dropping (Nureyev, Halston, Fonteyn, Madonna) that passes for an account of her final years, Graham does bestow upon us a sprinkling of gems: a rather lengthy commentary on the "mysteries" of *Night Journey* (1947); the information that *Frontier* (1935), with its Isamu Noguchi set of parallel and converging lines, is derived from the dancer's memory of the train tracks on her journey from Pittsburgh to Santa Barbara; and the fact that her dress in *Primitive Mysteries* (1931) was modeled on the flower of the night-blooming cereus that she and her mother and sisters delighted in admiring in their California backyard.

Graham's autobiography makes clear three very important connections between her life and her art. First, she successfully parlayed her childhood experience of being the dark, exotic, less-attractive Graham sister into an artistic persona as a wild creature—the strong, "ugly" one. She seized upon this role as the outsider, dramatizing it, for example, in her 1929 masterpiece, *Heretic*. Second, she centered great energy on the tension (which she, like St. Denis before her, seemed able to smooth out) between the notion of universal man and the fascination with ethnic and national identity. ("It is not that I tried to be either a Mexican or an Indian, but to gain the ability to identify myself with a culture that wasn't mine.") Third, the theatrical, ritualistic nature of her creations was an unorthodox distillation of her exposure to Roman Catholicism, Native American life in the Southwest, and Jungian theory.

In a way, *Martha* is de Mille's paean to a time when art was religion, not business. The controlling metaphor is that of the martyr: Graham is a prophet, a holy woman, who sacrifices herself at the altar of genius. She endures her lonely gift in order to provide the world with aesthetic redemption. Herself born into money, de Mille dwells upon the image of the young, impoverished, tortured genius. She stresses Graham's sexual life ("the key root to her dynamic organization") without any clear evidence and places far too much emphasis on the alleged sins committed against the dancer by her husband, Erick Hawkins.

She does, however, provide very valuable information about the early years of Graham's company, a compelling description of the early Graham technique, a frank account (very different from Graham's own) of Graham's wholesale purging of her company in the 1970s after recovering from alcoholism, and a clear-eyed evaluation of the recent deterioration of company style. The real co-stars in the book seem, to me, to be not the lovers, but the patrons—from Katherine Cornell to Bethsabee de Rothschild. Such patrons and their role in the development of American art before the days of government grants is a story that is yet to be told.

I have a final observation, about the books' photographs. It is trite but true: These images are worth more than any number of words about the dancer's love life or her celebrity collaborators. Imogen Cunningham's severely cropped, dramatically shadowed studies, from 1931, communicate Graham's unique projection of both strength and sensuousness. The very early Soichi Sunami photographs vividly reveal that amazing transitional moment when Graham was working through Denishawn decorativeness to her own austere, percussive style. Much of what makes Graham such a magnificent, mysterious figure is that she invented a completely new way of moving: She supplanted spectacle with intensity. In order to understand the scale of that achievement, to imagine its power and significance to its viewers, we need to spend more time considering the art—the body—itself.

—Journal of American History, 1992

Review: *A Cultural History of Gesture,* edited by Jan Bremmer and Herman Roodenburg

A COLLECTION of papers from a 1989 conference held in Utrecht, the Netherlands, *A Cultural History of Gesture* defines "gesture" very broadly, as "any kind of bodily movement or posture (including facial expression) which transmits a message to the observer" (1). No distinction is drawn between posture, gesture, etiquette, and paralinguistics, so the book addresses an unrestricted range of everyday movement practices, including standing, walking, sitting, hat tipping, bowing, hand shaking, kissing, and speech making. Written by scholars across the disciplines of folklore, anthropology, history, and philology, the ten papers aim to excavate the cultural meanings of human movement in a variety of times and places, from ancient Greece to present-day Andalusia, with a focus on ancient, medieval, and Renaissance Europe. Although the authors do not conceptualize gesture as performance per se, and although, as conference papers, the essays here are broadly brushed, the volume's significance for performance studies scholars lies in its articulation and demonstration of the moving body as a cultural and historical text. "The human body, in short," writes Keith Thomas in his introduction, "is as much a historical document as a charter or a diary or a parish register (though unfortunately one which is a good deal harder to preserve) and it deserves to be studied accordingly" (2).

The collection's first principle, then, is that movement practices are communicative acts. There are two other assumptions as well: first, that movement practices are cultural rather than universal; and second, that movement practices can only be interpreted in context. This framework echoes the work of Ray L. Birdwhistell, the founder of American kinesics and author of the groundbreaking *Kinesics and Context* (1970), but it is the European figures Norbert Elias (*The Civilizing Process,* 1978) and Marcel Mauss ("Techniques of the Body," reprinted in *Incorporations,* 1992) who loom large behind the work in *A Cultural History of Gesture.* To a lesser extent, the authors here also are working in dialogue with David Efron (*Gesture and Environment,* 1941) and Mary Douglas (*Purity and Danger,* 1992; *Natural Symbols,* 1982). And occasional reference is made to the work of E. T. Hall, Erving Goffman, Clifford Geertz, Paul Ekman, Michel Foucault, and Pierre Bourdieu. This volume recuperates the empirical approach to the body that marked kinesics, which has long since fallen out of intellectual favor, while integrating the theoretical/critical approach to the body that is now prevalent. I do not think that *A Cultural History of Gesture* completely bridges the empirical and the theoretical/critical, but it suggests the potential richness of the project. As medievalist Jean-Claude Schmitt writes, "gestures fulfil crucial ideological and practical functions" (62), and as such they need to be more specifically and extensively examined by cultural studies scholars, whether the subject matter is historical or contemporary.

What emerges most clearly in the collection is the function and significance of movement practices in constructing difference: difference between genders, between classes, and, given the European origin of the book, between northern and southern European nationalities. We see in the construction and evolution of "gestural communities," a term that Schmitt uses, the social distinction between Roman slave and free man, French working class and bourgeoisie, medieval laity and clerics. In "Gesture, Ritual, and Social Order in Sixteenth- to

Eighteenth-Century Poland," for example, historian Maria Bogucka explains how the Polish nobility, having just constructed its state, marked the distance between itself and others by elaborating a code of ritualized movement practices. In "Gestures and Conventions: The Gestures of Roman Actors and Orators," Latin scholar Fritz Graf points out how carefully oratory manuals demarcated the rhetorical movement style of distinguished orators, who were aristocrats, from the theatrical movement style of lower-status actors. In "The 'Hand of Friendship': Shaking Hands and Other Gestures in the Dutch Republic," cultural historian Herman Roodenburg demonstrates how greetings inscribe social hierarchy or equality.

Case studies also demonstrate that gender difference often is elided with class difference. In sixteenth-century Dutch portraiture, for example, the emphasis on the thrusting elbow, when an arm is placed on the hip, connoted the boldness, self-control, and masculinity of the upper-class gentleman. And in ancient Greece, the style of an Athenian aristocrat's gait could demean his status as "womanish." The aristocratic status of Roman orators, too, was enjoined with "manliness"—strength, valor, willpower, and self-control. Throughout the volume, self-control seems to persist across time and place as a central characteristic of manly/upper-class behavior.

The only essay that centrally addresses gender is anthropologist Henk Driessen's "Gestured Masculinity: Body and Sociability in Rural Andalusia." Refuting the common misrepresentation of Mediterranean gesticulation as the spontaneous outpouring of personal emotion (as opposed to the more restrained style of northern Europeans), Driessen argues that the movement practices of male drinking companions are "staged, evocative, ordered, stylized, and carry a message" (238). And, furthermore, this controlled and formalized behavior "enhances male companionship and helps to sustain the notion of masculine superiority" (249).

But the volume is not just important for its historical content. Perhaps more important are the methodological issues that almost every author explicitly confronts. By reflexively considering its own strategies of analysis and interpretation, each of the volume's ten case studies demonstrates, quite vividly, both the difficulties and possibilities of retrieving evidence of historic movement practices. Common sources include literature, etiquette books, theater, and painting. Schmitt makes an account of medieval sources: "theological, legal, literary, pedagogical, and medical texts; monastic rules and customaries; liturgical *ordines,* vision narratives, treatises on prayer and preaching, liturgical dramas; and mirrors of princes" (64). Cultural historian Peter Burke, in his attempt to reconstruct movement practices in early modern Italy, consulted formal treatises on gesture, the observations of foreign travelers, art, and judicial archives, which often recorded gestures of insult resulting in cases of assault and battery. Legal sources, explains historian Robert Muchembled, afford insight into "the point of honour amongst nobles, the protection of virgins' and women's purity by their fathers, husbands and others; the macho ethic of young men on the brink of marriage" (131–32). Further, he writes:

> The depositions of witnesses or letters of remission not only illuminate the actual crime, but numerous seemingly insignificant or accidental details relate the realities of the age. In fact, the most interesting social situations for a history of gestures are those of "social friction," i.e. the circumstances where people meet: the church, the tavern, festivals, crowds, and public places. (132)

The volume includes a selected bibliography, which, in conjunction with the works cited in the ten papers, reveals the extensiveness of the non-English literature. As a whole, the book goes quite a distance in proving what Thomas claims in his introduction: "behind the apparently most trivial differences of gesture and comportment there lie fundamental differences of social relationship and attitude. To interpret and account for a gesture is to unlock the whole social and cultural system of which it is a part" (11).

—*TDR: The Journal of Performance Studies,* 1995

Alvin Ailey Revealed

WHEN ALVIN AILEY turned from dancing and acting to choreography in the late 1950s, it was his Texas roots that inspired works such as *Blues Suite* (1958) and the classic *Revelations* (1960). These "blood memories," as Ailey called them, were of the African-American people, music, and religious rituals that he and his mother encountered as they moved from town to town in the Brazos Valley for the first twelve years of his life. The Baptist churches and the Dew Drop Inns, the house parties and the traveling vaudeville shows all impressed upon Ailey the soul, the rhythm, and the spectacle of his community's music. His Depression-era Texas childhood was filled with blues, spirituals, ragtime, Gospel, and work songs, and their intense emotion was what he poured into his dances decades later.

Ailey, of course, went on to international fame, as a choreographer and as artistic director of the Alvin Ailey American Dance Theater. He garnered just about every choreographic award and was commissioned for new works by prestigious companies from American Ballet Theatre to the Paris Opera Ballet.

In 1958 he founded his own troupe, which was the first African-American dance company sent abroad under President Kennedy's International Exchange Program, the first American modern dance company to perform in the Soviet Union since Isadora Duncan in the 1920s, the first African-American modern dance company to perform at the Metropolitan Opera, and the first modern dance company to make a U.S. government-sponsored tour of the People's Republic of China after the normalization of Sino-American relations. Even after his death in 1989, the company continues to rank as one of the country's most popular, under the artistic direction of longtime Ailey dancer Judith Jamison. *Revelations: The Autobiography of Alvin Ailey* (Birth Lane Press, 1995) is the compilation of interviews conducted by Virginia-based journalist A. Peter Bailey for a year or so before Ailey's death. And this is exactly how the volume reads: as a smoothed-out transcript of conversational remembrances, with many gaps and without much depth of reflection. Ailey impressionistically recalled his childhood, his entry into dance with West Coast choreographer Lester Horton, his partner Carmen de Lavallade, his early years in New York as a dancer and actor, the founding of his company, the famous personages he encountered, and his much-publicized breakdown and institutionalization in 1980. Presumably to compensate for the incompleteness of the autobiography, whose interview process was interrupted by Ailey's travels and subtle reluctance and then cut short by his untimely death, Bailey added his own introduction and an afterword of brief remembrances by friends and associates.

What does resonate in Ailey's account, however, is his rootless, fatherless upbringing, in segregated Texas towns such as Rogers, Temple, Cameron, and Navasota. Here is where he begins *Revelations:*

> My first memory of Texas is being glued to my mother's hip as we thrashed through the terrain looking for a place to call home. We never had a place, a house of our own. When I say "thrashed through the terrain," I mean branches slashing against a child's body that is glued to his mother's body as they walk through the mud in bare feet, going from one place to another. I'm talking about Texas mornings when the dew was lost in a hug of nothingness.

Ailey squarely blamed the racism of his Texas youth for his often-mentioned "inferiority complex." "That's one of the worst things about racism, what it does to young people. It tears down your insides so that no matter what you achieve, no matter what you write or choreograph, you feel it's not quite enough." Ailey recalled seeing Klansmen in their white robes; he remembered lynchings announced in newspaper headlines; he recounted seeing his mother come back from work late one night, bruised and crying. Only through intermediary Bailey did Ailey, years later, confirm that she had been raped by four white men.

And yet what we see in dances such as *Blues Suite* and *Revelations* is not so much the devastation of racism as the generative joy of African-American music and dance, both sacred and secular.

Ailey learned about the sacred from church, whose importance, intensity, and supreme theatricality greatly impressed him:

> At a church in Cameron, when I was about nine, I watched a procession of people, all in white, going down to a lake. The minister was baptizing everybody as the choir sang "Wade in the Water." After baptism we went into church where the minister's wife was singing a soulful version of "I've Been 'Buked, I've Been Scorned." The ladies had fans that fluttered while talking and singing. All of this is in my ballet *Revelations*.

For other sections of his signature work, Ailey drew upon the ladies who sold apples as they sang spirituals, songs his mother hummed around the house, and songs, such as "Rocka My Soul," that he sang in junior high school.

Ailey learned about the secular from the Dew Drop Inn, where Tampa Red and Big Boy Crudup played funky blues. He peered through the doors at the folks doing the "nasty dances," at the women in their flashy red dresses and the men with their large, "Texas Special" knives. "Many of the same people who went to the Dew Drop Inn on Saturday night went to church on Sunday morning," Ailey explained. "In dance I deal with these two very different worlds. *Blues Suite* is a Dew Drop Inn; *Revelations* is the church."

When Ailey choreographed *Blues Suite,* he wondered how its "down-home blackness" would be received. As it turned out, *Blues Suite,* as well as the rest of Ailey's repertory, has been received enthusiastically around the world, in no small part due to his commitment to an African-American vision of dance theater as an accessible community event. "I still dream," he wrote, "that my folks down on the farm in Texas can come to an Ailey concert and know and appreciate what's happening onstage."

—Texas Observer, 1995

SEASONS AND OCCASIONS

The Disco Project by Neil Greenberg. Photo by Paula Court. Used by permission.

Postmodernism and American New Dance

Several seasons ago, when Pina Bausch and tanztheater dominated the Brooklyn Academy of Music's Next Wave festival, the Goethe House New York sponsored a symposium on German and American dance. The panel discussion on contemporary dance in both countries turned out to be a partisan event: choreographers, dancers, and critics vehemently defending their own tradition to the disparagement of the other. The debate dichotomized the two so-called national aesthetics into American formalism and German expressionism, doing both a disservice. It became clear that American dance had become typecast, both here and abroad, as the radical formalism of the 1960s.

Two decades have elapsed since the emergence of postmodern dance. Since then, the aesthetic, social, and political climate here has changed drastically. Though choreographers such as Trisha Brown, Lucinda Childs, and David Gordon remain major figures, several generations of dance innovators have helped to shape the profile of current dance. And many of these younger choreographers have very different agendas than their postmodern predecessors.

The paradigm of 1960s postmodernism was Susan Sontag's essay "Against Interpretation." Choreographers, like other artists, were struggling to strip from the work of art what they saw as its oversaturated, overdetermined referents—the clichéd stories, the overdone emotions. It was the form they were interested in, not "the meaning," for "the meaning" had come to be a screen between work and spectator. They endeavored, with the most noble of intentions, to reaffirm the immediate, phenomenological experience of art. But that utopian paradigm has long since run its course. In a time of rampant anti-feminism, of AIDS paranoia, of evangelical exploitation of the poor and the airwaves, of yuppies, Irangate, and Reaganomics, the notion of a pure signifier, without ideology or connotation, is completely untenable.

The most innovative and satisfying dances today share a desire not to find new movement per se but to find new ways of communicating through movement. "Content," no longer a dirty word, seems to have wedged its way back into acceptability via all the recent experimentation with narrative, fractured and oblique as it was. (Ironically, when Yvonne Rainer's interest in specific emotions led her to narrative, she felt that she had to leave dance for film.) Connotations are both intended and encouraged these days, and dancers implore critics not just to describe but to interpret, too. These changing attitudes have been influenced by a decade of performance art, with its unabashed political messages, as well as by tanztheater and butoh, whose grippingly visceral performances provoked a maelstrom of controversy when they arrived here.

American choreographers such as Jane Comfort, Johanna Boyce, Dana Reitz, Eva Karczag, and Kinematic (the collaborative trio of Tamar Kotoske, Maria Lakis, and Mary Richter) seem to be throwing open the doors of exploration again, asking, in intelligently ingenuous ways, what is the meaning of movement? The answers are neither rigid nor explicit; in fact, what is remarkable about these performers and companies is that their work is so resplendently suggestive and yet so ineffable. Their work plays at the edges of semantics, registering itself at a kinesthetically expressive level that bypasses language. Their movement is intimately related to inner states, past experiences, future possibilities, community, fantasy, reality, identity, social conventions, and ideology. After so many years of left-brain activity in the arts, these choreographers are again embracing the eloquence and humanity of the moving body—but with a very sophisticated understanding of how culture manipulates the body, both physically and politically.

Dana Reitz and Eva Karczag are two soloists whose movement studies transcend mere formalism, the former with her sensual polyrhythms and extraordinary sense of space and place and the latter with her transportative—almost spiritual—presence. Kinematic's fractured fairy tales play in the powerful space between logic and absurdity, between the foreign and the familiar; their smooth layering of literal gesture and abstract movement is hardly "readable" in any linear way, and yet it makes perfect sense. Johanna Boyce's generous, women-centered dances suggest an implicit model of community. Her recent *Women, Water, and a Waltz* portrays a harmonious group of women whose Ingres-like arms elegantly intertwine in a sensuous water-pouring ritual. Jane Comfort's dances can be inscrutably evocative, and they can be stridently critical (but always with humor) of the way mass media clichés construct our lives. Her idiom is an unlikely blend of vibrant Latin rhythms, verbal text, and gestures that come from everyday life, sign language, and her own rich imagination.

But at the same time, another, more popularized strain of new dance is characterized by pastiche and appropriation. The most often quoted source is classical ballet, which has seduced choreographers as disparate as Twyla Tharp, Laura Dean, Lucinda Childs, and Karole Armitage. From an aesthetic point of view, the balleticization of new dance seems like an evasion of responsibility, but from an economic point of view, it makes good sense. In the 1980s "success" requires making it into the chic press (such as *Vanity Fair*) and into the bigger houses (such as the Brooklyn Academy of Music), both of whose mass public seems most impressed with technique and presentation—that is to say, spectacle. And ballet is the best shortcut to proscenium spectacle.

From a cultural point of view, the appropriation of ballet and other movement forms in new dance is right in step with the nostalgic accumulation of retro images that pervades everything from advertising to fashion to architecture to political rhetoric. The implications of this historical eclecticism—the hallmark of what architectural and cultural critics call "postmodernism," distinct from the dance critic's use of the same term to indicate 1960s formalism—are important. They tell us quite a bit about how we envision ourselves in the 1980s.

The rhetorical battle between modern dance and classical ballet, which is still being played out in the daily and specialized press, has long centered around the morality of individual expression. For the moderns, authentic art must spring from one's inner resources. For the classicists, the "cult of individuality" represents decadent self-indulgence; only the subordination of the self to the classical code will yield absolute perfection. The increasing dependence of new dance on the classical vocabulary bespeaks a growing confidence in the truth of the code over the truth of individual originality.

The sanguine modernist belief (shared by the postmodern choreographers) that the artist can autonomously create the universe anew in performance, based on her/his own unique grit and vision, has eroded. As critical as we have become of our representational codes, as trapped as we often feel before them and inside them, they have captured many a choreographer's imagination. And most choreographers are not ready to face the lie of the code. The appropriation of ballet is particularly disconcerting, because of its tacit endorsement of rigid hierarchy, of mastery, and of dichotomized gender roles.

Mark Morris's dances, at least a certain group of them, are jam-packed with facile glosses on such highly recognizable material as Laura Dean, Isadora Duncan, Doris Humphrey, Indian dance, baroque ballet, and folk forms. These dances are soundly crafted, and some of the conceits are downright ingenious, but, at end, I am usually left wondering what it all adds up to. I don't see any cracks in the veneer. What is the choreographer's point of view? By refusing commitment to a single aesthetic (whether his own or someone else's), Morris pretends to a tabula rasa innocence that is, of course, a hoax. By playing the quotes straight, without any critical reflexiveness or metacommentary, he goes nowhere in deconstructing them. Pastiche, in this instance, remains suspiciously aloof and gratuitous.

This is an issue, of course, that faces all the arts: is postmodern eclecticism an inherently conservative style for a conservative age? Is it possible for a dance to freely play among representational codes reflexively without sinking into relativism, or without valorizing its own representation?

That such divergent streams of new dance coexist is not surprising, for even the most pervasive aesthetic is never monolithic. But then again, the extreme contrast between the savvy dancers in P.S. 1's *He/She: Love Sex and Gender* series, for example, and Laura Dean's men dancers doing fancy overhead lifts with her women dancers, really seems to signal a dance community in transition. Even within individual companies, such as Dean's or Tharp's, the influx of young blood has radically changed the look and the meaning of the dances. In Dean's case, many of her newer dancers, instead of kneading down into their shifts of weight, look like they are flirtatiously swinging their hips. And in Tharp's case, her ballet-trained newcomers don't have the tongue-in-cheek edge that the original dancers gave to works such as *Nine Sinatra Songs*. In the midst of all these shifting, opposing aesthetics, only one thing is clear: that new dance is just too wide-ranging to be typecast.

—Festival international de nouvelle danse program, 1987

BAM and Beyond
The Postmoderns Get Balleticized

LINCOLN KIRSTEIN may have been right all along. Since the 1930s this leading apologist for classical ballet—the man who brought George Balanchine to America and helped to found him a company—has insisted that modern dance could not endure. Certainly the Brooklyn Academy of Music's (BAM) 1986 Next Wave festival demonstrated that, among its showcased choreographers, only a rigorous few such as Anne Teresa de Keersmaeker and Eiko and Koma can get along without ballet.

Really, the period of enmity between ballet and modern dance was brief. By the 1930s Martha Graham was incorporating ballet into her technique; in 1941 she sent Merce Cunningham to study at Balanchine's School of American Ballet. In 1959, she and Balanchine co-created a dance called *Episodes,* and today her dancers are as concerned with fluidity and extension as their counterparts at the New York City Ballet.

The death of Balanchine in 1983 symbolized the passing of a golden age for ballet. The classical choreographic genius of our century gone, there was no heir apparent within the ranks to continue expanding the idiom. As a stopgap measure, ballet companies began to mine experimental dance for fresh choreographic ideas. Companies such as the Joffrey Ballet and American Ballet Theatre commissioned works by the likes of Twyla Tharp, Laura Dean, Karole Armitage, and David Gordon. The practice of pairing choreographers and companies from different traditions was institutionalized in the National Choreography Project, founded in 1984 to "enable talented choreographers to develop new work on larger repertory companies" and to "enable participating companies to expand the scope of their repertories and to experiment with new ideas."

But these crossover projects have not proved synergistic, and in a good-intentioned way they may be thwarting the development of young ballet choreographers. Ironically, though it was the ballet companies that were looking for fresh blood, they have remained relatively unchanged but for the few novel additions to their repertories. The experimental choreographers, however, have been heavily influenced by ballet, whose technique, vocabulary, and stage conventions provide some ready solutions to the challenge of the BAM Opera House.

Ballet technique has never really been superseded as a general foundation for building flexibility, strength, and control. Most program bios nowadays make mention of some ballet training. In the case of Twyla Tharp's newly revamped company, many of the women have had quite serious ballet training, at the likes of the School of American Ballet. Even in the heyday of the Judson Dance Theater in the early 1960s, when the standard images of the ethereal ballerina and of Graham's bigger-than-life matriarchs had been banished and replaced with mere mortals who lugged around mattresses or crawled on the floor, Yvonne Rainer was taking ballet classes.

It is largely through training that ballet has infiltrated the "Next Wave" productions. Choreographers such as David Gordon, who was a member of the Judson Dance Theater and of the subsequent Grand Union (both of which eschewed technique and formal presentation), must now look for dancers whose amplitude will hold BAM's huge Opera House stage. Gordon has twice been commissioned to create works on the ballerinas and danseurs of American Ballet Theatre; he could not have been unaffected by their superhuman capabilities. His Pick Up Company, which performed three pieces on its BAM program, looked sleek and proper, displaying well-pointed toes and elegant turnout. But except for a poignant duet between Gordon and Valda Setterfield in *The Seasons,* the dancing in the two newest works was surprisingly unengaging.

But I bet no one in the cheap seats had trouble seeing what was going on. This large, limb-intensive kind of movement comes from ballet; it is today and was centuries ago calculated to project clearly from a proscenium stage to the last row of the balcony. This movement style—which in *Transparent Means for Travelling Light* was so big and yet so bland as to be immediately forgettable—befits its grand and gilded environs as well as his older pieces suited their intimate, unorthodox settings. In lofts and gyms Gordon worked with everyday movement and intricate structures whose success depended more on his ingeniousness as a creator than on how well his dancers projected themselves. In *Transparent Means for Travelling Light* (which *was* remarkable for the way Gordon kept recasting the quality and scale of the stage space) and *The Seasons,* the polish of the dancing took the edge off Gordon's stock-in-trade, his wit.

Unlike Gordon, who came relatively late in life to dance from the visual arts, Michael Clark was trained at the Royal Ballet School. With shaved head, pouty lips, and ass-revealing tutu, he descended on Brooklyn with all the pop British glamour of Boy George—and as much depth. *No Fire Escape in Hell* started with Clark alone, whose exquisite feet and line were astonishing. But that was about all the actual dancing there was to it. From there, the work degenerated into artistic puerilism. Stuff that had become passé after the 1960s (sex, aggressive action in the audience's space, lights glaring in the spectators' eyes) was done as if it were still naughty, when the only shocking thing about Clark's production was how unredeemably bad it was.

At the same time that Clark is working hard to conceal his classical framework, choreographers such as Karole Armitage, Twyla Tharp, and Molissa Fenley are eagerly flaunting theirs. Jetés, port de bras, arabesques and the like are becoming the lingua franca of the 1980s. Minimalism has taken choreographers such as Laura Dean just so far; in their scramble for something new, more and more of them are turning to the classical vocabulary.

Armitage and Tharp have hoisted upon themselves the Balanchine mantle. Armitage, a former Cunningham and Balanchine dancer, declared her allegiance with the recent change of her company's name to The Armitage Ballet. In her January season at the Joyce Theater, Armitage made a fetish of arabesques, leaving me with the indelible image of a Betty Grable pin-up. Though Armitage seemed to create a feminist heroine at the center of *The Watteau Duets,* those exotic/erotic toe shoes proved little more than theatrical substitutes for a femme fatale's stiletto heels, which Armitage did indeed slip on for the final duet.

Neither has Tharp really showed us anything new about pointe work. In fact, being on pointe seems to limit her women dancers; in her February season (at BAM, coincidentally), the men looked infinitely more interesting. For Tharp, ballet is the newest phase in a long history of borrowing from popular culture (such as jazz, ballroom dancing, graffiti). I do think ballet has become, in the most broadly archetypal way, popular culture. Balanchine surely did enough Hollywood musicals and whiz-bang stage numbers such as *Stars and Stripes* and *Who Cares?* to make it so. What Tharp brings to bear on her balletic forays that Armitage lacks, however, is Balanchine's dramatic sense of contrast and scale.

Throughout the season, viewers could trace how Tharp has come to terms with ballet. In *As Time Goes By* (1973) the dancers performed a complex, witty combination of proper balletic moves and Tharp's own idiosyncratic movement style. The two genres found their affinities, paradoxically, through their exaggerated differences—erectness vs. a pelvic slouch, balance vs. off-balance, controlled energy vs. a loose flow. With *Ballare* (1986), Tharp made a stab at a white ballet. With the apocalyptic *In the Upper Room* (1986), she managed to reconcile the modern and ballet idioms. It's telling, I think, of the fundamental distance between these two idioms that she did so through structural rather than through stylistic means. Most dancers performed signature Tharp style in sneakers, while a few women wore flaming red toe shoes. The two contingents were kept discrete even when they shared the stage; what made them look so right together was the misty black hole of a stage setting.

Fenley's homage to ballet in *Geologic Moments* was much more fleeting than Tharp's or Armitage's. In Fenley's previous seasons, I had admired the company's strong, resilient, self-possessed women. Her dances hurtled along nonstop, at full speed. The material was minimal, but it wasn't rigorously sharp-edged. There might be a motif weaving its unobtrusive way through a piece, but in the end the work had an inscrutable, organic inevitability. I thought Fenley and her dancers looked best when they were capitalizing on their physical exoticism; and when they were, the communal energy reminded me of a ritual or worship ceremony. Fenley's body is the prototype—a strong, hyperextended back and an ecstatic way of weaving her arms about her as if they had their own life. So I was taken aback when Fenley's company at BAM included two men. That the pair was so cookie-cutter proper—and that the material tended toward superficial classicism—prevented the company from achieving its trademark intensity.

Geologic Moments began coolly, infused with crisp arcs and spirals. There were very obvious steps from ballet, including a port de bras that stuttered downward in abrupt intervals. The second half was lyrical and Romantic, the women even wearing bits of tutu-esque tulle. In deep lunges, they curved their arms downward; everything was soft and sustained, with the barest bit of men partnering women. After a pause for the removal of two pianos from the stage, the dance resumed with a woman standing resolutely on half-toe, downstage center, as I recall. A little later Fenley unwrapped a luscious développé. And in the closing sequence, very deliberate and simple, the five dancers stood in a line holding hands. In unison they progressed from plié to arabesque into a lunge, and then exited one by one. Fenley handled the polemic material rather deftly throughout, but I don't know why it was there in the first place. It appeared to be a gloss—an excuse for content, something reassuring that the audience could latch on to, like finding the pipe in a Cubist still life.

Geologic Moments was a case of déjà vu. In the 1985 Next Wave season, minimalist Laura Dean, too, had gotten "balleticized." The dances that had established her reputation consisted of continual spinning in subtly kaleidoscoping floor patterns. For all their seeming simplicity, her dances were richly textured and deeply satisfying. But her BAM premiere, *Transformer,* was gratuitously fitted out with very pretty, very vapid arabesques and fancy lifts. The ballet vocabulary is enormously expandable and manipulable, but, extracted piecemeal, that vocabulary loses its logic and integrity.

In his more than forty years as a choreographer, Merce Cunningham has succeeded in developing a systematic logic of movement. Drawing on ballet's emphasis on the limbs and on modern dance's interest in the torso, he created a technique and vocabulary based on the relationship between the back and the legs. Using the considerable strength of their backs, Cunningham dancers can articulate very complex combinations of movement in their legs and trunk. On the surface they may look a lot like ballet dancers, very vertical and technically accomplished, but there is much more activity at the core than is allowed in classical ballet. As their legs jump, extend, or bend under them, their middles curve, tilt, arch, twist, or remain upright.

Roaratorio: An Irish Circus on Finnegans Wake (which opened the festival) was no exception. Although it took off on the quick-stepping of Irish dance, which shares with ballet an insistent verticality, *Roaratorio* was full of the quirky movement inflections that remove Cunningham style from the realm of the classical. Partnering, for instance, was one of the dance's motifs, and it definitely outstepped the boundaries of the pas de deux: friendly duets of pattered-out rhythms of the feet; measured, elegant duets; awkward, clomping duets; la-dee-da, stroll-in-the-park duets.

Though in a more stylistic than technical way, Bill T. Jones and Arnie Zane have also combined genres to come up with something of their own. With backgrounds in athletics and photography, Jones and Zane were seen by some as having sold out their renegade roots for the big time when they blatantly exploited the trappings of ballet in *Secret Pastures,* their contribution to the 1984 Next Wave festival. But I think that Jones and Zane have done the most thorough and creative job of completely transforming ballet—as well as jazz, gymnastics, social dance, sports, folk dance, and vernacular gesture—into their own pastiched style. Not only do they mix movement vocabularies but choreographic quotations and cross-genre witticisms as well. In *The Animal Trilogy,* Jones and Zane made references to Balanchine, Cunningham, and Graham; continuing their interest in filmic techniques, the choreographers created a processional entrance that immediately "rewound" itself, like a film run backward. Whereas Fenley's and Dean's dances were undermined by the classical sheen, Jones and Zane are in complete control of their variegated material.

And through the persistence of their own fanciful ideas, they have been able to deal unabashedly with the virtuosity of their company's dancing without needing the rhetoric of classicism to justify it. The dancers pack these disparate steps together with utmost clarity and invest them with all-out exuberance. There is no mistaking these explosive contemporary dancers—despite their balletic carriage and ballon—for "proper" classical dancers.

Besides the renewed concentration on line, projection, and technique, ballet is embedding itself in contemporary dance by negation—through parody. Choreographer Jean Erdman once argued that "pointed toes and turned-out feet" had made their entree into modern dance through satire; that's how it appears to be creeping into current dance, too. Choreographers as different as Trisha Brown, Charles Moulton, Senta Driver, Jones and Zane, Mark Dendy, and Mark Morris have all used ballet as a model to poke fun at.

Among Morris's offerings on the Next Wave program was *Pieces en Concert,* a parody on baroque ballet that effectively mastered and then broke its fussy rules of decorum and artistic convention. The two men and one woman inverted the proper fifth position, performed an excess of leg beats, and did rubber-legged jetés. They moved too fast, or too forcefully, or too awkwardly. Morris, at his florid best, stole the show with his uproarious poses of oozing rapture.

The current blend of ballet and postmodern dance is avant-garde chic with all the old-money respectability of ballet—a successful formula for pulling in both the art gallery owners and the corporate execs. BAM has managed brilliantly to create a Next Wave audience, but somewhere along the line the avant-garde disappeared. What used to be a provocateur has been made over into a social entertainment, and what better shortcut to spectacle than ballet? Ballet is aristocratic, devoted to the ideal of mastery, and resistant to clutter. It's the paragon of gentility, of surface, and of image—perfect for an age when social crises are rendered invisible and presidential scandals smoothed over with placid rhetoric.

There is nothing inherently wrong about the current adoption of ballet—in varying degrees and ways—by experimental choreographers. Fresh ideas can come from anywhere, and certainly ballet is a rich source. But it is disturbing that the dance forms that were originally created as an alternative and a challenge to the values of the ballet tradition are in the process of being leveled. Choreographers and dancers seem more interested in perfecting steps than in exploring the body's subtle, complex expressiveness. The exigencies of mass-market packaging and an opera house stage, in tandem with the postmodern impulse toward eclecticism, have produced a lot of dance that's surface-shiny but substance-dull.

—High Performance, 1987

The Closet Classicist

ROBERT WILSON, the theatrical auteur who changed the face of contempo-
rary performance with his and Philip Glass's now-legendary *Einstein on the
Beach* (1976), spent a month during the 1992 spring semester in residence in the
Department of Theatre and Dance at the University of Texas (UT) at Austin.
In two separate two-week periods, he conducted workshops on *Four Saints in
Three Acts,* the opera by Gertrude Stein and Virgil Thomson, and Jean Genet's
The Balcony. The open-rehearsal residency, for productions that will be mounted
elsewhere, culminated in a symposium on various aspects of Wilson's work, fol-
lowed by what was billed as a slide lecture by Wilson himself.

During the symposium, one student, who had written a master's thesis on Wilson, lamented the fact that scholars have no vocabulary for dealing with Wilson's
unique brand of theater, whose text is primarily visual rather than verbal. Her comment was symptomatic of Wilson scholarship, which claims his work for theater
and ignores its relationship to dance. It seems to me, after having seen a half-dozen
Wilson productions and sat in on a number of the workshop sessions, observing
what seemed to me a clearly choreographic process, that Wilson's practice is essentially about the movement of persons, objects, light, and words across time and
through space. Scholars in the field of dance have a quite adequate vocabulary and
methodology for dealing with such nonliterary performance.

Wilson himself soon took the stage and set the record straight. Less a slide lecture
than an autobiographical performance, complete with vaudevillian turns, he began
his three-hour tour de force with a characteristically lengthy and dramatic pause
at the podium. "Our responsibility as artists is to ask questions," he began. "To say,
'What is it?' and not to say what something is." Looking back on his work, he continued, there were three primary influences. And the first of these was dance.

Now, I am not interested in resurrecting the brouhaha sparked by Arlene
Croce's comment, in a 1980 *New Yorker* article, that Wilson was mentor to avant-
garde choreographers such as Lucinda Childs, Andy DeGroat, Meredith Monk,
and Kenneth King. What seems more apt today, given the trajectory of Wilson's
twenty-year career (from untrained performers to professionals, from low-tech
to high-tech, from nonverbal performances to canonical plays), is his connection
to classical dance, with its emphasis on technique and form.

Wilson recalls going to the New York City Ballet not long after he arrived in
Brooklyn in 1963 to study architecture at Pratt Institute. He attended Broadway
theater and opera, and disliked both. "Then I went to see the work of George
Balanchine, and I liked that very much. I go back, and it still fascinates me. One
reason is because of the space that Mr. Balanchine created—the physical space, the
virtual space, the mental space." Having been fascinated with architecture, music,

and pattern since childhood, Wilson particularly admired Balanchine's abstract works. "With Balanchine, I could see the architecture, the pattern being arranged in space. And I could listen to the music. I could see and hear easily. I liked the way the performers danced. They didn't push too hard, or insist too much.

"Later, I saw the work of Merce Cunningham and John Cage, and I liked that very much also, because they were classical artists and their constructions were classical." As with Balanchine, Wilson enjoyed the distinction between the visual and the aural. "What I saw was what I saw," he recalled. "What I heard was what I heard." He found in their collaborations what he seeks to achieve in his own: visual and aural texts that "counterpoint each other without destroying one another." For Wilson, counterpoint produces clarity.

Typically, as with the Stein/Thomson *Four Saints in Three Acts,* Wilson listens to the music, reads the libretto, and then puts it away. He beings work in the theater by choreographing the movement/lights/set apart from the music and words, and then assigning numbers to this visual text. Only then does he listen closely to the music, matching up the numbers of the visual score with the music and words. At this point, unlike Cage/Cunningham, Wilson does consciously edit the mise-en-scène so that it supports and reinforces the libretto without becoming illustration.

At its best, Wilson's work opens up a space—a fluid, playful, sensuous space—for the viewer to move around in. For me, this is its fundamental distinction from traditionally linear and narrative theater, which largely closes off the production from any intervention by the spectator. Wilson achieves his effect by conceiving of a production as structured by two independent but overlapping grids, the audio and visual, that he visualizes by placing one hand atop the other, with his spread-out fingers cross-hatching each other. The two layers of screens can be diametrically opposed, or lined up, or shifted, coming in and out of focus. "If you think of it in terms of a silent movie, then you can imagine the text or score, but if you hear a radio drama you're free to imagine the picture to some extent. Imagine putting those two together so that your audiovisual screens are boundless."

One of the problems with Western theater, he says, is that the two frames become defined, limited, and bounded by literature. Traditionally, the theatrical language of movement, lighting, and scenery has been considered mere decoration, subservient to the literary text. "But when we look at the history of theater, when we look at cultures outside of our own, we see that it's not necessarily the case. We look at Africa, South America, Indonesia, the Far East, we see that they have developed a language that is notated, recorded, learned, and it's visual—the movement of an eye, the movement of a finger."

Wilson is very interested in the classical theater of Japan, whose highly theatricalized movement style can be discerned in some of Wilson's recent work. In the middle of a fourteenth- or fifteenth-century narrative Noh play, he explains, "there can be a section in the middle that is purely abstract, that has absolutely no meaning. And that's what you have in Shakespeare. Or Molière. Sections that have absolutely no meaning. You just do the thing. It's so incomprehensible in some ways for us to do something that has no meaning. If you do, you're [considered to be] neglecting your intellectual responsibilities."

Although Wilson in recent years has undertaken the direction of "straight" plays (which he liberally edits) by the likes of Shakespeare, Ibsen, and Euripides, the body remains the center of his practice. ("You have to know your body," he says. "I learned about my body when I started painting and making drawings.") Words, however, are not primary, but only another layer of text in the mise-en-scène. And, in cases such as Ibsen's *When We Dead Awaken* (1991), the slipping and sliding between the verbal and the nonverbal make the spectator's space that much more exciting. Wilson negotiates this tension between the verbal and the nonverbal masterfully. I think it fairly significant in this regard that he stuttered as a child, and that it was a dance teacher, Bird Hoffmann, after whom he named his Byrd Hoffman Foundation, who cured him. It was Wilson's body, then, that delivered him into language.

"One has to start with the body," he tells the students in the workshop. "It is our instrument." Whether his performers are actors, dancers, or singers, Wilson, who taught classes in body movement and awareness in the 1960s, does not approach things any differently. "Theater is about one thing first. A continuous line."

Training, Wilson insists, must begin with technique. He talks often about performers whose technique he admires—Marlene Dietrich ("A woman who didn't need to sing with her arms. . . . She knew how to stand!"), Jessye Norman, Honi Coles, Lucinda Childs ("She's even more interesting now in *Einstein on the Beach* than she was in '76"), and Jack Benny (Wilson loves the timing of vaudeville actors' verbal patter). What he finds "interesting" (an adjective he is fond of) is a performer who can maintain a certain distance from her material.

Ballet dancers, too, figure prominently in his conversation. "Sylvie Guillem," he says, "has the same kind of remove as Suzanne Farrell, but not as soft—colder, harder. A certain strength, very intense." He says that Guillem, who played the title role in Wilson's *Le Martyre de Saint-Sébastien* (1988) for the Paris Opera, is "my kind of dancer." Which means, he explains, very, very cold. "It's something inside of her that you can't ever put your finger on, like Allegra Kent." Strange, he says, terrifying. It is clear that what draws him to performers is what he aims to achieve with his productions: a kind of surface impenetrability that suggests the mastery of the depths within. "The mystery," as he likes to say, "is in the surface."

Besides *Saint-Sébastien,* Wilson has received other requests to set dances, which, he admits, "is not what I do best." He has been asked to do *Swan Lake* in Florence and to make dances in East Berlin and Rome. The *Swan Lake* idea intrigues him—maybe, he muses, with a new text by his sometime collaborator, Berlin playwright Heiner Müller. Already in the works is a film project with Trisha Brown.

It is walking, Wilson insists, that is the most difficult thing to do onstage. So when he auditions performers, he likes to see two things—walking (a short distance sustained for an extended period of time) and sitting in a chair. He can tell "everything" from a walk—balance, use of weight, sense of timing. In workshop, the performers are called "walkers," presumably since they execute the movement without singing or speaking lines. At UT walkers were admonished to walk correctly.

"Don't walk with the beat. Walk against it."

"Be calm. Contained. Be careful about swinging your arms. Remember, walking onstage is not running to the cafeteria. It's a different awareness. About the line of the body. The placement of the fingers."

The director wants one continuous line, unbroken by bounces or awkward adjustments. (The way I see it, Wilson's performers need to be connected fully, with the pelvis coordinating seamless shifts of weight.) As one walker takes her cue, he has her repeat it several times, until he can no longer see an obvious initiation. "How do you turn to get your balance," he asks her. "Shift your weight to one foot, control the line with the other foot, so you don't jerk. And don't swing your arms." The result, in production, is the impression that movement, if it is never seen to begin, has never ended. In this way, the bodies onstage participate in the same mythic sense of timeless time that the lighting and moving scenery possess.

"There's no such thing as no movement," Wilson declares flatly. "The balance between tension and relaxation in standing is all movement. The movement of the hand is only a continuation of the movement that's already there. You see movement more when [the body] is *not* moving."

Wilson's commitment to body movement as a crucial subliminal element in the process of communication was greatly influenced by the mother-infant films of child psychiatrist Daniel N. Stern, who became a familiar face at Wilson's loft gatherings in the 1960s. Despite the mothers' professed and unquestioned love for their infants, the films of mothers tending to their crying babies, when slowed down, registered aggressive lunges unapparent in the interactions seen at regular speed. The screeching response of the babies was to the mothers' physical lunging, not to the soothing speech. Movement, then, adds another layer to what is normally accepted as the transparent meaning of words.

Naturalism, as Wilson often says, is a lie. "My theater is a theater of formalism. The movement style is somehow both neutral and stylized at the same time. The neutral face is already complicated," he tells the walkers. "It tells so many stories." *Four Saints* is impossible, he says, to do naturalistically. "The only way to think about it, to me, is dance. For me, all theater is dance, whether you're performing in a naturalistic or psychological way. It's all dance. Maybe this production is 'more dance.'"

In workshop, Wilson seems to generate movement in three modes. First, he choreographs intuitively, within his own vocabulary, which emphasizes gross motor patterns such as flexions of the joints, bending from the waist, walking, sitting, standing, turning, gesturing. (He directs from a desk out in the theater: "David, sit down. With your legs out in front of you. Turn on a diagonal. Open your legs up more. Put your arms in back of you.") The prologue to *Four Saints* also included a number of references to kabuki (an *onnogata* walk and the wide, strapping walk of the *roppo* style) as well as gestures (like a single finger pointing upward) taken from the iconography of saints. Wilson sees the stage architecturally, and the performer's bodies are often used as a diagonal foil to its insistent horizontal and vertical dimensions. Whole bodies take on a lunge, or arms stretch toward a corner of the proscenium.

Second, he uses "chance," and his directions become more open-ended: "Everyone who's standing on a red line, sidestep as far as you can to the side of the stage. Everyone take seven steps in any direction (but don't hit the tree). Everyone change direction. Everyone change direction again. Everyone go to a partner. Everyone change partners. . . . All the women standing who were born on an odd day, sit down."

Third, when he has enough time, he has the performers improvise, and makes drawings of what they have done in order to help structure the piece.

All this raw material is videotaped and scrupulously notated by an assistant director. When the movement of the bodies, light, and scenery is performed alongside the music and singing, "then I'll find there are some strange accidents I never would have thought about. Sometimes they work and sometimes they don't, and then I go back and correct. So it's not like what Merce and John do. Mine is more of a critical selection. It's not arbitrary."

Once the form is set, it is up to the performers to make it live, and Wilson's paradoxical demand for a fully present but yet distanced performance style is crucial to the success of a production. (It remained elusive for Richard Thomas in his performance of the title role in the 1992 *Danton's Death* in Houston.) Much like Balanchine, who exhorted his dances not to express themselves, but just to do the steps, Wilson, too, believes that form executed faithfully transcends mere technique. Precision begets freedom. "The only way to beat the machine," he reasons, "is to be mechanical." The performance style he is after is functional, he says, but not *just* functional. "With Shakespeare and Mozart, the music is there. You can't make music with it. How you do it is simple. To make music out of it is false. You have to play every note so clear and so simple. This is formal theater, but form is boring. When you see a ballet by Balanchine, it's classical construction. He died in 1983. He made over four hundred ballets. Fifty will be around years from now. The reason they will be around is that it's classical construction and form in terms of its architecture.

"You can analyze and figure out the construction. That's interesting to a point. But it's what you do within the form. That's what's important. It's what you're feeling about what you're doing that makes it special. Too much theater today is too intellectual. There's too much thinking going on. What's important is what you experience, what you feel. No one can ever tell you the structure of your space—how you move through it. That's real. I can respond authentically."

—*DanceView*, 1993–94

Darkness into Light
A Decade in the West Transforms a Butoh Troupe

B UTOH HIT New York in the fall of 1985, like a thunderbolt from the gods. Tanztheater also took hold that season, and critics and choreographers were forced, kicking and screaming, to reconsider expressionism.

Both forms of dance—one incubated in postwar Japan, the other in post-Adenauer Germany—wrestled with demons internal, external, and existential. Butoh, with its contorted, oozing, naked bodies, expressed its suffering and joy through the grotesque. *Anokoku butoh,* as founder Tatsumi Hijikata named it, was literally a "dance of darkness," developed not as a technique or a vocabulary to be mastered but as a practice to be lived. For Hijikata, butoh was a transgressive gesture, one that aimed to surpass, and displace, the limits of acceptable social behavior.

But Hijikata died in 1986, before his planned American debut. Today, butoh has become another dance technique—the *butoh* (dance) without the *anokoku* (darkness). You can sign up for a workshop in butoh almost as easily as you can one in contact improvisation. Min Tanaka, who worked closely with Hijikata, has felt the need to renounce—if only rhetorically—any connection with "butoh" as it has evolved in the West.

Tanaka's improvisatory work is still raw and gritty, still focused on the moment of performance as a space of transformation, still opting for "freedom" over "beauty." After his 15 October performance of *I . . . Sit* at P.S. 122, Tanaka took questions from the SRO audience. Asked about the presence of the butoh tradition in his solo, Tanaka bristled. "People want to fix it. Why? It's good for making money. It's good for teaching."

But is it good for what Hijikata called the "unlimited power of butoh," its "hidden violence"?

Of the half-dozen or so butoh groups to appear in New York during the form's heyday in the mid-1980s, Sankai Juku has become the most popular. The five-member company is in the midst of an eighteen-city U.S. and Canadian tour, performing *Yuragi: In a Space of Perpetual Motion* (1993), the sixth of seven commissions garnered from the Theatre de la Ville, a key player in the increasingly institutionalized international touring circuit. It continues at the Brooklyn Academy of Music 14–16 November.

Yuragi has been described by *Seattle Times* critic Jean Lenthan as "a satisfying, highly accessible blend" of "dancerly phrases" and trademark butoh. She sees in it shades of Martha Graham and Trisha Brown, and the "haunted open-mouth expressions" she finds "downright pleasurable."

This taming of the inscrutable and therefore dangerous Other has been crucial to Sankai Juku's success in the West. (In 1990, a *New York Newsday* headline on a review of Sankai Juku's *Unetsu* proclaimed gleefully, "Buto Takes a Western Step at Last.") Almost from the beginning, during the company's second American tour, artistic director Ushio Amagatsu proved quite savvy, staging for the media in every city an outdoor performance (which read more like a daredevil stunt) in which the dancers descended long ropes. In Seattle, one performer plunged to his death.

Typically, *Yuragi* reads as "beautiful," a stage picture whose elegant production values are mesmerizing. The internal impulse has become theatricalized, the grotesque banished. The *difference* of butoh has been erased: it has become another Western spectacle, like ballet, in which audiences can admire the decor or gasp at the technique. There remains just enough of the "exotic" (bald heads, powdered bodies) to arouse an appetite.

"But please be careful," Tanaka has warned his audience, "not to become an easygoing fan."

—*Village Voice,* 1996

Finding the Logic of Difference

THE ALTOGETHER DIFFERENT series at New York's Joyce Theater boasts a respected history. Since 1986, the 472-seat, dance-only house has presented the almost-new-and-noteworthy. Its purpose is "to encourage the growth of talented artists by offering them a chance to expand their audiences and perform in a larger space." Physically, geographically, and economically, the Joyce is a halfway-house coming between the downtown scene, with its small, rough-and-tumble venues such as P.S. 122, La Mama, and the Ohio Theatre, and the "official" uptown gargantuans such as City Center Theater and Lincoln Center.

For the New York dance community, the series has become an institution. We trudge to the bright marquee in the dead of January, that dull interlude between the fall and winter seasons, to look at what's "hot," in a slicker venue than the downtown haunts (where we discover what's actually new). Among the festival's seventy-plus alumni: Ann Carlson, Jane Comfort, Molissa Fenley, Joe Goode, Ralph Lemon, Bebe Miller, and Stephen Petronio.

Tuesday, 7 January

THIS YEAR I sleuth for *Dance Theatre Journal.* My assignment: to find the source of dance's new impetus. The time: 7–26 January. The evidence: seven companies performing in rotation; nine world premieres.

Poppo and the GoGo Boys are well known from their butoh-inspired performances in the 1980s downtown club scene. A new company called Complexions—A Concept in Dance suggests a multicultural agenda. Shapiro & Smith Dance are a husband-wife team who danced with Alwin Nikolais and Murray Louis. Former Cunningham dancer Neil Greenberg formed his company, Dance by Neil Greenberg, in 1986. There's another choreographic duo: Sara Pearson/Patrik Widrig & Co. Neta Pulvermacher, artistic director of Neta Pulvermacher & Dancers, and Zvi Gotheiner, artistic director of Zvi Gotheiner and Dancers, both grew up on a kibbutz in Israel.

Thursday, 9 January

THE COMPANY's two-tiered name says it all. Complexions is not about dance, but about its subheading: A Concept in Dance. "Dance is a universal language—a means to communicate human emotions, concerns, outlooks and experiences," writes co-artistic director and former Ailey principal Dwight Rhoden. This naively well-meaning, but ill-wrought, evening featured five dances (*Gravel,* an excerpt from *Fractal Boundaries, Diction, Cake* and *Ave Maria*) and consisted of men's puffed-up chests, women's long legs, and more awkwardly labyrinthine limb-limning and butt shots than I've ever seen on a legitimate stage. I want to call it "muscle ballet." It seemed like so much effort just to mimic sex—and in an absurdly outdated, unintentionally parodic way. Why don't they just have it off for real? I began to suspect that might be more interesting.

Even before reading the bios, I could tell that somebody had seen too much William Forsythe. It turned out to be co-artistic director Desmond Richardson, formerly with the Alvin Ailey American Dance Theater and more recently with the Frankfurt Ballet. The company is long on postmodernish styling (smart costuming, pseudo-smart texts, fragmentation, hip attitude, white-noise "music," and hyperclassicism), but short on choreographic skill and conceptual depth.

Friday, 10 January

I'VE BEEN considering: although its reach far outstrips its grasp, Complexions does at least attempt to connect with life in 1997. American culture has become visual/virtual. Fashion designers are our culture heroes, and everyday dressing constitutes conceptual art for the masses. Designers are artists, artists are theorists. Films and magazines reign supreme. Even the *New York Times'* surprisingly hip new advertising campaign trades in the exchange of visual and verbal slippage (a pretty ironic move for the "paper of record"). Postmodernism is no longer an abstract term, some academic flotsam. It's a lifestyle—a dense, kinetic, complex approach/response to the seduction of surface. The borders between art, life, and entertainment have been liberated.

As a whole, New York's Western concert dance community (which still prevails, barely) feels like a twilight zone, bizarrely unaffected by the changing buzz of the world. I find it increasingly difficult to sit through concerts of "pure" dance whose modernist certainty about the transparency of abstract bodily expression is neither relevant nor tenable.

I wish it were. I wish that I could find the same pleasure in Molissa Fenley and Sally Gross, for example, as I did ten years ago. I wish Western concert dance had the cultural vibrancy it did thirty years ago. But dance has fallen behind art, film, print, and fashion, and now cyberspace, holding on to its long-lost authority over a body that "never lies." Well, the dancing body may lie or not—it doesn't much matter if no one is paying attention.

Sunday, 12 January

I ADMIRE the husband-wife team of Danial Shapiro and Joanie Smith, if for no other reason than that they have managed to forge their own choreographic voices after years of performing the specific, embedded aesthetic of Nikolais and Louis. Leaving visual abstraction behind, they investigate emotions and relationships. The matinee started with the premiere of *Piano,* a luscious, quiet, three-part duet to Erik Satie; continued with *What Dark/Falling into Light* (1996), a psychologically intense ensemble piece, featuring a Stein-like spoken text; and ended with *Never Enough* (1992), a black comedy about childhood terrors ("ogre mothers and fractured fairy tales"). In these last two highly theatricalized pieces, the choreographers demonstrate lessons well-learned from their mentors about the theatrical effectiveness of light and scene design.

After Complexions, this comparatively innocuous concert granted me physical relief. Here is solid craftsmanship, some moments even hitting a poetic note. But as a whole, it was a throwback—past Louis and Nikolais—to the dance that comes "from the inside out." The duet belongs to the familiar you-me-us, heterosexual "relationship" genre. The two ensemble works explore a dark vision of life, one from a private perspective, the other from a social perspective.

It is the kind of modernist art that implicitly connects its spectacle with the moral. It says, "Here I am showing you the difficulties of life, the dark side of life, so that we may better understand." We don't necessarily connect with it emotionally, although that is the apparent hook. Its power, if any, is an intellectual, even didactic one because of its distanced theatrical style.

But the well-made dance leaves me parched, still thirsty for more.

Wednesday, 15 January

ZVI GOTHEINER typifies the phenomenon of international modernism. Originally from Israel, he lands in New York in 1977 and his studies run the gamut—ballet, Graham, Ailey. Goes on to dance with Joyce Trisler, Feld Ballets/NY, Garden State Ballet, Bat-Sheva, and so on. Founds his own company in 1989 and travels round the world to teach.

So, what happens when you add-and-stir? Soup, judging from the dances I saw last night: excerpts from *Solos for Men to Scarlatti* (1996); *Oh, Moon of Alabama* (1997); and *Lash* (1996). Although Gotheiner works in a distinct style (luscious, curvaceous movement that suited Scarlatti—that suite of solos looked like a successful male update of Isadora Duncan—but completely missed the point of Kurt Weill), it's a single flavor, without undertones, that quickly exhausts its appeal. And when Gotheiner adds his dash of pantomimic gesture, it leaves a sour aftertaste.

I went home despairing: how is it possible to move today? Certainly not as if there is no world beyond the fire wall.

After a performance several weeks ago, Bill T. Jones was asked what he looks for in a dancer. "A dancer," he replied, "who is convincing in her physicality." The implication of Jones's analysis gives lie to the seductive, but fallacious, notion that all movement is valuable because, since the body does not lie, all bodily behavior is therefore "truthful" and, by extension, valid. The dancing body does lie, all the time, most noticeably when it has been borrowed, adapted, or inherited uncritically.

So the question remains: what makes a dancer, or a choreographer, convincing?

Thursday, 16 January

THIS MORNING I charged out of the elevator into the lobby, headlong into a large pushcart piled with old toilets. I flashbacked to the opening image in last night's performance by Poppo and the GoGo Boys (which now has plenty of GoGo girls, too): gleaming porcelain bowls scattered across the stage, a dancer perched upon each.

If Gotheiner's dance flows unmistakably from the dance-to-the-music genre of modern dance, Poppo Shiraishi's springs just as obviously from the anti-tradition tradition of butoh.

The five-part *Crazy Me, Crazy You* (1997), a series of visions, or vignettes, reaches for the transcendent through absurdity, juxtaposition, and the power of performative presence. Ten years ago, Poppo's raw-edged mix of Japanese metaphysics and downtown hip sparkled (literally: gold body paint remains his trademark). Last night, the magic didn't happen. Maybe it was the proscenium stage space, maybe the lack of depth in his performers, maybe our image-saturated world, which leaves little margin for error in this kind of work. I don't know. In any case, butoh proves to be just as vulnerable to the shifting sands of culture as any other aging dance form.

Friday, 17 January

NEIL GREENBERG is the real thing: a thoughtful, playful, skilled, imaginative choreographer who loves to move, and who has followed his own path. The result is plenty convincing.

Three dances formed tonight's evening-length trilogy: Greenberg's solo from *Not-About-AIDS-Dance* (1994), *The Disco Project* (1995), and the premiere of *Part Three (My Fair Lady)*.

All share a movement vocabulary set forth in the opening solo, a fitful internal monologue of remembrance, longing, and confusion, concerned with loss and survival. By contrasting abstract movement with verbal commentary (projected on slides, like the intertitles in silent movies) and silence with music, the solo's subtle, sophisticated choreographic structure literally embodies the condition of absence, void, and especially interruption.

The effect of the dances depends upon spaciousness, in every sense of the word. Each one spreads out in time and around the stage (dancers even come and sit at the edge of the stage, their legs dangling). The preliminary silence, which seems to go on forever when you're expecting to hear disco or tunes from *My Fair Lady,* sets up the sense of longing, or punctuated stillness, that is the foundation of the work.

A complex layering of anticipation, loss, and grief accumulates as the music drops in and out in unpredictable intervals, as blackouts further protract the sense of time, and as the self-referential texts introduce a specificity of emotional narrative that shrinks the distance between me and the performers. (The projected texts include sentences such as: "This is the song that was big the summer my brother died"; "We set out to have fun"; "Time for Neil's big solo.")

But exuberant dancing leaks out of the silence. Greenberg's solos are the showstoppers. He swishes through the romantic Broadway numbers and pumps through that disco as if his life depended on it. And, of course, it does: as the intertitles reveal, he is HIV-positive. He throws himself into the music with an irresistible abandon bordering on camp, his head tossed back like Duncan and Dionysus. His is an ecstatic body, outside itself, reaching beyond its own mortality.

Saturday, 18 January

LAST NIGHT, as Judy and I practically skipped down Eighth Avenue from the theater to the subway, I was giddy with the lyrics of Lerner and Loewe.

"Why can't all choreographers," I adapted Professor Higgins's earnest words, "be like Neil Greenberg?"

"That isn't quite right," Judy replied. "Not all choreographers should be like Neil Greenberg."

"Of course," I said, and tried again. "Why can't all choreographers make us feel as good as Neil Greenberg?"

Judy helped to round off the line, her voice considerably closer to pitch than mine.

Why, indeed. It wasn't that Greenberg gave us a "feel good" evening, although he certainly did choose music with immediate metakinetic power. On the contrary, I was stricken during his "Never Can Say Goodbye" solo. Loss infused the entire concert.

What Greenberg gave us was depth of experience (not necessarily feeling) and complexity of experience. Pathos infused with irony, the intellect's sense of humor. He made his points through the language of the stage, straight through the muscle memory of dancing disco and singing along with "My Fair Lady."

That makes the difference—whether a show aims for my head or seeps through my pores. How did Antonin Artaud put it? "In our present state of degeneration it is through the skin that metaphysics must be made to re-enter our minds."

Sunday, 19 January

I THOUGHT Bill T. Jones and Arnie Zane were the only two guys crazy enough to tackle choreography as a collaborative effort, and the Joyce brings me not one but two more teams.

Sara Pearson and Patrik Widrig's concert last night actually pulled me forward in my seat. His solo, *Muezzin* (1997), to live Arabic singing, and their joint ensemble work, *Ordinary Festivals* (1995), a paean to the sorrows and joys of community ritual via oranges and Italian folk music, were a delight.

But Pearson's solo, *Dr. Pearson's Guide to Loss and Fear* (premiere), kept me rapt. With a deftly spun blanket of movement and words, including a running dialogue between Pearson-the-patient and Pearson-the-German-accented-psychoanalyst, she caresses and tickles all our sensitive spots, where the fear of loss threatens to overcome us. The piece is so intelligent, so funny, so deeply human, so, well, profound.

But it doesn't break new formal ground (the talking/moving solo is the warhorse of post-postmodernism), or directly engage with the upheaval of life in the face of the millennium, as I've been ranting on about. Pearson's dance suggests to me that I've been misdirected: it's not necessarily the artistic forms that are failing us, but the artistic imagination. Self-involvement, or self-deception, does not substitute for self-scrutiny. Is that what it takes to be convincing?

Monday, 20 January

THE MORE company bios I read, the more revealing they become. What am I being told? Not much about what a company stands for, aesthetically or otherwise. But a lot about which institutions are considered to legitimize the company's existence: funders, producers, and presenters. It's about economic validation.

Tuesday, 21 January

WHAT ARE the odds that oranges would play the leading role in two programs? Pretty darned long, I'd bet.

But there they were, this time set to Schumann, if you can imagine, by Neta Pulvermacher. A tepid program. Dancers who perform the groove, but never actually jump into it. (The convincing thing again.)

Altogether Different bows out with a whimper.

Friday, 24 January

THE DOWNTOWN buzz on Altogether Different has been low and grumbly, despite the merrily sold-out houses. Located in Chelsea, a freshly gentrified neighborhood filled with relocated Soho galleries, chic restaurants, and a flourishing gay community, the Joyce Theater consistently attracts a healthy number of well-made suits, as well as blue-rinsed hairdos on weekend matinees. It's gratifying that the city's most prominent dance-only theater is packing 'em in.

But I wonder to what extent economic necessity has influenced the programming decisions for this year's Altogether Different season, whose stated goal, since 1986, has been "to present exceptionally talented artists in the process of developing and expanding their companies and audiences." And who presumably will become successful enough, with the aid of the administrative seminars provided as part of Altogether Different, to book the Joyce for their future self-produced seasons.

Except for Greenberg's program, Altogether Different was not at all. Different, that is. But neither was much else I've seen in New York this year, no matter whether the production was shoestring chic or extravagantly funded (Karole Armitage's Michael Milken ballet springs to mind).

I don't think that tells us as much about choreographers as it does about the state of American culture, which is to say, the state of capitalism. Most concerts in New York are driven by the need to offer a product that, if properly marketed by the critics (whose own role in the system has been hopelessly perverted), will draw enough of a paying audience to land the next gig. In the meantime, choreographers and performers are working maniacally at whatever flextime jobs will pay the absurd rent bills.

The 1960s avant-garde—those years of exuberant experimentation—is long dead. The price of living in New York City is just too high for art really to be the center of an artistic community. Government and private funding used to take enough of the edge off, but now that's all but disappeared.

Life outside New York, from Philadelphia to Austin to Seattle, offers more freedom for artists to make work driven by reflection and necessity. And more and more national and international productions tour the university circuit outside New York before being imported here. In the meantime, the New York season continues to limp along, and I continue to search for something "altogether different."

—*Dance Theatre Journal,* 1997

Dancing: A Letter from New York City

ME AND JULIA Kristeva are feeling glum about culture these days.

Here in Manhattan at the height of the fall 1996 season, delivering a lecture on the occasion of the "Antonin Artaud: Works on Paper" exhibit at the Museum of Modern Art, Kristeva began by describing a television program she had recently viewed, a documentary on political, sexual, and artistic movements since the 1960s. She recalled both the hope and desperation that constituted the transformative moment of 1968: "A time paved with fear, but that paved the way."[1] In contrast, she saw the punk and skinhead images of the 1980s as conventional, despite their purported radicalism. "I saw neither experiment nor fervor," she explained, "but fragmentation, posturing, fear, and anguish."

Kristeva went on to argue that Artaud was able to offer up himself as a "guardian" in "the liberating transformation of the subject and of society," because he was situated within the twentieth-century "culture of revolt," which is enacted by artists in a tragic encounter with "the wish of freedom." But, according to Kristeva, that era of revolutionary potential died with the 1960s, when the desire to satisfy consumer needs displaced that "wish of freedom." Describing our present moment as "a low point" in human history, she offered little optimism: "The simple fact that we can still speak of Artaud," she concluded, "while trying not to enclose him within the context of these years . . . and the simple fact of our own meeting this evening means, perhaps, that the culture of revolt still has a chance. Maybe later. In the meantime, it's something to think about."

Whether or not Kristeva is wholly correct in her dour diagnosis (one could argue that consumer desire overtook American culture as early as the 1920s, but, then again, her periodization of the "culture of revolt" from the late nineteenth century to the 1960s accurately charts the rise and fall of the avant-garde), it still provides the perfect frame for my reflections on the 1996/1997 dance season. Kristeva's gloominess resonates in the disappointment that I feel, returned to New York after a seven-year hiatus, toward a tepid dance community whose cultural isolation seems to be accelerating in direct relation to its desire for market share.

At a time when Kmart fashion, the redesign of the Coca-Cola can, and the Broadway debut of *Men Are from Mars, Women Are from Venus* by author John Gray are big news, even at the *New York Times,* dance slips further and further from the flow of American culture, which, like it or not, is vibrantly pop. At the same time that choreographers, producers, and critics strain to attract an audience with slick packaging techniques tweaked from street cool, the dance performances themselves remain aloof. When choreographers do try to connect, it is more often about style (the staples of 1980s performance—sex, violence, autobiography—have all been absorbed into style) than genuine engagement.

Dance, like any art, is not an amorphous "scene," as journalist parlance has it; rather, it is a mappable community of communities, with identifiable members, institutions, and practices. Today, dance is defined primarily by its producing institutions. You hear more about P.S. 122, BAM (the Brooklyn Academy of Music), and DTW (Dance Theater Workshop) than you do about any choreographer, company, teacher, technique, critic, or style. There are certainly no new artistic "movements" afoot. Symptomatically, program biographies supply nary a clue about a choreographer's aesthetics or concerns but scrupulously catalog the funders, producers, and presenters who have granted their imprimatur.

With studio and performance space at a premium, choreographers rely upon producing institutions rather than self-production in order to deliver their work to the public. In turn, the producing institutions depend upon market-driven strategies to make up for the loss of government funding, which, while never adequate, was at least helpful. The twenty-year-old P.S. 122, for example, received nearly $79,000 in government funding in 1993, but next year it will receive nothing. Similarly, the twenty-five-year-old Kitchen was granted no support from the National Endowment for the Arts for next year, after banner years such as 1983, when it received $442,300.[2]

The "festival" has become the standard gambit. The original cool-hunter was BAM, whose fall Next Wave festival set the pace in the mid-1980s; the Joyce Theater's Altogether Different festival picks up the slack every January, in that cold spot between the fall and spring seasons; most recently, Lincoln Center has assembled its own summer extravaganza.

The once-prescient Next Wave festival, afforded by the 1980s affair between Wall Street and SoHo, this season offered familiar formulas: the bankrupt extravaganza of Karole Armitage's *The Predators' Ball: Hucksters of the Soul;* Susan Marshall, a solid oldie-but-goodie; Donald Byrd's *Harlem Nutcracker,* a transparent attempt to cash in on the notorious success of *The Hard Nut,* Mark Morris's 1992 Nutcracker parody; the also-ran tanztheater of former Pina Bausch dancer Meryl Tankard; and Sankai Juku's tamed butoh. The delights were less frequent: Trisha Brown's twenty-fifth anniversary celebration, and Zingaro, the French equestrian theater troupe.

How can I justify my response to *Chimère,* Zingaro's "collaboration" with musicians and dancers from Rajasthan? Despite every crass Orientalist trick pulled by "Bartabas," the self-named artistic director, and despite every obvious circus stage business he exploited, I could not resist the purity of his theatricality: the deployment of bodies (whether animal or human) through time and space. (I felt the same physical elation during the Wooster Group's *The Hairy Ape;* even when my interest in the arcane agitprop narrative faltered, the depth of aural, kinetic, and visual forces buoyed me.) And the climactic solo—when the man Bartabas and his horse become one—was some of the most poignant dancing of the season.

Trisha Brown's jam session with Steve Paxton on the BAM Opera House stage easily could have turned nostalgic, but the stunning new dances that followed their duet marked Brown as an innovator who has managed to maintain her center while moving forward. Although the trappings may appear different, the Judson choreographer is still conducting the same physics experiment, begun decades ago when she walked down the side of a building and around the walls of a room. It is Brown's peculiar talent to demonstrate, with lush physicality, how the structure of space/time teeters at the edge of visibility, and to capture the little gaps where it falls into view.

Neil Greenberg was the bright light in the otherwise dim Altogether Different festival. Located in Chelsea, a recently gentrified neighborhood filled with relocated SoHo galleries, chic restaurants, and a flourishing gay community, the

Joyce Theater consistently attracts an audience wearing well-cut suits. Physically, geographically, and economically, the 472-seat theater, used for dance exclusively, is literally a halfway-house between downtown's small, rough-and-tumble venues such as P.S. 122, La Mama, and the Ohio Theatre, and the "official" uptown gargantuans such as City Center and Lincoln Center. Judging from the choice of the Altogether Different participants—who were, with more or less success, retreading old artistic ground—the Joyce festival has embraced its middling comfort zone.

The market mentality is supported not only by the production machine, but also by criticism, whose journalistic institutions and genres are little respected anymore. Preview features, functionally speaking, are unpaid advertising, which producers and choreographers consider a means of filling seats. Reviews are press kit fodder, which choreographers abide as a necessary evil for securing their next grant or commission. Previews remain at the level of reportage; reviews are either descriptive or evaluative. Rarely is dance discussed as part of a cultural conversation beyond the studio or the stage. And when it is, the topic is money: the Martha Graham Dance Company's fund-raising crisis, Paul Taylor's face-off with Musician's Union 802, the Kitchen's precarious future.[3] Or the topic is sports. The first suggestion of the *Village Voice*'s new editor-in-chief to dance editor Elizabeth Zimmer was a story on the top-ten asses in the NBA.[4] A few months later, the *Voice* devoted its special dance section to sports—an old ploy for convincing the masses that dance isn't sissy after all. Apparently, it failed. A few months later, the already-meager space allotted to dance was reduced to a single page.

Conspicuously absent from the season was the Pina Bausch Tanztheater Wuppertal, a staple of BAM's Next Wave festival since the mid-1980s, which bypassed New York on its first American tour. The company took *Nur Du* (Only You) to four southwest cities (Los Angeles, Berkeley, Tempe, and Austin), where educational and cultural institutions co-produced the new work, which was workshopped at the University of California at Los Angeles. Inflected by American source imagery (pop tunes, a redwood grove, Hollywood stars, fast food, a cheerleader) and a deeper sense of American rhythm and energy, the three-and-a-half-hour revue playfully and mournfully explored, once again, Bausch's obsessive question: Why do fools fall in love?

The *Nur Du* tour is indicative of the move toward decentralization. Top- and middle-level companies are producing and premiering more work out-of-town, through the patronage of an increasingly savvy and ambitious national network of university and community presenters. (I saw Urban Bush Women's *Bones and Ash—A Gilda Story,* for example, in San Antonio, Texas, six months before its New York premiere in November.) And not only are premieres dispersing from New

York, but so are the dancers and choreographers. The cost of living and making dance in New York is so high that art has been displaced by economics as the center of its artistic community. Life outside New York, from Philadelphia to Austin to Seattle, offers an appealingly cheaper and simpler (if not more lucrative) setting for artists to make work driven by internal, rather than external, forces.

Tanztheater, for all the critical furor and audience enthusiasm it provoked here a decade ago, has left only the slightest dents in homegrown dance; however, the dance theater aesthetic still permeates the European imports. The best of the season was Les Ballets C. de la B., from Ghent, Belgium, whose *La Tristeza Complice* (The Shared Sorrow) exhibited a compelling cast of social misfits acting out with and on each other in a London underground station.

Overall, the season was a matter of déjà vu. Too many of the names were familiar, and if the names weren't, the work—warmed-over postmodernism—was. It is unpleasantly ironic that dance is so complacent at a time when "the body" is so provocative, at least in theory. Too many of even the freshest faces were working in a conventional formalist mode, which, although radical thirty-five years ago, has hardened into formula: these young choreographers seem to have learned their lessons too well, both from the old masters and from college dance teachers. (Of notable exception is the way that Philadelphia's Headlong Dance Theatre, which appeared at both P.S. 122 and DTW, squints sideways at traditional postmodernism and makes it grin.) While most performances aimed either toward the physical ("movement exploration") or the intellectual ("identity politics"), very few manage to harness them both. Artaud stands as correct today as he did sixty-five years ago: "In our present state of degeneration it is through the skin that metaphysics must be made to re-enter our minds."[5]

That is an apt description of the best work I saw: dance so physical that it becomes metaphysical—without gimmicks, hype, or spin. (Beware the theoretically hip program note or press release; it usually functions as overcompensation for impoverished choreography.) By "physical" I do not mean extreme exertion, high energy, or technical virtuosity, although those qualities may make an appearance. The choreographers I have in mind—Neil Greenberg (a trilogy at the Joyce Theater), Lance Gries (*Half Life*, presented by Danspace Project in a private SoHo studio), Deborah Hay (*Voilà* at the Kitchen), and John Jasperse (*Waving to you from here* at DTW)—understand that the material expressiveness of the dancing body, in guises ordinary or extraordinary, is a text that already wonders and wishes, whispers and wails. They understand that the dancing body is not a construct (either mental or physical) unto itself but rather is constituted in relation to its environment—to time and space, and to other bodies in time and space, and to the dust balls of life's dramas that cling to every little movement.

Using popular music, a revamped Cunningham-esque vocabulary, and fragments of personal narrative for his trilogy (solo from *Not-About-AIDS-Dance*, *The Disco Project*, and *Part Three [My Fair Lady]*), Greenberg pressed grief and joy through a sophisticated camp sensibility, a strategy capable of embracing the contradiction of those experiences without denying either one its distinctness. Generated by a grid of movement variables displayed on the sidewall of the loft performance space, Gries's *Half Life* hosted a collective of haunted souls perched not so far from the edge of sanity, in a clinical mise-en-scène featuring gleaming gurneys and clanging surgical steel instruments. Hay's concert was an experiment in dance transmission: after she performed her solo *Voilà*, which mined the sublime and absurd powers of exuberant, silly, uncensored movement behavior, it was "repeated" by two other soloists, who, without ever having seen Hay's original, reconstructed their own radical versions from its libretto. Jasperse's *Waving to you from here* was a meditation, quietly but fiercely focused on that place between inside and out where longing and loneliness seed themselves.

Beyond the sanctions of the legitimate stages, the monthly thematic nightclub series called Martha at Mother took a significant, if not entirely serious, hold on downtown dance-makers and -lovers. Each revue-style evening—featuring video by Charles Atlas and live performances on a tiny basement stage—was devoted to a different landmark figure or movement in twentieth-century dance. The April installment, "Martha Meets the Expressionists," featured the Dancenoise duo as Valeska Gert and Hanya Holm; other evenings, filled with performer/choreographers ranging from Molissa Fenley to John Kelly, paid tribute to Nijinsky and to the postmoderns as well. Dragster Richard Move hosted each event as the magnificent modern-dance-diva-turned-emcee, bracing her overwrought monologues, accented by the demonstrative contraction or two, with impeccable dance history. Within this historical frame, the smoky, raucous evenings reached beyond entertainment to community-building. The institutional coherence of the dance community may be threatened on all sides by funding agencies, newspaper editors, landlords, and the academy, but this parodic embrace of tradition, with all its ambivalence toward the remote aptness of the dance avant-garde's own "culture of revolt," uses that past in order to re-create a space of identification (literally, a "club") for the future.

But then, the question needs to be asked: Has this tradition run its course? Is there nothing but the past to embrace? "Western culture," critic Marcia B. Siegel has decided, "is tired. I think it's at a point where it's played out. Or at least this phase of it. . . . [B]allet and modern dance as we've understood it is in a fallow period."[6] But non-Western dance, she quickly added, is a wealth of movement practice yet to be discovered. New York offers so much non-Western performance that I could only skim the surface, choosing in particular the plentiful Korean performances, both traditional and contemporary, presented at venues from the American Museum of Natural History to the Asia Society to the Ohio Theatre. As compatible as avant-garde and world dance viewing practices are,[7] and despite the intense avant-garde interest in non-Western performances, which peaked with the 1990 Los Angeles Festival of the Arts, world dance has not been integrated into the New York dance community, either by choreographers or audiences.

As for Western classical dance, City Ballet-bashing has become a bore, even for the most fundamentalist Balanchine devotees, because it is too easy to be fun anymore. For balletomanes who thrill to the nuances of technique, style, and interpretation, visits from the Pacific Northwest Ballet and Les Ballets de Monte Carlo, both with significant Balanchine repertories, provided the feast for a feeding frenzy. And I admit it: I indulged, just as I eagerly pay the big bucks for the all-Balanchine programs at City Ballet. His dances still make me marvel. Although the out-of-towners lacked the edge and élan of pedigreed Balanchine dancers (who can cop an attitude at top speed, with enough room left over for effortless precision), they offered instead the opportunity to re-view the choreography. Pacific Northwest Ballet's *La Valse,* Balanchine's psychologically noir tale about the temptation and death of a woman in white, prompted me for different questions about the "Balanchine ballerina," this time as a figure yoking sex and death into a phallic dagger, an angel of death. Again, in City Ballet's *Prodigal Son,* and in *La Sonnambula,* it was Balanchine's dark female erotica that suggested a deeper connection with the Freudian complexity of the femme fatale in late-twentieth-century popular culture rather than with the dangerous pleasure of the romantic ballerina. I suspect that the story of Balanchine, now stalled, would gain a new impetus if we reconstructed his context.

Modern masters brought their wares to market, as usual: Alvin Ailey American Dance Theater, Paul Taylor Dance Company (whose embarrassing radio advertisements touted him as the greatest living choreographer), and José Limón Dance Company. Missing in action: the Martha Graham Dance Company and the Merce Cunningham Dance Company, neither of which could afford their annual rites at the City Center.

Times dance critic Anna Kisselgoff, whose eyes are favorably focused uptown on upscale venues such as City Center, penned an uncharacteristically negative midyear lament over the "scattershot and essentially mediocre fall," concluding that dance, as of January 1997, "finds itself in a holding pattern; much of what we saw in the last few months in New York was interesting but not significant." She concluded: "The spectator, faced with this trend toward uniformity and the routine, demands something else. Having been served the blockbuster event, the dance audience expects it. Hence a hunger for the controversial or the spectacular. What dance needs is to find another way to proclaim its self-importance."[8]

But this was a season that fed the appetite for spectacle, particularly the vernacular step dancing that has persisted throughout the century on vaudeville and burlesque stages and Hollywood screens: *Bring in 'Da Noise, Bring in 'Da Funk* continued its Broadway run, transplanted from the Joseph Papp Public Theatre; *Riverdance* gave a sold-out reprise at Radio City Music Hall; *Lord of the Dance* cashed in on the craze for green; *Tap Dogs* rode on the coattails of *Stomp.* There were big tango and flamenco touring shows, as savvy about the art, science, and economics of the musical theater extravaganza as the ones now dominating Broadway.

Riverdance was an inadvertently instructive counterpoint to *Noise.* The former, with its New Age distortion of Irish acoustical music, its disconcertingly miked floor, its overblown epic format, and its confused importation of other dance forms, was as vague and questionable a paean to a mythic immigrant utopia as *Noise* was a precise and incisive history of African-American culture. Several friends—smart and sophisticated ones—had warned me that *Noise* was just great dancing with a slim pretext, so I expected little; what I found was an imaginative and efficacious cultural critique.

Ironically, what my (Euro-American) friends could not "see" is precisely the African- American survival mechanism that this episodic history brings into view: the "invisibility" of the black body's textuality. Whether enslaved to the plantation or the factory, the African-American body itself became a site of resistance for its own community, while remaining safely invisible to whites. Invisible, but not inaudible. What begins as shuffling becomes an explosive hitting several centuries later. *Noise* argues for an African-American genealogy of hoofin' that displaces Hollywood's whitewashed "flash and grin" acts (such as the Nicholas Brothers) and "shuffling fools" (such as Bill "Bojangles" Robinson) for a funk-based lineage privileging a more "real" expressive beat and rhythm of the legs. At root, the production is a brilliantly theatricalized intersection of Savion Glover's personal history with African-American cultural history. When "The Tap Dance Kid" belatedly discovered hitters Jimmy Slyde, Chuck Green, Buster Brown, and Lon Chaney, his conversion had as much to do with racial identification as with artistic style. *Noise* reclaims the story of tap dancing as the history of African-American community, whose bonds were rhythmically forged.

Back in October, after Kristeva finished her lecture on Artaud, I attended a late-night performance by the Japanese butoh master Min Tanaka at P.S. 122. During *I . . . Sit*, a journey through the space of bodily memory, the sound of Artaud's recorded voice saturated the room, and Tanaka launched himself through an exemplary improvisational cruelty. During the post-performance question-and-answer session, Tanaka refused to recognize the term "butoh" and renounced any connection with it. Why, he asked in return, has the practice become such a fixed term? Because it is only good for making money, for teaching. Commerce, he was telling us, had absconded with butoh, whose taboo-taunting practices had incubated in the nightclub underworld of postwar Tokyo. Despite the pressure to package and market, Tanaka's revolt presses forward, willfully nameless.

But how long can the avant-garde continue without its supporting context, its community, its "culture of revolt"? By definition, the avant-garde does not limp along. And the infusion of butoh and tanztheater in the 1980s has proven to have been only a temporary transfusion. It is one thing to see Sally Gross continue the conviction of her private rituals after twenty-five years, but to witness twenty-something dancers proffering formalist explorations, without a glimmer of irony, or a spark of vitality? I may remain cool to Douglas Dunn's physical idiosyncrasies, but his experimentation with wireless headphones in *Spell for Opening the Mouth of N* at least suggested an artist in conversation with the contemporary world.

In May, Movement Research rounded out the season with a performance tribute to Robert Ellis Dunn (1928–1996), leader of the early 1960s composition workshops that launched the Judson Dance Theater and postmodern dance. It was a conspicuous memorial, marking not just the end of another season, but the end of a "culture of revolt" already slipped away.

—TDR: The Journal of Performance Studies, 1998

Some Sentences by and about Merce Cunningham

About Merce Cunningham

IT IS DELIGHTFULLY ironic, and only appropriately so, that the man who exploded our need for a place called "center stage" came from a town named "Centralia."

By Merce Cunningham

IF PEOPLE are going to stay alive, they're going to have to deal with complexity. One of my earliest solos, *Root of an Unfocus,* was about fear; not how not to be frightened but how, with fear, to continue. Because I don't like to make decisions. In a sense, nothing was a mistake because each time you did something you'd say, "Oh, I never saw that!" This is not feeling about something, this is a whipping of the mind and body into an action that is so intense, that for the brief moment involved, the mind and body are one. I can hear the kind of sound she made, the rhythm was remarkable. Yes, in the beginning my titles were much longer than now, perhaps because the solos I did then were short. . . . I am a practical man (the theater demands it). If I saw something that I didn't understand then I would try it. It is simply a matter of allowing it to happen. Of course, if you make mistakes, you get something extraordinary. Incredibly, it was impossible. So you have to put yourself, it seems to me, in a situation in which you don't count on anything, and then deal with whatever arises. You do one thing, and that can lead to another. Sometimes I have finished a whole notebook of material before they arrive. We did the driving and packed the clothes and unpacked them, and we carried food and our personal clothing—and went trouping. Anyway, I've kept diaries for years and the first thing I do is write. My use of chance methods in finding continuity for dances is not a position which I wish to establish and die defending. We give ourselves away at every moment. I hope it's dazzling rather than willy-nilly. I work alone for a couple of hours every morning in the studio. I think dance is more primal than that. Now when you find something you don't know about or don't know how to do, you have to find a way to do it, like a child stumbling and trying to walk, or a little colt getting up.

About Merce Cunningham

I NEVER saw the young Cunningham, he of the elastic leaps. I know the Cunningham of the hobbled feet and flying hands. And I loved to watch him. The last time I saw Cunningham dance was in *Trackers*. It was a duet of sorts, with a portable barre that doubled for an old folk's walker.

By Merce Cunningham

WELL, YOU see for me drama is contrast. I watched and understood. My answer was "Appetite." On two legs or one. As Christian Wolff once said, it does imply good faith between people. The rhythm in each case was the inflecting force that gave each particular dance its style and color. Actually, the dance is quite dramatic. This all comes from Dostoevsky. What makes a movement at one moment grave, and the same at the next, humorous? Isn't that the way life is? It means: this is where I live. Anyway, there is so much in life, if you ever stop and think, you simply wouldn't do it. I dance because it gives me deep pleasure. Mannerism is an excuse or lack of vision. But if you abandon that idea you discover another way of looking. The most revealing and absorbing moments of life are the ones that have not past or future—that happen, as it were, without relevance—when the action, the actor, and the spectator are unidentified—when the mind, also, is caught in midair. The trick is to keep them both. It takes anybody a long time to really see something new. It was about fear—one of the predominant things in my life. Finally she hurried back, took one look at the four of us, and smiled and said, "All right, kids, we haven't any makeup, so bite your lips and pinch your cheeks, and you're on." Don't be surprised, if you find it difficult to find words to describe those movements. In fact, it's like a landscape. The idea of tranquility.

About Merce Cunningham

THE FIRST time I saw the Merce Cunningham Dance Company was compliments of People Express airline, in 1982. I could afford to fly round-trip from Pittsburgh, where I was attending college, to Newark. I spent the weekend with my parents nearby, and together we attended the dance concert at the McCarter Theatre. This was new territory for my parents, as well as for me. I remember best their responses. My mother got stuck on the sounds of babies crying. My father was struck by the fact that a sixty-year-old man was still dancing in public. A week or so later, my father called to tell me that he had heard Cunningham on the radio, and that he had explained the need to get up every morning and dance. My father sounded satisfied, and even envious.

By Merce Cunningham

CLIMAX IS for those who are swept by New Year's Eve. In that way, I do not think of each dance as an object, rather a short stop on the way. You see how it is no trouble at all to get profound about dance. That would be done not just to be complex but to open up unexplored possibilities. Dance is not social relationships. I wanted to make a dance about falling, so I worked on falls. Instead of saying no, you say yes. It can fulfill us in a way—give us something we know is there but don't get to see or experience very often. So I attempted to try them out, to ride the horse close to the chasm. No, but that's okay. So it becomes a technical problem. And I just say, "Well, you walk around the street without music." What I would like would be sunsets, *real* sunsets. I didn't *become* a dancer, I've always danced. We simply continued so as to be able to continue. By doing it. Like a pratfall, and you take off from that. As a matter of course a separation happens. And it was nine weeks of just daily work. There are two legs; the arms move a certain number of ways; the knees only bend forwards. Style is the dancer's being appearing through the dance. I'm trying to say in all this is that it remains always interesting if you get outside yourself. But my main interest is, as always, in discovery. It was wonderful, and absolutely maddening.

About Merce Cunningham

DURING A residency at the University of Texas at Austin, Cunningham had agreed to speak to my "Dance Criticism" class. We met that day over in the big old gymnasium, where he was rehearsing the dancers for a premiere. The students asked him some painfully naive questions, and he addressed them, after fifty years of addressing them, with striking patience and graciousness. In the midst of all this, he gestured down toward the sheaf of papers laying fitfully by his feet. "Choreography," he said, "is all paperwork."

—Essay delivered at Cornell University, 1999

New World A-Comin'
A Century of Jazz and Modern Dance

TWENTIETH-CENTURY America produced two great and enduring performing art forms: jazz music and modern dance. Both incubated in vernacular cultures of the fin-de-siècle. Both embraced the expressive vitality of a brave new century. And both were ambitious to be taken seriously, which meant that, sooner or later, the dancers (sooner) and the musicians (later) would need to assert their artistic autonomy.

Modern dance had no pedigree in "high" culture. On one side, it defined itself in opposition to classical ballet; on the other side, it fought long and hard to distinguish itself from vaudeville, skirt dancing, burlesque, and other popular dance entertainments. In order to elevate the status of dance from a suspect profession of "ill repute" to a fine art, early choreographers severed any connection to leg dancing, instead claiming for dance an ancient heritage as a sacred and noble art form. Isadora Duncan invoked the Greeks, and Ruth St. Denis recalled the traditions of Asia.

Jazz music-and-dance (the two were inseparable back then) was anathema to modern dance, not just because of its roots in jook joints and honky-tonks, but because of its racial origins. Isadora Duncan railed against jazz in the 1920s, describing its "tottering, ape-like" movements as "the sensual convulsions of the Negro," unclean and ignoble. Ted Shawn called jazz "the scum of the great boiling that is now going on," and dismissed it as the material of an "alien" race. (Nevertheless, Shawn later went on to make dances with African-American themes.) As a result, jazz music was largely absent from the early years of modern dance. Even during its Americana phase, in the 1930s, the leading choreographers bypassed contemporary jazz. Instead, "American" turned out to mean pioneers, Native Indians, cowboys—and, on occasion, slaves. The irony of this estrangement is that jazz and modern dance were such compatibly self-conscious expressions of artistic and social freedom.

"Freedom," however, is itself subject to regulation. Jazz was too free for white America. Duncan, a counter-culture heroine, espoused freedom all her life, but she condemned "this deplorable modern dancing, which has its roots in the ceremonies of African primitives" as uncontrollably chaotic. And when society dancers Irene and Vernon Castle, guided by bandleader James Reese Europe, popularized African-American social dances for their tony cabaret audiences, they whitewashed the originals, rendering them acceptably genteel. These "modern dances" (so named before the concert form) in the early 1910s fed the appetite of white audiences for unfettered self-expression. As the poet James Weldon Johnson observed: "On occasions, I have been amazed and amused watching white people dancing to a Negro band in a Harlem cabaret; attempting to throw off the crusts and layers of inhibitions laid on by sophisticated civilization; striving to yield to the feel and experience of abandon; seeking to recapture a state of primitive joy in life and living; trying to work their way back into that jungle which was the original Garden of Eden; in a word, doing their best to pass for colored." Most Euro-Americans, however, were not frequenting Harlem nightclubs. They did not want to pass for, or even pass close to, colored. But they did desire—from a safe distance—the sense of exotic freedom that they saw in jazz. The Jazz Age ushered in American modernism, its fantasized Africanist body making possible a new definition of white "American" culture.

Paul Taylor implies as much in *Oh, You Kid!* (1999), his collaboration with Rick Benjamin and the Paragon Ragtime Orchestra. In characteristic Taylor fashion, he chose a musical suite—in this case, ragtime dance tunes—with potent cultural associations, and then proceeded to deconstruct them. The pre-WWI music conjures up playful, nostalgic images—Keystone Kops, cooch dancers, and music hall follies. But when we look around back of those images, what we find is a Ku Klux Klan kickline. Ragtime, like every incarnation of jazz, bespeaks an age, a people, a cultural dynamic, a particular set of race relations. As one audience member suggested during a forum with collaborators Bill T. Jones and pianist/composer Fred Hersch, we need to ask, "freedom" for whom?

The cultural divide between jazz music and modern dance was perpetuated institutionally during the mid-1930s by the Federal Dance Project, which excluded vaudeville, variety, and musical theater dancers from eligibility for employment, because those forms were defined as entertainment rather than art. As dance historian Ellen Graff has pointed out, dancers such as Mura Dehn and Edna Ocko, who honed their techniques uptown at the Savoy Ballroom rather than a Greenwich Village studio, did not meet the criteria for a "real" dancer. And neither did the majority of African-American dancers, whose choices in professional dance were limited to popular venues.

Dance historian John Perpener has noted that African-American choreographers who aimed for a stage career faced a dilemma, between the Eurocentrism of modern dance and the African-American tradition of vaudeville and musical theater, which had emerged out of minstrelsy—a form that Charles Williams, director of the Hampton Institute Creative Dance Group, called "the lowest type of theater." Many dancers aspired to become more than "Cotton-Club types," explains Perpener, and modern dance, notwithstanding its racialist practices, offered them an avenue of serious artistic study beyond the stereotypes that clung to vaudeville and musical theater. The question remained, would jazz music have a place in their work?

Eugene Von Grona's American Negro Ballet premiered in 1937, performing to Duke Ellington as well as Bach and George Gershwin. Hemsley Winfield presented concerts featuring black composers, including Ellington. But those were the exceptions, not the rule. For the most part, African-American pioneers turned to African sources (Williams, Pearl Primus, Katherine Dunham, Asadata Dafora) and slave spirituals (Edna Guy, Williams, and Winfield) rather than contemporary jazz. Dunham refused to honor the European distinction between art and entertainment, choreographing theater concerts as well as revues and musicals. The third act of her 1962 revue, *Bamboche,* featured African-American songs and dances—gospel, spiritual, the shimmy, Charleston, and cakewalk. The immensely popular *Le Jazz Hot* revue (1940) also featured a selection of barrelhouse social dances. Primus, too, included some spirituals, jazz, and blues in a repertory that addressed a variety of African and African-American practices and experiences.

Jazz music made more frequent appearances in the work of second-generation modern choreographers, many of whom emerged from the companies and classes of Katherine Dunham, Martha Graham, Hanya Holm, Doris Humphrey, and Helen Tamiris. Jean Erdman's *The Castle* (1970), for example, was co-choreographed by clarinetist Jimmy Giuffre, who, along with the dancers, improvised parts of the work. The former Graham dancer also choreographed *Four Portraits from Duke Ellington's Shakespeare Album,* a semi-improvised satire that premiered in 1958. Esther Junger, who had danced in musicals and with Tamiris, created productions such as *Negro Themes* (1935), *Judgment Day* (1940), and *Go Down Death* (1930), the latter two both performed to poems by James Weldon Johnson. She adopted Ellington music for *Negro Sketches* (1940).

Anna Sokolow, a former Graham dancer whose work emphasized social commentary on contemporary life, saw jazz as one of the most profoundly expressive forms of her day. Concerned with the existential plight of the human condition, Sokolow often used jazz scores, many by third stream jazzman Teo Macero (*Le Grand Spectacle,* 1956; *Session '58,* 1958; *Dreams,* 1961; *Forms,* 1964; *Opus '60,* 1960; *Opus '65,* 1965; *Time Plus Six,* 1966; *Memories,* 1967; *Time Plus Seven,* 1968).

Kenyon Hopkins composed the score for her 1955 masterwork, *Rooms,* and she choreographed Jelly Roll Morton's *A Short Lecture and Demonstration on the Evolution of Ragtime* (1952).

The New Dance Group, formed in 1932 as a community organization that engaged social and political issues through its company and school, drew upon what was then called "folk material." In 1941 the group presented "America Dances," a program of "authentic Folk, Social, and Jazz dances and their influence on the Modern Concert Dance." It was a rare encounter between Euro-American modern dance and African-American vernacular dance-and-music. Besides Sophie Maslow's *Dust Bowl Ballads* (1941) to Woody Guthrie, Jane Dudley's *Harmonica Breakdown* (1941) to "Blind" Sonny Terry and Lee Sherman's *Jazz Trio,* the concert featured the Lindy Hoppers and Margot Mayo and her American Square Dance Group. Dudley had already made use of a Billie Holiday song in 1937; in 1945, she composed *New World A-Comin',* again to music by Terry. For *Poem* (1963), Maslow fused an Ellington score with Lawrence Ferlinghetti poetry. She used Ellington again for *Such Sweet Thunder* in 1975.

By the mid-1940s, the popularity of the big bands was waning, and the same issue of artistic autonomy and cultural legitimacy that choreographers had faced decades earlier came to a flash point for jazz composers. Like the African-American dancers of the 1920s and 1930s, African-American jazz musicians struggled with their complicated connection to dominant culture. "The music of my race is something which is going to live," Ellington said, "something which posterity will honor in a higher sense than merely that of the music of the ballroom." As much as he respected the ballroom—that was his source—he reached for something "higher." He spent his career negotiating this tricky balance, between roots in the honky-tonk and aspirations toward Carnegie Hall. He challenged the line between high and low, serious and popular, white and black. Ellington's ambitions fueled the debate about the relationship of jazz music to dance.

According to dancer and writer Roger Pryor Dodge, jazz was a dance music, but it, like all art, needed to evolve. Dodge was a classically trained dancer who discovered jazz in the mid-1920s and partnered Mura Dehn in the 1930s. He had been featured in *Skyscrapers,* billed as the first jazz-ballet in 1926, and then began choreographing his own jazz dances to the likes of Ellington's "East St. Louis Toodle-Oo" and "Black and Tan Fantasy." In his 1945 article, "The Dance-Basis of Jazz," Dodge took a long view on the debate, neither condemning jazz to the dance hall nor condoning its complete divorce from the rhythm of dance. Cautioning that the jazz musician should never lose touch with the rhythm of the dance floor, he anticipated that the jam session would develop jazz as a "listener's music." That split, observes saxophonist/composer Phil Woods, did have repercussions. "When they stopped dancing to jazz, jazz lost a lot of credibility and popularity. People don't really understand what jazz is anymore."

It was largely Ellington who facilitated the infiltration of jazz music into modern dance in the 1950s and 1960s, because, by bridging the breach between art and popular music, he made jazz music more acceptable to a modern dance community that had self-consciously constructed itself as a legitimate art form. For Donald McKayle, Talley Beatty, and Alvin Ailey, modern dance had found its soul mate. Their approach to choreography came less from a drive for modernist purity than from personal experience and artistic training that integrated art and life and social concerns.

McKayle studied on scholarship at the New Dance Group studio and performed with Maslow, Dudley, Erdman, and Graham, among others. His signature work, *Games*, about children's ghetto street life, debuted on a joint concert with Daniel Nagrin in 1951. (Jazz music would prove integral to Nagrin's repertory, too, which included *Strange Hero* [1948], a "dance portrait" of a gangster-character set to a progressive jazz score for large orchestra by Stan Kenton and Pete Rugolo.) Accompanied by New Orleans jazz, *District Storyville* (1962) depicted the birth of jazz, set in a turn-of-the-last-century bordello and loosely based on Louis Armstrong's early career. The score itself reflects the evolution of jazz, beginning with a funeral procession brass band and climaxing with a battle of the horn players. *Reflections in the Park,* an episodic look at city life—sometimes romantic, sometimes violent—through the eyes of a young couple in Central Park, was specially commissioned by the Modern Jazz Society of Hunter College. McKayle collaborated with composer Gary McFarland; for the premiere in 1964, the musicians assembled across the back of the stage, while the dancers performed in front of them.

Beatty, whose work reflects both his sense of musicality and his deep engagement with issues of race and culture, was a principal dancer with Dunham before making his choreographic debut in 1948. His breakthrough came with *The Road of the Phoebe Snow* (1959), set to an Ellington (and Strayhorn) score, as were *The "Way Out" East St. Louis Toodle-oo* (1958), *Congo Tango Palace* (1960), *The Black Belt* (1967), and *Black, Brown and Beige* (1974). His tribute to the composer, *Ellingtonia,* premiered at the American Dance Festival in 1994. Beatty set *Come and Get the Beauty of It Hot* (1960) to a variety of jazz composers—Gillespie, Dave Brubeck, Charlie Mingus, Miles Davis, Gil Evans, and Lalo Schiffrin. In *Montgomery Variations* (1967), a study in violence, Beatty spliced in the sound of bomb explosions and shouts of "Freedom" by the dancers to a score by Mingus and Davis. Often called a "jazz choreographer," Beatty was much more influenced by Graham's technique and choreography. "I use all her connective steps," he says, "and I put a little hot sauce on it." *Phoebe Snow* contains only one jazz step, and there are none in *Beauty of It Hot* or *Black Belt*. The jazz component of those dances, he explains, was "our spirit."

Ailey was deeply influenced by the honky-tonks of his Texas childhood and by his training with Lester Horton, whose aesthetic was highly theatrical and thematically multicultural. In 1952 Horton choreographed Ellington's *Liberian Suite*, which dancer James Truitte adapted for Ailey's company several decades later. So when Ailey founded the Alvin Ailey American Dance Theater in 1958, he was primed for a career-long dialogue with jazz, whose myriad forms—spirituals, blues, jazz—helped him to explore the roots of African-American culture past and present. From beginning (*Blues Suite*, 1958, and *Revelations*, 1960) to end (the Ellington cycle), Ailey focused on jazz, including composers such as Gillespie, Mingus, and Charlie "Bird" Parker. His most persistent inspiration, however, was Ellington. Ailey choreographed a dozen of his compositions, culminating in the multiyear "Ailey Celebrates Ellington" project of the mid-1970s, and invited into the repertory Ellington dances by other choreographers as well.

Eleo Pomare came of age in Harlem in the 1960s, during the heyday of black consciousness, and his dances took a more critical stance toward the black experience in America. He brought to modern dance a voice of protest, and he insisted that jazz be used as a way to break with the dominant Eurocentric aesthetic. His studies were based on the reality and characters of contemporary life, rather than historic or literary sources. His classic *Blues for the Jungle* (1962) used a combination of jazz and blues overlain with radio broadcasts, tracing the bleakness of African-American oppression from the slave auction to the ghetto.

In the 1970s jazz made its mark on another group of modern dancers, who adapted for movement the principle of jazz improvisation. Richard Bull started out as a jazz pianist and worked with Lennie Tristano, while supporting himself in part by playing for modern dance classes at Juilliard and the Graham school. After study with Alwin Nikolais exposed him to the use of improvisation in the generation of set choreography, Bull set out to transpose the techniques of jazz improvisation to establish the field of "structured improvisation" in dance. He choreographed more than one hundred dances for the Richard Bull Dance Theater, produced in his New York City loft the work of improvisational dancers for twenty years, and taught, among many others, Blondell Cummings and Bill T. Jones. Cummings is known for her improvisational solos, including *The Ladies and Me* (1979), set to recordings of female blues singers. Jones adapted the structured improvisation for his early solos. In the years since then, he has jammed with Max Roach, sung old blues songs, and, most recently, collaborated with Fred Hersch on *Out Some Place* (1999). Ironically, in a reversal of influence, it was Jones's method of improvising in front of a video camera to generate movement material that inspired Hersch to improvise at the keyboard for a tape recorder.

Dianne McIntyre, for sixteen years the director of the Sounds in Motion Dance Company, has exploited improvisation as a compositional and some-times performative process since the 1970s. Aiming to merge movement and music, she explores an eclectic range of African-American music, including avant-garde jazz, rhythm and blues, and spirituals, in close collaboration with live musicians such as Roach, Cecil Taylor, and Lester Bowie. She describes the process of creating together the work's dynamics and flow as "a conversation that becomes composition." Judith Dunn worked in tandem with jazz musician Bill Dixon, producing formal, nonnarrative improvisations such as *Nightfall Pieces* (1967) and *1972–1973* (1973). Their collaborations began with discussion of types of movement or relationships, the performance context, and the performance space, in order to produce a situation in which the dance and music existed separately, with equal importance.

Innovator Twyla Tharp, known for her eclectic taste in popular music, used jazz to great advantage for her spine-slipping movement style. She scored one of her early hits, in 1971, with *Eight Jelly Rolls,* a suite of Jelly Roll Morton songs. *The Bix Pieces,* which premiered the same year, was performed to Paul Whiteman's big band rendition of the trumpeter Bix Beiderbecke's music, with a coda to a Thelonious Monk arrangement of "Abide With Me." And for *The Raggedy Dances* (1972) she used a pastiche of Scott Joplin rags, Mozart variations on "Baa Baa Black Sheep," and modern piano.

At the close of the century, jazz is making new inroads into modern dance. Choreographers as diverse as Ronald K. Brown and Trisha Brown are exploring with fresh eyes a now-classic musical tradition. As part of an ongoing investiga-tion of his African-American identity, Donald Byrd has turned to jazz for source material. In 1996, he created *The Harlem Nutcracker,* using Duke Ellington and Billy Strayhorn's 1960 arrangement of "The Nutcracker Suite." Byrd made an explicit inquiry into the meaning of jazz in *Jazz Train* (1998), a three-part col-laboration with Geri Allen, Vernon Reid, and Max Roach. "What the process was about for me was to realize that I really don't know anything about jazz, and to listen in a new way, like a novice, and to share that experience with an audi-ence," says Byrd. "Jazz doesn't mean just one thing. It's actually a part of a living tradition. And it is as diverse as the artists who create it. It's a risk-taking kind of music, that encourages you to enter this space of not knowing, and entering that space with enthusiasm."

David Parsons, before teaming up with Phil Woods for *Fill the Woods with Light* (1998), had already gotten hooked on jazz because of the kinship he felt with improvisation and with the musicians' nocturnal, gypsy lifestyle. His very first work was a small jazz dance, and since then he has worked with pianist/composer Billy Taylor, the Turtle Island String Quartet, and clarinetist Tony Scott. Parsons sees a strong affinity between the two arts, both "small ensembles of people who work together and are very committed to something that's not hugely popular in the way that rock and roll or MTV are."

At century's end, modern dance and jazz music have become revered traditions, their revolutionary moments long passed. It's a postmodern world, where genres, styles, and cultures are all so much grist for the creative mill. Like everything else, modern dance and jazz music get reabsorbed and reconstituted—and in the process, reanimated. But that's how they began, really, as concocted hybrids, radical riffs on a culture emerging into the modern world. Dance historian Brenda Dixon-Gottschild argues that modern dance, with its torso articulation, pelvic contraction, and barefoot groundedness, is the product of a "Creolization-cum-segregation" with African dance. So, we have come roundabout to the same fluid place where we started the century, and you have to wonder if the intervening modernist dictum of "purity" wasn't just an attempt to conceal its gumbo origins. Jazz is an African-American gift, says Woods. "But if we haven't come to terms with our Afro-Americans, how are we going to come to terms with Afro-American music? It's an American problem, and it must be solved."

Orchestral composer/arranger Maria Schneider, who joined forces with Pilobolus to create *The Hand That Knocked, the Heart That Fed* (1998), combines modern jazz and modern classical writing. Hersch invokes Bach as easily as hambone, or tango. Woods is unsure that his music for Parsons even satisfies the requirements of jazz. "There's a love song, there's a rock 'n' roll section which we call a belly roll, there's a waltz, which is very romantic, and there's a bossa nova. None of those templates qualify as a jazz beat." Such fusion and fracture suits modern dance, which has largely abandoned any pretense of "purity." Jazz, explains Byrd, represents "the diversity of our culture and our uncanny ability to assimilate and transform all kinds of sources into making something new."

—*Modern Dance, Jazz Music and American Culture,*
season program, American Dance Festival
and the Kennedy Center, 2000

In Dance, Preserving a Precarious Legacy Begins Onstage

ONCE THE arcane domain of historians and librarians, preservation has become a veritable rallying cry throughout the dance world. Maybe it's a sign of the flagging energy of contemporary dance, or a case of millennial self-consciousness about the past and future, or the result of conservative funding priorities, but preservation now occupies a top spot in the field's agenda. Organizations such as the Dance Heritage Coalition, the National Initiative to Preserve America's Dance, and the George Balanchine Foundation have succeeded in raising consciousness about the critical and immediate need to safeguard the notoriously precarious legacy of American dance.

The call for preservation raises a fundamental question: what is lost to us if a dance tradition dies? It's a question to be considered not just by the preservation movement but by everyone interested in cultural policy.

Take the case of Martha Graham. After suspending operations nearly nine months ago, the Martha Graham School reopened on 16 January. The company remains in limbo, however, and its modern dance repertory, one of the great documents of twentieth-century America, is at risk of perishing. Paradoxically, Graham, who died in 1991 at the age of ninety-six, was named by the Dance Heritage Coalition as one of "America's Irreplaceable Dance Treasures" a few months after the board of her nearly bankrupt dance center announced the shutdown last May.

A dance treasure, however, is not a sunken chest of gold doubloons. Once buried, it can never truly be retrieved. In order to maintain the integrity of a classical repertory, a dancer must be in constant training for a specific technique and style.

Videotape and notation notwithstanding, dance is an oral tradition, whose fullness of history, meaning, and conditions of creation are passed along from generation to generation. It is not a treasure that can be framed, stored, or polished. Dance is a practice, not an object.

This is not to say that dance should not be documented. It should be documented, preserved, and made accessible. The Library of Congress, which acquired the Martha Graham Archives in 1998, has planned to create a "living history" on video, produce multimedia reference works, and sponsor live performances.

But preservation does not substitute for actual performance, in which individuals gather in a public arena for a shared experience and, potentially, a shared conversation.

At a conference on cultural policy last October in Washington (sponsored by Americans for the Arts and the Center for Arts and Culture), Julia Foulkes, a dance historian and professor at the New School University, called the fate of Graham's company "a dramatic exposé of the fragile existence of modern dance."

Ms. Foulkes traced the difficulties of modern dance in American culture: "Its relatively short history, the high labor costs involved in a performing art, the lack of permanence of the artworks, compounded by the difficulty in recording and preserving dance or reproducing it in any commodified form." And she concluded with an impassioned plea: "If Graham's company and school do not survive, I hope we can at least carry forth this insight into formulating cultural policy for the twenty-first century."

The federal government officially maintains a "no policy" cultural policy—despite its myriad tax codes, military bands, arts agencies, fellowship and exchange programs, educational standards, archives and museums, monuments, national parks, cultural attachés, broadcast regulations and copyright laws, and the First Amendment.

In the last two decades, however, a cultural policy network has developed among researchers, administrators, and policy makers. Literature has been published, university programs established, and annual conferences organized. By last August, when the Pew Charitable Trusts announced an initiative to "usher in a new era of cultural policy development," the idea had gained critical mass. Beginning in March, the Center for Arts and Culture, an independent research organization, will release a series of recommendations and issue briefs on "Art, Culture, and the National Agenda."

During the debates over money for the National Endowment for the Arts and the National Endowment for the Humanities, the scarcity of reliable research on the arts hampered the cultural sector in making a compelling case for them. As a result, a flurry of dollars has been directed toward data collection, much of it economic. Many a researcher is now gathering numbers to prove that the arts produce a measurable, significant, and meritorious impact on the economy.

The problem with this approach is its implication that the arts are justifiable only through their market value. If Graham's company generated less local restaurant and parking revenue one year than the year before, would it then be that much less valuable to us? The case to be made for Graham—or any other artist—is as a public good, not as an economic good.

When the arts endowment was founded in the 1960s, art—defined specifically as high art—was seen as needing protection against the pernicious incursion of popular culture (not to mention communist culture). As such, support for artists served as an antidote to an increasingly commercialized society. By the 1980s, the social role of the artist had shifted, for two reasons. First, popular culture was no longer the enemy. Second, what qualified as art was no longer restricted to high art.

Mary Schmidt Campbell, a former Cultural Affairs Commissioner of New York City and now dean of the Tisch School of the Arts at New York University, interprets the past decade's "culture wars"—intense public debates over the nature, purpose, and financial support of art—as a backlash against this thriving cultural pluralism. "Diversity was the mandate of the Endowments," she wrote in a 1998 essay. "Having achieved this diversity, however, the Endowments are now witnessing a public deeply uncomfortable with its ramifications."

If diversity was a mandate, it turned out not to be an end in itself. As the variety of artistic practices in America proliferates, their vital, if underrecognized, role in the democratic process becomes more pronounced.

The arts are a public forum where we tell one another—in symbolic language—who we are, who we've been, and who we'd like to become. Every artwork is, as Graham titled one of her dances, an "American Document" that can incite and engage the imagination of its audience. The arts frame an opportunity for civic dialogue, when commonalities as well as differences can be debated and elaborated. That was the message in Pittsburgh last November when leading business and foundation executives signed the Pittsburgh Arts Accords, affirming private sector support of the arts. The arts "empower people to participate effectively in a democratic society," the accords said, "by developing skills of perception, reflection, interpretation and communication, which promote understanding of diverse and cross-cultural values."

Graham tackled some of the most fundamental, enduring, and contested issues of American identity: the tension between individual and community, the mastery of space, the dilemma of womanhood, and the social role of ritual and religion. For a young generation just discovering the Graham company last season, and eager for more, her languishing repertory is a lost opportunity to participate in the continuing creation of our national life.

—*New York Times*, 2001

II

MAKING HISTORY

Review: From the Repertory of Isadora Duncan's "Soviet Workers' Songs"

THROUGH HER convincing and revealing dance reconstructions, Annabelle Gamson helped to provide the catalyst for a new generation of scholarship on Isadora Duncan in the 1970s. Today the number of Duncan dancers has multiplied. A half-dozen soloists and companies (by now the fourth and fifth generations) are continuing to produce more and more of Duncan's dances.

A company specializing in the group works, called From the Repertory of Isadora Duncan, has made a significant contribution to Duncan scholarship by mounting a more complete reconstruction of "Soviet Workers' Songs" than has been produced in the United States since the 1930s. The program featured the range of Duncan works, from the lyrical Brahms waltzes to the dark and somber *Marche Funèbre*. This reconstruction of "Soviet Workers' Songs," staged by third-generation dancers Julia Levien and Hortense Kooluris, suggested new—and important—insights into Duncan's oeuvre.

"Sovet Workers' Songs" is a modified assemblage of the dances originally choreographed as a choral suite by Duncan for the children of her Moscow school in 1924—her last completed works, before her death in 1927. Inspired by the way the children sang and marched to and from the stadium where classes were being held, she composed seven group dances to seven popular folk songs. This reconstruction featured five workers' songs: *Warshawianka; Dubinushka;* a later addition to the suite, *Labor, Famine, Labor Triumphant* (choreographed by Duncan's adopted daughter, Irma Duncan, who ran the Moscow school); *The Blacksmith;* and *One, Two, Three.*

In *Warshawianka* a succession of revolutionaries rushes across the stage diagonally, one or two at a time. Each one faces the onrushing battle with flag held high and is wounded. As one falls, the next enters to take up the flag again. While the last one is dying, the first one lifts herself up in time to claim the flag, exhorting all to rise again, triumphant. *Dubinushka* features a group in two parallel lines working together rhythmically to pull a rope, as a heroic figure leads them in their effort. Irma Duncan's trilogy, *Labor, Famine, Labor Triumphant,* also focuses on work movements. Labor is portrayed first; then a peasant places her fist in her gaping mouth, symbolizing famine; and in the last section, persistent work is shown overcoming hunger. In *The Blacksmith* one member rises from bondage, encouraging the others to follow suit and, through hard work (this time, hammering at the forge), to overcome their adversity. The finale, *One, Two, Three,* is a joyful round dance for young girl scouts.

In contrast to the lyrical, free-flowing style usually associated with Duncan, most of these dances have a blunt, bound, rooted look to them. There are few of those swelling waves of energy that Duncan usually sent out into space with her lilting arms, tempering the strength of the deep plush steps she took into the earth. The body image emphasizes tension, especially through lunging thighs, laboring arms, and clenched fists. The body is self-contained, a sculptural mass displacing empty space as it goes, rather than a porous entity gliding through its airy surrounds. The group formations are decidedly architectural. Even the garments are different—the short, squarish tunics frame the materiality of the body, rather than flowing with the body as the gauzy, shapeless chitons did.

These dances suggest that Duncan had more in common with the generation of modern dancers that followed her than is usually conceded. Martha Graham and Doris Humphrey did not begin to make their breakthroughs until after Duncan's last trip to America, but it is possible that Duncan was acquainted with the work of Mary Wigman and Rudolf von Laban. Duncan was an avid reader and an active theater-goer. In view of the strength of the avant-garde internationally in the 1920s, Duncan must have been familiar with the new currents of theater and dance in Germany and Russia. Certainly Duncan shared with them, in the "Soviet Workers' Songs," a more austere body image and group design. Probable links between Duncan and the Kamerny Theatre, Stanislavski's Art Theatre, Goleizovsky's constructivist ballets, and Meyerhold's biomechanics remain to be explored. Although the mystique that Duncan herself cultivated has come to overshadow the significance of her art, reconstructions such as this one of "Soviet Workers' Songs" are helping scholars probe the full and subtle complexities of her choreographic career.

—Theatre Journal, 1990

The Continuing Beauty of the Curve
Isadora Duncan and Her Last Compositions

THE AMERICAN fascination with Isadora Duncan surfaced in New York this season, thanks to Martin Sherman's new play, *When She Danced.* The scenario focuses on the later Duncan, past her prime and saddled with a variety of hangers-on, when already the question is being raised of what had made her such a great stage presence. A largely self-constructed legend, Duncan carefully cultivated a mystique to support her evanescent performing style. She encouraged people to think that her dancing was spontaneous, when it was quite definitely premeditated, and she made very sure that she was never filmed properly.

In 1921 Duncan lured the famed photographer Edward Steichen to Athens, on the promise that she would let him take moving pictures of her dancing on the Acropolis, but she reneged when they arrived, explaining that she wanted her dancing to be remembered as a legend. In this she succeeded. A large part of Duncan's enduring appeal is that at the center of her sensational, tragic, utopian story is a magnificent void. Duncan, the dancer in motion, is missing. This mystery perpetuates her legend, as she knew it would; it creates in us a longing that was so fundamental to Duncan's own romantic sensibility.

Although we do not have a proper filmic record, we do have enough documentation to get pretty close to Duncan, if only in our mind's eye. Between the photographs, drawings, reviews, memoirs, letters, costumes and lighting gels, notebook entries, programs, biographies, and the growing body of reconstructed repertoire, Duncan's dancing emerges quite vividly—and with much more depth and complexity than was previously suspected. Of major importance are the reconstructions, which are proliferating. Annabelle Gamson initiated the current wave of Duncan dancing in the 1970s; today, the tradition is continued by Lori Belilove, Jeanne Bresciani, Jodi Liss, Andrea Seidel, and Shain Stodt, among others.

This past season offered a variety of Duncan evenings, and among the most important reconstructions was that of "Impressions of Revolutionary Russia," a suite of dances that Duncan choreographed for the children of her Moscow school in August 1924. Having just finished a disastrous tour of Russia's more faraway districts, Duncan was enthralled by the classes that Irma Duncan, the functional head of the school, had organized for six hundred of the city children in the Sparrow Hills sports arena. "It was a beautiful sight," Duncan wrote to her friend and later biographer, Allan Ross Macdougall, "to see them all in their red tunics and red scarves, dancing and singing the 'Internationale.'" [1]

Inspired by the way the children sang and marched to and from the stadium, she composed seven group dances to seven popular folk songs: *With Courage Comrades March in Step; One, Two, Three, Pioneers Are We; The Young Guard; The Blacksmith* (or *Forging the Keys of Freedom*); *Dubinushka; The Warshavianka (In Memory of 1905);* and *The Young Pioneers.* They were her last completed compositions, premiered on one of her September farewell programs in the Kamerny Theatre. The program, an evening of revolutionary dances, included these seven choral dances, two funeral dances to commemorate the death of Lenin earlier that year, and a series of revolutionary dances from Ireland, Hungary, and France. The Moscow school children sang as they danced the suite, and they participated in the finale—with a large number of the summer students—for a rousing performance of the *Internationale*.

"Impressions of Revolutionary Russia," in slightly modified form (Irma Duncan added her own compositions—a Labor-Famine-Labor Triumphant trilogy and a suite of Russian folk songs by Gretchaninoff), continued to be performed by the Moscow School children when Irma Duncan toured the United States with them as the Isadora Duncan Dancers of Moscow in 1928–1930. She didn't return with the children to Russia in 1930, instead staying in the United States and starting up a new company. Among those girls, who continued dancing the "Impressions" suite, were Julia Levien and Hortense Kooluris. Key to our understanding of the Duncan legacy, these third-generation Duncan dancers helped to stage the current reconstructions.

The suite as a whole has not been performed here since the 1930s, but the most popular works, *The Warshivianka* and *Dubinushka*, have been available through groups such as Lori Belilove's. In a recent concert, Belilove made the decision to costume the dancers in jeans and men's oversized shirts rather than in Greek tunics in order to help the audience identify more directly with the heroic women onstage. Recently, From the Repertory of Isadora Duncan, a company that specializes in the group works, performed five of the workers' songs: *The Warshavianka, Dubinushka,* Irma Duncan's trilogy, *The Blacksmith,* and *One, Two, Three.* The suite initially took me by surprise. Most of the dances did not fall in line with the lyrical, floating, joyous image of Duncan as it has been etched in dance history. At some moments, I saw flashes of Mary Wigman or Martha Graham; at other moments, Rudolf von Laban's movement choirs.

In *The Warshavianka* a succession of revolutionaries rushes across the stage diagonally, one or several at a time. Each one faces the onrushing battle with flag held high and is then wounded. As one falls, the next enters to take up the flag again. When the last one lay dying on the ground, the first one lifts herself up in time to claim the flag, exhorting all to rise again, triumphant. *Dubinushka* features a group in two parallel lines working together rhythmically to haul a rope, as a heroic figure leads them in their efforts. Irma Duncan's trilogy also uses work motions to portray labor; then a peasant places her fist in her gaping mouth, symbolizing famine; in the last section, their persistent work serves to overcome hunger. In *The Blacksmith* one member rises from bondage, encouraging the others to follow suit and, through hard work (this time, hammering at the forge), to dismantle their own shackles. The finale, *One, Two, Three,* is more familiar territory: a joyful round dance for young girl scouts.

Unlike the airy, free-flowing style usually associated with Duncan, these dances have a blunt, bound, rooted look to them. There are few of those swelling waves of energy that Duncan usually sent out into space with her lilting arms, tempering the strength of the deep plush steps she took into the earth. The body image emphasizes tension, especially through lunging thighs, laboring arms, and clenched fists. The body is self-contained, a twisting sculptural mass displacing empty space as it goes, rather than a porous entity gliding through its airy surrounds. The group formations are muscularly sculptural in feeling. Even the garments are different—the short squarish tunics frame the materiality of the body, rather than flowing with the body as the gauzy, shapeless chitons did. If Duncan's prototypical style embodied a "feminine" ideal, this dancing was about the "masculine." It was boys, rather than girls, she said after one of the final Moscow performances, who were "better able to express the heroism of which we have so much need in this Age."[2]

As surprising as the dances are, they also make perfect sense, on a number of levels. First, the pragmatic. The pictorial style of the dancing (what Belilove describes as "energetic stasis") is a function of its agitprop theme: that hard work and group effort will triumph over all adversity. The desired image of strength seemed to require bent knees and feet planted flat on the ground. The pictorial style is also a function of the fact that these are basically songs translated into movement, not unlike the Delsartean pantomimes that catapulted Duncan into dancing in the first place. From the song "Dubinushka": "The time has come and the people awoke. Straightened their backs bent as long. Shook themselves free of century-old burdens And against its foes raised the 'dubina' [workman's song]."

Lastly, the pictorial style is a function of the music. Duncan's dancing, from beginning to end, was not so much about her own personality as it was about the music to which she chose to dance. In the case of the "Impressions" suite, she chose very programmatic music whose folksy simplicity and utopian sentiments appealed to her childlike vision of a better world. The melodies, rhythms, and images lent themselves to blunt, recurring gestures.

Considered in the larger context of Duncan's choreographic oeuvre, the "Impressions" suite begins to wear the Duncan label even more easily. For one thing, Duncan's own dancing had evolved over the years—from a gestural narrative to a transcendent musicality to a sculptural, nearly immobile minimalism; therefore, it should not be so surprising for her to develop in yet another direction. This direction would not have been so off-course, either. By the time she choreographed "Impressions," Duncan had established a history of portraying women of heroic stature, often embodying a call to action. The strong, bound arms are already apparent in *Revolutionary*, to Scriabin's "Etude op. 8, No. 12." The taut, angular body image had been used in *The Furies*, from Gluck's "Orpheus," and Tchaikovsky's *Pathétique*, third movement. The rhythmic appeal of the suite of dances also marks them clearly as Duncan's. In *Dubinushka*, the two parallel rows of workers, spread across upstage with a horizontal beam of light slashing across their arms, pull back an invisible rope in unison, then arc their arms down and forward to their starting position again. This pulling-arcing motion is done rhythmically, to the shifting tempo of the men's choral refrain. As with Duncan's most effectively musical works, the movement—its space and its materiality—can effectively disappear into time, when executed just right.

A 1929 photograph of *Dubinushka* suggests another important stylistic subtlety. The dancers in the front row are bending forward, over lunging front legs, with their hands held together behind their backs, as if greatly burdened, or perhaps enchained. The dancers in the back row, however, are raising their pliant arms (as well as their chests) upward, one wrist draped over the other, with the fists closed but not clenched. The point is that the bodies, though strongly grounded and sculpturally massed together, are not all tense. There is exhibited here a contrast between weighted mass in the front row and an aspiration upward in the back row, the literal and metaphorical mediation between the pulls of heaven and earth (or of freedom and servitude) that was the hallmark of Duncan's style from the very beginning.

This concern with the expressiveness of formal opposition is shared by the moderns of the next generation: the German tension-and-relaxation, Graham's contraction-and-release, Humphrey's fall-and-recovery. Graham and Humphrey did not begin to make their marks until after Duncan's last trip to America, but it is possible that Duncan encountered Wigman's and Laban's work, although nothing appears to be documented. Duncan was an avid reader and an active theater-goer; given the artistic avant-garde that thrived internationally in the 1920s, it is inconceivable that she would have been impervious to the currents of theater and dance in Germany and Russia. Certainly Duncan shared with them, in the "Impressions" suite, a more austere body image and the sculptural design of bodies in space.

Like Wigman, Duncan believed in the ugly as well as the beautiful as a legitimate subject of art, insofar as it was an expression of inner truth. Duncan's dancing did not have the nervous energy of Wigman's; it remained calm at the center, even when inflamed with revolutionary zeal. While Wigman primarily manipulated space, Duncan subsumed space into time (which is why she seemed to be improvising, and why she is often accused of having no technique or choreographic talent). With Laban, Duncan shared a belief in group dance as an expression and model of harmony in an inharmonious world. Dancing was not merely a training ground for the stage but for life itself. A photograph of one of the classes at the Sparrow Hill stadium bears striking resemblance to a Laban movement choir: a tight concentration of many youths, in short tunics, intertwining their arms, both from the front and behind. Closer to Moscow, however, was the Russian avant-garde—theater, dance, and visual artists all influenced by the vision of a new political and social order. We do know that Duncan admired the work of the Kamerny Theatre, as well as Stanislavski's Art Theatre. George Balanchine in Petrograd, Fedor Lopukhov in Petrograd/Leningrad, and Kasian Goleizovsky in Moscow were expanding the boundaries of ballet during Duncan's years there. Constructivist choreographer Goleizovsky, in a manifesto published in 1922, intimated that Duncan was, in fact, learning from the Russian experimentalists.[3]

If Duncan had lived and regained her generativity, would she have made the transition into full-fledged modernism, as her younger German, Russian, and American colleagues did? Amidst all the similarities and differences between Duncan and the next generation (the differences generally seem to be over-emphasized at the expense of the similarities), the essential distinction can be distilled into the dichotomy between the curve and the angle. Duncan believed in an ultimate harmony that could embrace opposites (the curve), while the next generation felt no need to reconcile the dissonances of modern life (the angle). The Russian worker songs, despite the hammering arms and lunging legs, contain neither Wigman's frenetic energy nor Graham's steel infrastructure. Duncan never abandoned her devotion to "the continuing beauty of the curve."[4] It is the swinging and arcing of limbs that keep the massive, blunt, weighted look of the "Impressions" suite from becoming caustic, sharp, or brittle.

By the time Duncan choreographed "Impressions of Revolutionary Russia," she realized that she had fallen out of step with the times. She railed bitterly against what she considered the freneticism and barbarism of jazz dancing. She protested so bitterly, in fact, that it sounded as if she were conceding defeat. "My art was the flower of an epoch, but that epoch is dead and Europe is the past," she wrote to Irma Duncan shortly before composing the revolutionary dances. "These red tunicked kids are the future."[5] Duncan, whose vision had always been so focused on the future, had become mired in the past. This she was smart enough to realize. However futile, it remains tempting to speculate that "Impressions of Revolutionary Russia," sparked by the forward-looking spirit of the times, might have broken a new path to the future carved out of the best of Duncan's past.

—*Ballet International,* 1990

Review: Millicent Dillon's *After Egypt*

OF ALL THE stories and anecdotes and remembrances that have been written about Isadora Duncan, the one that has been most instructive to me about her dancing is one that Irma Duncan tells. It took place in Egypt, at the Kom Ombo temple overlooking the Nile. Irma was a child then, and, quite unexpectedly, Duncan asked her to perform solo in the temple, in front of the entire entourage. Irma complied, grudgingly and, ultimately, unsuccessfully. Disappointed, Duncan proceeded to lecture Irma and her guests on the importance of the connection between gesture and its surroundings. Then she herself demonstrated:

> Adjusting her flowing white shawl, she strode across the court and disappeared into the shadows in the background. . . .
>
> Presently, as we peered into the background, we saw her emerge from the deep shadows cast by a peristyle of such massive proportions that it dwarfed her white-clad figure. But as soon as she started to move in and out of the tall lotus columns she seemed to grow in stature. The long shadows cast by the columns on the floor of the court formed a symmetrical pattern. And each time she stepped in her stately dance from the shadows into the strip of bright moonlight in between, there was a sudden flash created by her appearance. Alternating in this manner the entire length of the colonnade, slowly in one direction and faster coming back, she created a striking rhythm of brilliant flashes, which in a strange way suggested the beat of music.[1]

This is one of the many accounts that Millicent Dillon catalogs in *After Egypt: Isadora Duncan and Mary Cassatt* (William Abrahams/E. P. Dutton, 1990). It is Egypt—the country, the myth, the timelessness—that Dillon uses as the controlling metaphor for her piece of dual portraiture. Both Duncan and Cassatt were artists, both women, both American expatriates in Europe, and roughly contemporaries at the turn of the century. And both visited Egypt.

Subtitled *A Dual Biography,* the book is an ambitious experiment not just in biography, but in the limits of knowledge and history as well. Dillon, a biographer and fiction writer, is as interested in the telling as she is in the tale. She begins her book with an eloquent introduction on the subjects of time, death, and memory. It is not the accumulation of fact nor the neat linearity of narrative that reveals the life of another, she writes:

> This book will attempt a telling of another kind. Awkwardly, one step forward and two steps back, it will go in pursuit of a different kind of knowing, to search for explanation that proves the limitation of explanation, to break sequence to establish another kind of sequence through odd juxtapositions, abrupt branching

out and obsessive tunneling, through heavy-handed intrusion and even purposeful turning away. (2)

Dillon is an acutely self-aware writer. The book is full of heavy-handed interpretations (too often in the form of heavy-handed reflexive questions), and it is also mysteriously distanced, as when she reprints and then immediately abandons a sexually explicit love letter sent by Duncan to Mercedes de Acosta.

Actually, I think her strategy with the Acosta letter—one of the products of Dillon's fine research—is quite sound. Dillon sets up Duncan's lifetime pattern of romantic interludes as well as her implacable, desperate neediness at the end of her life, so it comes as no surprise that Duncan falls in love with her new "angel," whether male or female. The letter is enough said.

The book is episodic. Beginning with both women's trips on the Nile (Duncan in 1910 and 1912, Cassatt in 1911), it jumps back and forth in their lives, and then ends with their deaths. Sometimes the brief chapters simply provide quote after quote from a variety of sources. Others consist of extensive quotations of writings by Duncan's friends, lovers, and associates (Mary Desti, Victor Seroff, Maurice Dumesnil, Irma Duncan, and Florence Treadwell figure prominently), interspersed with Dillon's own speculations about these passages. Some chapters are analyses of Duncan's and Cassatt's own writings (mostly familiar material for scholars, in Duncan's case). Some offer paraphrased narrations of particular incidents. At some moments, Dillon pulls back entirely from her subjects and writes about writing biography. Often Duncan and Cassatt remain discrete within their separate chapters: less frequently, and in the final analysis (literally), they meet each other in the author's comparison.

Of particular interest to dance scholars are Duncan's poem and letter to Acosta, which are published in the book for the first time. Also, Dillon quotes directly from Duncan's childhood friend Florence Treadwell's memoirs. Previously, in the late 1970s, they had been reported on only through brief paraphrase, by Oakland journalist Paul Hertelendy. (To have Treadwell's entire memoir published would be a significant event for Duncan scholars.) Dillon quotes sparingly from Duncan's letters to poet Douglas Ainslie, whom the naive young dancer met and became infatuated with in London in 1899. The letters, housed at the University of Texas at Austin, are, in toto, a really rare and direct glimpse at Duncan as she was before she mythologized herself.

For the most part, what is new for dance scholars familiar with Duncan territory is how Dillon makes use of the material, both old and new. The book yields some fine insights into Duncan. Some of my favorites:

> There is, in this process [of writing her autobiography], a willed certainty in Isadora of her place in eternity that negates ordinary space and time. Yet she tells her

story in space and in time. So the reader is alternately pushed and pulled, led and overwhelmed, repelled and seduced by the doubleness of our own human desire for the creating of myth and the destroying of it. (159)

Isadora's encounter with intellect—with thought—is something that is difficult to even begin to understand. Ideas do not seem to come to her as idea. They are bathed in an aura of excitation, of eroticism. Certain words and expressions seem to become talismanic to her, work on her so as to create a readiness within her for her own expressivity, her own creativity through movement, for the creation of her own personal myth. (212)

And my most favorite, which I think accurately pinpoints why Duncan was so compelling a performer:

a simultaneous surrendering and asserting of her will in performance, the ability to convey to the audience the image of her body as if it were their own, and the ability to see herself in their eyes and to have them see her as she feels herself seen. (170)

The significance of Dillon's project to create a different kind of biography, one that acknowledges the unknown as well as the known, cannot be regarded too highly. There are many pleasures in the reading. But in the end, the book misses her mark. And I think it has something to do with those heavy-handed interpretations.

Although the disjunctive nature of the book's structure would seem a feasible strategy in which to lay bare the discontinuities of a life story and, subsequently, to provide spaces for the reader to enter those discontinuities, Dillon's insistence on interpolating her own interpretations actually kept me at a distance, dutifully deferring to the author's continuous presence. The overabundance of quotations (aggravated by Dillon's wooden descriptions of Cassatt's paintings) further intensified the feeling of claustrophobia. Dillon may have acknowledged the gaps in the narrative of her subjects' lives, and she may not have tried to smooth over those gaps by imposing a linear narrative on them, but she effectively smoothed them over anyway by embracing them into a master narrative—that of Egypt. Despite the expectations Dillon sets up in her introduction, *After Egypt* felt like traditional narrative to me, and I spent most of my time wiggling in the straitjacket.

Dillon does not suggest a way beyond the paradoxical impasse of narrative as limited in its grasp of knowledge but as total in its power over the subject, and neither does she allow the reader to live in that paradox. *After Egypt* offers a thesis, which is developed from nearly the beginning of the book: the theme of containment. Dillon wraps up her treatment of Duncan and Cassatt by saying:

One woman who came to Egypt had embraced the mythic as Ideal and the Ideal as mythic in her own being, in her own body, and if she did not refuse the daily, she thought of it as what had to be transcended. The other woman who came to Egypt had refused the Ideal, refused the mythic, had found her being, her purpose, in that which she saw—in surface, on surface, in the visible object, in the way light reflected from surface, a woman who lived in and through the daily. (340)

Dillon finishes her book as she begins it, with doubt about the limits of knowledge in biography: "There remains something beyond our reach in the telling" (364). She has explicitly acknowledged those limits by opening up the narrative's temporal structure, by refusing to fix these women's lives in chronological order. The problem remains, however, that narrative closure (and the illusion of complete knowledge) is produced not only by temporal sequence but also by spatial configuration—the shape—given a narrative by virtue of its ending.

Dillon ends, conventionally, with the artists' deaths, and then she succinctly ties everything together. The temporal structure of the book may be opened up, but its spatial configuration is crisply, classically circumscribed. The gaps are all filled in with interpretation, which functions to close off Duncan's and Cassatt's lives and to close off the book from the reader. In the end, Dillon ties Duncan (the idealist), Cassatt (the materialist), and Egypt neatly together: "It [ancient Egypt] was a world in which a single word meant both 'celestial glory' and 'daily utility'" (340), leaving the traditional narrative structure intact.

—Dance Research Journal, 1991

Isadora Duncan in 1920s America: "A Bolshevik Shade of Red"

IN THIS PAPER I am defining "criticism" very broadly, from the viewpoint of the cultural historian, opening out the term "criticism" from the aesthetic to the social and the political. As part of a larger project interpreting the meaning that Isadora Duncan held for her American audiences during her lifetime, I am interested here in analyzing the popular press's hostile reaction to Duncan's final American tour, from October 1922 to February 1923. By contextualizing Duncan's "bad press," so to speak, we can see that just as she had been a medium for the discourse of the artistic radicals and cultural nationalists during the teens, so she became a discursive ground for the reactionary conservatives of the early 1920s. Situated in a period of widespread xenophobia and paranoia (of blacks, unions, immigrants, and communists), Duncan's social critics read her dancing body through her perceived associations with Soviet Russia. Even though her repertoire was largely unchanged, she was no longer seen as a Greek goddess or revolutionary heroine, but rather as a seditious traitor. Soon after her departure, the State Department stripped her of her citizenship.

When the Russians overthrew their tsar in March 1917, Duncan paid tribute to the rebel peasants with a celebratory performance at the Metropolitan Opera House. In April 1917 she added to her nationalistic repertoire another allegorical solo like the *Marseillaise,* this one to Tchaikovsky's "Marche Slave." It was similar to the French anthem in its dramatic trajectory, but this new solo represented the Russian moujik rising from slavery to freedom. The *Marche Slave* was greeted almost as enthusiastically as the *Marseillaise* had been, by the press and the public.

Besides America and France, Russia had been, and would continue to be, an important host to Duncan's art. She had toured there at least six times since 1904, when she experienced a great success. And seventeen years later it was the young Soviet government that offered her state sponsorship for a school.

With the Russian Revolution, Duncan's liberation philosophy found its ideal domain. The revolution gave substance to her vision of a communal dance school, where none of the students, who lived, learned, and played together, had to pay. It gave content to her utopian vision. It renewed her antipathy toward the rich, toward those who had the things she never had as a child, toward those who commercialized art. Duncan was enthralled by urgent human drama, such as grief and oppression: that which is driven by inner necessity, which resists legislation. Thus the Russian Revolution appealed to her, with its upwelling of human suffering and injustice against its oppressor.

At this point, before the Bolsheviks seized power, Duncan could intertwine the Russian revolution with Allied patriotism, by appealing to her audience's sympathy for the politically oppressed and to their belief in the might of the right. But when Duncan returned to America in October 1922, after having established a school in Moscow, and with a Russian husband, poet Sergei Essenin, in tow, the sympathies of the press and public had shifted radically. The sort of innocent, nondoctrinaire "revolution" that Duncan represented was no longer possible. Being a "revolutionary" was no longer a romantic badge of honor associated with the fight for democratic reforms, as it had been during her heyday, hailed by the Progressives, the Villagers, and cultural nationalists; it now denoted a dangerous communist sympathizer out to destroy the American way of life.

Sol Hurok, Duncan's manager for the last American tour, recalled in his autobiography just how ignorant Duncan was of the America to which she had returned: "This, remember, was 1922," he wrote. "The wave of reaction to the war, to Wilson, to liberalism, was rolling up in a fearful tide. It was a year when red was the color of all evil, and to call a man a Bolshevik was to damn his eternal soul as well as to send his earthly body to jail." [1]

Duncan, however, was naive enough to believe in revolution without ideology. To her, communism was the renewal of democracy without the "greed" and "villainy" and "class injustice" of capitalism. [2] She saw no contradiction between her own transcendentalist American ideals and those of the Soviets. Thus she described the streets of Moscow as "the picture of the song of the 'Open Road' of Walt Whitman," whom she claimed as the first Bolshevik. [3] She could never understand why America, itself borne of a revolution, did not support all revolutions, including the Russians' and including her own. "I am not an anarchist or a Bolshevik," she told reporters as she left America for the last time. "My husband and I are revolutionists. All geniuses worthy of the name are. Every artist has to be one to make a mark in the world today." [4]

Although the Red Scare peaked in late 1919/early 1920, when striking workers were automatically labeled "Reds" and dissidents were rounded up and deported en masse, America was still acting out its vindictive xenophobia and revolutionary paranoia when Duncan arrived. Provincial politicians and sensational newspapers fanned the flames. To the average American, who had read the propaganda planted by the Justice Department in the general press, Bolshevism meant chaos, wholesale murder, and the utter destruction of civilization. Even more, it threatened to infect the rest of the world—even our own shores—as communist revolution had already spread to Hungary and Germany. The Soviet famine elicited pity, and the National Economic Policy, an apparent turn toward capitalism, inspired optimism, but Americans still abided by the Wilsonian principle of "100 per cent Americanism." While new legislation was proposed to curb immigration, and as race riots rocked major cities, observers smugly predicted the failure of the communist experiment. [5]

The press fanned the nativist and antiradical hysteria. The banner of the *New York American* (the flagship paper of William Randolph Hearst's national chain and news service), for example, included a bald eagle on whose wings were emblazoned the words "Character," "Quality," "Accuracy," and "Enterprise." Above the eagle's head were printed the words "America First," and below, a banner read "An American Paper for the American People."

Headlines celebrated heroes such as Henry Ford and Charles A. Lindbergh and sensationalized sordid dramas. The Hearst chain, the most adroit at exploiting sex, crime, and scandal, seemed to dog Duncan around the country. Feeling badgered by questions about her personal life, she blamed the papers in general and Hearst in particular for the failure of her tour.

Long before, however, the moment Duncan had accepted an invitation to create a school for the fledgling communist country, she had been labeled by the popular press as a "Soviet Dancer" who had "joined the reddest ranks of Bolshevism," according to the *San Francisco Examiner*.[6] Her comments and activities, her marriage, her performance to commemorate the fourth anniversary of the Revolution, were covered in the American press, so by the time she returned here, she had already been deemed a traitor.[7] The former Lady Liberty herself, maternal and majestic in her rendering of the *Marseillaise*, had transgressed a geographical/sexual/ideological border and was thus branded a communist whore.

Even though she repeatedly disavowed any interest in preaching politics during her last tour, and preferred to talk about her needy Moscow school children, Duncan was held responsible for the evils of communism, through her dancing, through her marriage to Essenin, and even through the color of her costumes. Red—the color that had signified life and passion to an entire generation of American physical culturalists—had once fueled the nationalist spectacles of the *Marseillaise* and the *Pathétique*. Now, after displaying a red flag had actually been prohibited in twenty-eight states,[8] red was seen as brazen communist propaganda. Even her hennaed hair was described as "a Bolshevik shade of red."[9]

Although her Carnegie Hall audiences—constituted, at least in part, by pro-Soviet liberals, leftists, and intellectuals—cheered her as ever, and even demonstrated Soviet sympathy, some of her old bourgeois friends and radical followers did abandon her. The larger population saw her as she was constructed in the newspapers, as the traitorous whore. Where they once had seen freedom in the dancer's body, now they saw sedition. And that image was dramatized upon her very arrival, when she was denied entry at the New York harbor, pending questioning by immigration officials about her communist sympathies.[10]

Most of her repertoire during the last American tour was familiar: Tchaikovsky's *Pathétique Symphony* and *Marche Slave;* Beethoven's Seventh Symphony; Schubert's *Ave Maria, Marche Militaire,* and *Unfinished Symphony;* selections from the Brahms waltzes; and Wagner's "Liebestod" from *Tristan and Isolde* and his "Bacchanale" from *Tannhäuser.* New to her American audiences were two other Wagner works ("Siegfried's Funeral March" from *Die Götterdämmerung* and "Ride of the Valkyries" from *Die Walküre*); four by Alexander Scriabin (Sonata No. 4 and three etudes); and two by Franz Liszt ("Benediction de Dieu" and "Les Funérailles").

Duncan was now forty-five, even though she told the press she was thirty-eight. She dressed quite fashionably, without a hint of the Greek. Although her body was shorn of its lithe and supple youth, she appeared surprisingly slender and fit. Still, she no longer was a dancer of vivid motion, but rather a tragic actress. *Boston Evening Transcript* critic H. T. Parker explained: "Instead, she is becoming [a] sculptress, while the medium upon which she works is her own body, her own mantling raiment. . . . Becoming sculptural, she becomes also more independent of the music."[11] With the late solos she seemed to be coming ever closer to the "divine presence" that she had so admired in Eleonora Duse: that tremendous force of dynamic movement communicated through stillness.[12]

By now, Duncan's New York audience rather expected her to make curtain speeches. They started out mildly, with the dancer invoking Whitman and talking of building a bridge between America and the Soviet Union. Duncan told a Carnegie Hall audience that she did not preach Bolshevism, but only love—the love of mother for child, lover for beloved, and her own for the top gallery.[13] But Duncan grew impatient as the papers became more insistent on interpreting her as a communist sympathizer, ensconced in the power structure of the Soviets. So, she baited them. "There is a new idea of living now," she told an audience in November. "It is not home life. It isn't family life. It isn't patriotism, but the International."[14]

From New York Duncan went to Boston, where another brouhaha made the national headlines, setting the tone for the rest of the tour's coverage. After her opening night at Symphony Hall, many of the local papers ridiculed her performance, taking issue with the looseness of her tunics. She retaliated in her Saturday performance with a certain speech, defending her theories. "If canned Greek art is permitted," she asked, pointing to the nude statues in the niches around the hall, "why object to the beauty of the living body?" As she waved her red scarf, the dancer proclaimed that "this is red; that is what I am. Don't let them tame you." Red, she explained, is "the color of life and vigor," while gray, the color of New Englanders, is "dull and gray." Only thirteen years before, Duncan had declared that Boston was Bacchic, but now it was "the hot-bed of Puritan prudery and vulgarity."[15]

When the mayor himself publicly accused Duncan's dancing of being indecent, she denied the charges, letting go her bluestocking indignation: "Every time I come to America they [the press] howl around me like a pack of wolves," she complained. "They treat me as though I were a criminal. They say I am a Bolshevist propagandist. It is not true."[16] Nevertheless, she was banned from the city, and three government departments ordered complete reports on her alleged Bolshevik declarations. The officials were not so much outraged by the nudity, they explained, but by the spread of Red propaganda.[17]

The Boston scandal framed the rest of the tour. In Washington the evangelist Billy Sunday demanded that the "Bolshevik hussy" be deported. In Indianapolis the mayor ordered policemen to monitor her performance, lest the "nude dancer" sully his fair city. Back in New York, St. Marks-in-the-Bouwerie withdrew an invitation for Duncan to lecture on "the moralizing effect of dancing on the human soul." Essenin, in one of his drunken, violent spells, made anti-Semitic remarks at a gathering of Russian-Jewish poets in the Bronx, causing a scandal. At the Brooklyn Academy of Music, Duncan's pianist left the stage as she began an encore, which ended abruptly after she bumped into the piano. "The lurid headlines which trumpeted her march across the country caused mayoral apoplexy and occasional cancellations," Hurok recalled later on, "but they also assured long lines at the box offices where she did appear." [18]

Duncan left America for good on 3 February 1923. Like many other artists and intellectuals after her, she rejected the rampant materialism that had accompanied America's postwar rise to economic preeminence. She was part of a generation of artists and intellectuals—many of them, like her, expatriates—who found America disgustingly materialistic, artistically and intellectually barren, and generally repressive. She criticized American culture, which, she pointed out, "still ha[s] child labor, and only the rich can see the opera, and beauty is commercialized by theater managers and motion picture magnates. All they want is money, money, money." [19] The theater in America, as she saw it, was no longer a temple but a house of prostitution.

Duncan was bitter about the scandal-mongering newspapers and about the petty parochial politicians. She abhorred Prohibition and despised the billboards cluttering the landscape. Among other things, she called America narrowminded, hypocritical, and intolerant. She criticized the country's marriage laws, child-rearing practices, commercialism, and overall mental and spiritual slavishness. "Routine, weary routine," she said, "the same old table in the middle of the same old floor, the same old books on the same old table—that's America." [20]

I hope that during this brief time I have been able to at least suggest, through a contextual reading of the popular press, how Duncan's body functioned as a site of political struggle during her final tour. What is of particular interest to me about Duncan's career in America is that, during each of her three major periods spent here, her body was a ground upon which social, political, and aesthetic issues were negotiated. In the cultural historian's quest for the larger meaning of dance as a cultural practice, criticism can yield important information about the cultural field in which dancer, critic, and spectator operate together.

> —Paper delivered to the 1993 joint conference
> of the Congress on Research in Dance
> and the Society of Dance History Scholars

Review: Lillian Loewenthal's *The Search for Isadora*

L ILLIAN LOEWENTHAL HAS contributed at least two scholarly articles to the Isadora Duncan literature, one on the dancer's early tours in the Netherlands and the other on her use of Chopin's music.[1] The articles are distinguished by their detailed research and sensitive analysis; unfortunately, the same cannot be said for Loewenthal's new book, *The Search for Isadora: The Legend & Legacy of Isadora Duncan* (Princeton Book Company, 1993).

The book is divided into three sections. "The Dance of Isadora Duncan" focuses on her aesthetics, stage practices (dancing, costuming, design), and use of music. "The Isadorables" deals with two of her schools (Grunewald and Bellevue) and her studio-home in Neuilly, as well as the Isadora Duncan Dancers, as a group and in separate portraits. "The Legend and Legacy" looks at Duncan's portrayal both in the French press and by artists and chroniclers such as Abraham Walkowitz, Antoine Bourdelle, and Michel Georges-Michel; at the career of Raymond Duncan; and at the dancer's death and burial. The epilogue considers the legacy of the Duncan repertory, what Loewenthal calls the "choreographies."

This oddly organized book, which skips idiosyncratically among various aspects of Duncan's life and career, is framed and shaped by the author's literal "search" for Isadora, a "self-styled odyssey" (x) to Europe that Loewenthal began in the early 1960s. The book's lack of coherence probably reflects the non-goal-oriented nature of Loewenthal's expeditions. She did not set out to write a book, she says, and what results seems to be an attempt to knit together accounts of her visits to Duncan landmarks, with the familiar outline of Duncan's dance practice serving as a necessary prelude. The book, which tells a familiar story, lacks a point of view other than that of the admirer. Loewenthal's voyages are both personal, inspired by her childhood epiphany in 1928 when she saw a performance of Duncan's Russian students, and intellectual, motivated by her desire "to enlarge my comprehension of Duncan and her dance as an esthetic phenomenon" (xii). Loewenthal cannot help but see through the eyes of the eleven-year-old girl who found herself

> in the midst of a riveting enchantment of bare legs and arms moving so deliriously free as they danced the dances of Isadora. The rhythmic life of their running and skipping across a seemingly limitless space in playful freedom and blissful joy produced an intoxication in itself. The graceful contours of their more contained and deliberate movements, like the freezing of motion by a photographer, firmly set images in my mind. Around this memory circled the thoughts that would attach me to the subject of Isadora Duncan—her dance and her music. I was moved to seek what there was about this art that had touched me so. (xv)

Isadora Duncan presents any researcher with a classic challenge: how to deal with an overexposed subject. Loewenthal responded by choosing what she considered the road less taken, seeking out artists who portrayed the dancer, surviving associates and friends, the Duncan repertory, her French press accounts, and Duncan's homes, schools, and burial site. I would guess that many scholars, fans, and biographers visit the architectural ruins of their subject's lives, but, in most cases, such visits do more for the writer's imagination than the subject's reality. In this case, Loewenthal's accounts of her "odyssey" do very little to reveal anything new about Duncan (or about Loewenthal, for that matter). There is no reason to doubt Loewenthal's word that she consulted a multitude of sources—written, visual, architectural, and human—in her thirty years of research, but that research is not analyzed and interpreted in the text in any substantial way. The book does include plentiful photographs, a handy chronology (which does not include dates of dance premieres), and an extensive bibliography, marked by breadth rather than depth. Sketchy and uneven, the book lives in a nether land between scholarship (footnotes are used, but not consistently enough) and travel literature (without the literary grace).

As a result, *The Search for Isadora* cannot equal its more focused predecessors. For biography, Fredrika Blair's *Isadora: Portrait of the Artist as a Woman* still prevails. For a concise synthesis of Duncan's aesthetic practice and sources, there is Deborah Jowitt's "The Search for Motion." For Duncan's place within the American cultural milieu, there is Elizabeth Kendall's *Where She Danced: The Birth of American Art-Dance.* For a portrait of her intimate life, there is Francis Steegmuller's *"Your Isadora": The Love Story of Isadora Duncan and Gordon Craig.* For a definitive photographic portrait, there is the new *Life into Art: Isadora Duncan and Her World,* edited by Doree Duncan, Carol Pratl, and Cynthia Splatt.[2]

—*Dance Research Journal,* 1994

Isadora Duncan and the Distinction of Dance

IN TURN-OF-THE-CENTURY America, Edith Wharton wrote in her autobiography, "Only two kinds of dancing were familiar . . . : waltzing in the ball-room and pirouetting on the stage."[1] Wharton missed her earliest opportunity to see the pioneering modern dancer Isadora Duncan (1877–1927), in 1899, when a Boston philanthropist and Newport hostess featured the aspiring young dancer at a garden party:

"Isadora Duncan?" People repeated the unknown name, wondering why it had been used to bait Miss Mason's invitation. . . . I hated pirouetting, and did not go to Miss Mason's. Those who did smiled, and said they supposed their hostess had asked the young woman to dance out of charity—as I daresay she did. Nobody had ever seen anything like it; you couldn't call it dancing, they said. No other Newport hostess engaged Miss Duncan, and her name vanished from everybody's mind.[2]

No doubt, the young Duncan's performances, sponsored by New York and Newport socialites, must have looked peculiar. She neither waltzed nor pirouetted. She did not kick up her legs; she manipulated no skirts; she rarely portrayed any specific character. In her more semantically polemical moments, Duncan rejected the label "dancer" altogether, in order to distinguish herself from the questionable antics of her colleagues.[3] Instead, she set herself apart as an "artiste," which is how she listed her occupation on the birth certificate for her second child, Patrick Augustus Duncan, in 1910.[4]

In late-nineteenth-century America, the popularity of the dancing girl grew alongside the development of theatrical syndicates, whose escapist entertainments reflected the increasing commercialism of the theater. The typical scenario, recalled by *Modern Dance Magazine* staffer Louis C. Fraina, went like this: "You enter. The audience, mostly male, eagerly eyes the stage. The air is heavy—the audience seems prepared for a 'good time.' They know about exactly what's coming—the blaze of color, the stupendous efforts to amaze, pretty chorus girls and clever principals—legs, toes, arms, hips, breasts, eyes, hair, the whole melange of stage femininity."[5] Thus, the female body was a staple ingredient in the spectacle extravaganzas that dominated the stage. The dancers' apparently nude legs (actually covered in "fleshings") were just another part of the mise-en-scène, to be marveled at along with the lavish costumes and incredible sets. (Ironically, it was the legs that were objectified, and the scenery that was mobilized.) By the turn of the century, the "dancer" was implicitly female, with little distinction between the trained ballerina, the entertaining skirt dancer, and the moonlighting factory-worker-cum-chorus-girl. She was constructed as a highly paid, empty-headed—and probably blonde—soubrette of ill repute. Subject to the whims of the novelty-hungry audiences through the theater manager, she was hired and fired largely on the basis of her looks.

It is no surprise, then, that Duncan was flatly rejected in her early auditions in San Francisco. Her dancing, one manager commented, was more suitable for church than theater.[6] Such managers, with their fingers on the pulse of the public's desires, were not interested in grace and art but in shapely legs, unveiled silhouettes, smiles, and availability. Audiences had clamored for the likes of Lola Montez, with her convulsing spider dance; Little Egypt's shimmying hootchy-cootchy; and "The Naked Lady" herself, Ada Isaacs Mencken, so named for her apparently nude ride strapped atop a "wild stallion" in *Mazeppa*. They flocked to see Lydia Thompson and her British Blondes, who transformed burlesque from its nineteenth-century emphasis on satire and parody into the twentieth-century striptease.[7]

But by World War I, in large part due to Isadora Duncan,[8] dance had been transformed from entertainment into "Culture," at least in New York.[9] Duncan reimagined the form and content of dance as an aesthetic object and convinced an audience of its legitimacy as a "high" art.[10] She created a "taste" for dance, and, furthermore, made it a matter of "good taste." Her style of dancing became so widespread that, by the 1910s, local dance teachers added it to their list of offerings, identified variably as "Natural dancing," or "Classic dancing," or "Aesthetic dancing." For working-class and immigrant girls and women, this style of dance literally added "class" to their lives, because it had become an emblem of Cultural refinement.

Duncan managed to accomplish what historian Lawrence W. Levine has described as the "sacralization of culture." By the end of the nineteenth century, Levine has shown, opera and the production of Shakespeare—arts that had enjoyed a status both popular and elite in this country—underwent a process by which they were reconceived as unquestionably elite. Although symphonic music and the visual arts were never quite as popular, they, too, gained their Cultural legitimacy through a newly institutionalized hierarchy that established standards and elevated taste. This process of sacralization endowed these arts "with unique aesthetic and spiritual properties that rendered it inviolate, exclusive, and eternal. This was not the mere ephemera of the world of entertainment but something lasting, something permanent."[11] Culture became synonymous with the European products of the symphonic hall, the opera house, the museum, and the library, now seen as veritable temples, "all of which, the American people were taught, must be approached with a disciplined, knowledgeable seriousness of purpose, and—most of all—with a feeling of reverence."[12]

How, in less than two decades, did Duncan gain this reverence for dance? By deconstructing and reconstructing it as a practice of high, white, Western Culture for the privileged classes of northeastern cities. She used strategies of difference and exclusion, exploiting the conventional distinctions between high and low and appropriating the legitimacy of established European practices and discourses.

Taste, according to French sociologist Pierre Bourdieu, is not disinterested; rather, it is rooted in social origin and in education. As an arbiter of taste, Culture is not just reflective, but also productive. That is to say, it is not just "the state of that which is cultivated," but also "the process of cultivating."[13] This process of cultivating—which, similarly to Levine, Bourdieu calls "cultural consecration"—confers "on the objects, persons and situations it touches, a sort of onto-logical promotion akin to a transubstantiation." [14] By inscribing into perception and practice a "distinction" (difference that produces hierarchy) between the sacred sphere of legitimate, or high, Culture, and the mere vulgarity of enter-tainment, Cultural practice thus fulfills a social function, whether conscious or not, of legitimating social—and specifically class—difference. In this essay, I want to identify the strategies that Duncan employed in order to establish the distinction of dance and then consider their social implications. But first I will outline some larger contours of her early relationship with American Culture as a "classical" dancer.

Culture and Nature, Greeks and "Primitives"

UNABLE TO FIND encouragement for her fledgling dance, Duncan fled her na-tive San Francisco for Chicago, and then New York. In 1899, at the age of twenty-two, she abandoned America altogether for Europe: first London, then Paris. The American press's amused depiction of Duncan as a "Greek" dancer began in reports from Paris salon society in 1901 and peaked during her first trip to the land of Apollo and Dionysus in 1903. Her rhetorical dependence on classical precedents lasted from about 1901 to 1904,[15] when her experiment with a Greek boys choir, singing "authentic" Greek music for her performances, ended unsuc-cessfully. Although she would return to the Greeks later, in the 1910s, for different reasons, during this early period she was stressing the ancients' discovery of beauty in Nature and of Nature in the human form. And, not inconsequently, Duncan's Greek rhetoric ended up functioning as a novelty in an era of novelty-driven theater and journalism. Just as Ruth St. Denis's gimmick was the "exotic" and Loie Fuller's was the "picturesque," so Duncan's was the "classical."

For America in the several decades before and after the turn of the century, "Greece" (conceived more from the likes of John Keats's "Ode on a Grecian Urn" than anything archeological) was an idea about Cultural legitimacy. An animating Cultural fantasy since the Greek Revival in the early 1800s, Hellenist enthusiasm indicated the renewed, post–Civil War aspirations of a burgeoning nation, without its own pedigreed past, to flourish in all its aspects—scientific, industrial, politi-cal, social, and cultural. The renewal of the Olympic Games in 1896 had sparked interest in the Greek ideal of the body, helping to reinforce Duncan's insistence on its beauty and nobility. Greek games were held at colleges such as Barnard and Berkeley, and outdoor Greek theaters, like the one at Berkeley, were built in cities large and small. In the wake of the 1893 World's Columbian Exposition, whose organizers purposefully chose a neoclassical architectural style over an incipient American modernism, civic and commercial buildings across the country—the courthouse, the state capitol, the university, the commemorative statue, even the firehouse—were being built in the image of the great Greek temple, its soaring columns and monumentality a visual declaration of collective ambition. In the flush of its imminent world-class status, America—as well as Britain, Germany, and France—envisioned itself as the true heir of the great Greek civilization, in all its political, economic, and artistic glory.

When Duncan returned to America in August 1908, after ten years abroad, producer Charles Frohman's press agents began spreading word of Duncan's "celebrated classical dances" before she even reached shore.[16] After several seasons of Indian incantations, Salome dances, and Loie Fuller look-alikes, the Greek dance was a welcome distraction. Despite Frohman's efforts to sell her as a Greek dancer, however, the Criterion Theatre audiences were not responsive to such refined references. As a *Variety* reviewer explained:

> To one whose vision is perhaps somewhat warped by too frequent attendance upon vaudeville performances and whose culture in classic Art is rather less than inconsiderable, Isadora Duncan's attempt to monopolize a whole audience—and a $2 audience at that—for an entire evening, has very much the complexion of Paul McAllister's untoward experiment as a condensed "Hamlet" in vaudeville. . . .
>
> Now comes along Miss Duncan with an immense success in Europe as a recommendation and offers Broadway (as distinguished from East 125th Street) an entertainment the lofty pretension of Art of which is in about the same relation to the established standard of entertainment.
>
> . . . It is a fairly safe venture that a goodly percentage of the Criterion's audience who lent their applause to the none too plentiful gaiety of the evening did so because they thought that it was the proper thing to do and not because they found real delight in Miss Duncan's performances.[17]

The theater audiences, who were accustomed to even lighter entertainment than usual during the summer season, were suspicious of anything pretending to "Art." (And, yet, the *Variety* review makes clear the social pressure to recognize and acknowledge "Art.") Duncan had better luck with her northeastern out-of-town engagements, but when she returned to New York, she and Frohman canceled their contract. She began, instead, a series of immensely successful engagements with Walter Damrosch's prestigious New York Symphony Orchestra.

Her appearances with Damrosch were in concert halls and opera houses, such as the Metropolitan, with a considerably different audience and set of critics. The audience was upper class, predominantly female, and thirsty for "Art." The critics flattered Duncan with comparisons grand and undiscriminating: not only to Greek sculptures and vases, but also to Keats's "Ode on a Grecian Urn" and even to Wedgewood pottery. In order to describe Duncan, *New York Daily Tribune*'s highly respected music critic, H. E. Krehbiel, invoked the British minister Charles

Kingsley's fanciful description of Greek dancing, "in which every motion was a word, and rest as eloquent as motion; in which every attitude was a fresh motion for a sculptor of the purest school, and the highest physical activity was manifested, not, as in coarse pantomime, in fantastic bounds and unnatural distortions, but in perpetual, delicate modulations of a stately and self-sustained grace."[18] Duncan performed excerpts from Gluck's *Iphigenia in Aulis,* portraying the Greek maidens as they played ball and knuckle-bones and spied the Greek fleet in the dance. Then she added *Iphigenia in Tauris* and *Orpheus* to her repertoire, strongly reinforcing her reputation as the "Greek" dancer. Duncan may not have intended to copy ancient Greek dances per se,[19] but she did admit to imitating their gauzy, tunic-style clothing, and her audiences immediately recognized the reference.

Despite the identification of this "Natural" body with "nudity," Duncan never performed nude. Her Greek costume left her breasts free (early versions of the brassiere were not widely marketed as an alternative to the corset until the 1920s) and modestly covered her groin, eradicating any pubic hair, as did the ancient statuary. Duncan's audiences accepted the tunic as a sign of nudity; moreover, they accepted it as a sign of *classical* nudity, whose claim to the Natural guaranteed the moral and the noble. The warm glow of Duncan's stage lighting helped to create that ideal image, since it softened the reality of bare flesh, as did pancake makeup later in her career.[20]

In the eyes of these moneyed, educated, largely female Americans, Classical art had made the liberating connection between nudity and nobility that had been impossible within the Puritan tradition. As they saw it, the body, as depicted on the vases and in the statuary, was endowed with an ideal form both moral and beautiful. For women such as Mrs. William K. Kavanaugh of St. Louis, who defended Duncan against a minister who had characterized the dancer as a Midway come-on, Duncan was "an exquisite figure on an old vase that we are allowed to admire with all propriety."[21] As Americans constructed it, the unquestioned authority of Greek art allowed even a woman to contemplate the naked body with a good conscience and at the same time to congratulate herself on possessing an elevated taste—an elevation not only moral but social as well.

In this way, Duncan, who believed that "Education of the young is the only way to bring taste and understanding to the working class,"[22] was not so different from the self-described "merchants of culture, professional men and artists"[23] who started the Metropolitan Museum of Art. These robber-barons-cum-Culture-brokers sought to establish Culture from the top down, so that eventually even the uneducated manual laborer could gain enlightenment through the love of the "Beautiful." For regardless of the country's industrial and commercial prosperity, explained one Metropolitan patron, it still needed to prove itself Culturally:

> The wealth of a nation lies not in its material pursuits alone. In a new country like ours they are the first to occupy its people, but when the forests are cleared, the roads built, the mines opened, the land tilled, manufactories in operation, and habitations are built, unless the higher part of man's nature is developed in the realm of art, whether useful, beautiful or romantic, like music and poetry, the nation relapses into barbarism.[24]

Duncan, too, was concerned that the masses not sink back into "primitivism," that is to say, Africanism, which functioned in her practice as the paradigm of that precivilized state of being she endeavored to elevate.

Unlike her experiences in Germany, France, and the Soviet Union, where she opened free schools for all kinds of children, Duncan never was able to put her egalitarian educational ideas into practice in America. It was not Duncan herself, but the Duncan-style dance schools that opened across the country in the wake of her appearances that forged contact between her ideas and the immigrant/working class.[25] For example, modern dancer Helen Tamiris's father, a Russian Jewish immigrant, sent her to Duncan-style classes at the Henry Street Settlement in order to get her off the streets of the Lower East Side.[26] For decades, thousands of women and young girls like Tamiris flocked to classes in Classic, Natural, or Aesthetic dancing, and, in this process, hoped to acquire "Culture."

Strategies of Distinction

BOURDIEU CONCEIVES of society as being organized into "fields," each of which is a structured and structuring system of social relations with its own logic. Any field, including that of Culture, has its own economy, so to speak, in which capital—economic, social, educational, symbolic—must be accumulated in order to advance or dominate in that field. The strategies for accumulating such capital and for gaining legitimacy, or distinction, are regulated by the field itself. These predisposed strategies, a generative constellation of tacit, internalized, embodied principles and practices, are what Bourdieu calls a field's "habitus." These unwritten rules are learned not explicitly, but implicitly, through practice in the field. Although the general contours of the habitus are shared by each player in the field, each individual, having come from a different background and thus occupying a different position within the field, have a slightly different habitus.[27]

Duncan internalized the habitus of the Cultural field early in her life, although much of her childhood was spent in poverty and on the outskirts of polite society. Duncan's parents, Joseph Charles and Mary Dora Duncan, apparently divorced shortly after the birth of their fourth child, Angela Isadora.[28] Without support, the thirty-year-old divorcee had to eke out a living for herself and her children by selling knitted goods and giving music lessons. Fleeing more expensive San Francisco, the Duncan clan crossed the Bay to Oakland, where they moved frequently from one rented room to the next. Perhaps because she was the youngest and thus would garner the most sympathy, little "Dora" was the one sent to charm the credit from the baker. Sometimes cold and hungry, the four young Duncans enjoyed a rather unsupervised childhood: Dora dropped out of school around age twelve. Whenever a little money did come their way, they spent it profligately on treats and luxuries, as if in defiance of their actual economic circumstances.

The Duncans' poverty was compounded by a considerable fall from social grace. Before the divorce, the Duncans had been a respected San Francisco family. Joseph C. Duncan was an art connoisseur and a cunning businessman. The suave and cultured man had been a lifelong poet and an accomplished journalist. Early on, he had published the poetry of Ina Coolbrith (an Oakland librarian familiar to young Dora) who later would become poet laureate of California. For a time he had run an auction house, and then became an art dealer, traveling to Europe to purchase his goods. A private art collector and one of the first presidents of the San Francisco Art Association, he was a leading force in establishing the fine arts there. Unfortunately, art dealing was not consistently profitable, so he turned to real estate, back to journalism, and then on to banking. He founded both the Safe Deposit Company, of which he was primary stockholder, and the Pioneer Land and Loan Bank of Savings, of which he was secretary and manager. But with a wildly erratic economy, the tapering off of the silver mines, and hence the failure or suspension of other, more established banks, Duncan himself ran into trouble. He attempted to keep his bank afloat through some shady dealings, but it collapsed, nonetheless, in October 1877. Accused of forgery, embezzlement, and grand larceny, Duncan ignominiously fled the charges but was eventually found. After four inconclusive trials, the charges finally were dismissed on a technicality, in January 1882.[29]

Despite—or because of—the poverty and the social stigma of jail and divorce, the Duncans clung to their artistic aspirations. For Isadora, it substituted for formal schooling. "My real education," she wrote in her autobiography, *My Life,* "came during the evenings when my mother played to us Beethoven, Schumann, Schubert, Mozart, Chopin or read aloud to us from Shakespeare, Shelley, Keats, or Burns."[30] Their living room functioned as a salon, where Mother played piano; Aunt Augusta, in shorts, recited Hamlet; and Isadora, of course, danced. On the wall hung a reproduction of Botticelli's "Primavera," which she later would transform into a dance.

The family's last two years in California, however, were spent more comfortably, back in San Francisco. By 1893, Joseph Duncan had collected a new family and a new fortune, with which he bought Mary Dora and the four children a stately home called Castle Mansion. The clan's private theatricals expanded into a barn theater, run by brother Augustin, which developed into a brief tour down the

California coast. For several years, the family enjoyed a higher standard of living. They gained some reputation among the town's better families for the dancing school run by Isadora and her older sister, Elizabeth. Accompanied by her mother, Elizabeth also had taught at exclusive girls schools, bringing the family to the edges of, but hardly inside, high society. But by 1895 Joseph Duncan lost his fortune, and the occupants of Castle Mansion again fell on hard times.

Duncan claimed—and I do believe her—that even as a child she knew she was destined for greatness. Without any educational, social, or economic capital, however, her acceptance into the domain of Culture was largely unlikely, especially since dancing itself held no currency in that realm. But Duncan learned at a young age about the intimacy between class and taste, between social and artistic prestige. Denied the illusion of meritocracy that inheres in a comfortable middle-class upbringing, Duncan became a remarkable master of the signs and emblems of dominant taste, and she used that practical knowledge to gain distinction for her art. Duncan's savvy for positioning her dancing vis-à-vis major social institutions or practices (alignment with science, for example, or opposition to ballet) was as brilliant a performance as her dancing.

With the nineteenth-century sacralization of culture, the arts had become implicated in class status. The Duncans, with Joseph at their head, established class status not just by virtue of his income but also by virtue of his publicly demonstrated aesthetic mastery. When the Duncans, sans Joseph, lost all their money and their social position, they endeavored to maintain and, later, to elevate their status through their refined Cultural sensibilities. Those evening salons functioned not merely as self-amusement but as the private performance of class. Duncan dealt with the considerable anxiety of her changing childhood fortunes by adopting a flagrant lifelong disinterest in the management of money and thus a denial of its importance; she displaced the definition of class from money to art. If class brought Culture (as the nouveau riche took great pains to demonstrate), then could not Culture bring class? Duncan, and the girls and women who would later flock to Duncan-style dance classes, believed so.

The usefulness of Bourdieu's scheme to an analysis of Duncan's elevation of dance as an American art form is its attention to the ways an artist constructs distinction/difference, in both practice and in the perception of that practice. Using Bourdieu's model, we can look at how Duncan made specific choices in preexisting, intersecting fields: how she strategically engaged economic, social, intellectual, and Cultural institutions and practices.

Duncan's choices consistently aligned her dancing with upper-class white Euro-America. Dancing was considered cheap, so she associated herself with the great Greeks, who deemed the art noble, and she associated herself with upper-class audiences, by carefully courting her patrons and selecting her performance venues. Dancing was considered mindless, so she invoked a pantheon of great minds, from Darwin to Whitman and Plato to Nietzsche, to prove otherwise. Dancing was considered feminine, and thus trivial, so she chose well her liaisons and mentors—men whose cultural or economic power accrued, by association, to her. Dancing was considered profane, so she elevated her own practice by contrasting it to that of "African primitives." The fundamental strategy of Duncan's project to gain Cultural legitimacy for dancing was one of exclusion. In order to reinvent the idea of the "dancer," that is to say, to make dancing (but, specifically, her kind of dancing) a matter of good taste, within the existing Cultural field, Duncan employed the dominant logic of difference along a number of axes, and used it to construct distinction. Effectively, she elevated dancing from low to high, from sexual to spiritual, from black to white, from profane to sacred, from woman to goddess, from entertainment to art.

She accomplished this through a range of communicative means—kinesthetic, visual, and verbal. In performance, she embedded references to the Greeks in her costuming, music, mise-en-scène, and movement vocabulary. In photographs, whose relative scarcity (considering her fame) evidences Duncan's great concern about the circulation of her image, clothed herself *à la grecque,* sometimes explicitly quoting Greek iconography in her prose. The visual was predominated by the verbal, with which she felt quite comfortable. Her father, after all, was a writer, and she had begun writing (a novel, a neighborhood newspaper, a journal) at a young age. Duncan's speeches, both off- and onstage, increased as her career progressed. She preached (usually freedom) and pleaded (usually for money, for a school) like a bluestocking. She freely granted newspaper interviews (and learned well how to meet their need for good copy), and wrote letters-to-the-editor as well. Program notes (poems, blurbs from reviews, dramaturgical notes on the Greek productions) supplemented her performances; booklets, such as the early and enduring manifesto, "Dance of the Future," and a short-lived magazine also functioned to establish and extend the legitimacy of her art.

Of particular interest is a booklet titled "Dionysion," published in 1914, presumably to accompany her performances. Printed on beautiful, deckle-edged paper, it consists of nothing but a series of quotes, one per page or spread, simply designed, in an elegant typeface. Auguste Rodin's and Eugène Carrière's eulogies to her are included, and her own paean to the dance of the future is sandwiched between Walt Whitman and Friedrich Nietzsche. Duncan's meditation on the Greek theater precedes Percy Bysshe Shelley's "Hellas," and there are passages on Isadora's school and pupils (for which she was then raising money) by poet Percy MacKaye and writer/editor Mary Fanton Roberts. Nothing less than the Bible is given the final word: "Thou hast turned for me my mourning into dancing," a reference to Duncan's loss of three children. Thus Duncan wove herself into the center of a network of both Euro-American and local New York Cultural authorities. The appropriation is made complete by twin images that frame the text, a picture of a Greek statue on the front cover, and one of Duncan on the back, making clear the dancer's desire to be seen as a Greek goddess. This strategy helped to lift her from the realm of the physical, with its emphasis on female body parts, to that of the aesthetic.

Except for a very early vaudeville turn in Chicago and the ill-fated season at Frohman's Criterion Theatre in 1908, Duncan refused to perform in theatrical venues. Rather, she positioned herself, both literally and symbolically, in high-priced opera houses and concert halls mostly in northeastern urban centers, allying herself with symphony orchestras such as Walter Damrosch's, whose cache was already established. In one of her boldest moves, she dared to appropriate the canon of great symphonic works, notably with Beethoven's Seventh Symphony in A Major. To some New York music critics, who had only recently won their own victory for the sacralization of absolute music, such an idea cried heresy. It was perhaps justifiable for her to use Chopin's mazurkas and polonaises, or Gluck's dance interludes, or even Wagner's dance music, but it was an indefensible breach of aesthetic convention to attempt any "interpretation" of the great concert and operatic works. Despite the immediate indignant furor by music critics, Duncan prevailed, and her dancing came to be identified with the names of Tchaikovsky, Schubert, and Liszt as well.

But before Duncan ever got to the point of public performance, she was cultivating—and being cultivated by—wealthy women, whose patronage was an important factor in the establishment of Culture at the turn of the century. Symphonies, art galleries, and, later, the little theater movement were largely spearheaded by these philanthropic women.[31] Duncan's early drawing-room performances in Chicago, New York, and Newport were sponsored by the likes of Mrs. A. M. Dodge and Mrs. Nicholas Beach, whose afternoon soirées attracted attention from the most well-known society reporters. Duncan's Delsarte-based performances resonated with the likes of Mrs. W. C. Whitney, Mrs. William Astor, and Mrs. Stuyvesant Fish, who had met twice weekly in Delsarte-style classes in a distant Newport summer, "to writhe, wriggle, bend and sway; to relax and decompose [and to] form spiral curves and make corkscrews of themselves."[32] In her earliest New York performances, Duncan attracted the same female audience that had patronized Delsarte-based classes and performances, both of which often employed Greek imagery. Duncan's dancing, and the classical statue-posing of Genevieve Stebbins before her, presented women with a rare theatrical opportunity to identify with Woman as both the source and emblem of Art.

When, after a Newport lecture-demonstration of Duncan's version of Omar Khayám's then-fashionable *Rubáiyát*, Mrs. Astor herself "invited Miss Duncan to sit by her upon a divan and talked with her for twenty minutes upon the music and poetry of movement, the young lecturer's future was settled as far as the Four Hundred are concerned."[33] Similarly, when Duncan later returned to New York, her reputation was based in no small measure on her reported associations with the cultural, intellectual, and social elite: "The Alma Tademas saw her dance, and so succumbed to her charm that she became thenceforth their protege and was made much of by London's exclusive aesthetic set. The 'smart' and the titled sets followed after. The Prince of Wales himself applauded her."[34] The imprimatur of elite patrons—kings and capitalists—gained Duncan an aura of economic leisure and social pedigree.

Social capital, Bourdieu explains, encompasses a number of culturally, economically, politically, and sexually useful personal relations. Besides overcoming the disadvantages of an impoverished background by cultivating the patronage of upper-crust hostesses and royalty, Duncan also overcame the disadvantages of being a woman by associating herself—sexually, socially, artistically, and intellectually—with well-placed men. Edward Gordon Craig, a brilliant theater theorist and designer and father of her first child, reinforced her early aesthetic hunches (although, truth be told, he gained much more from the liaison than she did). Paris Singer, heir to the Singer sewing machine fortune and father of her second child, gave her economic freedom and entree into moneyed European society. Walter Damrosch's eager collaboration was especially important to Duncan's early artistic reputation in America. And, of course, Duncan was not shy about dropping names—Wagner, Rodin, Haeckel, Nietzsche, Schopenhauer, Darwin. I am not saying that Duncan consciously chose male associations because of their gender per se, but rather that, given the sexually divided social, cultural, and intellectual fields at that time, the almost exclusive dependence on men (aside from her early patronesses) was a logical—and effective—means of increasing her capital.[35]

Duncan's most successful strategy in sacralizing dance was "Greece," a symbolic matrix whose set of signifiers cut across the aesthetic, economic, intellectual, and social fields. It was embedded not only in her flowery prose, but also in her dancing—the stories, the costumes, the movement vocabulary—and the grand manner of her lifestyle (her clothing, as well as her widely publicized trips to Greece). By invoking the classical ideal, Duncan effectively displayed her education and refinement. The Hellenistic practices also presupposed a certain class of spectator: not the likes of the *Variety* reviewer who mocked the artistic pretension of "the celebrated classical dancer," but rather an educated viewer reared on classical literature and philosophy.

In the Greeks, Duncan constructed an origin for her "Natural" dancing, as opposed to ballet, which she described as physically, aesthetically, and morally deforming. No doubt genuine in her stance, Duncan was, nevertheless, capitalizing on a preexisting discourse. Even before Duncan ever trod the boards, cultural and intellectual leaders were interested in reclaiming dancing as something more than mere "amusement," which implied a lack of social import or, worse, moral degeneracy. Duncan galvanized discourses that had already been established by American and Continental intellectuals, who had begun to make quite serious inquiries into the nature and status of dancing. From the 1860s to the turn of the century, and especially around 1890, dancing became a legitimate topic of consideration in respected books, such as Mrs. Lilly Grove's *Dancing*, and in journals such as *Popular Science Monthly, Eclectic Magazine, Lippincott's* and *Contemporary Review*.[36] Authors criticized the state of the art: acrobatic entertainment, ta-ra-ra-boom-de-ay skirt dancing, and the ballet, with its ever-shortening tutu. Although it was generally agreed that dancing was in serious decline, authors recounted its past glories and called for its "renaissance."

The Social Origins/Effects of Modern Dance

I HAVE ARGUED elsewhere that Isadora Duncan offered her American audiences a means of imagining themselves in the radical process of transformation.[37] For artists and intellectuals, she did embody in her dance practice a revolutionary ethos. "This solitary figure on the lonely stage suddenly confronts each of us with the secret of a primal desire invincibly inhering in the fibre of each," wrote the poet Shaemus O'Sheel, "a secret we had securely hidden beneath our conventional behaviors, and we yearn for a new and liberated order in which we may indeed dance."[38] It also needs to be said, however, that, for the upper class, she reproduced a seemingly apolitical, disinterested Platonic "Beauty." And, later on, for her middle-class "audiences," who experienced Duncan mostly secondhand, in the press and through imitators, she represented taste and breeding. Without dismissing the very real subversive meaning of her dancing for some of her audience, we also must recognize that Duncan's project was no less about cultural legitimacy than it was about aesthetics. And that this aesthetic practice was produced by and, in turn, continued to reproduce social differences.

Duncan's idea and use of Greece was really about the aesthetic of a "Natural" body. It was not a willful flight from high culture, off to some precivilized utopia. Neither was it a Whitmanesque celebration of the common folk, despite her genuine love for the poet's earthy vision. Duncan emphasized the noble over the savage; her model, after all, was the Nike of Samothrace, not Pocahontas. This "Natural" body, the foundational trope from which she theorized both her aesthetic and social agenda, was the artistic transformation of Nature into Culture. It was artless artifice. And "Nature" was only "Nature" when it was thus ennobled;[39] otherwise, it remained base primitivism: "People ask me, do you consider love making an art and I would answer that not only love but every part of life should be practiced as an art. For we are no longer in the state of the primitive savage, but the whole expression of our life must be created through culture and the transformation of intuition and instinct into art."[40] In other words, the "Natural" body is a "civilized" body. Duncan wanted to establish dance as "civilized," which she did, at least in part, by establishing its essential difference from the "primitive savage" she saw as manifesting itself in the African-rooted social dances of the early teens.

Despite its roots in the classical world (by way of modern European thinkers such as Winckelmann and Nietzsche), Duncan's "Natural" body paradoxically offered the paradigm for what she felt to be a uniquely new, uniquely American culture. Although Duncan's noble Hellenic associations failed to make much connection with the Criterion's working-class audience, the link with Greek Culture found believers among the wealthy, educated class of white Americans who could afford tickets to see her at the opera house or concert hall—a class deeply invested in the establishment of a national Cultural identity.[41] And despite whatever initial resistance the working class may have had to such highfalutin Hellenism, the imperative of upward mobility to revere "Art" later brought them to the altar of dance as well, if not as spectators (which assumes a certain habitus), then as students (which entrains habitus).

Duncan was specifically interested in appropriating the roots of *Western* (white) Culture, with the Greeks. The Egyptians, she said, were origin of an-*other* (black) race.[42] During her Argentinian tour of 1916, Duncan called her unfriendly audiences "niggers," asserting that they were simply not advanced enough to appreciate her Art.[43] As for ragtime and jazz, whose popularity provided her with fierce competition during her second set of American tours, she scornfully dismissed them on many an occasion as "this deplorable modern dancing, which has its roots in the ceremonies of African primitives."[44] Unlike some of her European contemporaries, Duncan found neither beauty nor inspiration in what she perceived as a vulgar practice lacking in all taste.

Many social leaders agreed with Duncan that this modern dancing that saturated the country from 1911 to 1915 was unbecomingly violent and spastic.[45] While many criticized what they saw as the seething sexuality of dances such as the black bottom or the fox trot, Duncan objected to them as vulgar on different grounds. In literal and metaphorical terms, the popularity of modern dancing, which she identified with "African primitivism," threatened Duncan's social vision of unity and harmony. She railed against the uncontrolled character—the presumed *chaos*— of ragtime and jazz, because it symbolically threatened the moral *order* of civilization, which was precisely that moral order engendered by Duncan's first principle, the harmonious ideal of "Nature" that she had gleaned from the Greece of Winckelmann and Botticelli and from the monism of Ernst Haeckel. According to Haeckel, God inhered within the singular web of the cosmos.

After reading Haeckel, Duncan came to understand "Nature" as a comprehensive system whose inherent harmony she mapped onto her body. "Nature" signified order. "Nature" served as a comforting, orderly matrix for all the fiercely multiplying, often contrary, elements in the universe—a universe whose microscopic and extraterrestrial boundaries were expanding daily, through the rapidly paced discoveries of science. "I always put into my movements," she wrote, "a little of that divine continuity which gives to all of Nature its beauty and life."[46] The "Natural" body, which represented her ideal society, was one that moved harmoniously, as a single unit whose each minute part functioned interdependently. It embodied the basic wavelike patterns and principles of movement in "Nature."

Although a large part of Duncan's appeal was her seeming spontaneity (and she fed this illusion, that her dancing was improvised onstage), Duncan's dancing was far from wild. It was, according to *Masses* editor Max Eastman, a perfect proportion of "art with nature, restraint with abandon."[47] Although "spontaneous," her movement style had a decided sense of flowing, unhurried gentility. Compared to what was described as the "spasms" or "paroxysms" of Africanist dances, she embodied a spontaneity tempered with the unspoken, unquestioned control that marked good breeding. This particular bodily hexis (to borrow Bourdieu's term for embodied dispositions of belief)—ease borne of effortless control—was that of the upper class.[48]

By constituting a "Natural" body as the basis for dance practice, Duncan effectively removed from it any vulgar requirement of *labor,* which would have smacked of the working class; instead, it could be imbued with an aura of the innate—of good taste, which is, by definition, effortless. Something that ballet, constituted as it was by its demanding technique, could not claim. Since the popular perception of the ballet dancer was collapsed into that of untrained chorus girls, its social position was associated with lower-class women who turned to dancing as a means of making a living. Thus, even though ballet could claim the history of kings, it still required and connoted work.[49] Onstage or off, Duncan always aligned herself with leisure, luxury, and ease—never with necessity. "When in doubt," she often said, "always go to the best hotel."[50]

This is not to say, however, that Duncan was a calculating aristocrat. She was hardly unsympathetic toward the American masses; in her late career, after encountering the Soviet experiment, she claimed them as her true audience. Inhering in Duncan's art was a curious tension between the desire to legitimize dance as an aesthetic object through a strategy of exclusion, and the desire to spread dance as a social practice through a strategy of inclusion. Part of her desired to see the whole world liberate itself through dancing. But, really, she only accepted the "masses" on her own terms: as those who could be "uplifted" through the experience of Culture and, thus, affirming through their uplift the class difference that is ostensibly being erased. When she lauded the abilities of the tenement-dwellers on the Lower East Side to appreciate her Art, she did so primarily as a means of shaming unresponsive millionaires into contributing money for her to start a school.

Thus, when Duncan was denouncing African primitivism, or invoking Nietzsche, or constructing herself as a Greek goddess, she was producing and reproducing the social divisions between high and low. By operating strategically within the structures of the upper class, she was developing an audience and thus a "taste" for her art that drew upon and reinforced its distinction from all others—blacks, immigrants, the poor, the uneducated, the middle class. Bourdieu calls this effective social exclusion "symbolic violence: a symbolic means of per-petuating social difference in an age when overt violence has become unacceptable." [51]

Approaching Dance as Social Practice

Founded, at least in part, as a rebellion against ballet, the genre of American modern dance has long been approached by dance historians as embodying a democratic ethos. If ballet was about the subservience of the self to a male, European, aristocratic tradition, then modern dance was about the discovery of the self through a female, American, democratic experiment. A Bourdieu-modeled analysis of Duncan's practice, which looks closely at the social and historical bases of that Cultural production, yields a different, more complex story.

In order to gain legitimacy for what would later become institutionalized as American modern dance, Duncan engaged strategies whose ideological sources and effects were at odds with the democratic reputation that modern dance has come to enjoy. In fact, modern dance in America was constructed from and for high Culture, that is to say, white, Western, male Culture. And at the heart of this construction, silent and unacknowledged, is the Africanist presence against which Duncan established her art as acceptable to an upper-crust audience. [52] At the heart of St. Denis's Orientalist practice, too, lay the "darkie," this one from the East, through whose negotiation of sexuality and spirituality she appealed to a specifically middle-class audience. In both cases, the Americanness of modern dance (one of our few indigenous genres of art) was established through the use of an Africanist body as "surrogate and enabler," to quote Toni Morrison. "Africanism is the vehicle," she has written, "by which the American self knows itself as not enslaved, but free; not repulsive, but desirable; not helpless, but licensed and powerful; not history-less, but historical; not damned, but innocent; not a blind accident of evolution, but a progressive fulfillment of destiny."[53] And, I would add, Africanism is the vehicle by which the American self posited by Duncan knew itself as not primitive, but Cultured.

For the study of modern dance as social practice (rather than just aesthetic object), Bourdieu's framework offers a plausible alternative to the two extremes of cultural interpretation: on the one hand, "rational-actor" subjectivism, and on the other hand, objective determinism. It offers us a way to see that Duncan was neither a "genius," forging new practices out of thin air, nor a passive function of her cultural context. Yes, Duncan's choices and strategies were delimited by the institutions and practices of her day, but they were choices, nonetheless. Bourdieu's concept of the habitus yokes together internal choice and external conditions into a mutually conditional and—this is most important—generative dynamic. He posits the artist as occupying a relational, potentially changeable position in an equally changeable field. Thus we can recognize the social structures and practices through which Duncan negotiated her art while also acknowledging her agency. And vice versa. We can recognize her agency and still acknowledge the social structures that gave rise to that agency.

Such an approach to dance as social practice could push the field of American early modern dance scholarship past its focus on individual figures and their oeuvres and facilitate inquiry into some of the larger, underinvestigated questions, such as: Why was modern dance founded by women? Was it or was it not a subversive practice? What were the origins and effects of its bodily hexis in other fields? What was the nature of its patronage by colleges? How did it spread, geographically? What were the meanings of its Americana phase, in the 1930s? How and why was it institutionalized? By what means did ballet and modern dance struggle for predominance? Isadora Duncan's own struggle for distinction is merely the beginning, rather than the end, of an inquiry into the cultural production of modern dance in America.

—American Studies, 1994

Isadora Duncan's Dance Theory

IN AMERICA, around 1900, Edith Wharton wrote in her autobiography that "Only two kinds of dancing were familiar . . . : waltzing in the ballroom and pirouetting on the stage."[1] Wharton missed her earliest opportunity to see Duncan, in 1899, when a Boston philanthropist and Newport hostess featured the young dancer at a garden party:

"Isadora Duncan?" People repeated the unknown name, wondering why it had been used to bait Miss Mason's invitation. . . . I hated pirouetting, and did not go to Miss Mason's. Those who did smiled, and said they supposed their hostess had asked the young woman to dance out of charity—as I daresay she did. Nobody had ever seen anything like it; you couldn't call it dancing, they said. No other Newport hostess engaged Miss Duncan, and her name vanished from everybody's mind.[2]

No doubt, the young Duncan's earliest performances must have looked peculiar. She neither waltzed nor pirouetted. She did not kick up her legs; she manipulated no skirts; she rarely portrayed any specific character. Legend even has it (though not quite accurately) that she was maverick enough at a very tender age to disavow her toe dancing lessons. In her more semantically polemical moments, Duncan rejected the label "dancer" altogether, in order to disassociate herself from the questionable antics of her colleagues.[3] Instead, she set herself apart as an "artiste." That is what she listed as her occupation on the birth certificate for her second child, Patrick Augustus Duncan, in 1910.[4]

Duncan's dancing was something very new. And yet it did not spring whole from the head of Zeus, as she preferred people to think.[5] Rather, she emerged into—and galvanized—discourses and practices that had already been established by American and European intellectuals, who had begun to make quite serious inquiries into the nature and status of dancing. "How has dancing [as a social institution] reached its present recognition as an important function of civilised life," inquired one such writer, "and can that position be justified on rational, moral, or aesthetic grounds?"[6] From the 1860s to the turn of the century, and especially around 1890, dancing became a legitimate topic of consideration in respected journals and books. Authors criticized the current state of the art: acrobatic entertainment, ta-ra-ra-boom-de-ay skirt dancing, and the ballet, with its ever-shortening tutu. Although it was generally agreed that dancing was in serious decline ("This first-born and eldest sister of the arts has fallen upon evil times in this old age of the world"[7]) authors recounted its past glories and called for its "renaissance."

Even before Duncan ever trod the boards, cultural and intellectual leaders were interested in reclaiming dancing as something more than mere "amusement," which implied a lack of social import or, worse, moral degeneracy. By 1893, according to a presentation at the World's Congress of Representative Women, social dancing was taught in primary schools, enjoyed in "modern girls' clubs" and at parties, and even sanctioned as church recreation. "The ethical value of the dance," observed Lady Battersea, "must depend upon the wholesome exercises it entails, upon the fine spirits is engenders, and upon the healthy social tone it imparts."[8]

Furthermore, dancing became an appropriate subject of legitimate scholarly study, not under the aegis of the arts but in the spirit of scientific inquiry, whose desire for causality and classification lent respectability to the study of dancing, both historically and anthropologically. One writer laid out the necessities of such a discipline: "Why do people dance? How have they danced? What (if any) is the essential difference between the dancing of the South Sea Islands and the dancing of Queen's Gate? . . . These are the essential problems of the virgin study of comparative chorology, a science which is still, in 1885, awaiting its exponent."[9]

Evolution theory, in particular, gave new impetus to the study of dance in "primitive" cultures; such dances were seen as living artifacts for the study of humankind's past. Herbert Spencer, the leading social Darwinist of the mid- to late nineteenth century, wrote about the evolution and professionalization of dance and music in *Contemporary Review* and *Popular Science Monthly*.[10] In 1895, Mrs. Lilly Grove, influenced by the work of late Victorian anthropologists such as E. B. Tylor (author of *Primitive Culture*) and James George Frazer (Grove's second husband and author of *The Golden Bough*), authored a detailed accounting of dance through history and across cultures. In addition to covering the traditional story of dance history, *Dancing: A Handbook of the Terpsichorean Arts in Diverse Places and Times, Savage and Civilized* also included sections on the dances of "savages," ritual dance, and the dances of the East.[11]

Serious studies—historical, anthropological, and philosophical—were published in reputable journals such as *Popular Science Monthly, Eclectic Magazine,* and *Lippincott's*.[12] Throughout these articles runs a still-familiar story. Told largely through the writings of figures such as Lucian, Soame Jenyns, Thoinot Arbeau, Sir John Davies, and Jean-Georges Noverre, the history of dance traversed from the glory of religious and military dance of the ancient Greeks to the Romans and the Christians, to the flowering of ballet in Italy, and through to its development in the French court. Curtain drawn, the stage was readied for a new act.

THE "NEW DANCE," as Duncan referred to it, was forged, practically and discursively, out of three American movement traditions: social dance, physical culture, and ballet.

From social dance Duncan inherited the tradition of dance as a model of social, sexual, and moral behavior and as a means of promoting healthy exercise and achieving graceful refinement. Manuals such as the distinguished New York dance teacher Allen Dodworth's (1885) stressed the importance of ballroom dancing as a means of modeling social intercourse. "With children," he wrote, "the effort to move gracefully produces a desire also to be gracious in manner, and this is one of the best influences of a dancing-school."[13]

Dancing, then, was a matter of manners, or etiquette—a body "technique," both physical and social, which, by disciplining the range and repertoire of body movement, marks a person's class and, thus, suitability for courtship. Dodworth himself made the connection, defining manners as "morality of motion." He believed that dancing—if taught correctly—could encourage moral, healthy living. Of the many popular "do-it-yourself" dance manuals available at the end of the nineteenth century, Judson Sause's *The Art of Dancing*, published in Chicago, was typical. It cited the benefits of dancing (in descending order of importance) as: physical development, freedom and grace of motion, social culture, morality, recreation, and, at the end of the list, enjoyment.[14]

From the physical culture movement Duncan appropriated an upper- and upper-middle-class interest in behavior as the visible expression of the inner self. Physical culture, a blending of Delsartean practices with the fields of elocution and gymnastics, emphasized not only the fitness of the body-in-motion, but also the expressive and social implications of that body-in- motion. It displaced the notion of the self's essential (and thus unchangeable) "character" with that of the self's malleable "personality." The message of physical culture—that by changing your outward behavior, you could improve your inner being (and thus your worldly standing, as well)—was extremely important for Duncan, who conceived of dance not as entertainment, but as social betterment. It was not simply a matter of what dance should be, but what it should do—what it should accomplish within the social sphere.

While social dance and physical culture contributed the positive arguments of Duncan's discourse, she used ballet to construct her negative argument. She was by no means alone in her disdain for ballet. Philip Hayman, in the May 1891 issue of *Theatre*, articulated the growing disillusionment with the art near the turn of the century:

> Now is there anything rhythmic, expressive, or descriptive about the movements of the ballerina? I harden my heart to say "certainly not." When on the tips of her toes she palpitates from the footlights to the fringe of coryphées, and whirls down again in a series of lightning pirouettes; when she springs into the air making her heels vibrate to each other; when she is held head downwards with one limb extended in the air; when she finishes in an astounding whirl of pink tights and tulle frills—in all these postures and motions she may be active, agile, athletic, gymnastic, acrobatic, but *not* expressive, *not* descriptive, and certainly *not* rhythmic.[15]

To Duncan, and to many of her admirers, ballet was the older order that needed to be overthrown, a concrete symbol of all that was wrong with overcivilized nineteenth-century living. Americans had lost their connection with the earth, and that loss was enacted onstage by ballerinas on pointe. Americans had lost their connection with their own bodies, and that loss was enacted onstage by ballerinas in corsets. The question of ballet vs. the new dance went beyond aesthetics, for, as Duncan wrote in her "Dance of the Future" manifesto, echoing the rhetoric of eugenics, "It is a question of the development of perfect mothers and the birth of healthy and beautiful children."[16]

As DUNCAN'S EXPERIENCE at Miss Mason's must have taught her, merely demonstrating her novel art form was not enough. Somehow her audiences must be convinced otherwise of the worthiness of her new dance. And eventually they were, as Duncan's verbal discourse began running alongside her nonverbal one. Although the young dancer's Newport appearances stirred no significant enthusiasm, her New York performances in the homes of society women and at theaters such as the Lyceum did garner modest attention from the press. She spoke eloquently to her interviewer from the *New York Herald*, for example, of the importance of dancing as a means of "character formation" for children.[17] This term she perhaps learned from the local kindergarten proponents who were spreading the work of Friedrich Froebel, which was, as he described it, a "means of emancipating the bound up forces of the body and the soul."[18] By yoking the mind to the evolution of the body, Darwin had made the continued separation of mind and body untenable,[19] and Duncan proposed dancing as the connective tissue between the two. By sharpening the skills of the young body, Duncan argued, dancing would concomitantly sharpen the skills of the mind. "The dance," she said, "is a series of movements being the expression of connected thought, and is in its higher exercises a concentration of mind and body on the understanding of a form or emotion, thus being a means of supporting the mind with the strength of the body, and thereby obtaining greater understanding."[20]

As Duncan's career progressed, she never neglected to seize the opportunity to render her theories of dance verbally. Second only to her talent for movement was her uncanny instinct for tapping into the discourses of her day and using them as a way to lead people to her dancing. When she published a "Dionysion" pamphlet in 1914, for example, it consisted of nothing but quotable quotes, from the likes of Percy Bysshe Shelley and the Bible.[21] Auguste Rodin's and Eugène Carrière's eulogies to her were included, and her own paean to the dancer of the future was sandwiched between Walt Whitman and Friedrich Nietzsche.

Duncan displayed a much greater interest in working out her theory on paper than most other choreographers of her stature. Her writing is unsurprisingly florid and high-minded: Beauty, Rhythm, Dance, and like terms are reverently capitalized. Her notebook drafts indicate that she wrote swiftly, without much revising. Her words ebb and flow one into the next, as do her sentences, with punctuation clearly implied but not always indicated. In both early and final forms, her essays dart quickly from topic to topic, often threading back and again to important themes. Like her dancing, her writing does not find its power through linear logic. (On the rare occasion when assertion opens into a modestly extended argument, it tends to beat a circular path.) Rather, the power of Duncan's writing lay in its sheer force of belief—a kind of ingenuous, sometimes breathless force rather than a sharply insistent one. As Whitman wrote in "Song of the Open Road": "(I and mine do not convince by arguments, similes, rhymes, / We convince by our presence)." [22]

Duncan may have quit school at about age twelve, but she was a voracious reader whose choices (other than the dime novels) were guided at an early age by Oakland librarian Ina Coolbrith, who later became the poet laureate of California. There is also indication that she received sporadic private instruction in French, German, and English at the Anna Head School. [23] But, in fact, only a small percentage of the women of Duncan's generation gained a college education. Instead, they did, on a collective basis, what Duncan did on an individual basis: they taught themselves. Women's clubs, large and small, flourished across America during the late nineteenth century. Having been largely excluded from higher education and public opportunities for self-improvement, the clubwomen turned to the private drawing room. They took turns giving reports on various social and intellectual subjects, as well as inviting guest speakers. [24]

Unlike most clubwomen, however, Duncan soon became a Continental artist-celebrity of great personal charm who could gain access to some of the great minds and imaginations of her time—Rodin, Ernst Haeckel, and Edward Gordon Craig, for example. She may not have systematically understood their thinking ("It is not for us to arrive at knowledge," she wrote, "we know, as we love, by instinct, faith, emotion" [25]), but she was smart enough to know what would be of use to her, and how to make it useful. A selective learner, Duncan did not need to master the depth and breadth and nuances of an aesthetic theory or scientific principle; she needed only to discover that which helped to articulate and legitimate her dancing.

Despite this lack of rigor in her arguments, Duncan's writings yield a consistent theoretical framework that dates back to those early interviews and lectures in New York. The theory is stated most comprehensively in her 1903 manifesto, "The Dance of the Future," a published essay that was originally a speech delivered to the Berlin Press Club, invited as a response to the clash of opinions surrounding her performances. Afterward, she wrote to her friend Douglas Ainslie, the young British poet, that she was received with "much sympathy & the journals write about it as seriously as if I were a Member of Parliament." [26] It was here that she learned firsthand about the power of the word as an aid to her dancing.

"The Dance of the Future," written in a blue copybook amidst quotes from Descartes's studies of mind in relation to body, Rousseau's ideas on education, and notes on ballet history, touched on all the main points of Duncan's dance theory, which she would spend a lifetime elaborating.[27] Most significantly, Duncan used this opportunity to build upon a compelling, but largely imaginary, past—specifically, the ancient splendors of the Greeks—to create a foundation for the "Dance of the Future." Beginning with a tribute to Darwin and Haeckel, Duncan immediately tapped into the power of the evolutionist discourse to invent a pedigree, so to speak, for her dancing: "If we seek the real source of the dance, if we go to nature, we find that the dance of the future is the dance of the past, the dance of eternity and has been and will always be the same."[28]

While "The Dance of the Future" pays its obvious debt to Wagner's "The Artwork of the Future," and to the evolutionary premise that life will progress to higher levels of development, much of her optimistic infatuation with this "dancer of the future" is also attributable to Nietzsche's concept of the Superman.[29] Like an entire generation of American radicals, Duncan embraced the iconoclastic philosopher's exhortation to break with the narrow, bankrupt morals and values of a Christian civilization and to harness the expansive, life-affirming creativity of the Superman.[30] This dancing body that Duncan constructed—"The highest intelligence in the freest body!"[31]—was, essentially, her version of Nietzsche's Zarathustra, the philosopher-dancer who bitterly chastised the "despisers of the body" for their failure to recognize its wisdom and will. Dancing was far more than a physical activity, for the body is the self incarnate; it is reason, soul, and spirit; it is the self's means of creating beyond itself. Like laughter, the upward bounding of the dancing body is a symbol of all that resists death and affirms life.[32]

Duncan defined dance as "not only the art that gives expression to the human soul through movement, but also the foundation of a complete conception of life."[33] This theory—both aesthetic and social—was based on seven basic tenets, which I summarize here.[34]

I. Our first conception of beauty is gained from the human body.

The body, according to Duncan, is the first principle of any aesthetics, for our fundamental understanding of proportion and symmetry arises from our experience of embodiment. She wrote in an early, unpublished notebook entry that without this bodily consciousness,

> men could have no consciousness of the Beauty surrounding him—his knowledge of the beauty of Earth forms—& from that his conception of architure painting sculpture and all art comes originally from his first consciousness of the nobility & Beauty in the lines of his own body—And when we study accurately the proportion & symmetry of a noble form—we see how from this form as first idea all noble forms follow as natural sequence.[35]

It is as a corollary to this first principle that Duncan addresses the issue of dress reform. The body is an eternal constant, subject to change only through evolution, not through fashion. Not only are the disfiguring properties of the corset physically and morally degenerate, but they are also aesthetically distasteful. Again, from the same early notebook entry:

> I have before me on my desk the correct drawing of a woman's skeleton—The form of the skeleton is beautiful & its chief beauty rests in the fact that the ribs rest *lightly* & far separated—This gives to the [form] its lightness & strength. I look from this beautiful design of a woman's skeleton on my desk to the dummy forms accross the way [in a dressmaker's shop] on which the girls are fitting the dresses—and I can not find any analogy between the form of this woman's skeleton & those dummy forms whose ribs are pressed tightly together. But if I am bewildered at the complete difference of these dummy figures to the skeleton what is my complete astonishment when I further regard another chart on which is represented the muscles—which clothe this skeleton & the organs which are protected within it—Then it appears to me plainly that there is no analogy of woman's form with the dummy forms across the way without the deformation of the beautiful skeleton—the displacing of the internal organs—and the decadence of at least a part of the muscles of the woman's body—[36]

The body, in its extraordinarily rich relationships with nature and art and will and movement, is the centerpiece of Duncan's aesthetic. From the body, she connects with the entire universe. She creates religion. She harnesses "Nature." She participates in the forces of evolution. As Whitman wrote, in a poem called "Kosmos": "Who, out of the theory of the earth and of his or her body understands by subtle analogies all other theories, / The theory of a city, a poem, and of the large politics of these States."[37]

II. The source of dance is "Nature."

Up until Duncan, the only alternative to technical mastery in theatrical dance was, at best, amateurism and, at worst, incompetency. Duncan challenged the paradigm of technique with that of the "Natural." That is not to say that there was no technique to her dancing, but that she ennobled an "artless" aesthetic, turning it into a virtue rather than a vice. According to Duncan, the true dancer—whether amateur or professional—participates in "Nature," thereby engaging in a universal rhythm that embraces the entire cosmos.

For Duncan, only the movement of the naked body can be perfectly "Natural." Although Duncan used the words "naked" and "nude," she never danced that way and probably never intended complete undress, as we understand those words today. A "naked" dancer here means an unsheathed, unshod dancer, whose bodily *form* is clearly visible—but whose details are modestly veiled, as were the fifth-century Greek statues she so admired.

III. Dancing should be the natural language of the "soul."

Duncan stared in the face of a long, strong Puritan belief that the spirit is sacred and the body profane. Cartesian dualism and Christian denial of the body had disqualified dance a priori as a legitimate form of significant expression. But Duncan looked to another precedent, to Nietzsche, who wrote that "body am I entirely, and nothing else; and soul is only a word for something about the body."[38] Duncan understood the American temperament—after all, she had spent her early years here trying to gain recognition for her dancing, without much encouragement, even from fellow artists. She realized that dancing would never be considered more than an "amusement" unless people were made to understand that it was religious: "art which is not religious is not art, is mere merchandise."[39]

Since 1899, Duncan had been asserting the intimate connection between body and soul as a fundamental basis from which to legitimize the body in motion as an artistic means of expression. Duncan made this idea acceptable by retaining the conventional distinction between moral and immoral but displacing the terms: the dancing body is sacred when it aspires to express the spiritual, but it is profane when it remains at the level of sensuality.[40] As an outward expression of the soul—of its upward yearning toward the good and the beautiful—the dancing body thus gained acceptance *within* the existing moral code.

Dance was Duncan's religion, and it was the gospel that she preached. Through dance, as either dancer or spectator, each "soul" could partake in divine unity with "Nature." Each "soul" could participate in the harmonious "Beauty" that merged self with God through the medium of "Nature." Thus Duncan endeavored to guide the world back to "Nature," whose evolutionary process, if we permit it, would deliver us to God.

IV. The will of the individual is expressed through the dancer's use of gravity.

Duncan cohered body and "soul" into one entity: that inner mechanism called "will," which she explicitly adapted from Nietzsche and Schopenhauer, who conceived of the body as objectified will. She used the term and concept as the German philosophers generally outlined it: as the essence of being—an endless striving. Just as the "soul" yearns upward, so does the body. "Upward goes our way, from genus to over-genus," says Nietzsche's Zarathustra. "Upward flies our sense: thus it is a parable of our body, a parable of elevation."[41]

Yet the will could not aspire heavenward without a solid basis on the earth, that is to say, within the stabilizing force of gravity. Duncan's theory echoes Schopenhauer's assertion that the pull of gravity is the simplest form of the objectification of will. Rejecting the extreme and unvarying lightness of ballet, Duncan instead emphasized groundedness as its necessary complement and foundation. Though her upper body soared, her lower body was resiliently strong and well-rooted, giving the appearance of a "will"—or, in other words, an inner force—very present in, responding to, and acting upon the world.

V. Movement should correspond to the form of the mover.

The natural correspondence between form and movement was part of the bedrock of Duncan's theory and practice. Besides discussion of this principle in a number of essays, Duncan entitled one of her notebook essays (ca. 1915), an unusually lengthy one, "Form and Movement." Taking on the tone and empirical logic of scientific inquiry, she aimed to discover the true nature of dance movement. She began:

> In my pamphlet *The Dance of the Future* I have endeavored to touch on the subject of form and movement in their relation to the Dance. That is that the form of an organism and the movement of an organism are one and grow together—The study of this subject is most beautifully illustrated in Charles Darwins Movements of Plants—where he shows how the movement and form of the plant are one manifestation Any one who has watched the movements of fishes must have noticed how the long & light fish move in long & light undulating lines just the lines of their form. how the round stodgy fish move in short thick curves—The porpoise describes a curve through the air which is exactly conforming to the curve of the line of its back—The whale moves in great pondrous lines—[42]

From there she launched into a further litany of impressionistic thumbnail sketches of various birds, throwing in a kitten for good domestic measure. She then continued:

> In other words Form and Movement are one—Now through this sequence of the form & movement of spheres—plants—fishes Birds and animals we come in sequence to consider the form & movement of Man—What the form & movement of man has been—what it is—is the study for the scientist The movement & form of man kind in general in its real state is the study of the scientist—in its ideal state the study of the Artist—That particular real ideal form in its realism to Harmonious movement is the study of the Dancer The True dance would be to find the Harmonious rhythmetic movement to the ideal form—[43]

Duncan turned to the tradition of art for further clues, but really she only succeeded in asserting her prior assumption:

> All this is so well known I would hesitate to repeat it if it were not for the fact that I am endeavoring to prove that the study of the Beautiful in form & movement which is considered as a knowledge a priori in all art should also be considered on the basis of the art of the Dance. We have seen through all Nature that form & movement are one in line & character—There fore may we not say that we should take this as our foundation text of the School of the Dance[44]

So, taking her "evidence" from Darwin's study of the natural kingdom, and secondarily from visual art, Duncan "proved" that the movement of a dancer must correspond harmoniously and naturally to the line, proportion, and symmetry of the human form. Reacting against ballet, whose artificial movements Duncan found an offense against the "Natural beauty" of the human body, she aimed to discover movements so suited to the human form that they would be rendered virtually transparent on the body. "In my dance," she wrote in an early notebook, "I search those movements which are in direct proportion to the human form— so that the form & movement shall be *one* harmony." [45] This seeming transparency, itself the product of work and study, paradoxically facilitated the myth that Duncan's dancing was spontaneous, her body independent of technique.

Two corollaries follow. First, since individual human bodies vary greatly within the general form, every person will move differently. Duncan did not envision dancers duplicating her style (although in reality this is what she had the Isadorables do); she envisioned a multiplicity of forms of dance, based on each dancer's own form and vision. This ethos of the body-as-original constituted the fundamental aesthetic of modern dance as a genre. Second, since the form of the body changes over the course of a person's lifetime, movements will change accordingly. To Duncan, only movement that corresponds to the individual's particular stage of development could be properly termed "Natural." Duncan used this precept in her work with children, and she embodied it in her own career, modifying her vocabulary, style, and choreography to suit her aging body.

VI. Dancing must be successive, consisting of constantly evolving movements.

During Duncan's youth, stage dance consisted of a display of steps rather loosely strung together. Within that context, her idea that the dancer's every movement should be borne from its predecessor, obvious as it seems today, was quite new to the American theater. She herself felt that this was her most important innovation as an artist.[46]

With the term "successive," Duncan implied two things. First, that movement should spread seamlessly throughout adjacent body parts. Second, that each action should evolve seamlessly into the next. This was contrary to the ballet,

Duncan argued, whose geometrical figures were based on straight lines. Its energy stopped at the extremities of the limbs, and the rhythm constantly stopped and started, without a continuously rising and falling pulse.

Duncan's paradigm of successive movement was the wave, which, she argued, is the basic movement pattern of "Nature." It is the alternate attraction and resistance to gravity that creates this wave movement, in "Nature" both visible and invisible: "[A]ll energy expresses itself through this wave movement. For does not sound travel in waves, and light also?"[47] The waters, the winds, the plants, the living creatures, and the particles of matter all obey this controlling rhythm, and thus should the dancer:

> He starts with one slow movement and mounts from that gradually, following the rising curve of his inspiration, up to those gestures that exteriorize his fullness of feeling, spreading ever wider the impulse that has swayed him, fixing it in another expression.
>
> The movements should follow the rhythm of the waves: the rhythm that rises, penetrates, holding in itself the impulse and the aftermovement; call and response, bound endlessly in one cadence.[48]

Besides its roots in "Nature" and science, and its significance as a formal principle of dancing, the wave also held spiritual connotations for Duncan, as it did for the Romantics. Unlike the ballet, whose stop-and-start motion "is an expression of degeneration, of living death," the continuing line of the wave symbolizes eternal life: the conquest of death through perpetual rebirth.[49]

VII. Dancing must express humankind's most moral, beautiful, and healthful ideals.

From beginning to end, Duncan worked through the characteristically Progressivist discourses of her day: health, morality, womanhood and motherhood, and education. With Nietzschean confidence and fervor, Progressive era leaders sought to reform the social and political ills that had been wrought upon American society by urbanization, immigration, and industrialization. Duncan's was a quintessentially Progressivist program; she wanted nothing less than to "make over human life, down to its least details of costume, of morals, of way of living."[50]

Hers was not a material program, however; like many modern artists of her day, Duncan's program partook of a strong transcendental belief. Dancing was socially progressive because it could create "Beauty," both in the dancer and in the spectator. By "Beauty," she meant not just outward appearance, but essential human goodness—a state of being in harmony with self, others, and the cosmos. Irma Duncan recalled in her autobiography that "I had learned my first English words at Isadora's knee when she taught her pupils to recite Keats's immortal lines: 'Beauty is Truth, Truth Beauty,—that is all / Ye know on earth, and all ye need to know.'" [51]

Because the improvement of humankind's lot was truly the basis of her dancing, she was able to gain the approval of the educated, the radicals, and the upper classes during the first two decades of this century. She succeeded where no other American dancer ever had: by aiming to establish dancing as a social and not just aesthetic necessity, she managed to gain its public acceptance as a legitimate art form.

—*Dance Research Journal*, 1994

A Fearless Confession Heard Round the World

EARLIER THIS YEAR, a conference of dance scholars retired from a long day's meeting to an oyster house, where the oyster lovers set out to seduce the skeptics into sampling the delicacy. A quotation from the modern dancer Isadora Duncan's autobiography, *My Life*, persuaded the final holdout. "You know what Isadora wrote, don't you?" said a clever historian. "That she began to dance in her mother's womb, in response to her mother's diet of oysters and champagne, the food of Aphrodite."

My Life turns seventy-one this month, a lifetime much longer than that of its author. While seventy-one isn't a silver or gold anniversary, the longevity of the book is testament to the importance of what Duncan had to say. Sweeping episodically through her adventures and misadventures up until 1921, when Duncan was invited to create a dance school in the Soviet Union, the book is still quoted in oyster houses and classrooms, still a rite of initiation for aspiring dancers, and still a source of voyeuristic fascination.

Since December 1927, when it began a run of seven printings in six months, *My Life* has been reissued at least thirteen times and translated into as many languages. The Norton English-language paperback sold twenty-five hundred copies last year, and there is no indication that its shelf life nears exhaustion.

The book was completed just months before her death, at age fifty, in a bizarre car accident in which she was strangled by her scarf when it became snagged around a wheel as she was driving in Nice on 14 September 1927. Published posthumously, it turned out to be Duncan's final performance. One of our century's most significant choreographers, Duncan was never properly captured on film; instead, she was recorded for posterity in the pages of *My Life*. *New York Times* dance critic John Martin remarked that the book had arrived "like an epitaph of her own devising."

From the moment it was published, *My Life* was reduced in the popular imagination to the torrid escapades of a female Casanova. The story, after all, does start with oysters and champagne and proceeds through numerous love affairs and three pregnancies.

But a more subtle reading of *My Life,* afforded by the explosion in the study of women's autobiography in the last decade, reclassifies Duncan's story. Not just another romance, it is a quest for a life lived without compromise, as both a woman and an artist. Quests, however, have been the traditional domain of men, who wrote them as authoritative accounts of heroic battles against worldly and measurable obstacles. Duncan's quest, however, was internal, and she could find no literary precedent for expressing it. "No woman has ever told the whole truth of her life," she wrote in her introduction, citing autobiographies that merely reported the events of outward existence. Of their inner experiences, Duncan insisted, women "remain strangely silent."

Duncan breached the silence with her book's first words: "I confess." This was a nod backward toward Rousseau's *Confessions,* which she admired, and forward, unknowingly, toward the genre of women's confessional literature that would flourish several generations later. Unafraid of the reality and richness of what others might consider "petty, human feeling," Duncan tackled just about every taboo topic for a woman's public discussion—desire, despair, ambition, and jealousy. She also dealt with abortion, homosexuality, and suicide. She directly addressed the onset of middle age, extolling rather than mourning what she saw as "the magnificent and generous gift of the Autumn of Love."

Most of the book was dictated in a kind of free association that can be felt in its fluid structure and conversational tone. Duncan composed words the same way she did movement—in grand swelling rhythms. Stylistically, *My Life* duplicated the distinctive tension in her personality, between the sensuousness of the artist and the high-mindedness of the "cérébrale," which Duncan longed to be.

She delivered the manuscript and was paid in monthly installments, a contractual strategy devised by her American publisher, Boni & Liveright, in order to ensure the book's timely completion. Although Duncan complained of feeling harried and uncertain under such pressured circumstances, she was desperate for the cash to pay her hotel bills. The manuscript was published largely as she drafted it, but before she could further edit it. In the end, the publisher excised a number of passages in which she delved into her experiences (the physical pain of losing her virginity, for example, and the bodily flush of sexual excitement).

The original dust jacket proffered *My Life* as "probably the most intimate book ever written by a woman." These memoirs are indeed intimate, but not in the euphemistic sense that the word was being used, to sell sex. It's not even intimate in the sense that the author was whispering her innermost secrets to the reader. Duncan was not telling us her story; she was murmuring to herself, and allowing us to eavesdrop. *My Life* recorded the private, often painful process of recollecting the fragments and contradictions of her tumultuous past.

Here, then, is a portrait of the female artist at middle age. Artistically eclipsed by modernism and denied citizenship by her country, Duncan wrote with a sobering backward glance. It was as if she were sifting through the rubble, reconstructing the ruins of her dreams, much as she was then literally trying to reclaim her once-magnificent but long-abandoned home in Neuilly, France.

What strikes me now, rereading *My Life,* is not the frankness with which she described her love affairs but the frankness with which she observed her failures and follies. She was alert to her "deluded" schemes, kind toward her strident defiance, appreciative of her irrepressible emotions, and patient with her extravagances. She knew full well that she was "impractical and untimely and impulsive."

DUNCAN SUCCEEDED in living an extraordinary life only because she was willing to risk excess and self-absorption. But she was a woman, and, as such, her ambition was judged as hubris. The threat posed to the world by her driving desire for autonomy, the persistent theme of her life, was effectively neutralized by discounting it as mere sexual precociousness. Always an astute—and outspoken—cultural critic, Duncan reproached the public that, once having glorified her as a goddess, now dismissed her as a matron. Duncan had always battled the institution of marriage. Now, she also attacked the standard of youthful female beauty that disapproved of her thickened figure and proscribed her still-active libido. By writing a woman's life as sensual as it was idealistic, Duncan rejected the script that she was handed at midlife.

She wrestled with this impossible task, the fixing of her life in black and white. If only it were easier, she lamented, to dive down within herself "and bring up thought as the diver brings up pearls—precious pearls from the closed oysters of silence in the depths of our subconsciousness!"

She did not consider herself a skilled enough writer to avoid clichés and feared that the work would turn out an awful mess. Better to capture the truth of her life through fiction ("twenty novels or so"), she argued, than through fact.

Duncan understood that an autobiography is just a story, and that an identity is at best a moving target. She embraced her many metamorphoses—"the Chaste Madonna, or the Messalina, or the Magdalen, or the Blue Stocking"—but resisted the autobiographical imperative to choose one. "How can we write the truth about ourselves?" she agonized in her introduction. "Do we even know it?"

—*New York Times,* 1998

THEORIZING GENDER

The Balanchine Woman
Of Hummingbirds and Channel Swimmers

Man is a better cook, a better painter, a better musician, composer. Everything is man—sports—everything. Man is stronger, faster. Why? Because we have muscles, and we're made that way. And woman accepts this. It is her business to accept. She knows what's beautiful. Men are great poets, because they have to write beautiful poetry for women—odes to a beautiful woman. Woman accepts the beautiful poetry. You see, man is the servant—a good servant. In ballet, however, woman is first. Everywhere else man is first. But in ballet, it's the woman. All my life I have dedicated my art to her.

—GEORGE BALANCHINE, 1976

WHEN PEOPLE say that "Balanchine glorified Woman," it is generally considered a laudable accomplishment. But in an age of backlash against feminism, when women's efforts toward progressive social change are losing ground to blithe conservatism, "glorification" smacks of regressive sexual politics. Though artists and scholars in art, film, and theater have been deconstructing representations of "Woman" for fifteen years, such work is rarely found in Western theatrical dance. The issues surrounding the ballerina as a cultural icon of femininity have been left virtually unexplored in print and met with impatient, if polite, disinterest in most public discussions.[1]

If the ballerina has been only a passing subject of critical feminist thinking, the Balanchine ballerina has been strictly off-limits. During his life, Balanchine was enveloped by a mythology that ascribed to him near-mystical inspiration, and now, four years after his death, Balanchine's legacy is generally considered sacrosanct. Yet Balanchine's statements about his idealized "Woman" openly declared their patriarchal foundations. Familiar themes emerge: Woman is naturally inferior in matters requiring action and imagination. Woman obligingly accepts her lowly place. Woman is an object of beauty and desire. Woman is first in ballet by default, because she is more beautiful than the opposite gender.

The Balanchine ballerina is not simply an innocuous, isolated theatrical image. As much as Twiggy or Marilyn Monroe, she is an American icon. When, as in these cases, an artificial construction takes on a "natural" appearance, ideal representations (Woman) instead of realities (women) set standards for everyday life.[2] An iconographic hangover from the nineteenth century, the Balanchine ballerina now serves as a powerful but regressive model in a social milieu where women are struggling to claim their own voices.

Balanchine's choreographic framing of Woman came up briefly at the Dance Critics Association (DCA) seminar on *The Four Temperaments* (1946) on 25 January 1985. During one session, former New York City Ballet dancer Suki Schorer narrated a movement analysis of her role in the third theme pas de deux while two students from the School of American Ballet demonstrated.

She told the audience early on that the man "is manipulating [the ballerina] —controlling her." At one point, he lifts her straight up and sets her on the floor on one pointe, her free leg crossed over the bent, supporting leg. She looks as if she is perched in an invisible chair. With one hand he grasps his ballerina's upstretched arm like the throat of a cello; then he pulls on her free arm, spinning her repeatedly. "You see the boy totally controlling the girl," Schorer commented. "He opens her arm [to the] side and then puts her arm in front. He's doing her port de bras.... The boy should appear then to be strumming—playing—some sort of harp or cello. The girl is like an instrument."

During the later critics' panel, a member of the audience commented that she found the ballet somewhat misogynistic. Of the five panel members, only the two men responded. "I don't think there's any misogyny in Balanchine whatsoever," said David Daniel, a *New York Review of Books* staff member. "Whenever he has a man manipulate a woman it is pure metaphor."

Critic Robert Greskovic added:

> What happens in those three themes, for me, is that man's support is allowing this woman to be more powerful, more open, and in my sense of looking at it more beautiful than she could be by herself because she has this ... human ballet barre—I don't care what you call it. That man shows her in four arabesques that she couldn't do by herself, and each one is more powerful than the next because of his assistance or whatever you want to call it—manipulation.

"Nor is there any indication in a Balanchine ballet that a man is making a woman do anything that she doesn't want to do," Daniel concluded.

The gap between the choreography and the male rhetoric deserves investigation. The third theme of *The Four Temperaments* is but a few minutes in the many hours of Balanchine's repertory, but it is an emblematic starting point for a feminist discourse on ballet. If Balanchine did "glorify Woman," the question remains: whose idea of Woman is she?

Like the Madison Avenue model, *Playboy* centerfold, or Hollywood bombshell, Balanchine's ballerina is part of a "culture [that] is deeply committed to myths of demarcated sex differences, called 'masculine' and 'feminine,' which in turn revolve first on a complex [male] gaze apparatus and second on dominance-submission patterns. This positioning of two sex genders in representation clearly privileges the male."[3] The same questions E. Ann Kaplan asks about the cinema can be used to probe the Balanchine ballerina. In the third theme of *The Four Temperaments,* how is Woman represented? In a dance form that Balanchine called an instant love story, whose desire is being played out? Who occupies the position of privilege?

Balanchine choreographed *The Four Temperaments* to Paul Hindemith's 1940 "Theme with Four Variations (According to the Four Temperaments)." The ballet is not so much about the four humors as it is about the sometimes sweet, sometimes plaintive music, featuring the comings and goings of piano and strings. The score begins with three themes, each represented by a pas de deux; the subsequent variations are "Melancholic," "Sanguinic," "Phlegmatic," and "Choleric." This was the first of Balanchine's strain of so-called "modern ballets," which, though rooted in the classical vocabulary, inverted it, stretching it beyond the boundaries of conventional "good taste."

The third theme is adagio—a man and woman dancing together in a slow tempo. Its gender system is the traditional one "in which girls perform, supported by male partners."[4] The couple enters together, and, after a brief foray by the ballerina, the danseur puts her through an extraordinary sequence of precarious moves and off-kilter positions that render her totally vulnerable to his control. It is as if the man were experimenting with how far he could pull the ballerina off her own balance and still be performing classical ballet. The extreme to which the third theme exemplifies what a ballerina can look like with the support of her partner makes it an archetypal pas de deux.

A recurring motif is the arabesque, created and used in quite unconventional ways. The danseur lays the ballerina in arabesque against his leaned-back body or swings her around on the pivot of her supporting foot. As soon as an arabesque is formed or even before it is fully formed, the man pulls, lifts, or thrusts the ballerina into another phrase. However innovative the arabesques are, they still serve the traditional purpose of focusing on the ballerina's leg. The emphasis on the manipulated weight of the ballerina—passive weight, counterweight, displaced weight, the compression of balanced weight, no weight—forces a focus onto the women's support system: her legs. They are constantly drawn in and then extended outward, further intensifying the visual impact of her dynamic line. And as the couple exits, the man carrying the woman, she reverently unfolds her legs forward, as if she's rolling out a red carpet for her exquisitely arched feet. Displaying the line of her body, artificially elongated by her toe shoes, is the goal of their joint venture.

Because Balanchine created so many more starring roles for women than men, it is usually assumed that the ballerina is therefore the dominant figure.

But it is not enough to observe that the ballerina is of primary interest; it must be asked how the choreography positions her within the interaction. In the third theme of *The Four Temperaments,* the ballerina is the center of attention because she is the one being displayed. The "feminine" passivity that marks this display is a low-status activity in American culture; action is valued as "masculine" for its strength and self-assertiveness. In paintings, in films, in beauty pageants, in advertisements, women are constructed as to-be-looked-at; the men are the lookers, the voyeurs . . . the possessors. Men, on the other hand, are constructed as the doers in films, in television commercials, in sports, in politics, in business. That's why men who model are often seen as being "effeminate." As John Berger wrote, "men act and women appear."[5]

The Romantic ballerina—an important forerunner of the Balanchine ballerina—is similarly seen as dominant because of her legendary celebrity. Both Erik Aschengreen and John Chapman have debunked this myth. Only superficially, Aschengreen argues, did the Romantic ballet in France belong to the ballerinas; rather, Romantic ballet was the expression of a masculine society's desires. "Both *La Sylphide* and *Giselle* are named for the leading female characters, but the heroes, James and Albert [Albrecht], bear the problems of the ballets."[6] They bear the problems, and they make the choices: they act, while the heroines are acted upon. In *La Sylphide,* for example, James loves, and the Sylphide is loved: James rejects, and Effie is rejected.

Chapman writes about the paradox in which the Romantic ballerina was adored at the same time both she and her stage persona occupied a low status within the social order:

> The owned woman, the slave girl, and the harem girl occurred with great frequency in ballet and painting, reflecting the female's position in Parisian society. . . . Perhaps just as erotic as the harem girl was the supernatural spirit . . . and she was as free for the taking. . . . Yet the taking was not always so easy, at least on the Opera stage, where wilis lured men to their dooms and sylphs eluded the most eager grasp. The challenge and danger of the seductive femme fatale only heightened the erotic stimulation. Ballet was well suited to support this image of the female. On the stage real women, as slave girls, spirits or adventuresses, revealed themselves to the hungry eyes of the viewer. Off stage in the foyer de la danse, the wealthiest and most influential could mingle with the dancers in highly elegant surroundings. From this sophisticated market-place the rich buyers selected their mistresses. . . . Thus the female who was elevated to the position of a goddess was demeaned to the status of a possession, a sexual object.[7]

The ballerina in the third theme of *The Four Temperaments* is a blend of the Romantic ballerina's enticing elusiveness and the contemporary American woman. Arlene Croce writes that "in Balanchine the ballerina is unattainable simply because she is woman, not because she's a supernatural or enchanted being."[8] She is specifically a white, heterosexual American Woman: fast, precise, impassive. These qualities, exemplified in her modern technical prowess, seduce the male gaze, but the titillating danger—the threat—of her self-sufficient virtuosity is tamed by her submissive role within the interaction. Much as the Romantic ballerina was a "beautiful danger"[9] because of her narrative association with the erotic and the demonic, the third theme ballerina is a dualistic construction whose "danger" lies in the unattainable Otherness of her "daredevil" technique. And if she is feisty, her surrender is all the more delicious.

In the third theme, the ballerina does momentarily assert herself. After the danseur whirls her posed body seven times on the balance of one pointe, she bursts upward and turns triumphantly, in a split second. So when she does surrender, it is all the more oppressive. For instance, after a bit of typical Balanchine play with the presentation of hands and the intertwining of arms, the ballerina's arms are crossed over her chest, and her partner holds her hands from behind, like reins. Figuratively and literally, the man has the controlling hand. According to Schorer:

> The boy is lowering her arms so that she has to go to the floor, and she goes into a fetal position. It's like he's wrapped her up, and now by pulling her arms down she has to go into this teeny ball or form. . . . [About] the next step [in which she extricates herself from this bind], Mr. B. always said, "It should look like a struggle." From here she has to get her leg out, followed by hips, arms, and the last thing is her head: to "get born," so to speak. She should be a little bit lower and sort of almost awkward, struggling—but in a graceful way.

Struggling is not "feminine," but Balanchine's ballerina makes it so because Balanchine has choreographed it to emphasize the extension of her leg as she steps out of her cocoon. This episode, like the entire pas de deux, has violent undertones. They have to do not only with the physical extreme to which Balanchine stretches the classical vocabulary and the ballerina's body, but also with its sadomasochistic pattern: man manipulates powerless woman.

The erotic undercurrent in the theme surfaces when the ballerina's arabesques shoot between her partner's legs. In another sequence, the ballerina ends up in an elegant sitting position, with bent knees properly together and still poised on her toes. Before repeating the phrase, she briefly looks at him, then coyly lowers her gaze and cocks her head as she frames the sinuous curve of her face with an open palm. Like the Romantic image of the female and the image of a geisha girl in Japanese prints, she is revealing her feminine charms in a demure yet provocative way.

The Balanchine ballerina does have control over her body in the sense that she is a technical dynamo, but a distinction must be made between the athleticism and virtuosity of the steps and the worldview that the choreography expresses. Kirstein says: "Balanchine has been responsible for a philosophy that has treated girls as if they were as athletic as their brothers. He has proved that they can be fiery hummingbirds rather than dying swans, with the capacity of channel swimmers."[10] But why is a channel swimmer required for the part of a hummingbird, fiery or otherwise?

In the third theme, the manipulated ballerina looks less like a dominant dynamo than a submissive instrument, both literally and figuratively. Her partner is always the one who leads, initiates, maps out the territory, subsumes her space into his, and handles her waist, armpits, and thighs. She never touches him in the same way: she does not initiate the moves. Metaphorically, she makes no movement of her own; her position is contingent on the manipulations of her partner.

By arranging and rearranging the ballerina's body, the man (first the choreographer, then the partner, and voyeuristically the male-constructed spectator) creates the beauty he longs for. Croce says that "like Petipa's, his [Balanchine's] ballets are more likely to be expressed from the man's point of view, and he has used the unemotional style of American ballerinas as an object, a created effect."[11] In the third theme, that objectified, impassive style renders the woman a prop in perversely exquisite imagery. She is a bell to be swung to and fro, a figurine to be shown left and right, or an instrument to be strummed. In what Schorer called the "drag step," the man literally carries the ballerina on his back. Her legs are lifeless, following after her like limp paws.

As "abstract" as the third theme may be, it is rooted in the very concrete, very familiar code of chivalry. The chivalric tradition gives rise to the rhetoric that a woman is "more powerful, more open and . . . more beautiful than she could [be] by herself because she has this . . . man," as Greskovic put it in the DCA seminar. Edward Villella, one of Balanchine's greatest male dancers, makes implicit reference to the chivalric code when he explains why he does not feel subordinate to his women partners:

> My presenting the ballerina gives me great pleasure and I find it a very masculine thing to do. It's very masculine to hold a door for a woman or to take her elbow to help her across the street. The male dancer does the same kind of thing. We take the woman's arm and we take her waist, we lift her and present her. It's a social as well as a balletic tradition.[12]

Rather than glorifying women, chivalry has been linked to openly subordinating attitudes toward women.[13] Masculine deference such as Villella describes is false, Nadler and Morrow point out, "because it is accorded to women only insofar as they subordinate themselves to a narrow stereotype, and remain 'properly' submissive." [14] Women are accorded superficial amenities and ritual etiquettes provided that in important matters they "keep their place." [15] Positioning women as needy and "deserving" of male assistance, chivalry casts her as "feminine" against the privileged patriarchal "masculine." Preventing women from venturing out on their own in the name of chivalry precludes women from acquiring knowledge and capability and, therefore, power. [16] Power and prestige accrue to the men.

In the third theme, immediately following the couple's entrance, the woman ventures out on her own by carving out a big chunk of the stage space as she makes a semicircular path toward a back corner. The ballerina reaches toward a place in the distance, only to be pulled back in by her cavalier, who then restricts her to much smaller portions of floor space. According to Schorer: "It really looks like the boy takes her to make her stop." From then on, he succeeds in keeping her within arm's reach.

Pointe work often frames the ballerina as needy of her partner's help. In the third theme, the danseur is the upright, steadying force for the ballerina as he pulls her off-balance or positions her precariously on one pointe. This movement motif starts with their very entrance. Self-assured and impenetrable, the danseur moves sideways toward center stage with his arms broadly extended in a "T," stepping quickly up on half pointe and then descending squarely on his heels. When the ballerina follows suit, she steps laterally on both pointes in front of him, but then she gently lunges sideways off pointe, with her arms lilting. He is linear and stable; she is curvaceous and inconstant.

The male door-opening ceremony to which Villella compares partnering a ballerina is a notorious reinforcement of gender asymmetry. Laurel Richardson Walum underlines the importance of this social ritual as a means of perpetuating patriarchal order:

> The door ceremony, then, reaffirms for both sexes their sense of gender-identity, of being a "masculine" or "feminine" person. It is not accidentally structured. In a very profound way the simple ceremony daily makes a reality of the moral perspectives of their culture: the ideology of patriarchy. These virtues of "masculinity" are precisely those which are the dominant values of the culture: aggression, efficacy, authority, prowess, and independence. And these virtues are assigned to the dominant group, the males. Opening a door for a woman, presumably only a simple, common courtesy, is also a political act, an act which affirms a patriarchal ideology. [17]

Ballet is one of our culture's most powerful models of patriarchal ceremony. In the third theme, Balanchine sharply demarcates "feminine" and "masculine" behavior. Though the ballerina displays her beauty, power is associated with the masculine values of authority, strength, and independence that her partner, the manipulator, demonstrates. And by her compliance, she ratifies her subordination. The cultural model that Daniel passed off at the DCA seminar as harmless, "pure metaphor" in fact perpetuates male dominance, and the hegemonic result is women co-constituting their own oppression. As Daniel pointed out, Balanchine's ballerinas don't do anything they don't want to: they've bought into the system. Suzanne Farrell, Balanchine's most perfect "creation," once said: "I'd kill myself for a man, but I ain't going to kill myself for a woman. I think it works well that way also. It's not that a woman couldn't . . . not that a woman couldn't be president, but I think it works better if it's a man with a very powerful woman behind him." [18]

Balanchine glorified Woman because her Beauty pleased him, pleased the cavalier, and pleased the spectators' male gaze. The choreographer made no secret that his ballets were created for the male point of view: "'The principle of classical ballet is woman,' he said in his tiny backstage office during the second act of *Jewels.* 'The woman is queen. Maybe women come to watch men dance, but I'm a man. . . . The woman's function is to fascinate men.'" [19] Balanchine was a man who liked to watch women. He choreographed representations of Woman that conformed to his male idea of what she should be. In the third theme of *The Four Temperaments,* the ballerina is not represented as a subject; rather, she is Woman as object of male desire. This pas de deux may be an archetypal courtship, but the desire expressed by their relationship belongs only to the man. About her own desire, the compliant ballerina is silent.

All this is not to single out Balanchine; rather, it is to show that, despite the "ballet is woman" rhetoric, the representational form in which Balanchine worked is rooted in an ideology that denies women their own agency. No matter what the specific steps, no matter what the choreographic style, the interaction structure, pointe work, and movement style of classical ballet portrays women as objects of male desire rather than as agents of their own desire (like the woman in "The Unanswered Question" portion of Balanchine's *Ivesiana,* 1954). The only way a woman can be truly assertive and independent, from that male point of view, is as a venomous femme fatale (like the Siren in Balanchine's *The Prodigal Son,* 1929).

The question arises: can women ever represent themselves in classical ballet? During the New York City Ballet's Spring 1986 season, Merrill Ashley danced the adagio in Balanchine's *Symphony in C* (1947) so assuredly and so bravely that she literally and figuratively left her partner behind. Even when a spitfire ballerina such as Ashley does manage to transcend her choreographic frame, she is still seen against the model of the chivalric pas de deux. Her autonomy in the *Symphony in C* adagio emerged in spite of the choreography rather than because of it—Woman as the to-be-looked-at Other remains the norm. As long as classical ballet prescribes Woman as a lightweight creature on pointe and men as her supporters/lifters, women will never represent themselves on the ballet stage.

Because ballerinas are smaller and lighter than danseurs, some argue that they are biologically determined to be the supported rather than the supporter. The argument's premise is faulty, as Suzanne Gordon graphically described in *Off Balance,* for the ethereal look is not an anatomical given.[20] Many aspiring ballerinas practically starve themselves to achieve the ballerina image, turning into anorexics and bulimics in the process. Besides, Senta Driver and the contact improvisation dancers have demonstrated that actual weight has relatively little to do with the ability to lift someone.[21] Lifting and supporting are much more a matter of *how* a dancer uses her/his weight, of placement, and of timing.[22] And, of course, there is no biological reason for the exclusion of men from pointe work.

But if pointe work, support systems, and weight deployment were shared among individuals rather than divided between genders, the form would no longer be classical ballet. Ballet, as it has been molded since the arrival of the professional female dancer and even before, is based on dichotomized gender difference and, hence, dominance.[23] Martha Graham's very early works created a radical vision of strength for women, but today's modern dance is just as gender-dichotomized as ballet. A totally new way of dancing and choreographic form—if that is possible to imagine within the framework of patriarchy—is needed in order to encode a gender-multiple dance. In his effort to verbalize this dream of a future without gender asymmetry, Jacques Derrida talks about "the desire . . . to invent incalculable choreographies"[24]:

> [W]hat if we were to approach here . . . the area of a relationship to the other where the code of sexual marks would no longer be discriminating? . . . As I dream of saving the chance that this question offers I would like to believe in the multiplicity of sexually marked voices. I would like to believe in the masses, this indeterminable number of blended voices, this mobile of non-identified sexual marks whose choreography can carry, divide, multiply the body of each "individual," whether he be classified as "man" or as "woman" according to the criteria of usage. . . . Then too, I ask you, what kind of a dance would there be, or would there be one at all, if the sexes were not exchanged according to rhythms that vary considerably?[25]

Until that dance is created—if it ever is—the solution is not to abolish classical ballet; rather, the only chance of seeing "incalculable choreographies" hinges on a concomitant change in the audience. We must learn to look critically: past the chivalric rhetoric to the underlying ideology. Twenty-three years ago Ray Birdwhistell argued that, as a weakly dimorphic species, human beings express a constructed gender dichotomy at the level of movement, body position, and expressive behavior that "can be variably exploited for the division of labor."[26] The subtleties of movement as a regulator of social order have been explored in the social sciences,[27] and the same can and should be done in dance. To begin with, critics, practitioners, and scholars have got to recognize ballet as a cultural institution that represents and thus inscribes gender behavior in everyday life. Gender imaging must become as important a subject of discourse as the ubiquitous cataloging of style and technique. Otherwise, our channel swimmers will forever remain hummingbirds.

—*TDR: The Journal of Performance Studies,* 1987

Classical Ballet
A Discourse of Difference

WHEN MARIE CAMARGO leaped forward to substitute for a male soloist who had missed his entrance at the Paris Opera in the late 1720s, her fame was ensured. She was admired for her speed and her fiery style as well as for her ability to master difficult steps. Voltaire complimented her by saying that she was the first woman to dance like a man.[1] Thus, when the ballerina emerged as a great stage persona,[2] she was defined as difference. For to say that Camargo danced "like a man" was to imply that she appropriated the vigorous style and steps of the danseur rather than sticking with her native feminine abilities.

Those abilities had been quite clearly prescribed. The German dancing master Johann Pasch, for example, had written in his 1907 *Beschreibung wahrer Tanzkunst* that any sort of technical tours de force such as pirouettes or any movements not *gracieux* or *doux* were improper for women dancers.[3] Even the radical Camargo had internalized a degree of conventional femininity; according to an obituary, she "did not make use of *Gargouillade,* which she considered inappropriate for women."[4] Unlike Voltaire, who—however lefthandedly—appreciated Camargo's bravura, Jean-Georges Noverre disparaged her lively style, which, he implied, was carefully constructed so that spectators had little time to notice her shortcomings in female form.[5]

In ballet, the female form has long been inscribed as a representation of difference: as a spectacle, she is the bearer and object of male desire. The male onstage—the primary term against which the ballerina can only be compared—is not inscribed as a form, but rather as an active principle. As celebrated danseur Igor Youskevitch wrote only nineteen years ago, "the inborn feminine tendency to show herself physically, combined with the natural feminine movements that are the cornerstone of her dance vocabulary, is to me the golden key to feminine dance."[6] And, he continued, "For a man, the technical or athletic side of dance is a rational challenge. Once mastered, it provides him with the opportunity to display strength, skill and endurance, as well as with the vocabulary and means to achieve creativity."[7] Masculinity is not mere shallow display. Masculinity is the strong jumper, the narrative's driving force, the creator rather than the created.

Youskevitch's rhetoric is emblematic of ballet discourse as a whole: it is inextricably rooted in the notion of "inborn" or "natural" gender differences. Across the centuries, these differences have been an unabashed hallmark of classical ballet at every level: costuming, body image,[8] movement vocabulary, training, technique, narrative, and especially the pas de deux structure.[9] Like a thicket grown fat around a fencepost, discourse has entwined itself with stage practice in inscribing gender difference as an aesthetic virtue.

Because of dance's ephemerality and because of the relatively recent development of film and video, discourse has been privileged more completely in dance than in any other art form. And it is as much in discourse as in the stage practice itself that Woman (and Man) has been trapped. Instead of confronting patriarchy in representation, critical and scholarly writing has only rationalized it, often in the guise of "classicism" and "romanticism." Dance classicism is an ideology devoted to tradition and chivalry, and to hierarchy of all kinds—gender, performer's rank, the distinction between types of roles, spectator's placement, stage organization, the canon. Romanticism's emphasis on personal expression also relies on the theatricalized dichotomy of feminine and masculine temperaments.

Few critics and scholars have investigated the patriarchal underpinnings of ballet. This is largely due, I think, to dance's inferiority complex as a "feminine art." Any systemic criticism would undermine the constant struggle to establish dance as a legitimate art form. The first step in creating an alternative discourse is to ask questions—new, difficult, and even disturbing questions. Perhaps it is the only way to present any challenge to the ballerina icon, given that we can never posit who she would be outside of the male constructs that have created her. And it is only by asking questions that "difference"—the seemingly natural and innocent phenomenon in which the ballet discourse is rooted—will be exposed as a socially and politically constructed "opposition." For, as Monique Wittig has pointed out, the primacy of difference is that which constitutes dominance:

> [B]efore the conflict (rebellion, struggle) there are no categories of opposition but only difference. And it is not before the struggle breaks out that the violent reality

of the oppositions and the political nature of the differences become manifest. For as long as oppositions (differences) appear as given, already there, before all thought, "natural," as long as there is no conflict and no struggle, there is no dialectic, there is no change, no movement.[10]

Although there have been obvious historical changes in women's lives during three centuries of ballet, Woman's place in representation has never really changed, because its ideology has never really changed. Whether the surface rhetoric is Théophile Gautier's fetishization of the ballerina, or Lincoln Kirstein's separate-but-equal argument, or Clive Barnes's dancing-is-macho stance, the underlying assumption is of female difference/male dominance.

Writing during the Romantic period, Gautier's first requirements for ballet were grace and beauty. For him, dancing consisted of "nothing more than the art of displaying beautiful shapes in graceful positions and the development from them of lines agreeable to the eye."[11] He clearly differentiated, however, between female and male participation in this beauty, their respective roles being very narrowly defined. It was fine, he wrote, for men to take action parts—pantomime and character roles—but they were unsuited for the pure dance (i.e., pure display) parts, because these effeminized men: "that specious grace, that ambiguous, revolting, and mincing manner which has made the public disgusted with male dancing."[12] Pure dancing befit a shapely young woman, he believed, but it was beneath men, whose presence intruded on the illusion of the Eternal Feminine being played out onstage. To be female was grace incarnate; strength/action was the male's sole domain.

Critic Jules Janin in 1840 expressed a similar philosophy, making clear the derogatory feminization of Romantic ballet:

> Speak to us of a pretty dancing girl who displays the grace of her features and the elegance of her figure, who reveals so fleetingly all the treasures of her beauty. . . . But a man, a frightful man, as ugly as you and I, a wretched fellow who leaps about without knowing why, a creature specially made to carry a musket and a sword and to wear a uniform. That this fellow should dance as a woman does—impossible! That this bewhiskered individual who is a pillar of the community, an elector, a municipal councillor, a man whose business it is to make and above all unmake laws, should come before us in a tunic of sky-blue satin, his head covered with a waving plume amorously caressing his cheek, a frightful *danseuse* of the male sex, come to pirouette in the best place while the pretty ballet girls stand respectfully at a distance—this was surely impossible and intolerable, and we have done well to remove such great artists from our pleasures.[13]

Gautier and Janin abhorred men dancing because their participation in this spectacle emasculated Man's unquestioned power and authority. That men were effectively banned from engaging in this display during the height of Romanticism does not bespeak a subordination of men, as many critics and scholars interpret it, but rather an attempt to uphold the man's virile image—his dominance—untainted by the "feminine." It is no coincidence that the cult of the ballerina arose at the same time that the Paris Opera, cut loose into private enterprise, was trying (successfully) to turn a profit by appealing to the rising middle class's desire for entertainment.

Even though women's newfound pointe work monopolized the balletomanes' attention, the men onstage retained dominance in the representation by presenting and displaying (and "creating") these object-forms as their own possessions. And by identifying with these figures, the male gaze of the spectator[14] was active in creating and possessing—and "ogling"[15]—these female creatures. Such is the tone of Gautier's criticism: verbal ogling. He wrote as if each ballerina were but one more specimen in his private collection of femininity—minutely and sometimes cruelly making an inventory of what he considered her every asset and defect. For him, the ballerina embodied his desires. Fanny Elssler, he wrote, "in that hand which seems to skim the dazzling barrier of the footlights, ... gathers up all the desires and all the enthusiasm of the spectators."[16] And as she gathered them up, so she dutifully projected them back.

The rhetoric of gender differentiation continued into the twentieth century, superficially transformed by supposedly more enlightened times. Much of the discourse of this century unblinkingly posits the equality of male and female on the ballet stage. For instance, Balanchine apologist Lincoln Kirstein wrote in 1959:

> In the best dance theater, there is a polarity of male and female on an equal see-saw of elegance and muscularity. The power of the male for leaps in the lateral conquest of space sets off the softness, fragility, speed and multiplicity of the ballerina's action on pointe and in the sustainment of held, breathless equilibrium. Male dancers make girls more feminine and vice versa.[17]

Male and female—"power" and "fragility"—are "equal" only insofar as they maintain the asymmetrical *equilibrium* of patriarchy—which does not offer equality at all. Lauding women for their marginal characteristics, Kirstein and many like-minded writers never question these accepted notions of "femininity," let alone the bipolar opposition which, as Simone de Beauvoir explained, ensnares women in an illusion of complementarity. "Here," she wrote, "is to be found the basic trait of woman: she is the Other in a totality of which the two components are necessary to one another."[18] De Beauvoir could just as well have been describing the pas de deux, an emblem of classical gender asymmetry.

The ruse of ballet's equality-in-difference deconstructed itself by 1978, when *New York Post* critic Clive Barnes explicitly stated the implicit. Under the headline "How Men Have Come to Rule Ballet's Roost," he wrote:

> Male dancing is much more exciting than female dancing. It has more vigor, more obvious power, and an entirely more energetic brilliance. Of course there are different qualities—thank Heaven!—to female dancing, yet there is something about the male solo, its combination of sheer athleticism with art, that makes it unforgettable.[19]

Female dancing, he implied, is valuable *only* because it is different; the important—"unforgettable"—qualities are already and exclusively embodied in male dancing.

Male dancing rose to prominence during the 1970s—at the same time, ironically, that the women's rights movement reached its peak. The shift was accompanied by a lot of "dancing is masculine" propaganda in the press (à la Barnes) and in a spate of books. Rudolf Nureyev, Mikhail Baryshnikov, and Edward Villella were hyped as strong, virile, and athletic stars. They, however, were the exceptions that proved the rule. The fervor with which apologists invoked the rhetoric of difference in order to assert male dominance in ballet ironically echoed the very rhetoric—that some activities are "masculine" and others are "feminine"—that had contributed to the "emasculation" of the art form as a whole. The profession will never be truly destigmatized for men (or women) as long as the masculine-feminine difference is maintained, because it is due to this polarity that dance was dubbed "effeminate" in the first place. And yet an extreme version of this argument was used in the 1970s to "upgrade" the status of men dancers (masculine = big money = sports = motivation = action = dance).[20]

Symptomatically, a 1969 issue of *Dance Perspectives* was devoted to the "Male Image." Anthropologist and kinesics founder Ray L. Birdwhistell introduced the issue by discussing the invented nature of human gender display and concluding that "art is conventional and erroneous when it allows the binary logic of the primary sexual characteristics to determine the rhetoric expressing human interaction."[21] Despite Birdwhistell's visionary critique of gender codes, four danseurs—including Youskevitch—then proceeded to characterize the art form along rigidly "natural" gender lines: female/male, display/action, delicate/strong, emotional/rational, nature/culture.

The civil rights movement demonstrated that "separate but equal" is impossible and even vicious—that "separate" or "different" underlines and perpetuates inequality. Until the struggle—at least in discourse—breaks out in classical ballet, the political nature of male-female difference remains submerged. This is especially true today, when formerly experimental choreographers are one after the other turning to toe shoes and arabesques for their inspiration. In borrowing from the classical vocabulary, choreographers such as Karole Armitage, Laura Dean, Twyla Tharp, and Molissa Fenley are not being subversive or transformative. They may mix-it-up differently, laying their own twist or attitude on top of the classical, but it is essentially the traditional ballet and its ideology borrowed whole, particularly the romantic pas de deux. If choreographers such as these are not going to question themselves, at least the critical discourse can do so.

But contemporary writing, for the most part, has continued to collude in ballet's representation of Woman. When Bill T. Jones and Arnie Zane did some gender-bending of George Balanchine's classic *Serenade* in their 1985 *How to Walk an Elephant, New York Times* critic Anna Kisselgoff scolded them for daring to tangle with Balanchine's "ballet is woman" iconography:

> When they take one of the most celebrated and beautiful moments in "Serenade"—a woman in arabesque revolving in place because a man on the floor below turns the leg upon which she stands—and give us a gawky arabesque for a tall slim man, they are not being respectful of either the choreographer or one of his greatest ballets.
>
> It does matter whether the arabesque in this "quotation" belongs to a man or a woman. Mr. Zane and Mr. Jones might wish to make a valid point about changing attitudes toward traditional gender roles, about men and women sharing the same characteristics. But this was never Balanchine's belief and his well known creed that "ballet is woman" received one of its firmest statements in "Serenade."[22]

Kisselgoff's indignation underscores the integral role of Woman in ballet ideology and particularly in its inscription of pleasure. To her, the sacred authority of tradition is never to be desecrated by critical analysis. For what we risk in questioning pleasure is the very loss of that pleasure. But the liberating potential of the inquiry, as Laura Mulvey has pointed out, is "the thrill that comes from leaving the past behind without rejecting it, transcending outworn or oppressive forms, or daring to break with normal pleasurable expectations in order to conceive a new language of desire."[23]

—*Women & Performance: A Journal of Feminist Theory,* 1988

To Dance Is "Female"

I LEARNED A disconcerting lesson recently at a symposium called "Reclaiming or Effacing? How Women Artists Handle Sexist Images in Performance"[1]: there is very little understanding—even amidst the interested, intelligent people who attended this event—of the vigorous and extensive feminist inquiry that has been going on in the arts for the past decade. It finally hit home why practically no choreographers are investigating issues of women and representation, compared to their colleagues in film and the visual arts: the issues involved in the study of gender in dance are still generally misunderstood, if they are in circulation at all.

The panel's moderator, Peggy Shaw of the Split Britches Company, was most interested in exploring whether women performers' use of gender stereotypes serve to subvert or to reinforce those representations. This was an excellent and timely question, given the popularity of pastiche these days; but the discussion suffered from a naive concept of "sexism" that ended up scapegoating women in the process of mythologizing individual free choice, and from a general confusion about the complexity of the issues at hand.

Despite its comprehensive title, Judith Lynne Hanna's *Dance, Sex and Gender: Signs of Identity, Dominance, Defiance, and Desire* (University of Chicago Press, 1988) is no antidote to the confusion.

Addressing the whole of Western theatrical dance as well as selected dance around the globe, Hanna's stated goal is "to enrich the discourse on male/female body images and social change by spotlighting and clarifying how gender is socially and culturally constructed and transformed in a critical medium of human communication—the dance" (241). This is an unquestionably important aim, shared by a modest but growing number of dance scholars. Dance is an ideal laboratory for the study of gender, because its medium—the body—is where sex and gender are said to originate; it is where the discourses of the "natural" and the "cultural" thrash it out. Dance is a significant clue to the management of the female body in any given time and place. Furthermore, the politics of dance as an institution, sometimes dominated by women, more often dominated by men, demands its own inquiry.

Hanna's reach, however, far exceeds her grasp. Though she has identified the area of investigation, she fails to develop a coherent framework for analysis and neglects to ask fundamental questions. She calls her work a synthesis, but synthesis depends upon meaningful organization and insightful connections. On both counts, *Dance, Sex and Gender* fails. Hanna is uncritically dependent on the work of other anthropologists and critics—she uses citations as substitutes for analysis. Hanna darts, often tediously, from quote to quote (some so long as to be teetering at the edge of impropriety), without any apparent purpose other than to feign rhetorical legitimacy. Though the format of the book is much like a textbook, with an introductory chapter defining key words in italics and providing chapter summaries, *Dance, Sex and Gender* is muddled, beginning with her definition of terms.

Hanna's constant bobbing and weaving appears to stem from her determination to avoid becoming politically embroiled. In a footnote leading off her chapter entitled "Patterns of Dominance: Men, Women, and Homosexuality,"[2] Hanna writes that "After my 1984 presentation, a male colleague said he was disturbed that it was not clear where I stood; I sounded like a feminist who did not deliver. However, my intent is to present facts, issues, and perspectives of participants involved in a process, not to advocate" (119n). Gender, however, is not a matter of fact. It is a matter of ideology and its constantly evolving discourse.

For someone who insists on the historical and cultural nature of dance, Hanna's book is curiously ahistorical and acultural. It consists of an endless series of examples. She plucks out a few superficial aspects of a given dance to make a point, to fit it into a category, without setting any dance into its larger context. Thus specific dances are rendered meaningless. In the quest for "synthesis," Hanna resorts to strange lists (nine words that identify sexuality and sex roles in criticism: androgynous, erotic, gender, heterosexual, homosexual, sensual, sexual, sexy, and suggestive) and absurd compressions ("Nijinsky danced superbly, had an affair with the famous impresario Diaghilev, eventually married, and suffered from mental illness" [185]). Her fondness for tidy cause-and-effect leads to facile assertions, as with "Women created new fields such as modern dance, social work, kindergarten teaching, and librarianship rather than compete in male professions" (131) or "Gay men identify with the effeminate yearnings, feelings, and romantic idealizations of the ballet, which is not marked by sexual preference so much as by sexual grace for both sexes" (137).

Hanna pays lip service to the methods of Erving Goffman and Ray Birdwhistell, but the body of the book bears no resemblance to their brand of astute observation, rigorous analysis, and provocative theory. Hanna's perspective is a quaint hybrid of Darwinian functionalism, the sociologist's impulse to categorize types, and a kind of primitive communications theory predicated on a simplistic sender-receiver model—none of which gets us closer to understanding the ways gender and sexuality are constructed in dance. And because of her aversion to politics, the author never thinks to ask *why* gender is constructed the way it is. Though claiming to take a semiotic approach, she never gets to questions of meaning. And she commits the fatal error that gives semiotics such a bad reputation in dance: movement is treated as a series of static things rather than as an ongoing process.

The book's most serious flaw is its hazy use of such basic terms as sex, sexuality, gender, sexual identity, and sex role (which she uses as a synonym for gender). The terms tend to slip, even when Hanna appears to be neatly defining them. For example, at first "sexual identity" is said to depend "on biological criteria of genetic, anatomical, and physiological characteristics" (7). Not a few lines later, it is said to refer "to sexual interaction: heterosexual, homosexual (gay, lesbian), or bisexual" (8). Certainly if sexual orientation is tied to biological sex, then all women would have the same orientation and so would all men.

Hanna's definitions only make sense within her Darwinian paradigm, where sex is said to dictate sexuality and gender. There is no room in this scheme for the fundamental distinction that gender studies makes between biology and behavior. Hanna disregards the historical, cultural, and ideological factors that help to construct our notions of sex, sexuality, and the body.

Hanna sees not only sex—but also sexuality, which is really a separate matter—as the function of the survival of the species. This is an untenable position when analyzing dance in cultures where sexuality and reproduction have been wedged apart. In those cases, one's sexuality does not derive necessarily from the drive to procreate. Within Hanna's functionalist scheme, homosexuality and lesbianism are completely marginalized.

Although she rightly emphasizes the intertwined relationship between sexuality and gender in the dancing body, she leaves it at that, never attempting to untangle the vines. Because she identifies sex with sexuality and sexuality with gender,[3] she therefore links sex and gender, implicitly affirming that "biology is destiny." Hanna starts and ends with the assumption of difference, so she will never "enrich the discourse on . . . social change" (241), for it is the insistence on difference that leads inevitably to dominance.

Like the "Reclaiming or Effacing?" symposium, Hanna operates on the superficial level of "sexism," as if the problem were simply a matter of a bad attitude. For all its rhetoric about anthropology and the cultural construction of gender, *Dance, Sex and Gender* is naive concerning the dissemination of culture, reducing the process to simplistic notions of modeling and "vicarious learning" (11). Hanna sees this as a conscious, cognitive process. Actually, gender is a much more complex, culturally entrenched process of representation, which encompasses the spectator and her process of interpretation as well. Looking at "images," the way Hanna does, only deals with half the phenomenon, which in recent feminist scholarship has been dubbed the "male gaze."[4] As tiresome as this term has become to some, it remains a fundamental concept: that, in modern Western culture, the one who sees and the one who is seen are gendered positions. The possessive gaze is "male," while the passive object of the gaze is "female"—regardless of the dancer's or spectator's sex.

Gender studies is not yet widely accepted among dance scholars, and Hanna's book will do nothing to recommend what is, to my mind, the field's most intellectually compelling frontier.[5] For to scrutinize the construction of gender in the dancing body requires the most subtle of analyses. Indeed, what is so fascinating about this project is its greatest challenge: to figure out, and then to verbalize, the ineffable experience of the dance spectator—to find the clear, accurate, and necessarily poetic language to express how it is that a dancer's focus, or the way she activates her skin, or the palpable feeling of the spatial environment, signifies a particular way of seeing and being seen.

In the effort to theorize alternatives to the male gaze, we need to think a lot more about performative presence. Presence is the silent yet screeching excitement of physical vibrancy, of "being there." It is one of the thrills of watching dance, to see someone radiate pure energy, whether it is in stillness or in flight. Questions abound: What constitutes presence? How do we know it when we see it? Is it pan-cultural, or is it highly coded? How is it related to the structure of spectacle? Why is it so seductive? Does that seductiveness demand possession? Can that seductiveness be derailed? There appears to be an affinity between presence and the male gaze. At one end of a continuum, ballet strives for presence and, concomitantly, is a highly coded spectacle that reifies the male gaze. At the other end, performance art in its early, most radical moments aimed to undercut traditional conventions of performing and presence, opting instead to try to confound the usual audience-performer relationship. Postmodern dancer Deborah Hay straddles both ends of that continuum. She is striving toward a kind of movement-in-stillness that she calls pure "consciousness" at the same time she insists on inviting the audience to share in her performance rather than consuming it from afar.[6]

The concept of the male gaze comes from feminist film theory. In film, the woman performer is literally a celluloid object. She has no presence in the movie theater; she cannot look back at the spectator and is thus rendered passive. In dance the situation is not as clear-cut. The dancer does have a literal, if not always effective, presence. S/he can participate in a give-and-take with the audience. A highly accomplished technician looks anything but passive. Nevertheless, the dancer becomes more than just a technician within the stage frame. S/he becomes part of a dense thicket of completely familiar codes and conventions that conspire to position her/him as the willing object of our desire. We need to face squarely the risk factor in trying to jam those conventions: much of the beauty and pleasure of dance as we know them are tied up with the erotics of display and spectatorship.

There are times and places, however, when the conventions are in such flux that it seems possible for the gaze to be unfixed and for the performer to elude possession. I don't happen to think we're living in that time and place. Our existence is too overcoded. But very early modern dance, or early postmodern dance, for example, may have been such a time and place. In order to find out, we need to examine those dances and dance-makers both in the minute details of their performance and in the full context of their culture. The late 1920s and early 1930s as well as the 1960s were a time of great change—old rules were being discarded and new ones were being invented at an alarming speed. In that space of radical cultural change, the confounding of the gaze in dance may have reinvented gender, too—until the new conventions became entrenched. Modern and postmodern dance today are as much a spectacle as ballet.

It is ironic that when feminist literary theorists come to a point where words no longer suffice, they often invoke dancing as a metaphor. And yet dance is too infrequently the subject of feminist inquiry. I still think Jacques Derrida's words, in a published interview called "Choreographies," are ones to look and think and write by:

> [W]hat if we were to approach here . . . the area of a relationship to the other where the code of sexual marks would no longer be discriminating? . . . As I dream of saving the chance that this question offers I would like to believe in the multiplicity of sexually marked voices. I would like to believe in the masses, this indetermin-able number of blended voices, this mobile of non-identified sexual marks whose choreography can carry, divide, multiply the body of each "individual," whether he be classified as "man" or as "woman" according to the criteria of usage. . . . Then too, I ask you, what kind of dance would there be, or would there be one at all, if the sexes were not exchanged according to rhythms that vary considerably?[7]

I admire Hanna's attempt to tackle the analysis of gender in dance across cultures. At a time when everything in our own culture seems to lead unrelent-ingly to the difference between "man" and "woman," cross-cultural study holds the promise of freeing up our imaginations. What is gender in a culture that is not bound to bipolar opposites: to the mutual exclusivity of here and there, of you and me, of male and female? And what is its dance?

—*TDR: The Journal of Performance Studies*, 1989

Unlimited Partnership
Dance and Feminist Analysis

AMONG ALL THE arts in Western culture, dance may have the most to gain from feminist analysis. Certainly the two are highly compatible. Dance is an art form of the body, and the body is where gender distinctions are gener-ally understood to originate. The inquiries that feminist analysis makes into the ways that the body is shaped and comes to have meaning are directly and immediately applicable to the study of dance, which is, after all, a kind of living laboratory for the study of the body—its training, its stories, its way of being and being seen in the world. As a traditionally female-populated (but not necessarily female-dominated) field that perpetuates some of our culture's most potent symbols of femininity, Western theatrical dance provides feminist analysis with its potentially richest material.

Like any kind of analysis, feminist analysis is a quest to determine how something is put together—how it works. Feminist analysis draws upon a variety of methodologies: newer ones such as semiotics (the study of symbolic systems) and deconstruction (loosely speaking, a kind of reading "against the grain" to unearth an underlying ideology), and more traditional ones such as ethnography and movement analysis. Rather than being defined by any particular methodology, feminist analysis is distinguished by its point of view.

Earlier in this century, when the social sciences were still identifying and defining themselves with the "hard" sciences in their bid for legitimacy, admitting a point of view was as good as confessing sin. But today that patina of objectivity has been tarnished. No analysis, no interpretation, no history, no criticism is ever disinterested. Every inquiry, inasmuch as it asks certain questions and not others, is governed by some point of view. Ideology exists everywhere, whether acknowledged or unacknowledged. The traditional social sciences, whose white, male, middle-class, high modern ideology has long passed for disinterested, has been invigorated in the past twenty years by a host of other points of view. These alternative perspectives—including those of feminists—have yielded a much richer understanding of history, anthropology, literature, and the arts.

The feminist point of view in the United States can be defined only broadly. Really, one cannot talk about *the* feminist point of view at all, for beyond the specific concern with women, feminism at this moment of entry into the 1990s is a widely varying phenomenon.[1] The variety is part generational, part personal, and part theoretical.[2]

Late-twentieth-century feminism burst onto the social and academic scenes in the late 1960s–early 1970s as "Women's Lib." At that point, generally speaking, feminism was concerned with ennobling the history, culture, and social reality of Woman. Literary scholars initiated a kind of analysis that focused on images of women, separating the regressive from the progressive. In the burgeoning genre of performance art, ritual enactments that reclaimed the archetypal Goddess helped to empower women on a personal as well as an aesthetic level.

Today, a generation later, the context for feminist analysis is very different. The backlash against feminism is fierce and, if you can believe the "New Traditionalist" advertising campaign of *Good Housekeeping,* an overwhelming trend.[3] The framework for feminist analysis of the arts has changed radically, too. With the introduction of semiotics and psychoanalysis into the feminist discourse by cinema studies in the 1970s, the terms of analysis shifted from a social to a theoretical ground. Two key changes in thinking occurred that underlie most of current American feminist analysis in the arts.

First, feminist scholars no longer accept blindly a category of Mankind known as Woman. Although the earlier generation of feminists embraced and found empowerment in the notion of their fundamental difference from men, an outspoken segment of the current generation of feminist scholars (along with postmodernists in all fields) has called into question the very concept of "difference." For difference, Monique Wittig wrote in 1982, necessarily implies dominance. It separates the world into an "us" and a "them," with the "us" always providing the measuring stick and the "them" inevitably failing to measure up.[4] In modern Western culture, Woman has always been the Other, defined according to the fantasies and power structures of men.

Second, the object of analysis has been shifted from just the image itself, in isolation, to the entire *process* of representation, which also encompasses the spectator and her/his process of interpretation. The power of the spectator in constructing the representation has been dubbed the "male gaze."[5] As tiresome as this term has become to feminists and nonfeminists alike, it remains a fundamental concept: that, in modern Western culture, the one who sees and the one who is seen are gendered positions, despite the actual sex of the participants. The one who is looked at—the performer who puts her/himself on display for the spectator—is in a passive, traditionally female position. The spectator, again regardless of her/his actual sex, is the one who looks—who consumes, who possesses—the image on display. The spectator is in the position of power: a traditionally male position. Thus, the term the "male gaze."[6]

As fragmented as the current intellectual climate seems—deconstruction, semiotics, postmodernism, ethnography, etc.—it all revolves around the issue of representation. How is a representation created? Whose point of view does it embody? What role does it have in the spectator's construction of everyday reality? Feminist scholars today are concerned with the schism between cultural or aesthetic representations of Woman and the lives of real women. How does our culture—a patriarchal one—construct representations of Woman that somehow come to determine our standards of femininity in everyday life, where women are not usually sylphs or pin-up girls? How can women represent themselves onstage without being co-opted by the conventions and expectations of the male gaze? Is it possible for women to reconstruct their own standards of beauty that need not depend on becoming the object of male desire?

The theory of the male gaze has obvious implications for dance, and dance has much to offer to the development of that theory. In film, where the concept of the male gaze originated, the performer is flat on a piece of celluloid; in dance, the performer is live. How does that affect the dynamics of the male gaze? Is the male gaze then more vulnerable to being dismantled when the performer is live? How can a dancer—who fundamentally displays her/his body for the viewer—avoid being objectified? Does some dance create a literal and metaphorical space in which spectator and performer can share the dance together, on equal terms, rather than the one serving her/himself up for the other? Are there dancers who have been able to achieve this?

At this time, most feminist dance analysis is brewing informally in discussion groups, individual exchanges, and classrooms, as well as at conferences.[7] Some of this activity has made its way into print, taking a variety of forms: criticism,[8] history, biography, formal analysis, ethnography, interviews, and roundtable discussions.[9] The subject matter ranges from nineteenth-century travesty dancing to the pas de deux and dance criticism, from George Balanchine to Pooh Kaye and Martha Graham.

Several years ago an entire issue of *Women & Performance: A Journal of Feminist Theory* was devoted to dance. It was called "The Body as Discourse." The variety of articles in this special issue indicates the range of content, methodology, and point of view in feminist dance scholarship. Issue editor Marianne Goldberg's essay was a poetic text that probed the theoretical underpinnings and cultural connotations of the female body in dance. Carol Martin reflected on the complexity of analyzing gender across culture, pointing out both the imperialistic dangers of imposing one's own agenda on another culture and the potential benefits of finding new ways of thinking about gender. Goldberg and Ann Cooper Albright held a roundtable discussion with postmodern choreographers Wendy Perron, Johanna Boyce, and Pooh Kaye to record their perspectives on the problems and possibilities of being female onstage. My own essay attempted to deconstruct some of the critical rhetoric that has conspired to preserve the notion of difference and of male superiority in classical ballet. Two other authors focused on women artists who have been marginalized by mainstream history and criticism: Ann Gavere Kilkelly on tap dancer Brenda Bufalino and Lynn Garafola on choreographer Bronislava Nijinska, most often referred to as the sister of Vaslav Nijinsky.[10]

Once you start thinking about the kinds of questions that might be prompted by feminist analysis, the list seems endless: Why was it almost exclusively women who invented modern dance? Is a dance of universal emotion possible, or is it always colored by gender expectations, based on the sex of the performer? What was Marie Sallé's theory and practice of the ballet d'action? Was Delsartism a liberating outlet for women's creativity in the late nineteenth century, or was it a restrictive, sanctioned outlet for women's potentially hysterical "emotionalism"? How did Isadora Duncan's radical reconfiguration of the conventions of dance allow her to defuse the issue of "sex" in her stage presentation? What is the relative importance of anatomy, training, and cultural conditioning in the construction of female and male body images in dance? How has the female and male body image of modern dance, or ballet, changed over the past hundred years, and what do those changes tell us about shifts in culture? What are the differences between dance forms that depend on the mirror in the training process and those that do not? What were the feminist implications of Yvonne Rainer's "dances of denial"? How does the social hierarchy of the dance world embody sexist attitudes? Does Pina Bausch's tanztheater effectively condemn or glorify gender warfare?

The value of feminist analysis to dance studies, however, is not just for feminists. It promises to contribute to the development of the field at large, in at least four ways. First, the emphasis on the process of representation is leading to new insights into the ways that dance produces meaning. Second, research about dance figures overlooked by the canon (the list of dances, choreographers, and dancers that our field generally agrees are the most important) is enriching and expanding our understanding of dance history. Third, the introduction of theories and ideas from other disciplines is a potential stimulant to dance scholars of all persuasions. And fourth, the broadened view of dance as a cultural practice, rather than as a purely aesthetic phenomenon, will lead dance into a more prominent place in the social sciences. In this sense, feminist analysis is part of a larger trend in our discipline toward an expanded concept of dance studies as a field of significant social, political, and cultural relevance.[11]

—Dance Research Journal, 1991

Dance History and Feminist Theory
Reconsidering Isadora Duncan and the Male Gaze

ISADORA DUNCAN (1877–1927) is unarguably one of the seminal figures in twentieth-century American dance.[1] Her importance lay neither in the extension of an existing form, as did George Balanchine's, nor in her progeny, as did Ruth St. Denis's, but rather in the fact that she created an entirely new form of dance. Duncan's choreography offered her spectators a new kind of meaning and demanded from them a new way of seeing. She ennobled the previously suspect image of the human body and succeeded in her bid to legitimize dance as high art. As an international celebrity who lived out her beliefs in the corsetless figure and in voluntary motherhood, Duncan is commonly held to be an exemplary feminist, although she never explicitly labeled herself as such.[2]

Duncan has been set forth as a symbol of the feminist impulse since Floyd Dell's *Women as World Builders: Studies in Modern Feminism.* Published in 1913, this book was the first of many written by Dell, a radical intellectual and assistant editor of the *Masses,* the quintessential Greenwich Village magazine. He astutely realized that the woman's movement was in large part a product of nineteenth-century evolutionary theory, "which, by giving us a new view of the body, its functions, its needs, its claim upon the world, has laid the basis for a successful feminist movement." [3] In his chapter devoted to Duncan and writer/ crusader Olive Schreiner, he wrote that Duncan expressed "the goodness of the whole body." [4] This new view of the body, he believed, was "as much a part of the woman's movement as the demand for a vote (or, rather, it is more central and essential a part); and only by realizing this is it possible to understand that movement." [5] Since Dell, scholarly and popular critics alike—many less perspicacious than he—have painted Duncan as the larger-than-life symbol (sometimes the caricature) of Woman, who is casting off her corset, taking on lovers as she chooses, bearing children out of wedlock, and generally flouting the last-gasping strictures of oppressive Victorian culture.

Duncan did, of course, invite her status as a feminist spokeswoman. She began to articulate a specifically female dancer very early in her career in her famous "The Dance of the Future" manifesto, delivered in 1903 to the Berlin Press Club. (It was here that she first encountered—and embraced—the extraordinary power of the reported word as a rhetorical adjunct to her dancing.) The following passage is one of the most often quoted in dance:

> [The dancer of the future] will dance not in the form of nymph, nor fairy, nor coquette but in the form of woman in its greatest and purest expression. She will realize the mission of woman's body and the holiness of all its parts. She will dance the changing life of nature, showing how each part is transformed into the other. From all parts of her body shall shine radiant intelligence, bringing to the world the message of the thoughts and aspirations of thousands of women. She shall dance the freedom of woman. O, what a field is here awaiting her! Do you not feel that she is near, that she is coming, this dancer of the future! She will help womankind to a new knowledge of the possible strength and beauty of their bodies and the relation of their bodies to the earth nature and to the children of the future.
>
> . . . O, she is coming, the dancer of the future: the free spirit, who will inhabit the body of new women; more glorious than any woman that has yet been; more beautiful than the Egyptian, than the Greek, the early Italian, than all woman in past centuries: The highest intelligence in the freest body! [6]

Those words have become a large part of the Duncan mythology, which has grown as unwieldy as the woman herself. For a number of reasons—the lack of a film record of her dancing, the lack of a codified technique, the anecdotal nature of much dance history, the colorful drama of Duncan's personal life, and her own Irish flair for the well-spun tale—Duncan's career as a choreographer/dancer has been distorted in the American imagination. For one thing, there is no single "Isadora" to be embraced. Her dancing and her rhetoric changed over time, as did the meaning they held for her spectators. The popular image of Duncan as a liberated woman and an advocate of free love (embedded in the popular imagination by Vanessa Redgrave in the film *The Loves of Isadora*) may be more a product of our own social and political desires than a reasonable historical interpretation of her significance for American audiences during her own day.

Up until the last decade or so, dance history, which is a young discipline, consisted largely of the accretion of personal anecdotes, memories, impressions, and interpretations. The Duncan history is no exception; developing out of recycled interpretations rather than primary sources,[7] it has followed two broad veins: the first, a romantic celebration of her liberated ways (usually by women); and the second, a classical dismissal of her antitechnical "dilettantism" (usually by men). Both interpretations oversimplify her artistry and concentrate on her personality.

In large part, the Duncan history began with the posthumous publication of her autobiography, *My Life,* a few months after her tragic, well-publicized death in September 1927.[8] The autobiography, the first of two projected parts, is clearly written from the perspective of a middle-aged woman who realized that her era had passed. "My Art was the flower of an Epoch," she had written to Irma Duncan in 1924, "but that Epoch is dead and Europe is the past."[9] She made it no secret that she was writing the memoirs for the money. A strictly commercial venture, the book necessarily stressed the personal rather than the professional and was indeed successful in terms of its international sales and newspaper serialization.

My Life clearly belongs more on the side of fiction than history.[10] It tells us much more about Duncan's psychic state in 1926–1927 than it does about the course of her lifetime. But it made a legend out of her love life, thus setting the tone for much of the Duncan history. Most of what has been written about Duncan since her death focuses on her sexuality, as it was "revealed" through the book. Yet Duncan's love life was not reported in the American newspapers during her lifetime until her very last tour, in 1922–1923, when she was accompanied by her properly wedded young Russian poet lover, Sergei Esenin. Duncan's own sexuality did not provide the primary framework for understanding her dances, yet it has taken interpretive precedence in much of the Duncan history.

In the hands of balletomanes, *My Life* has become the basis for a critique of Duncan's dancing. "The Sexual Idiom," Rayner Heppenstall's notorious essay on

Duncan still circulating today in a dance anthology text, serves as prototype. A British essayist and balletomane, Heppenstall baldly reduces Duncan to an erotic, bare-legged spectacle:

> Isadora's Art was, in effect, then, merely an art of sexual display, and I would stress the "merely." Isadora was not conscious of the fact. Nor, I suppose, were most of the spectators. She and they thought they were enjoying a spiritual experience. Perhaps they were, but it was only in the mass stimulation of private phantasies. There was no communication, or no communication in terms exact enough to be terms of art.... Her art was aphrodisiac.[11]

Heppenstall criticizes her for a lack of theatrical clarity and legibility. She stands for "Phantasy," while he values "Tradition." She does not mediate her body (her self) through the self-sacrificing, external objectification of a traditional *form*, that is, balletic technique. In Heppenstall's explicitly Freudian terms, she did not adequately "sublimate" her sexual impulses, which would have transformed them into art.[12] The British balletomane blithely accepted the myth that Duncan was improvising and that her dances were a spontaneous outpouring of inner emotion. In fact, they were choreographed;[13] they were rooted in a technique; and, they had form, although in different form than ballet's.

In a sense, this reaction is part of a willful denial of Duncan as *choreographer*, as creator—in a traditionally male domain. Instead, she is defined (even by sympathetic writers) as a *dancer*, emphasizing only the immanence of her body—a traditionally female domain. From here, it is a short leap to the conclusion that Duncan was merely acting out an erotic fantasy: "Isadora Duncan was not concerned to dance, not concerned with any clarity of plastic forms," concluded Heppenstall. "She was concerned with the Dance only as part of her primarily sexual phantasy."[14]

As extreme as Heppenstall's rhetoric is, it is not atypical. The tension between an elitist ideology of the sacrifice of self to tradition (ballet) and a democratic ideology of the expression of self through an original form (modern dance) still runs deep. In 1986, close on the heels of Gelsey Kirkland's stinging critique of the Balanchine aesthetic as oppressive and inexpressive, Balanchine apologist Lincoln Kirstein dredged up the very same rhetoric in a *New York Times* article entitled "The Curse of Isadora."[15] From Heppenstall to Kirstein and beyond, all sorts of imaginatively revisionist writers have made out of Isadora a suspect female who capitalized on her near-naked body in the guise of art.

Between the balletomanes' outright dismissal of Duncan as a dilettante and the more sympathetic, feminist claim for her as the mother of us all, where is the reality of Duncan's significance to her American audiences? What role did gender play in her dancing? It is time to revise the revisionists.

ALTHOUGH IT IS the youthful gamboling that most people associate with Duncan, her choreography, as well as its meanings, changed significantly over the course of her lifetime. Her American tours can be separated into three distinct groups: her initial tours (twice in 1908, once each in 1909 and 1911), during which spectators learned to "read" this new art form; the second group of tours (1914–1915, 1916–1918) during World War I and after the much-publicized deaths of her children, during which she came to symbolize motherhood and nationalistic pride; and the third group (1922–1923) when she returned from Soviet Russia with a young poet husband to a suspicious and increasingly hostile audience. I am interested here in examining her initial American tours, when her dancing was a startling phenomenon.[16] Given the sexual interpretations often connected with her dancing, it would seem appealing to use the "male gaze" theory of representation as a framework for analysis.

Contemporary American feminist criticism was developed, in the mid- to late 1970s, through the discourses of psychoanalysis, semiotics, and film theory. It concerned itself mainly with a series of dichotomous relationships: the male and female of the Oedipal construction, the subject and object of the performer-spectator relationship (the male gaze), and the verbal and nonverbal phases of human development. The male gaze, as much a theory of Western cultural communication as anything else, refers to the way in which the structure of representation is gendered. The subject (spectator) and the object (performer)—each assumed to have a stable position in their encounter—operate in two dimensions, on a linear basis of binary opposition. The spectator, the one who looks (who consumes, who possesses), is in the position of power: a traditionally male position. The one who is looked at—the performer who puts her/himself on display for the gaze—is in a passive, traditionally female position. Much of the early feminist project in performance, as in all the arts, was to deconstruct how this model of binary opposition had rendered women secondary in—and even absent from—representation.

Before long, however, feminist critics began calling for more than just *decon*struction. They sought to *re*construct a feminist subject[17] in representation. It has become clear that the logic of binary opposition and its corollaries—the singular subject and the male gaze—though they have been crucial in understanding how the present system works, are not terribly useful in advancing beyond the problem; for, if patriarchy were truly so monolithic, then there would be no room within it for a feminist subject. And, seductive as they are, utopian visions of a world "elsewhere" are cultural and theoretical impossibilities.

Asking whether or not a choreographer such as Duncan managed to "subvert" or "break" the male gaze will neither advance the feminist project nor necessarily tell us anything about Duncan. In fact, the male gaze theory forces the feminist dance scholar into a no-win situation that turns on an exceedingly unproductive "succeed or fail" criterion. We expect the choreographer to topple a power structure that we have theorized as monolithic. The dancer or choreographer under consideration will always be condemned as a reinforcement of the patriarchal status quo, despite any transgressive behavior, because, by definition, whatever is communicated arises from within the fabric of culture, that is to say, within patriarchy.

This view really leaves little room for the work of the dance scholar: The outcome of analysis—whether the dancer or choreographer in question is a "success" or "failure" from a feminist point of view—is decided before the analysis is even begun. She will always be a "failure." Historical study is left in an especially problematic situation, because the male gaze has been theorized as a transhistorical model for Western culture, impermeable to the specifics of time and place. But as we clearly know, the body and its meanings, as well as the nature of display (and, concomitantly, the gaze), do certainly change with period and culture. Furthermore, the metaphor of representation as a "gaze" is not as suited to dance as it is to static visual media such as cinema and art. Dance, although it has a visual component, is fundamentally a kinesthetic art whose apperception is grounded not just in the eye but in the entire body.

The case of Isadora Duncan is much too rich and too complex to be reduced to a fait accompli. To understand the significance Duncan had to her American audiences from 1908 to 1911, a new theory of representation is required: one that includes within its very structure the capacity for change. I propose that we shift the terms of our inquiry from the two dimensional to the three dimensional. We need to understand culture as a full space (not an empty one) that encompasses transgression without necessarily co-opting it, or else we are doomed to a history without change.

A number of feminist theorists have already devised space-intensive models of representation: Laura Mulvey's emphasis on the carnival as a ludic space,[18] Teresa de Lauretis's notion of the space-off,[19] Jessica Benjamin's use of the concept of intersubjective space,[20] and Julia Kristeva's model of the chora.[21] Mulvey, whose "Visual Pleasure and Narrative Cinema"[22] largely initiated the inquiry into what E. Ann Kaplan dubbed the "male gaze,"[23] has criticized her own groundbreaking essay precisely because of its dependence on binary logic: "The either/or binary pattern seemed to leave the argument trapped within its own conceptual frame of reference, unable to advance politically into a new terrain or suggest an alternative theory of spectatorship in the cinema."[24]

Julia Kristeva, in *Revolution in Poetic Language,* sets forth a theory of representation, really a semiotics of art, that provides an excellent framework within which to analyze the cultural significance of Duncan's dancing body. Kristeva starts with the notion that the self is not a thing situated in one position and unchanging over time; rather, the self is a process that fluctuates through space and through time. In other words, we are always in the process of becoming, a phenomenon Kristeva calls a "subject in process/on trial."

She criticizes traditional semiology because it is based upon the static model of information theory, which emphasizes the message as the final *product* of codes.[25] Kristeva instead posits semiotics as a *process* of communication whose complexity and subtlety exceeds any simple transfer of information. She therefore conceptualizes literature, or any signifying practice, not as monolithic structure of simple communication but rather as consisting of two inseparable, simultaneous realms: the semiotic and the symbolic.[26]

The realm of the symbolic is linear and logical; it is social and syntactical. By participating in these rules of order, we are able to communicate easily with one another. But the semiotic realm, on the other hand, is a kind of "underground" communication. It is a pulsing, kinetic, heterogeneous space whose meanings are much more fluid and imprecise, yet no less powerful. Kristeva describes this realm as a "chora" (from the Greek for enclosed space, womb), a term borrowed from Plato's *Timaeus*, defined as "an invisible and formless being which receives all things and in some mysterious way partakes of the intelligible, and is most incomprehensible."[27] The chora denotes something "[i]ndifferent to language, enigmatic . . . rhythmic, unfettered, irreducible to its intelligible verbal translation; it is musical, anterior to judgment."[28]

All signifying practices contain both the semiotic and the symbolic, although one realm usually suppresses the other. Thus a *potentially* subversive element is posited even in the most traditional signifying system. The extent to which the semiotic is pulled out to rupture the symbolic—thus pulverizing, imploding, infinitizing its meanings—determines the potential "production of a different kind of subject, one capable of bringing about new social relations."[29] This is the "revolution" to which Kristeva refers in the title of her book. Revolutionary art need not be overtly political in content; what is more important is that it demand a new means of perception on the part of its spectators. The subject in process/on trial can thus be fundamentally transformed. Change here, at the level of individual consciousness, is a necessary element of social change. Seen in this way, the arts are not merely *reflective* of social relations but are *productive* of social relations.

For a feminist dance historian, this schema is particularly congenial, for several reasons. First, Kristeva's theory conceives of representation as a process, not as a vocabulary, syntax, and grammar of discrete units like letters or words. Dance, an art by definition in constant evolution over time and through space, cannot be explained through linguistic semiotics, as a building-block arrangement of fixed units. Unlike many theories generated from nonperforming arts, Kristeva's processual semiotics is suited to dance *sui generis.*

Second, the schema recognizes representation as historically embedded. Because the theory is based on positionality rather than essence, what constitutes the symbolic and the semiotic changes with period and culture. Positions shift, and codes evolve. The body does not remain static; it is as potentially semiotic as it is potentially symbolic.

Third, Kristeva's theory explains art as a process that is intelligible in its unintelligibility; that is, although some poetry, abstract art, or nonnarrative dance may not operate through normative codes of communication and may not be expressible in words, it is still meaningful. We can still "understand" it. Although there is no single fixed language of dance (indeed, one of the great things about modern dance in particular is that it is constantly re-creating itself), it is eminently understandable. At its best, when the realm of the semiotic prevails, dance's power to indicate meaning far exceeds its capacity to be reduced to the symbolic, that is, into a message expressed through the ordinary structure of language.

This paradox is what the theory of the male gaze cannot accommodate: that what is ineffable, what consequently poses a threat to the ordered realm of the symbolic, can be rendered intelligible without being co-opted by the symbolic, even though the symbolic to some degree is engaged. The semiotic and the symbolic realms exist in precarious, paradoxical relation to each other, and a large part of the appeal of Kristeva's framework, for me, is that it accepts and indeed poises itself at the center of paradox. For dance scholars whose job it is to render what is nonverbal into words, paradox is a familiar state of being.

Fourth, the idea that all signifying practices contain both the semiotic and the symbolic is an especially important one for dance, because dance is commonly conceived of as purely primitive, "pre-verbal," idiosyncratic, infantile, female, and uncoded, in opposition to the civilized, social, adult, male reasoned code of language. The nonverbal, and with it the body and dance, have become the "other"—marginalized and feminized—to the privileged signifying system of language. Kristeva challenges this opposition by positing that all signifying practices, literature and dance equally, include both the semiotic and symbolic realms. Like literature, most dance does emphasize the symbolic, following the codes and conventions that render the nonverbal very "readable."

The term "pre-verbal" has always been a subtle way of marginalizing movement, of relegating it to the negative role of "other" in a world supposedly constructed solely in language. This marginalization of the nonverbal in Western culture has been institutionalized in (among other places) psychoanalysis, which theorizes infant development before the acquisition of language as a great wash of nonsubjective symbiosis with the mother. The self as a separate entity is constituted only with the entrance into language. Because psychoanalysis has been the basis of so much feminist theory in literature and cinema,[30] it has been difficult for dance scholars to appropriators those logocentric models.

Daniel Stern, however, has refigured some of the basic psychoanalytic assumptions that pit the verbal against the nonverbal in a developmental hierarchy. By reconsidering psychoanalytic theory in light of what developmental psychologists have learned empirically about infancy in the past decade, he has defused the rhetoric of the "pre-verbal" by suggesting that (1) the infant progresses not from symbiosis to differentiation but from differentiation to relatedness; (2) the infant does relate as a sense of self to others through movement before learning to talk; and (3) these bodily senses of self and their corresponding nonverbal means of relatedness persist even after the acquisition of language. Whether verbal or nonverbal, these various means of relatedness are not temporal "phases" that are eclipsed with each developmental step; rather, they are spatial "domains" that accumulate into a full complement of adult interpersonal processes.[31]

Stern's revised psychoanalytic model suspends the classic binary opposition between the verbal and its negative term, the "pre-verbal" (that is, the body, movement, nonverbal behavior, dance). Furthermore, it renders unfounded our culture's romantic, and sexist, notions of pre-verbal existence as the feminine realm of the "other." Nevertheless, the cultural marginalization of the nonverbal is deeply ingrained. The nonverbal stream of our everyday encounters, Stern observes, are eminently deniable. We cannot deny our words, but we can always deny the "body language" with which we deliver them. Similarly, Kristeva sees gesture as highly marginal.[32] Ideally, gesture (and dance, by extension) is an excessively semiotic process—a trace, really—whose significance we can understand without its being embedded in literal meaning. It lives in between and across the semiotic and the symbolic, testing the outer limits of what it takes to produce signification.

That which is so marginal as to be deniable has obvious subversive potential. Kristeva's project of paradox is to appropriate marginality—whether it be femininity, race, or class—for subversive ends: "to make intelligible, and therefore socializable, what rocks the foundations of sociality."[33] It is only by working through the semiotic, she suggests, that we can implode the symbolic. The study of gesturality, which may be as close as one can get to a pure chora, would be "a possible preparation for the study of all subversive and 'deviant' practices in a given society."[34] It is partly because dance (which is, after all, culture's aestheticized gesturality) had such a marginal status in American culture at the turn of the century that Isadora Duncan was able to manipulate it so successfully as a means of social critique and that her spectators were able to appropriate it so successfully as an enactment of their respective agendas. To her liberal yet mainstream Progressivist spectators, she embodied an optimistic belief in the re-formability of the social and political system. To her radical spectators—including suffragists, anarchists, and socialists—she enacted a paradigm of complete social rupture.

WHEN DUNCAN toured America in 1908, 1909, and 1911, her reputation as the "Barefoot Classic Dancer" had preceded her from Europe. Newspaper accounts had reported on her rise to fame and her colorful lifestyle ever since her first Parisian appearances in 1900. Broadway producer Charles Frohman initially imported the dancer as a Broadway novelty in late summer 1908, pushing up the original September debut in order to preempt the appearances of Duncan imitators who were spreading across two continents. She fared poorly in the summer Broadway venue, whose audiences expected light entertainment. When her subsequent Frohman tour also began badly, she released the producer from his contract in order to tour with the esteemed conductor Walter Damrosch and the New York Symphony Orchestra, beginning with a second "debut" in November, this time at the Metropolitan Opera House. The Duncan/Damrosch tour was a success, as were her subsequent American appearances when she traveled primarily to large northeastern cities. Duncan's repertoire included the dance interludes from Gluck's *Iphigénie en Aulide,* scenes from Gluck's *Orpheus,* Beethoven's Seventh Symphony, and a Bach/Wagner program, as well as selections from Chopin and Tchaikovsky. Her encores included Schubert's *Moment Musicale* and the ever-beloved Blue Danube Waltz by Johann Strauss.

What did Duncan's American audiences see onstage during those early tours? What did it mean for them? Although Duncan's bare limbs were certainly an issue for her audiences, I am not willing to begin with the premise of the male gaze theory, that what they saw was first and foremost an objectified female body. That may be what we, from the late twentieth century, would see, but our way of seeing was not necessarily their way of seeing.

Just because Duncan's limbs were bare does not mean her performance was necessarily seen as erotic. Her bare legs and feet were as potentially distasteful to some as they were titillating to others. Her homemade, nip-and-tuck tunics were anything but glamorous. They emphasized an abundant figure, quite the contrary of the hourglass curves that were then the erotic ideal. The tunics were quite modest, because attached inside the shoulders of each one was a leotard-style undergarment, made of the same cloth as the outer tunic. Furthermore, Duncan danced with her entire body, as an integrated whole; she did nothing to isolate and thereby heighten the sensuality of her breasts, legs, or pelvis.

Without exception, newspapermen (primarily music critics) felt compelled to make immediate comment upon whether or not the barefoot dancer was indeed a proper sight. The public was ripe for indignation, in no small part because Duncan's American debut came in the midst of an epidemic of Salome acts—no less than twenty-four in vaudeville in October 1908.[35] But reviewer after reviewer stated unequivocally that there was nothing "sensational" about Duncan's dancing; it was, rather, quite "chaste."[36] *Current Literature* reported that

> Miss Isadora Duncan has not given the Salome dance in her present tour through the United States. She refuses to sacrifice her art to the sensationalism and the vulgarity of the hour. In her dance the purely physical plays no part. She dances scantily clad, remarks a writer in the New York *Sun*. "The fact that her feet and legs are unclothed is forgotten. It is part of the picture. Miss Duncan therefore does not rely upon physical charms to add to her success, as do some of the so-called dancers who are at present doing various sorts of stunts on both sides of the water. Her success comes through her grace and ease of movement, not on account of her ability to kick or wiggle or do acrobatic tricks."[37]

Even before her actual appearances, it was clear that Duncan offered something different, if only for the reason that no one else had ever devoted an entire evening to dancing solo, without respite of song, skit, or recitation. Before they set foot in the theater, the public was predisposed to accept Duncan on legitimately artistic terms for two main reasons. First, she placed herself within the Hellenistic tradition, which was then considered the pinnacle of genuine artistry. Second, she had been acclaimed by European royalty, artists, and intellectuals. At a time when America was struggling to develop a cultural tradition of its own, the imprimatur of European high culture held ultimate authority. It did not hurt, either, that this high priestess of the Terpsichorean Art could be claimed as one of America's own daughters.

That is not to say, however, that Duncan's reputation as a barefoot dancer was not in some cases a drawing card for the curious and for the erotic appetite. Since the 1880s, images of ballet girls and actresses ("stage beauties") had functioned as pinups in dubious publications such as the *National Police Gazette* and even in more respectable ones such as *Munsey's*.[38]

Whatever her audience's expectations, they were confounded by the dancer's actual performance. Duncan's dancing was different than anything that had previously hit the American stage. She did not construct herself as a visual spectacle, as her contemporaries did, performing a string of steps in mechanical time in some thematic costume, complete with backdrop. Ballet girls and vaudeville dancers were step dancers; their legs were their stock-in-trade, and not much of interest happened in the rest of their bodies. They operated in a pictorial mode, striking pose after pose or performing trick after trick. This was entertainment, whose appeal lay in the shapeliness of the female form, the successful (maybe even graceful) achievement of physical feats, and the novelty of the mise-en-scène. This image was what filled the pages of the *Police Gazette*. In Kristeva's terms, the entertainment was the countenance of the symbolic realm of early-twentieth-century dance.

Because Duncan's dancing did not conform to these easily readable conventions, many of her reviewers found themselves at a loss for words. (Dance criticism, it should be noted, was only in its infancy. The first full-time dance critic would not be appointed for twenty years.) The critics spent a lot moral space rhapsodizing on the aesthetic beauty of her dancing rather than describing how she achieved her effects. Although they knew not exactly what she was intending in some of her dances, they assured their readers that it was a "poetic" experience all the same. Interestingly enough, Kristeva's own term for the expression of the inexpressible was the same one used widely in Duncan's time by critics of theater and art to denote the same thing: an expression that is beyond the grasp of conventional communication, whose meaning is deeper, more oblique, and more profound. Other critics voiced that same feeling in stronger terms, declaring outright that the exquisiteness and depth of Duncan's expression defied being put into words at all. She was revealing something about the powers of the dancing body that had never been enacted onstage before, and neither her audience nor the critics had discovered the vocabulary to articulate this strangely ephemeral, transcendent, elusive vision.

In the meantime, they turned—quite reasonably—to the discourse on the academic nude, rooted in the classical visual arts.[39] It gave the critics at least some way to discuss the beauty and nobility of her dancing body. By this late date, however, the Victorian discourse was fraught with hypocrisy. It often functioned as a thinly disguised sanction of erotic spectacle in the name of "art." Despite the use of this suspect rhetoric in Duncan's review, it is clear from their uniformly serious and respectful tone that she did appeal to them on artistic grounds. Unfortunately, the only language they possessed to discuss this phenomenon was one that belied the nature of their experience.

The line between the chaste and the erotic is hardly a solid one, anyway. "The barriers between what is deemed licit and illicit, acceptably seductive or wantonly salacious, aesthetic or prurient," Abigail Solomon-Godeau has written, "are never solid because contingent, never steadfast because they traffic with each other—are indeed dependent upon each another."[40] Just as Solomon-Godeau has shown that for photography in late-nineteenth-century Paris the "chaste" had become "erotic," so, for a brief time when Duncan's choreographic invention was new to America, the "erotic" became "chaste."

The press's reaction is typified by the *Chicago Daily Tribune's* description of her debut in Chicago in 1908:

> Of Miss Duncan's dancing it is not the easiest thing in the world to write. It is so elusive, so fine, so delicate in its grace, and so perfect in its technic that it needs to be seen rather than read about. To say that she appears with bared feet, legs, and arms, and so gauzily draped for many of the dances that the whole form is clearly defined, is to suggest to the reader something of the sensational and possibly the prurient.
>
> Nothing could be further from the truth. Miss Duncan, when she is dancing, gives no hint to the onlooker of her being in anywise naked or unusually bared. The idea of sex seems wholly obliterated when watching her. The spirit of youth and of joyousness seems embodied for the moment before you, and there is nothing more of sex in her appearance than there is in boyhood or maidenhood.
>
> When the dancer comes forward to acknowledge applause she is unmistakably feminine—girlish, perhaps, but essentially of the woman conscious and confident. But when she is dancing, the fact of her being a woman and of her feet and limbs being bare never makes itself realized. This is sincere commendation of her art and in fullest justification of her manner of dressing for her dances.[41]

Duncan had made it a rule never to perform in vaudeville houses or music halls.[42] She played in legitimate theaters, concert halls, and opera houses, where she transformed the stage into a mythic space. She effectively metamorphosed the stage, paradoxically, by *not* attempting to make it into something other than itself. There were no illusionary sets or props. A simple set of tall, voluminous, blue-gray curtains surrounded the stage on three sides, and there was a similarly colored carpet underfoot. Having dispensed with the harsh glare of the footlights, Duncan placed the light sources in either wing. They were soft tones—ambers and pinks mostly, but never stark white—that gently mottled the stage in shadow and light.

Into this awaiting space, unmoored from any particular time and place, flooded the sound of the orchestra. It always played for a while first, sometimes as much as the first movement of a symphony. Only after the space bad been enshrouded in melody and rhythm would the dancer slip through the shadows into the audience's awareness. She did not play characters per se; instead, she preferred to function as did the Greek chorus, allowing the movement to convey universal emotion. In this dim radiance, Duncan surged and floated, gathering inward and spreading outward, without a hint of self-consciousness. Duncan looked a vision, her tunic as alive as her body, the garment's light gauze catching the force of her curving, swaying, onrushing motion.

Her vocabulary was simple. She used basic ambulatory steps, adapted from the social dances of her childhood. She stopped, skipped, hopped, and jumped; but that was merely *what* she did to get from here to there. It was *how* she moved (and sometimes how she stood still) that distinguished her dancing, that imploded the conventional syntax of the ballet girl or chorine.

First, Duncan's body was always moving of a single piece, the torso and the limbs integrated seemingly without any effort. Gesture and pantomime (she was a very talented mime) were never isolated; they were always woven into the flow of bodily movement. There was a strong oppositional pull in her movement—her torso twisting to the left while her arms motioned to the right, for example—that gave her a potent dynamism. The impulse of her movements visibly originated from the center of her body (the solar plexus), and that energy flowed freely outward, like a wave, through her head, arms, legs, and into the furthest reaches of space. She achieved a kind of groundedness at the same time that her arms floated—a rare mixture of strength and grace. While the ballet girl's arms etched static lines, Duncan's were always carving out sculptural space in three dimensions. And unlike the typical dancer of her day who went mechanically from pose to pose, Duncan's movements melted one into the next, into the next, into the next, with seamless ease.

She was extraordinarily sensitive to the dynamic qualities of movement. In fact, much of her effect was communicated through her genius for choreographing the drama of the kinesthetic—the sense of intentionality communicated through activated weight, the attentiveness signaled through spatial sensitivity, and the impression of decisiveness or indecisiveness gained through the manipulation of time. Today we take for granted the expressive potential of these formal means of movement, but in Duncan's day, they were revolutionary. Her powers of focus and concentration—her ability to stay fully alive inside each moment—produced a compelling sense of presence.

Duncan had an uncanny instinct for musicality, which is the temporal expressiveness within the way music unexpectedly stretches out or rushes ahead. Instead of dancing squarely on the beat, she played with the elasticity of her accompaniment's rhythm, embedding hesitancy, fear, longing, or a whole host of inner states by variously quickening or suspending her movement through time. Paradoxically, although Duncan revealed her flesh in unprecedented quantity, she effectively dematerialized her body in the expressive force of the music.

Reviewers constantly articulated this distinction between what they *perceived* in Duncan's dancing and what they actually *saw,* because the stuff of her dancing was not physical. It was virtual;[43] that is, there was more happening onstage than a dancer simply moving her body parts. As writer/reformer Bolton Hall wrote:

> It is not dancing, tho' dancing is of it. It is vital motion, expressing emotion. Unlike the ordinary dancing, it has no set pattern or subordinate motif increasingly repeated.

315

It has structure and design, but so closely allied to its beauty and grace that it can only be perceived, not seen.[44]

Duncan gave the impression of dancing spontaneously, even though her dances were choreographed.[45] As Hall wrote, there was "structure and design," but spectators could not discern it while they were experiencing the dancing. They were not meant to discern it. The choreography was very simple, usually a gently repetitious, symmetrical scheme supporting the kinesthetic drama of the piece, primarily through the use of body level (up and down) and floor pattern (side to side, front to back, diagonal to diagonal). Again, as with her vocabulary, structure served only as a framework, meant to recede from view as the work was performed.

Thus, for her American spectators between 1908 and 1911, Duncan's body effectively dissolved in the act of performance. H. T. Parker (a fine writer who worked as a theater, music, and dance critic) of the *Boston Transcript* described this phenomenon as "this innocence, this spontaneity, this idealized and disembodied quality in her dancing."[46] A perceptive, anonymous critic from the *Philadelphia Telegraph* wrote similarly that Duncan was "an absolutely rare and lovely impersonation of the spirit of music, more like a sweet thought than a woman, more like a dream creation than an actual flesh and blood entity."[47]

Duncan's dancing was a paradigm of the late-nineteenth-century symbolist aesthetic, captured in Walter Pater's dictum that "all art constantly aspires towards the condition of music." Unfettered by character, plot, mise-en-scène, or the conventions of the ballet girl, Duncan stirred the imagination with her poetic, nonrational form of communication. In Kristeva's terms, she was enacting the chora, tapping into a realm of meaning that was not linear, not logical, not mimetic. When Duncan began dancing, whether her spectators' preconceptions were sacred or profane, it was clear that she was neither an entertainer nor a performer in the theater's realistic tradition. She was, instead, as a number of reviewers called her, a "symbolic dancer," whose capacity to communicate meaning went beyond that of apparent convention. (What they called symbolic at that time is what Kristeva called semiotic almost a century later.) The poet Shaemas O'Sheel wrote that

> Isadora Duncan's dancing is no less than an interpretation of life in symbols. Watching her I have felt that I was watching the Soul of Man moving in the Dance of Destiny. The term "dance" has a very different and very much more serious significance when used to indicate Miss Duncan's work than it has when standing for even the most talented and delightful of ordinary stage dancing. It connotes not merely something pretty and happy, something to beguile and amuse; it is an expression of the impulse which is a dream of all beauty; it is a questioning, an aspiration, a thrill with hopes and fears, desires and joys and melancholies, and ever with wonder.[48]

What was so extraordinary about Duncan for those early, American audiences was that she made visible the inner impulses, stirrings, vibrations of the soul. When Duncan initiated a motion from her solar plexus, then successively lifted her chest and raised her head heavenward or threw it backward Dionysically, it was a stunning embodiment of Nietzschean Will. Ongoing movement became a metaphor for what they then termed "soul," what we call the self. The dancing body was no longer a product—of training, of narrative, of consumption—but rather a process. The dance was about becoming a self (the subject-in-process/on trial) rather than about displaying a body.

Duncan essentially played out the drama of a self yearning for something, or somebody— an ideal, really—that continually obsessed her. All her life she was dogged by the inability to integrate all the different aspects of herself, and her early choreography was about a person—not necessarily a woman, not necessarily a man—yearning and searching and, in that process, finding beauty and pleasure. Even today, the choreography is not taught as a series of steps but as narratives of someone moving forward but being pushed backward by an unseen force, for example, or of someone repeatedly looking here and there for something beyond reach. Those were the virtual forces that drove the choreography; and, at a time when America was obsessed with finding for itself a national selfhood, a cultural identity, and a means of individual self-expression, spectators were primed to participate in this dancing subject-in-process.

America was poised on the threshold of modernism, a moment when corporate organization threatened the primacy of the individual and mass production threatened the uniqueness of the individual. According to cultural historian Jackson Lears:

> For many, individual identities began to seem fragmented, diffuse, perhaps even unreal. A weightless culture of material comfort and spiritual blandness was breeding weightless persons who longed for intense experience to give some definition, some distinct outline and substance to their vaporous lives.[49]

Duncan's dancing provided that intense experience, connecting with the innermost reaches of the soul. As a teenager, she had been influenced by Delsartism, which was absorbed into the larger physical cultural movement at the turn of the century. Delsarte and physical culture manuals[50] (forerunners of the contemporary self-help guide) circulated widely, promoting the idea that the individual *did* indeed have control over her fate through physical activity, whether calisthenics, dance, or sport. The message of these manuals spread through popular magazines and women's clubs: outward behavior could be changed as a means of improving one's inner being.

The origin of the self was thus effectively relocated from God to human. The self could be constructed and reconstructed through behavior, which became a conspicuous mark of identity that embedded the theatrical into everyday life. If you changed the way you carried yourself, the way you walked, and the way you gestured, you could then bring about fundamental changes: physical health, moral improvement, aesthetic grace. In effect, you could be whomever you wanted to be. America soon found its longed-for identity in the "self-made man."

Duncan was one of America's first self-made women. She was constantly reimagining herself, both onstage and in her interviews. (*My Life* was only the last in a long line of autobiographical narratives.) She embraced the importance of this connection between the internal and the external, and out of it she created a new art of the dance. Dance was no longer about the spectacular display of the legs for entertainment's sake; it was now about the self's inner impulses made manifest through the rhythmic, dynamic expression of the whole body. To Duncan, freedom meant being able to give presence to those otherwise invisible stirrings (consequently, she did away with the studio mirror, because it emphasized external image rather than inner impetus). Her dances of the early period were essentially about the self in formation. Constantly ongoing movement provided the perfect metaphor for that fluid identity.

Moreover, hers was a kinesthetic experience in which the spectators actively participated. From the mythic stage space to the familiarity of the music, from the accessibility of the vocabulary to the flow and ease of her movement style, Duncan constructed a literal and metaphorical theater environment that included the spectators. Her Progressive-era audiences were filled with marginalized Americans—women, artists, radicals, intellectuals—whose vision of a new social order was marked by unchecked optimism. They moved *with* this universal being onstage, this subject-in-process whose unspecified longings they could fill in with their own specific agendas. One writer recalled:

> I remember when I first saw her. . . . I shuddered with awe. In this . . . free, simple, happy, expressive, rhythmic movement was focussed all I and a hundred others had been dreaming. This was our symbol, the symbol of a new art, a new literature, a new national polity, a new life.[51]

Duncan started with the known, normative discourses of the symbolic—Greek sculpture, physical culture, even the leg show—and took her spectators to what was unknown inside themselves: "This solitary figure on the lonely stage suddenly confronts each of us with the secret of a primal desire invincibly inhering in the fibre of each, a secret we had securely hidden beneath our conventional behaviors, and we yearn for a new and liberated order in which we may indeed dance."[52] She activated the chora, creating in the theater a fluid, porous pulsing space of representation that invited spectators to engage in the dancing as a subject-in-process. She created a space of intelligibility into which the unintelligible—in this case, the kinesthetic and all its attendant emotions—erupted. For a time, her spectators reveled in this freely moving self, for it offered them the possibility "to make intelligible, and therefore socializable, what rocks the foundations of sociality."

—*Gender and Performance,* ed. Laurence Senelick, 1992

About Interpretation
Joann McNamara Interviews Ann Daly

JOANN MCNAMARA: Can you describe the interpretive approach you used in your article "Dance History and Feminist Theory: Reconsidering Isadora Duncan and the Male Gaze"? You seem to be looking at Isadora Duncan's dancing rather than just a dance, per se.

ANN DALY: Dancing is a con/textual practice. I don't think that you can just look at the dance and not the context or that you can just look at the context without the dance. I'm devoted to both formal analysis and contextual analysis. I began this project with Duncan's practice—very closely tracking her writings and her dancing—and then I moved outward into the context and negotiated between the two.

MCNAMARA: Do you consider this an approach, a perspective, or an actual method?

DALY: I don't know what the difference is between an approach and a method. The term "method" comes from science, where it means that you have something that can be replicated by others to verify your findings. Obviously that's not possible, or even desirable, in the humanities. Is deconstruction a philosophy or a method? Is feminist theory an approach or a method?

MCNAMARA: What was the initial value of feminist theory when you began using it—or even now?

DALY: Feminist analysis is useful to me because it gets to the very issue of how dance means. How does this dance make meaning? Who makes meaning, where does it come from? What is it inside and outside the dance that gives us the clues to its meaning? Feminist theory was articulating a theory of representation in a fresh way and connecting to my semiotic interest in the production of meaning. The theorists said: "There is a structure of representation, which is a visual one. And it's gendered." This idea of the male gaze was a very powerful one, and it gave me a way to keep thinking about how meaning is constituted in dance. But as I started work on Duncan, within a historical rather than contemporary time period, I found the theory of the male gaze problematic. That is basically what this article is about. This theory, which was so tremendously rich and provoked so many different lines of analysis, had been around for enough time that we began to see that it was not perfect and that it was not all-encompassing. It was not necessarily going to help me to understand how audiences in late-nineteenth/early-twentieth-century America saw and made meaning of Duncan's dancing. Along parallel tracks, I had become interested in Kristeva in graduate school, because she posits a theory of culture—of patriarchy—that is not monolithic. Feminist analysis is political. It aims to bring about change. Any theory of culture has to be able to allow for change—or else, what's it for? If you buy into the male gaze theory, which posits that everything is constructed from a male point of view, and you also believe that we are all constructed within culture, there's nowhere to go. We're stuck. Which is rather depressing. And for several years I didn't engage feminist theory. I focused on historical work. Kristeva, however, posits a theory of culture that allows for change from within. There had been theorizing about how we can change culture from an "elsewhere." Is there an "elsewhere" outside culture? Well, no, there isn't. So for me Kristeva articulates a way that you *can* change from within, because that's the only place where you can create change. She also allows a space for nonverbal representation and the nonverbal basis of culture. This interests me a lot, and I'm going to pursue it in my next project. I think of this project as the beginning of an effort to tease out a cultural theory that will apply to dance as a nonverbal phenomenon. The feminism will be there, but not explicitly.

MCNAMARA: Can you describe your cognitive processes when you've used this approach? In other words, what were the cognitive processes that you went through?

DALY: I break it down into four intertwined, simultaneous processes: observation, analysis, interpretation and judgement. Each of us privileges or is more comfortable with one or several of these four. I consciously monitor and deploy them sequentially in my long-term working process. When I did the Duncan research—it's been about four years and I'm still working on it—I began by systematically looking at her documentation. I wasn't sure what all my lines of analysis would be. Some people might call that disingenuous, but I really wasn't sure what the issues were going to be. I knew gender was going to be an issue, but I didn't realize race and class would enter so clearly. I started by looking for clues to her movement. The first thing was to figure out what it was that she did. And to try to get a sense of historical/cultural specificity. It was very important to me to place her dancing in the specific contexts of her audiences at particular periods and locations. The same dances that she did in 1908 in the Criterion Theatre meant very different things than they did at the Metropolitan Opera House in 1922. I was very careful not to erase those differences. So, I wanted to establish what it was she did and when and in what context. I was trying to reconstruct, in my head—I use the word "reconstruct" very loosely—a picture of how she moved. Then I was also very interested in her words, how she was constructing her discourse through a verbal mode. I spent a lot of time trying to visualize her practice, and then I started to undertake analysis and interpretation. I'm not saying that I wasn't implicitly doing analysis and interpretation earlier on, but now it became explicit and conscious. At this point I am doing a critical rereading of the work, in particular the effects of Duncan's discourse on constructing African "savagery" and "primitivism."

MCNAMARA: What's your role as an interpreter when you're using this approach?

DALY: I'm creating meaning, the meaning made from my position. Everyone wants to think that her interpretation of Isadora is *the* interpretation, but there are many interpretations of Isadora. What's so interesting about her is that she intentionally and consciously created a myth of herself. There is no essential Isadora. I'm of two minds about my role, actually. You have to start with facts. I mean, you can't just hallucinate out of nothing. Then there is the narrative nature of history. It's a story, a fiction that we fashion. So, on the one hand, I researched like hell and went back to original sources and manuscript collections. Detailed primary research is the basis of it all. But once I've gotten as far as I can with trying to find all of my "evidence," it's still this scholar making up the story. You can look at the same material I did. You're a different person, so you will ask different questions and you will see different connections. So, I'd have to say that I am creating meaning and I can only be creating meaning from Ann Daly in 1993 as a female, white, middle-class, heterosexual American. But even the "facts," in the case of Isadora Duncan, are sometimes in dispute. One of the reasons I am studying her is that she is a void. We have no films of her dancing. She is an absence, palpably present, in our dance history. To me that's an irresistible challenge and fascination. I'm effectively reconstructing her dancing. My role is kind of as a sleuth, in a way, to try to find as much good information as I can, tracking down all of the leads—as a creator of meaning, and as a writer. I am a writer by profession. I think of my work in writerly terms. My role is also to make this live for the reader. I am very, very conscious of the reader.

MCNAMARA: Is the historical context of feminism important to you?

DALY: Well, yes. Part of the reason that you can't glom the male gaze onto Isadora is that feminism meant something different in her day. When we call her "the first liberated woman," we're using the term in the sense that we know it today. But the way they thought of feminism (and feminism wasn't even a word yet—it was called the "woman movement") was very important. I couldn't talk about Duncan's feminism without knowing what feminism meant during her lifetime. That was where I started. What was subversive about what she was doing within the context of women and the woman movement?

MCNAMARA: What do you think is the primary advantage of this interpretive approach and does it have any weaknesses?

DALY: Well, one of the big advantages is that it asks different questions and yields new information. New knowledge is only produced by asking different questions. And in a field where most of the artists have been women, it has its obvious advantage. Weaknesses—well, I think any approach has weaknesses. Its greatest strength is its greatest weakness, because it asks some questions and ignores others. Feminist analysis is looking at gender, but it doesn't address issues of race and class per se. In the past five or so years, though, feminist theory has developed in that direction.

MCNAMARA: What does this article say to you now and what do you think it says to its readers? Do you think that this has changed over time?

DALY: It tells me that I have a lot more work to do. It says that it's real hard to integrate history and theory. Some people glom theory onto history. Some historians are theory-phobic. It took me a long time to write that article, because it's a challenge to deeply intersect theory and history—in a synergistic way—without doing violence to either one. It says to me that I have some rich veins that I need to mine. It says to the reader—I don't know what it says to the reader. You'd have to ask the reader, I think.

MCNAMARA: What's the overall purpose of the article?

DALY: Several things. On one level its purpose was to say that we just can't keep repeating the same Duncan line, that the current history is too easy and that maybe there are new ways of thinking about it. Second, its purpose was to work toward creating a historically-informed model of feminist theory for dance. And, conversely, working toward a more theoretical model of dance history.

MCNAMARA: How does it negotiate the notion of body?

DALY: In part, I tried to suggest that, just because Duncan wasn't wearing clothing on her arms and legs, we should not assume her as having been read as erotic. As art historian Abigail Solomon-Godeau demonstrates, the line between the chaste and the erotic is a shifting one. So, I guess I was trying, again, to negotiate the body as something whose meanings change across time and space. How we'd read it today isn't necessarily how audiences would have read it back then.

MCNAMARA: What about the way that this article negotiates the notion of time?

DALY: There is a gap between today and yesterday, and our challenge as historians is to try to figure out the logic of their way of seeing, of their perceptual apparatus and of their ways of making meaning.

MCNAMARA: How does this article negotiate the notion of space?

DALY: Well, it suggests that the space of the dance and the body is constituted by a confluence of different discourses, which must be read in their conjunctions. One of my foundational ideas about Duncan is that her body was a volatile, lively, provocative intersection of many cultural discourses in her time and place. I see her as having constructed several bodies: the natural body, the expressive body, the dancing body, the body politic, and the female body. I'm not sure of the spatial metaphor yet. I started out saying that the bodies were "layered on top of each other," but I don't think that's right. I think of the space of the body as occupying the center, where her body is a matrix, as it were, for American culture at that time and all of these cultural discourses. What does it mean to be expressive? What does it mean to have an American culture? What does it mean to be American? What does it mean to be a woman? What does nature mean? It took me a long time to figure out what the heck that was all about. These questions, these discourses, all come together in her practice.

MCNAMARA: I'm going to ask some questions about the process of writing. Are you aware of your own body when you're observing a dance, and, if yes, can you describe that experience?

DALY: I do respond physically. I feel free to not stifle any strong kinesthetic response.

MCNAMARA: What about when writing about a dance? Are you aware of your body when you're writing?

DALY: Only if I'm uncomfortable.

MCNAMARA: Have you ever studied dance? In college? Did you take classes?

DALY: I did take classes, but I would never say I "danced." When I discovered dance, I took ballet and modern classes to understand more about it as a writer. I love social dancing. I met my best friend in high school on the dance floor. And I've learned a whole new style of dancing down in Texas.

MCNAMARA: Reflecting back on your personal space when you were writing your text, how would you describe it?

DALY: I wrote this over a long period of time, and I wrote it in my office at home on a kneeler chair. My space, when I am writing, is not outer, it's inner. Mihaly Csikszentmihalyi describes this experience as "flow." Flow is an optimal experience in which you're fully absorbed by a challenging activity. It's that sense of consuming absorption that seems to obliterate any sense of externality.

MCNAMARA: Are there any other components of space that seem meaningful to you as you recall your use of this approach?

DALY: With this essay I tried something different, structurally. I'm a very linear person, linear thinker, logical. And I know how to structure writing very well linearly. I wanted to write this piece more circularly, or in a spiral. It's divided into three parts, and they don't necessarily flow into each other seamlessly. There's a little bit of a conceptual space and a corresponding visual break between the three sections. The basic questions and historical details, as I recall, are discussed in the first section. Kristevan theory is deployed in the second section. In the third section I tried to pull together the history and theory. I think one of the possible weaknesses of the article is that the third section really doesn't close the loop. It's more suggestive than explicit, which echoes the form of Isadora herself. She suggested images; she never explicitly denoted them.

MCNAMARA: What, if any, are your experiences of time when you are, or when you were: observing a dance, writing about a dance, editing your writing, finished with your text?

DALY: It depends upon the dance, when I'm observing. There's lived time, as distinct from chronological time. With a really good dance, time is subsumed into space, and you're in that place where you're not measuring time, it just opens out three-dimensionally. Other times you're just marking time until the house lights come up again.

MCNAMARA: What was your sense of time when you were writing your article?

DALY: On a literal level, I had to find the time to write it while I was teaching. You have to find those pockets of time that are large enough that you can do something meaningful. So the sense of time was always about being squeezed in, or was a negotiation with other responsibilities. There was not a luxurious sense of time, but a quite pressured sense of time. But when I'm in that flow, time opens up into space. You kind of drop out of clock time. But for me that never lasts too, too long. It comes in spurts. You plod along in very metrical time, and then something clicks. You reach critical mass and you kind of get lost in that flow. Then, right after, I usually make a breakthrough. I figured out a connection, for example. Then I usually take a break. That always worried me, actually—why don't I just keep going with it after I've made a breakthrough? I was discussing this with a playwright. She described it as "the cigarette syndrome"—like needing a cigarette after you reached your climax. It makes sense—after reaching that moment of intensity, you kind of cool out for a while. Me, I usually eat. Now that was writing. Editing is more linear. I go through the text for grammar, I go through to check the quotes, I go through for continuity, I go through for logic of argument.

MCNAMARA: What about when you're finished with your text?

DALY: It's all gone.

—1993 (unpublished)

Gender Issues in Dance History Pedagogy

IN HIS BOOK *Beyond the Culture Wars,* English professor Gerald Graff recalls his early and persistent aversion to reading books.[1] Nevertheless, he drifted into a solidly liberal arts English major in college, and suffered tongue-tied in the face of the classics until graduate school. What finally turned him on to literature, history, and other intellectual pursuits, he writes, was not the books themselves, but critical debates. Even Mark Twain's *The Adventures of Huckleberry Finn* left him cold, until an instructor mentioned that there was disagreement over the last part of the novel.

Graff's central argument is that critical debate should be integral to teaching literature, that books do not inherently yield their "hidden meanings" to young minds. The point, he argues, is not to teach dogmatically one interpretation or the other, but to teach the conflict itself. That is, to present the various interpretations to students, who should learn to process the debate for themselves. Being invited to join in the discussion empowers students as active thinkers rather than passive memorizers.

The situation is not so different with dance history studies. Reading Graff's book was like looking into my own classroom. It challenged me to think about the ways that the critical debate surrounding gender and dance could be used to bring intellectual and personal excitement into dance academics.

Critical debate pertaining to issues of race, gender, and class are as applicable to dance as they are to literature and art. Students should be encouraged to question their textbooks, their curriculum, and yes, even their teachers. One of my students, for example, asked what the lower classes did during the Renaissance, because the text and my lecture specifically focused on court dances. I was thrilled when another student expressed her discomfort with a discussion of butoh (Japanese postmodern dance), in which references to white body paint and the darkness of the unconscious appeared to reinforce racial stereotypes. Her comment was followed by an amazing discussion about the construction of American modern dance as positioned against black jazz dance and the Oriental "darkie," as I suggested that we use Toni Morrison's theory[2] to examine the rhetoric of Isadora Duncan and Ruth St. Denis. These are, as they say, teachable moments.

Students are eager, even if at first shy, to discuss such issues. And it is important for educators to encourage these discussions, because gender analysis—along with social analyses of race, class, and sexuality—will lead to new knowledge. Not only new knowledge about dance as an aesthetic and a cultural practice, but also self-knowledge. In this way, dance education makes itself an integral part of the humanities curriculum.

My goals in using gender as a frame for critical debate in dance history studies are to (1) establish a relevant connection between dance history studies and the students' own dance practice, (2) establish a relevant connection between dance and society, (3) establish the classroom as an open forum for the exchange of student ideas, (4) teach critical thinking skills, (5) facilitate students' examination of their own assumptions, (6) help students develop independent viewpoints, and (7) encourage close reading of dance texts as analytical support for students' interpretive conclusions.

To these ends, I recommend the following teaching strategies for promoting productive debate:

Use the analysis of gender as an organizing principle of your dance history studies course. There are enough articles in print by now to frame almost every period with gender issues—from Fanny Elssler's to Isadora Duncan's, from Martha Graham's to Pina Bausch's. Consider using an alternative textbook, such as Christy Adair's *Women and Dance: Sylphs and Sirens.*[3] Using gender as an overarching method of inquiry will give students a coherent critical framework. They will learn not only to read for facts, but to ask questions about historical documentation and interpretation—to read between the lines. This independent critical thinking skill carries over into any kind of analysis, not just of gender.

Design units that supply students with contrasting viewpoints. Some of my most successful units have been structured this way. For example, try pairing the videotape, "Dancing for Mr. B: Six Balanchine Ballerinas"[4] with an article titled "The Balanchine Woman: Of Hummingbirds and Channel Swimmers."[5] Or make companions of the film series *Ballet for All* program on *How Ballet Was Saved*[6] with Lynn Garafola's article on "The Travesty Dancer in Nineteenth-Century Ballet."[7]

Confronted with conflicting perspectives, students need to identify authors' assumptions, define the key issues in the debate, assess evidence, and come to a reasonable conclusion about the material. When we make it clear that "Dance History" was not handed down on a stone tablet, but rather has been constructed by real people who often disagree, we make room for our students' ideas. By asking students not only to study history but to practice historiography, we make history a more accessible career choice. Whenever I am asked a question unanswered in the literature, I commend the student for her or his inquisitiveness and suggest that here is dance history waiting to be written.

Include guided, open discussion in every class session. Questions such as "Why was the Romantic ideal a woman?" and "By what criteria did Théophile Gautier judge ballerinas?" challenge students to probe gender issues that are often left unexamined in standard dance histories. Inevitably, such discussion leads to connections between gender construction in dance and gender construction in the culture.

An environment for productive discussion, however, must be cultivated. When I teach the freshman "Introduction to Dance Studies" course, I insist that the students speak in class, and I work hard to make every student feel valued. (This does lead, admittedly, to some meandering discussions, but I consider it a worthwhile price for long-term student enfranchisement.) The emphasis on class discussion causes initial discomfort. One student told me privately that no teacher had ever asked her to talk in class before. There is no more insidious myth about dance than that dancers are inarticulate. By the time the students enter the sophomore "Dance History" survey course, it's hard to keep some of them reined in! Our discipline has no trouble conceptualizing studio work as a means of self-expression that is important to the development of students as individuals; the same is true of academic work.

The other main reason for class discussion is cognitive, rather than developmental. Some of the most powerful pedagogy comes not from me, or from the textbook, but from the students themselves. If a safe classroom community has been established, students will respectfully disagree with one another and thereby encourage in each other a deeper and more complex thinking process. (Similarly, when students edit each other's writing, or when students read an assignment aloud, they will self-regulate. Without the judgement of an authority figure, they can see that their writing was unclear, for example, or that they got off track.)

Encourage class debates. On occasion I devote a class session to a semiformal debate. I preassign appropriate reading and viewing along with the issue to be debated, so that students come to class prepared with an answer and supportive data and analysis. Possible debate topics range from "Was early modern dance a female dance form?" (which forces the question "What is 'female'?") to "Is Mark Morris challenging or reinforcing the stereotype of the male dancer as effeminate?" (which forces the question, "what is 'masculine'?"). The point is not deciding the "right" answer, but the process of discovering that definitions are not always agreed upon, that assumptions influence analysis, that the same information can be used to reach opposite conclusions, and that not all arguments are equally convincing. Faced with the task of defending their positions, students must present reasonable arguments and lay bare their starting-point assumptions. It is here, where the assumptions are explicitly placed on the table for debate, that students have the opportunity for personal and intellectual growth.

In practical terms, students divide into two groups, select a member in each group to represent them in the debate proper, and devise a list of documented arguments for their point of view. Like small discussion groups and guided, open discussion, this encourages students to learn from each other, synergistically. Both sides offer an opening statement and a closing statement. In between, both groups ask one another three questions. Critical thinking is entrained, and everyone has fun "performing."

Assign micro-essays. Although writing might be considered an imposition on students, especially those whose talents are nonverbal, it is an important ingredient in developing students' abilities to identify issues, analyze dance, synthesize data, and argue a point of view. A microessay is only one page, single- or double-spaced. The key is assigning very specific questions that require attention to a specific skill. For example, any of the following assignments could accompany a unit on George Balanchine:

- Compare and contrast the Balanchine ballerina with the Romantic sylph.
- Define the Balanchine ballerina.
- In what ways does Merrill Ashley's role in *Ballo Della Regina* exemplify the Balanchine ballerina?
- What did Balanchine mean when he said that "ballet is woman"?
- What gender image does the Balanchine ballerina communicate, and how?
- Is the Balanchine ballerina a reinforcement or subversion of traditional gender stereotypes? (Some of the more subtle thinkers in the class bridle at my insistence here that they take a side; however, I think it necessary for students to learn how to convincingly sustain and support a single point of view.)

With a very specific question and a limited amount of space, students are required to conceptualize their answer clearly and succinctly. In a sense, there's nowhere to hide murky thinking or creative double-talk.

Assign body work. Verbal and visual experiences should be complemented by kinesthetic experiences. Movement assignments appeal to students' talents and bring the abstract issues onto a concrete level. For example, ask students to perform a phrase from technique class first in a "feminine" way and then in a "masculine" way. This opens up a discussion about what it is that makes certain ways of moving "feminine" or "masculine." Is either mode more "natural" for each student? Why? Is it the result of anatomy, or training, or both?

Gender is an unavoidable issue, whether articulated or not, for dance instructors. In the ways we teach both technique and dance history studies, we send powerful messages about the roles of men and women in society. By framing dance history studies as an inquiry into the cultural construction of gender, we enable students to reflect on their studio and stage practices in the larger contexts of their lives and their culture. We have the opportunity to produce not just dancers, but "thinking dancers," whose abilities to reflect critically on their profession and their society will enrich the rest of their lives as artists, citizens, and individuals.

—Journal of Physical Education, Recreation, and Dance, 1994

"Woman," Women, and Subversion
Some Nagging Questions from a Dance Historian

Today I will focus specifically on questions, rather than answers, for two reasons.[1] One, because I am at a place right now in my own research, between projects, where I am involved more with questions than with answers. Second, because I do believe that, in the long run, questions are more important than answers. For new knowledge or new ways of looking and understanding will never be produced if the same old questions keep getting asked. As Albert Einstein wrote, "The formulation of a problem is often more essential than its solution, which may be merely a matter of mathematical or experimental skill. To raise new questions, new possibilities, to regard old questions from a new angle, requires creative imagination and marks real advances in science."[2]

Addressed from a specifically feminist perspective, the gender issues that entered the discourse of dance history in the late 1980s encouraged us to ask new questions. The kinds of nagging questions that reframe the very field itself. Nagging questions that we recognize as the way that children make sense of the world in the first place. Questions such as "what if?", "how come?", "who says?", or, the perennial favorite of any creative soul, "why not?"

Inserting the question of gender into dance history also broke open the issues of truth and authority. It demonstrated that history can, and should, be written and rewritten and rewritten again. Different stories will be told, depending upon what questions are asked. No one story inherently holds truth and authority, and the basis upon which we evaluate the relative merit of one story over another is not the mere accumulation of facts. "Facts" are not at all the protagonists of dance history. They certainly are necessary, but they are not sufficient, for facts mean nothing until they are interpreted. Facts are highly unstable. They must be choreographed, given particular shape through the questions that are asked, the person doing the asking, and the context in which they are placed. Edwin Denby made the point eloquently:

> About facts, too, what interest me just now is how differently they can look, one sees them one way and one sees them another way another time, and yet one is still seeing the same fact. Facts have a way of dancing about, now performing a solo then reappearing in the chorus, linking themselves now with facts of one kind, now with facts of another, and quite changing their style as they do. Of course you have to know the facts so you can recognize them, or you can't appreciate how they move, how they keep dancing.[3]

Gender-based research in dance history succeeded in breaking open a whole new way of looking at old, so-called "facts." It has given us new eyes through which to tell more stories, and different stories.

When I began engaging feminist theory as a tool for looking at historical dance practices, some ten years ago, the questions focused on the mechanisms of representation of Woman. The theory of the "male gaze" was tremendously powerful, because it explained so much about the way that women had been positioned in dance and, indeed, in all the arts.[4] The theory prompted us to ask questions that had never been asked before. Like all paradigm shifts, it at first seemed to explain everything. And, like all paradigm shifts, after the first flush of discovery, its weaknesses began to appear. Feminist theory has been around long enough now that it needs to be renewed. I want to call for an interrogation of feminist theory with its own unflinching eye, so that we can continue to come up with new sets of questions, and new stories.

The emphasis here, I should make clear, is not on the new just for the sake of novelty. When I advocate the asking of new questions and the telling of new stories, I mean to communicate the importance of producing a deeper, a broader, and a more complex discourse. I use the word "discourse" instead of the term "dance history" because I want to frame and define our field not as a fixed thing, like a puzzle in which a "fact," once set in its place, is finished and fixed forever, but as an ongoing dialogue—no, a polylogue—in which the facts or stories are never fixed, because the big picture is always in process, always dancing.

THERE ARE TWO questions in particular that have been nagging at me during the past year. Each one—the first about developing a productive model of cultural change that acknowledges the agency of women, and the second about critiquing the gender politics of logocentrism—is crystallized in recent personal encounters.

THE FIRST ENCOUNTER occurred at the joint conference of the Congress on Research in Dance and the Society of Dance History Scholars, which took place last summer in New York City. The conference concentrated on American dance of the 1930s, a rather neglected period. What an epiphany the gala concert was for me, as I watched reconstructions of dances by members of the New Dance Group. It was a whole new world of visionary dances, most of them by women, that intrigued and exhilarated me. I remember listening to Doris Hering interview Sophie Maslow and Jane Dudley. Strong and generous and no-nonsense, these women recalled a life of tough but committed decisions, in less-than-easy circumstances. I felt great respect and affection for them, and it disconcerted me that some feminist theoretical models would see only that they had failed to overthrow patriarchy singlehandedly. This experience intensified my discomfort with a theory of identity and subjectivity that denies women any agency and cannot conceive of culture as potentially productive as well as inherently reproductive. The question nagged at me: Can't I find or construct a theory of cultural change that allows for women as potentially productive agents rather than as reproductive ciphers? Must I have to choose among equally unsatisfying frameworks: one that denies women the agency that men possess (e.g., the theory of the "male gaze"); one that denies everyone agency (e.g., Foucault); and one, the default model, that denies any cultural impediment to agency (e.g., the American Dream)?

During the years I spent researching Isadora Duncan, I came to realize that real women, as historical subjects rather than as cultural constructs called "Woman," engage in aesthetic practices that are complexly matrixed and many-layered. It is fruitless to ask whether her dancing was a subversion or reinforcement of the status quo, because in some ways it was a subversion, and in some ways it was a reinforcement. Duncan exploited certain dominant discourses, such as class distinction and nativistic nationalism, to propagate other, more oppositional discourses, such as female autonomy. And these discourses and their interrelationships never remained static.[5]

As a way out of this impasse, I have been reading the work of French anthropologist/sociologist Pierre Bourdieu.[6] Bourdieu conceives of society as being organized into "fields," each of which is a structured and structuring system of social relations with its own logic. Any field, including that of Culture, has its own economy, so to speak, in which capital—economic, social, educational, symbolic—must be accumulated in order to advance or dominate in that particular field. The strategies for accumulating such capital and for gaining legitimacy, or distinction, are regulated by the field itself. These predisposed strategies, a generative constellation of tacit, internalized, embodied principles and practices, are what Bourdieu calls a field's "habitus." These unwritten rules are learned not explicitly, but implicitly, through practice in the field. Although the general contours of the habitus are shared by each player in the field, each individual, having come from a different background and thus occupying a different position within the field, has a slightly different habitus. Cultural belief, Bourdieu argues, is not in our heads, but in our bodies, what he calls the bodily "hexis."

The usefulness of Bourdieu's scheme to a gender-based dance history is its attention to the ways an artist constructs difference and distinction, in practice and in the reception of that practice. Adapting Bourdieu's model, we can look at how women choreographers have made specific choices in preexisting, intersecting fields: how women strategically deployed economic, social, intellectual, as well as cultural institutions and practices.[7]

For the study of dance history as social practice (rather than just aesthetic object), Bourdieu's framework offers a plausible alternative to the two extremes of cultural interpretation: on the one hand, subjectivism, which attributes behavior solely to the agency of the individual, and on the other hand, objectivism, which attributes behavior to the rules of social structure. It offers us a way to see that women choreographers and dancers are neither "geniuses," forging new practices out of thin air, nor passive functions of their cultural contexts. Yes, a woman's choices and strategies are delimited by the institutions and practices of her day, but choices are made, nonetheless. Bourdieu's concept of the habitus yokes together internal choice and external conditions into a mutually conditional and —this is most important—*generative* dynamic. He posits the social agent as occupying a relational, potentially changeable position in an equally changeable field. Thus we can recognize the social structures and practices through which a woman negotiated her art while also acknowledging her agency. And vice versa. We can recognize her agency and still recognize the social structures that gave rise to the conditions of that agency. The feminist historical project is not simply about divining a woman's "intention," but about teasing apart her actual choices in relation to her possible choices. It is not about determining whether or not she lives up to current theoretical models, which seems fundamentally to disrespect women in a decidedly unfeminist way. We may critique her choices, but we need to acknowledge that choices were indeed made.

As feminist historians, we need to recognize both the limits and possibilities that constituted a woman's habitus. We need to take into account social limits and possibilities: the limits and possibilities of education, of money, of class, of race and ethnicity, of the body, of sexuality, of particular artistic genres. Just as important, we need to take into account the limits and possibilities of our own conditions and knowledge.

These days, it is impossible for me to read gender without reading its connection to race, class, and sexuality. By theorizing the interaction of various fields of social life, Bourdieu suggests the complexity of artistic practice. I am looking for a more complex understanding and analysis of how culture operates in constructing the gendered dancing body. I would like to expand the borders of the social context in which we make sense of women's artistry. I would like to take into consideration the meaning of patronage, performance venues, marketing, body techniques, and schools, as well as religious background, economic status, and social contacts.

THE SECOND ENCOUNTER took place not even a month ago, and it pulled to shore, so to speak, an issue that has been lapping at the edges of my work for some time now. I was attending a women's studies seminar at the University of Texas at Austin, where a visiting scholar had presented a fascinating paper on the dance craze in the 1910s in Australia. One of the questions posed to the visiting scholar went something like this: "It's interesting what happens when women have only their bodies with which to speak. In this time and place, why dance? In other words, why was it dance through which they communicated?" I had been quiet up until now, preferring to listen. But I could hardly remain silent any longer. To this question, "Why dance," I rather abruptly replied, "Why NOT dance?" I went on to suggest that women—and men, for that matter—are ALWAYS "speaking" with and through their bodies. Furthermore, I challenged the assumption that nonverbal communication is inferior and somehow less authentic or valid than verbal communication. Of course, the idea of the body as the essential realm of Woman is the larger context here. This idea has served to marginalize women, bodies, and dance, so it is a notion that we tend to reject, but in doing so, we are also rejecting the whole of nonverbal communication, and, by extension, dance itself. The question I have been asking in this regard has to do with the politics of logocentrism, and the resulting quandary for women in general and dance scholars in particular, who do not want to reject the non-verbal but, at the same time, do not want their involvement with the nonverbal to be read as "feminine" and therefore marginalized. It's not only a question about the status of dance in culture and its potential for producing change but also a question about the status of dance history and dance historians within the academy.

For all the volume of current writing on the "body," inspired largely by the groundbreaking work of theorists such as Foucault, Bakhtin, and the French school of *écriture féminine,* the body is still approached as a suspect "other." The body is still posited as a presence, in a deconstructive moment that privileges absence. The body, when it is taken into account, is treated, more often than not, as an inscriptive surface, a pretext for language. And the body, when its bodily practices are directly addressed, is treated, more often than not, as a means of cultural reproduction, rather than a means of cultural change.

In addition, many current theories of identity, subjectivity, language, and culture are rooted in Lacanian psychoanalysis, which constructs subjectivity and culture as the very break from an infantile (nonverbal) plenitude of the body into the world of (verbal) language. Within this model, nonverbal practices are relegated to the realm of the asocial, the maternal, the hysteric; obviously, then, within this model, nonverbal practices cannot produce cultural change. And, for women, alignment with nonverbal practices serves only to reinforce their marginality. This doesn't leave much work for the scholar studying dance as a cultural production, and especially for the scholar studying dance as a feminist practice.

So, as that scholar, I ask: What would result from a rereading of cultural theory that does not repress the body as "pre-verbal"; that does not marginalize dance as "nonverbal" and "feminine"; that, avoiding the privileging of either of the terms "verbal" or "nonverbal," underscores the dialectic between the two? The nature of this dialectic, I suggest, is a fundamental issue underlying any cultural theory of dance, including a gender-based cultural theory of dance.

I have been looking in four places for clues in dealing with the feminist implications of this dialectic: French theorist Julia Kristeva's *Revolution in Poetic Language,* psychoanalyst Daniel Stern's *The Interpersonal World of the Infant,* philosopher Mark Johnson's *The Body in the Mind,* and philosopher Drew Leder's *The Absent Body.*[8] I have found these works useful for questioning the privilege given to verbal language, and its alignment with the "masculine" in our culture. By deconstructing the opposition between the verbal and the nonverbal in many of our cultural theories, we can make a space for dance, and especially that of women, as a potentially productive cultural practice.

To BORROW a longstanding phrase from feminist literary critic Annette Kolodny,[9] I would like to advocate for a "playful pluralism" in our discipline's gender-based research. The goal is to accept all points of view but subject them all to fair and fundamental scrutiny. This principle of simultaneous acceptance and scrutiny captures our challenge as dance historians: to respect differences while remaining intellectually engaged. No one theory or framework or approach is appropriate for all objects of study or for all researchers and the questions they choose to ask. Only intellectual flexibility will enable us to broaden, deepen, and enrich the field of dance history. There are many women to write about, many questions to ask, and many stories to tell. Women's lives in dance are not reducible to a formula, and it is only appropriate to the spirit of a feminist project to respect and even encourage difference as the very condition of both change and knowledge.

—Choreography and Dance, 1998

Trends in Dance Scholarship
Feminist Theory across the Millennial Divide

I

Every so often I receive a request to anthologize my 1987 article, "The Balanchine Woman: Of Hummingbirds and Channel Swimmers," in which I used the feminist theory of the male gaze to analyze a prototypical pas de deux.[1] So far, I have declined each one, or proposed that the article be published in tandem with "Dance History and Feminist Theory: Reconsidering Isadora Duncan and the

Male Gaze," a 1992 essay that critiqued the very theory that had enabled the earlier work.[2] While I am grateful that "Hummingbirds" made a meaningful contribution to our understanding of how feminist theory could be a useful framework for dance scholarship, I also appreciate that both feminist theory and dance studies have come a long, long way since the groundbreaking paradigm of the male gaze.

When I wrote "Hummingbirds," feminist theory was the most creative, rigorous, and productive discourse around. It articulated what had emerged as the fundamental issue of twentieth-century arts and humanities: representation. Feminist theory infused dance studies with a fresh, compelling set of questions that were quickly taken up, especially by younger scholars, critics, and artists. We were challenged to shift our angle of vision and expand the field of our vision. As a result, our critical acuity was honed, the dancing we chose to study became more inclusive, dialogue was opened with other disciplines, and dance literature as a whole grew more incisive, complex, and engaged.

But no question, framework, or theory ever remains fixed. I began to question the theory of the male gaze almost as soon as "Hummingbirds" was published. When I attempted to adapt the model to my historical research on Isadora Duncan, I bumped up against its limits, which led me to other theories and more questions. It also led me to critique the then-flourishing "success-or-failure" brand of feminist criticism, whose brittle, reductive analyses were not only unconvincing scholarship but problematic politics as well. So I wrote "Dance History and Feminist Theory" as a companion piece to "Hummingbirds."

Theory is successful insofar as it is generative. Feminist theory proved so successful that it was superseded—by race theory, queer theory, and postcolonial/transnational theory. In 1994, when I was asked to deliver a keynote lecture on gender to the annual conference of the Congress on Research in Dance, it was impossible for me to address issues of feminist criticism without considering these new axes of critical analysis. Drawing upon Pierre Bourdieu's theory of habitus, I called for a more complex understanding and analysis of how culture operates in constructing the gendered dancing body, to include consideration of things such as patronage, performance venues, marketing, dance techniques, and schools, as well as religious background, national identification, economic status, sexual orientation, and social class. I had extended "Hummingbirds" and "Dance History and Feminist Theory" into a trilogy.[3]

Thirteen years later, "Hummingbirds" may make an exemplary argument clear enough for undergraduates to follow and debate, but it is also, if excised from its full discursive trajectory, misleading. "Feminist theory" (whenever my students throw around this term, I politely inquire, "Which one?") is not a simple matter of applying theory A to case X. I even dispute the very trope of the "gaze" as an adequate explanation of dance spectatorship. Of course, the overlooked methodology in "Hummingbirds" is movement analysis. If there remains any pedagogical currency in that article—besides as a historical document of early feminist dance criticism—it is in the necessary collaboration between theoretical analysis and close reading.

II

I loved theory at first sight, after having blindly stumbled into a graduate program stocked with every variety. The puzzlelike logic appealed to me; it felt like an especially intense, even erotic, form of play. Then why do I find myself snapping shut a book in the Women's Studies section of the local bookstore when I realize from a quick scan of the table of contents that it is a "theory book"? Because most new feminist theory—or most theory, for that matter—lacks both imagination and rigor. Because it has become insular, trafficking only to other theories. And because it is so poorly written, as if a plodding and veinless prose would compel us to take it more seriously. Theory is like classical ballet: unless it's world-class, it's painful to watch.

Once liberating, theory has become stifling (hence, the creative and intellectual energy invested in experimental writing and hypersubjectivity). The very shorthand itself—"theory"—is a noun rather than a verb, an unmovable object rather than the irresistible force that it should be. A theory, feminist or otherwise, is a tool for invention—a set of questions that provides the motor for research and reflection. It is not a substitute for imagination. It is only a tool, and a tool is only as effective as its user and the design of her project.

I sense that a younger generation of dance scholars is avoiding formulaic applications of feminist theory, creatively questioning the received wisdom of earlier work. I wish that more of the complexity of my love-hate relationship with Balanchine's ballerinas had been written into "Hummingbirds," but I am satisfied to know that others are challenging the then-prevailing assumption that classical ballet is an irredeemable enemy to womankind. And challenging it not just rhetorically, but with solid research and keen analysis.

Personally, I now find poetics more intellectually productive than "theory." Poets are immersed in issues of subjectivity and representation, without sacrificing the sensuousness of language or observation. (Charles Bernstein, who goes so far as to theorize in verse, provides sumptuous food for thought.[4]) My premises have shifted, too. Identity cannot be theorized as a static category; it is a shifting positionality. I don't think about "women" as a category anymore; I think of women in relationship to each other, to lovers, to the world. (This is the Kristevan approach begun in "Dance History and Feminist Theory" as preparatory work for my book, *Done Into Dance: Isadora Duncan in America*.[5])

What are the limits and possibilities of these relationships for women? Dance, an art of bodies across time and space, is particularly well suited to investigating such relationships. Whether this project is considered "feminist" anymore, I don't know. I would like to think that the term and the practice of feminism are evolving along with the rest of the world.

III

In October 1999, the *New York Times* published an essay of mine on Pina Bausch.[6] I am still curious and nervous about it, because it gestures toward a direction in my thinking that I do not yet fully comprehend. In the essay, I reappraise Bausch's aesthetic, sixteen years after her initial appearances in this country. Back then, I called her imagery nihilistic, taking the choreographer to task for failing to question and probe, and therefore to ultimately perpetuate, the unheard rage of the violated women she portrayed.[7] Today, after a lot more observation and research, I describe her as a "romantic postmodernist," recognizing that, for her, the fact of the theater as communal space where feelings can be shared and meaning generated constitutes its source of strength and beauty. In 1986 I faulted Bausch for not providing within her dances a mediating ideology with which spectators could critique the violence against women in works such as *Kontakthof* and *Gebirge*. I did not know—and neither did anyone else, judging from the journalistic and scholarly criticism—that a "kontakthof" is a hotel courtyard where men go to choose among the gathered prostitutes. That, I daresay, is crucial information for a feminist reading of the dance. Such an oversight reiterates that, while theory is necessary, it is not sufficient to critical analysis and interpretation.

Feminist critics were generally agreed that Bausch's neutral presentation of gender violence was a failure of political obligation. As then formulated, American feminist critical theory demanded intervention, or at least commentary. Our definitions of political efficacy are no longer so inflexible. To remain an effective strategic practice, feminist critical theory must evolve in relationship to its immediate community and larger contexts. (When narrative was recuperated as a subversive practice after having been summarily dismissed as inherently patriarchal, we should have learned never to say "never.")

Today it is possible to argue that dance-as-witness is a viable strategic alternative to dance-as-critique. The choreographer and her dance are witnesses to culture, as then become the spectators. I have heard witnessing eloquently described as "selling your faith"—as accurate a description of feminist performance as I've ever encountered. As a model of performance it posits not a passive spectator who requires a "mediating ideology" to make the connections. Instead it empowers an active spectator whose humanity can be depended upon to bear witness—to continue telling the story or spreading the word, and thereby making movement toward change. This schema may sound naive, but was it any less naive to expect to transform/enlighten/politicize/convert that same spectator in a single bound?

Bausch managed to jam the feminist machinery by acknowledging and heightening raw emotion. Feminist critics did not have any more of a theory of theatrical emotion than did the formalist critics, which impeded everyone's ability to assess the work. Emotion onstage was dismissed as uncommitted by the former, self-indulgent by the latter. Emotion is a human reality, however, that feminist theory can no longer ignore.

Theater critic Bonnie Marranca recently remarked that the failure to connect with the theater on an emotional level is largely responsible for our failure to discuss beauty. For several decades, "beauty" has been banished from critical discourse. And justifiably so, because as a category of disinterested evaluation, it had long been used as a facile criterion for replicating the form and privilege of dominant culture. But there was something lost when we ousted the experience, if not the category, of beauty. Artists and theorists alike are feeling that loss, and turning to address it. The terms of poststructuralist analysis are inverting, as if we have indeed crossed a millennial divide. From death to ecstasy. Oppression to utopia. Pain to beauty. Dance will have much to offer these new inquiries, without even having to disclaim its deep and many pleasures.

—*Dance Research Journal*, 2000

NOTES

INTRODUCTION

1. Antonin Artaud, *The Theater and Its Double* (New York: Grove Press, 1958), 71.

2. Quoted in "Action/Performance and the Photograph" exhibit. Sidney Mishkin Gallery, Baruch College, New York City, 17 March–18 April 2000.

3. Maurice Merleau-Ponty, *The Visible and the Invisible* (Evanston, Ill.: Northwestern University Press, 1968), 146.

REVIEW: DIANA THEODORES'S *FIRST WE TAKE MANHATTAN,* JILL JOHNSTON'S *MARMALADE ME,* AND LYNNE CONNER'S *SPREADING THE GOSPEL OF THE MODERN DANCE*

1. Maurice Berger, ed., *The Crisis of Criticism* (New York: The New Press, 1998).

2. See Judith H. Dobrzynski, "The Embarrassment Of Critics: Raters Rated," *New York Times,* 20 June 1998, A13, A15.

3. Arlene Croce, "Discussing the Undiscussable," *New Yorker,* 26 December 1994/2 January 1995, 54–60.

4. See Susan Manning, *Ecstasy and the Demon: Feminism and Nationalism in the Dances of Mary Wigman* (Berkeley: University of California Press, 1993), and Ellen Graff, *Stepping Left: Dance and Politics in New York City, 1928–1942* (Durham, N.C.: Duke University Press, 1997).

5. Clifford Gertz, *Works and Lives: The Anthropologist as Author* (Stanford, Calif.: Stanford University Press, 1988).

6. See Jill Johnston, *Jasper Johns: Privileged Information* (New York: Thames and Hudson, 1996).

7. Jill Johnston, "How Dance Artists & Critics Define Dance as Political," *Movement Research Performance Journal,* no. 3 (Fall 1991): 2–3.

8. Ibid., 3.

THE INTERESTED ACT OF DANCE CRITICISM

Epigraph from Marcia B. Siegel, "Looking at Dance from All Sides Now: On Multiculturality and Authenticity in Dance," *Ballett International* 14, no. 7/8 (July/August 1991): 16.

1. That is not to say that dance in *popular* culture is suffering the same fate. In fact, dance is probably one of the most vibrant areas of popular culture—witness the impact that MTV, Madonna, and Hammer are making in the lives of American youth. Critics slowly are getting around to looking beyond the theater, toward the TV screen, the streets, stadiums, and clubs.

2. Siegel, "Looking at Dance," 13.

3. June Vail, "World Dance: We'll Understand It When We Recognize That Bop and Ballroom Are Ethnic, Too," *DCA Newsletter* (Winter 1990): 6; reprint, *Maine Times,* 27 July 1990.

4. Arlene Croce, "Discussing the Undiscussable," *New Yorker*, 26 December 1994/2 January 1995, 54–60.

5. Ibid., 54.

6. Ibid., 55.

7. Ibid., 56.

8. Ibid., 54.

9. Ricardo D. Trimillos, professor of ethnomusicology at the University of Hawaii at Manoa, concluded his address to the 1990 DCA with this list of questions:

> 1. What is the responsibility of the critic to the performer and to the tradition he [*sic*] reviews?
>
> 2. In the age of television and of language diversity in urban America, is the critic effectively reaching an optimal audience using only an English-language and print medium?
>
> 3. What role should the reviewer's artistic criteria play in reviewing a performance of another culture? And finally
>
> 4. What is the responsibility of the critic in America as mediator between majority populations and minority ones?

Richard D. Trimillos, "More Than Art: The Politics of Performance in International Cultural Exchange," *DCA News* (Winter 1990): 9.

10. Nicole Plett, "Looking at Ritual Dance," *DCA News* (Summer 1988): 4.

11. Joann Kealiinohomoku, "An Anthropologist Looks at Ballet as a Form of Ethnic Dance," *What Is Dance?* ed. Roger Copeland and Marshall Cohen (Oxford: Oxford University Press, 1983), 533–49. For other early perspectives on dance criticism and anthropology, see Suzanne Walther, "A Cross-Cultural Approach to Dance Criticism," *Dance Research Collage*, ed. Patricia Rowe and Ernestine Stodelle (New York: Congress on Research in Dance, 1979), 65–76; and Ruth K. Abrahams, "Dance Criticism and Anthropology," *Journal for the Anthropological Study of Human Movement at New York University* 1, no. 1 (Spring 1980): 63–66.

12. This is a standard, and hardly new, journalistic practice. When I was coming up on a daily newspaper fifteen years ago, editors stressed the importance of context in reporting a story. So what if widget X is pulled out of production of the city's main steel plant? What place does that widget X have in the life of the employees, the plant profits, the local economy? Context produces meaning.

13. Sal Murgiyanto, "Seeing and Writing about World Dance: An Insider's View," *DCA News* (Summer 1990): 3.

14. Deidre Sklar, in the course of writing a movement ethnography of a religious fiesta performed annually in Las Cruces, New Mexico, developed five essential parameters for considering movement or dance in cultural context:

> 1. Movement knowledge is a kind of cultural knowledge.
>
> 2. Movement knowledge is conceptual and emotional as well as kinesthetic.
>
> 3. Movement knowledge is intertwined with other kinds of cultural knowledge.
>
> 4. One has to look beyond movement to get at its meaning.
>
> 5. Movement is always an immediate corporeal experience.

Deidre Sklar, "Five Premises for a Culturally Sensitive Approach to Dance," *DCA News* (Summer 1991): 4.

15. Clifford Geertz, "Thick Description: Toward an Interpretive Theory of Culture," *The Interpretation of Cultures* (New York: Basic Books), 18.

16. Brenda Dixon, "Born Too Late?" *DCA News* (Fall 1991): 5.

17. See Sally Banes, "The Critic as Ethnographer," *DCA News* (Spring 1990): 3, 8–10; Siegel, "Looking at Dance."

18. This was at issue in a 1987 exchange between critic Eva Resnikova and a host of other critics, including Arlene Croce, over Resnikova's article entitled "Mark Morris Superstar" (*New Criterion* [January 1987]: 59–62; letters to the editor and Resnikova's response were published in *New Criterion* [April 1987]: 82–87). On the surface a bit of professional infighting, below the surface lay a joust over the justification of elevating Morris into the canon, and who is empowered to do so. Resnikova thought not, and criticized Croce for her efforts to do so.

Resnikova, despite her severe criticism of Croce's approach to criticism (she mistakes Croce's emphasis on music as an end in itself; actually, the emphasis on music is about the emphasis on form and structure) is herself a tiger of the same stripe. She is every bit as interested in assessing Morris's worthiness as an inductee into the canon. Since she uses different criteria for her judgement, however, she comes to an opposite conclusion: "Balanchine's self-appointed apostles may have allowed despair to color their perceptions of a talented and promising, if still somewhat undisciplined and self-indulgent, aspirant, who is not, alas, the savior of the dance" (Resnikova, "Mark Morris Superstar," 62).

19. Hilton Kramer, "A Note on *The New Criterion:* September 1982," *The New Criterion Reader: The First Five Years,* ed. Hilton Kramer (New York: The Free Press, 1988), 3.

20. Lincoln Kirstein started off a posthumous essay on Balanchine by recounting the story of a woman who anxiously asked the dance master if her daughter would dance. Balanchine replied, "La Danse, Madame, c'est une question morale." *Portrait of Mr. B* (New York: The Viking Press, 1984), 16.

21. Pierre Bourdieu, *Distinction: A Social Critique of the Judgement of Taste,* trans. Richard Nice (Cambridge: Harvard University Press, 1984), 6.

22. Bourdieu, *Distinction,* 6.

23. Ibid., 7.

24. Jawole Willa Jo Zollar, "Listen: Our History Is Shouting at Us," *Update* (November/December 1990): 16.

25. Joan Acocella, "Purity," *Village Voice,* 14 April 1992, 95, 102.

26. Gus Solomons Jr., "Black Like Who?" *Village Voice,* 14 April 1992, 96.

27. Ibid.

28. Quoted in Yvonne Rainer, "Looking Myself in the Mouth: Sliding Out of Narrative and Lurching Back In, Not Once but . . . Is the 'New Talkie' Something to Chirp About? From Fiction to Theory (Kicking and Screaming) Death of the Maiden, I Mean Author, I Mean Artist . . . No, I Mean Character A Revisionist Narrativization of/with Myself as Subject (Still Kicking) via John Cage's Ample Back," *October* 17 (Summer 1981): 67.

29. Ibid.

30. Ibid., 76.

31. Ibid., 68.

32. Jack Anderson, "Political Dogma Fades. Social Awareness Remains." *New York Times,* 4 October 1992, sec. 2, p. 8.

33. Joseph R. Roach, "Power's Body: The Inscription of Morality as Style," *Interpreting*

the Theatrical Past: Essays in the Historiography of Performance, ed. Thomas Postlewait and Bruce A. McConachie (Iowa City: University of Iowa Press, 1989), 115.

34. Susan Sontag, "Against Interpretation," *A Susan Sontag Reader* (New York: Vintage Books, 1983), 104.

35. Ibid., 98.

36. Michael Kirby, "Criticism: Four Faults," *Drama Review* 18, no. 3 (T63, September 1974): 66.

37. Ibid.

38. Sontag, "Against Interpretation," 103.

39. Marcia B. Siegel, "On Encountering the 33rd Fouetté," *DCA News* (Spring 1989): 3.

40. Nancy Moore, "New Dance/Criticism: Is It Whatever You Say It Is?" *Dance Magazine* (April 1974): 60.

41. Siegel, "On Encountering," 11.

42. Brenda Dixon-Gottschild, "Some Thoughts on Choreographing History" (Paper presented at "Choreographing History" conference, University of California, Riverside, 16 February 1991), 5.

43. See Gregory Battcock's introduction to Jill Johnston, *Marmelade Me* (New York: E. P. Dutton, 1971).

44. Jill Johnston, "How Dance Artists & Critics Define Dance as Political," *Movement Research Performance Journal,* no. 3 (Fall 1991): 2.

45. June Vail, "To the Editors," *DCA News* (Summer 1989): 3.

46. Mindy Aloff, "Discomfort in the Driver's Seat," *Village Voice,* 17 November 1984, 110–11.

47. For a typology of feminisms, see Jill Dolan, *The Feminist Spectator as Critic* (Ann Arbor, Mich.: UMI Research Press, 1988).

48. For an overview, including a bibliography, of feminist analysis of dance, see Ann Daly, "Unlimited Partnership: Dance and Feminist Analysis," *Dance Research Journal* 23, no. 1 (Spring 1991): 2–5. Also reprinted in this volume.

49. Marianne Goldberg, "Preface," *Women & Performance: A Journal of Feminist Theory* 3, no. 2 (#6, 1987/1988): 4.

50. Johnston, "Dance Artists & Critics," 3. For an analysis of how gender hierarchy is produced through ballet criticism, see Ann Daly, "Classical Ballet: A Discourse of Difference," *Women & Performance: A Journal of Feminist Theory* 3, no. 2 (#6, 1987/88): 57–66.

51. Edwin Denby, *Dance Writings,* ed. Robert Cornfield and William Mackay (New York: Alfred A. Knopf, 1986), 541.

52. Yvonne Rainer, "A Quasi Survey of Some 'Minimalist' Tendencies in the Quantitatively Minimal Dance Activity Midst the Plethora, or an Analysis of Trio A," *Minimal Art: A Critical Anthology,* ed. Gregory Battcock (New York: E. P. Dutton, 1968), 263–73.

53. June Vail, "World Dance," 14.

THE PLAY OF DANCE: AN INTRODUCTION TO *LAMB, LAMB, LAMB, LAMB, LAMB, . . .*

The epigraph is from Deborah Hay, interview with author, 9 September 1989.

1. Deborah Hay, guest lecture to Dance History I class, University of Texas, Austin, 18 November 1990.

2. Hay, program notes, *The Man Who Grew Common in Wisdom*. University of Texas Opera Lab Theatre. Austin, Texas, 8–9 September 1989.

3. Hay, interview with author, Austin, Texas, 9 September 1989.

4. Ibid.

5. Hay, interview with author, New York City, 7 October 1988.

6. Hay, guest lecture to Dance History I class, University of Texas, Austin, 18 November 1990.

7. Ibid.

8. Hay, interview with author, New York City, 7 October 1988.

9. Hay, guest lecture to Dance History I class, University of Texas, Austin, 18 November 1990.

10. Hay, interview with author, New York City, 7 October 1988.

11. Solo enactment, *Lamb, lamb, lamb, lamb, lamb, . . .* , Hyde Park Theatre, Austin, Texas, 6 December 1991.

12. Hay, interview with author, New York City, 7 October 1988.

HORSE RIDER WOMAN PLAYING DANCING: ANN DALY INTERVIEWS DEBORAH HAY

1. This interview was conducted on 2 March 1997.

BILL T. JONES IN CONVERSATION WITH ANN DALY

1. Arnie Zane, born in 1948, was the second son of immigrants: an Italian Catholic from Brazil and an orthodox Jew from Lithuania. He was raised in Queens, New York.

2. *Monkey Run Road* (1979) was named after Monkey Run, a juke joint near Jones's childhood home in upstate New York. The duet was modeled after Richard Bull's *Making and Doing,* in which dancers performed ordinary, everyday movements repetitively until they evolved into pure form.

3. Contact improvisation is a partnering technique developed by dancer Steve Paxton that involves moments of countering and opposing touches. Jones and Zane learned the technique from Lois Welk at Binghamton in 1973, thus beginning their dance partnership. They later formed the American Dance Asylum with Welk.

4. *Last Supper at Uncle Tom's Cabin/The Promised Land* (1990) is a highly theatrical piece comprised of four distinct parts: "The Cabin," "Eliza on the Ice," "The Supper," and "The Promised Land." The work was defined by Huck Snyder's childlike, colorful sets; score by saxophonist Julius Hemphill; and influence ranging from Harriet Beecher Stowe's nineteenth-century antislavery novel, Leonardo da Vinci's masterpiece *The Last Supper,* Sojourner Truth's "Ain't I a Woman," and Leroi Jones's *Dutchman.*

5. See Bill T. Jones, *Last Night on Earth* (New York: Pantheon Books, 1995), 38–39.

"WHAT REVOLUTION?": THE NEW DANCE SCHOLARSHIP IN AMERICA

1. Lynn Garafola, *Diaghilev's Ballets Russes* (New York and Oxford: Oxford University Press, 1989), xii–xiii.

2. Ibid., 147–48.

3. Deborah Jowitt, *Time and the Dancing Image* (Berkeley and Los Angeles: University of California Press, 1988), 7.

4. Ibid.

5. Cynthia J. Novack, *Sharing the Dance: Contact Improvisation and American Culture* (Madison: University of Wisconsin Press, 1990), 3–4.

DANCING: A LETTER FROM NEW YORK CITY

1. Quotations from Julia Kristeva are from her lecture "Artaud: Between Psychosis and Revolt," delivered 20 November 1996, The Drawing Center, New York City.

2. Marina Isola, "Struggling to Stay Avant," *New York Times*, 4 May 1997, sec. 13, p. 3.

3. See Arlene Croce, "Facing the Music," *New Yorker*, 17 March 1997, 48, 50; Jennifer Dunning, "Struggling to Carry On the Graham Tradition," *New York Times*, 1 May 1997, C13; and Isola, "Struggling to Stay Avant."

4. See Elisabeth Bumiller, "New Editor Changes the Cadence of the Village Voice," *New York Times*, 13 February 1997, B1.

5. Antonin Artaud, *The Theater and Its Double* (New York: Grove Press, 1958), 99.

6. Marcia B. Siegel, "Looking at Dance from All Sides Now: On Multiculturality and Authenticity in Dance," *Ballett International* 14, no. 7/8 (July/August 1991): 16.

7. See Barbara Kirshenblatt-Gimblett, "Confusing Pleasures," in *The Traffic in Culture: Refiguring Art and Anthropology,* ed. George E. Marcus and Fred R. Myers (Berkeley: University of California Press, 1995), 224–55.

8. Anna Kisselgoff, "A Season Short on Truly Memorable Turns," *New York Times*, 12 January 1997, sec. 2, p. 8.

THE CONTINUING BEAUTY OF THE CURVE: ISADORA DUNCAN AND HER LAST COMPOSITIONS

1. Quoted in Irma Duncan and Allan Ross Mcdougall, *Isadora Duncan's Russian Days and Her Last Years in France* (New York: Covici-Friede, 1929), 262.

2. Ibid., 276.

3. Reprinted in Sally Banes, "Goleizovsky's Ballet Manifestoes," *Ballet Review* 11, no. 3 (1983): 64–75.

4. Isadora Duncan, *The Art of the Dance* (New York: Theatre Arts, 1928), 100.

5. Quoted in Irma Duncan, *Duncan Dancer: An Autobiography by Irma Duncan* (Middletown, Conn.: Wesleyan University Press, 1966), 252–53.

REVIEW: MILLICENT DILLON'S *AFTER EGYPT*

1. Irma Duncan, *Duncan Dancer: An Autobiography by Irma Duncan* (Middletown, Conn.: Wesleyan University Press, 1966): 122–23.

ISADORA DUNCAN IN 1920S AMERICA: "A BOLSHEVIK SHADE OF RED"

1. Sol Hurok, *Impresario* (New York: Random House, 1946), 98.

2. Isadora Duncan, *The Art of the Dance* (New York: Theatre Arts, 1928), 109.

3. Ibid., 111.

4. "Isadora Duncan Off, Will Never Return," *New York Times,* 4 February 1923, 15.

5. See Peter G. Filene, *Americans and the Soviet Experiment, 1917–1933* (Cambridge: Harvard University Press, 1967); Robert K. Murray, "The Red Scare," in *Assault on Victorianism: The Rise of Popular Culture, 1890–1945,* ed. John N. Ingham (Toronto: Canadian Scholars' Press, 1987); Francesco Nitti, "Russia's Plight Exposes Futility of Soviet Rule," *San Francisco Examiner,* 16 October 1921, N5; David A. Shannon, *Between the Wars: America, 1919–1942,* 2d ed. (Boston: Houghton Mifflin, 1979).

6. "Isadora Duncan Soviet Dancer," *San Francisco Examiner,* 16 October 1921, 9.

7. For an account of Duncan's Moscow days, see Ilya Ilyich Schneider, *Isadora Duncan: The Russian Years,* trans. David Magarshak (New York: Da Capo Press, 1968).

8. Shannon, *Between the Wars,* 33.

9. A. J. Lorenz, "Isadora Denies She's Nude; Skirt is 'Glued' to Form," *San Francisco Examiner,* 25 October 1922, 5.

10. According to Hurok, the media flap sold out three performances in twenty-four hours (Hurok, *Impresario,* 101).

11. H. T. Parker, *Motion Arrested: Dance Reviews of H. T. Parker,* ed. Olive Holmes (Middletown, Conn.: Wesleyan University Press, 1982), 69.

12. Duncan, *Art,* 121.

13. "Miss Duncan's Farewell," *New York Times,* 15 November 1922, 22.

14. "Miss Duncan Dances Again," *New York Times,* 16 November 1922, 26.

15. Henry Levine, "Boston Bars Isadora Duncan," *Musical America* 37, no. 1 (28 October 1922): 2.

16. "On With the Dance, Isadora's War City," *World,* Isadora Duncan Clippings, Dance Collection, New York Public Library for the Performing Arts, New York City, New York.

17. "US Probe Ordered," *San Francisco Examiner,* 24 October 1922, 10.

18. Hurok, *Impresario,* 118.

19. Isadora Duncan, *Isadora Speaks,* ed. Franklin Rosemont (San Francisco: City Lights Books, 1981), 63.

20. "America Makes Me Sick, Nauseates Me," *San Francisco Examiner Magazine,* 4 March 1923, 9.

REVIEW: LILLIAN LOEWENTHAL'S *THE SEARCH FOR ISADORA*

1. See Lillian Loewenthal, "Isadora Duncan in the Netherlands," *Dance Chronicle* 3 (1979–1980): 227–53; and Lillian Loewenthal, "Isadora Duncan and Her Relationship to the Music of Chopin," *Proceedings, Society of Dance History Scholars,* comp. Christena L. Schlundt (Riverside, Calif.: Dance History Scholars, 1987): 159–65.

2. Fredrika Blair, *Isadora: Portrait of the Artist as a Woman* (New York: William Morrow, 1986); Deborah Jowitt, "The Search for Motion," *Time and the Dancing Image* (New York: William Morrow, 1988): 67–102; Elizabeth Kendall, *Where She Danced: The Birth of American Art-Dance* (New York: Alfred A. Knopf, 1979); Francis Steegmuller, *"Your Isadora": The Love Story of Isadora Duncan and Gordon Craig* (New York: Random House and The New York Public Library, 1974); Doree Duncan, Carol Pratl, and Cynthia Splatt, eds. *Life into Art: Isadora Duncan and Her World* (New York and London: W. W. Norton, 1993).

ISADORA DUNCAN AND THE DISTINCTION OF DANCE

1. Edith Wharton, *A Backward Glance* (New York and London: D. Appleton-Century, 1934), 321.

2. Ibid.

3. George Seldes, "What Love Meant to Isadora Duncan," *Mentor,* February 1930, 64.

4. Folder 64, Irma Duncan Collection of Isadora Duncan Materials, Dance Collection, New York Public Library for the Performing Arts, New York City, New York.

5. Louis C. Fraina, "Lydia Kyasht—Spirit of Beauty," *Modern Dance Magazine* (April 1914): 12.

6. Isadora Duncan, *My Life* (New York: Boni & Liveright, 1927), 25.

7. See Robert C. Allen, *Horrible Prettiness: Burlesque and American Culture* (Chapel Hill: University of North Carolina Press, 1991).

8. Ruth St. Denis and, to a lesser extent, Loie Fuller and Maud Allan also pioneered modern dance. Unlike Duncan, however, St. Denis often performed in vaudeville venues. Fuller and Allan spent most of their careers in Europe, as did Duncan, but had much less of an impact in America.

9. For the purpose of distinguishing between "culture" in the anthropological sense, and "Culture" as high art, which is the subject of this essay, I will capitalize the latter. In keeping with the tenets of a sociohistorical analysis, I will also capitalize words (such as Beauty and Nature) as they were intentionally and meaningfully capitalized by Duncan and her contemporaries. Occasionally, I will place such words in quotation marks, as a way of emphasizing the gaps in belief between Duncan's day and our own.

10. Duncan's style of dancing was used in American pageants, too. Duncan was good friends with pageantry movement leader Percy MacKaye; it was most likely out of personal friendship than admiration for pageantry (she disdained amateurs) that she agreed to a cameo appearance in his *Caliban,* in 1916. On pageantry, see David Glassberg, *American Historical Pageantry: The Uses of Tradition in the Early Twentieth Century* (Chapel Hill: University of North Carolina Press, 1990); Naima Prevots, *American Pageantry: A Movement for Art & Democracy* (Ann Arbor, Mich.: UMI Research Press, 1990); Dorothy J. Olsson, "Arcadian Idylls: Dances of Early Twentieth-Century American Pageantry" (Ph.D. diss., New York University, 1992).

11. Lawrence W. Levine, *Highbrow/Lowbrow: The Emergence of Cultural Hierarchy in America* (Cambridge: Harvard University Press, 1988), 132.

12. Ibid., 146.

13. Pierre Bourdieu, *Distinction: A Social Critique of the Judgement of Taste,* trans. Richard Nice (Cambridge: Harvard University Press, 1984), 11.

14. Ibid., 6.

15. Duncan's discursive strategies shifted through the years. Her time in America can be divided into roughly three periods. During her early tours, 1908–1911, her pastoral Greek imagery appealed to upper-class spectators aspiring to a greatness on the scale of the Greek civilization. During the war years, she appealed to the pro-Allied spectators and their revived sense of patriotism, especially when she wrapped herself in the flag and danced, like Lady Liberty, to the Star Spangled Banner. During her last tour, 1922–1923, she insulted a rabidly xenophobic and anti-communist audience with her Soviet sympathies (even though her idea of communism was calling Walt Whitman the first Bolshevik). Afterward, when stripped of her citizenship, she seemed to compensate in her rhetoric, returning to Whitman and the Statue of Liberty.

16. This idea of translating Greek statuary into dance was hardly new. Back in 1890, for example, at about the same time that "living statues" became a popular pastime for women, the *San Francisco Examiner* ran an article (could Duncan have seen it?) on two rather sophisticated skirt dancers named Carmencita and Otero, who, "in her slow and sinuous movements, seems like a masterpiece of Phidias." "Wriggling into Wealth. Two Dancing Daughters of Sunny Spain, Carmencita and Otero. The Ballet of the Future Will Have Little Use for Legs. They are Children of Nature, But Their Mother Seems to Have Taught Them How to Dance—They Could Give Delsarte Points on Making Your Body Talk—Poetry of Motion Personified," *San Francisco Examiner,* 1890, Performing Arts Library and Museum, San Francisco, California.

17. Rush, "Isadora Duncan," *Variety,* 2 August 1908, Isadora Duncan Clippings, Dance Collection, New York Public Library for the Performing Arts, New York City, New York.

18. H. E. Krehbiel, "Miss Duncan's Dancing," *New York Daily Tribune,* 7 November 1908, Isadora Duncan Clippings, Dance Collection, New York Public Library for the Performing Arts, New York City, New York.

19. Collections of Greek vases and plaster cast collections of the great statuary circulated in the new urban museums of the late nineteenth century. Even before seeing the British Museum, Duncan herself may have seen San Francisco's brand new collection of Greek vases in the California Midwinter Exposition Memorial Museum, which opened in March 1895. In New York she may have seen the plaster casts at the Metropolitan Museum of Art.

20. Based on the available indirect evidence, it appears that Duncan wore undergarments, as a rule: either a teddy-type leotard fastened to the outer tunic at the shoulders, or a brief pair of tights, depending on the costume. See Mary Desti, *The Untold Story: The Life of Isadora Duncan 1921–1927* (1929; reprint New York: Da Capo Press, 1981), 218–19; Maurice Dumesnil, *An Amazing Journey: Isadora Duncan in South America* (New York: Ives Washburn, 1932), 154; Julia Levien, interview with author, New York City, New York, 10 July 1990.

21. "Isadora Duncan's Dance Causes War in St. Louis," *Kansas City Post,* 5 November 1909, Isadora Duncan Clippings, Dance Collection, New York Public Library for the Performing Arts, New York City, New York.

22. Isadora Duncan, *The Art of the Dance,* ed. Sheldon Cheney (New York: Theatre Arts, 1928), 118.

23. *The Metropolitan Museum of Art Twenty-fifth Annual Report of the Trustees of the Association* (New York, 1895), 23.

24. Ibid., 26.

25. "The agitated ripples that Isadora Duncan started have widened and divided until now there are many different schools of free dancing," reported *Woman Citizen* in 1926. "One of the most popular, whose appeal and influence is national, is the school of Florence Fleming Noyes." She had four schools in New York alone, and two summer camps in Cobalt, Connecticut. Mildred Adams, "The Rhythmic Way to Beauty," *Woman Citizen* 11 (October 1926): 27.

26. Helen Tamiris, "Tamiris in Her Own Voice: Draft of an Autobiography," ed. Daniel Nagrin, *Studies in Dance History* 1, no. 1 (Fall 1989/Winter 1990): 7.

27. On habitus, see Pierre Bourdieu, *The Logic of Practice,* trans. Richard Nice (Stanford, Calif.: Stanford University Press, 1990), 52–79; Bourdieu, *Distinction,* 169–225. On field, see Bourdieu, *Logic,* 122–34. The first half of *Logic* provides a coherent description of Bourdieu's overall project. On the cultural field in particular, see Pierre Bourdieu, *The*

Field of Cultural Production, ed. and trans. Randal Johnson (New York: Columbia University Press, 1993).

28. Because of the San Francisco earthquake and fire in 1906, in which city records were destroyed, there is no birth record available on Duncan. Her baptismal record at Old Saint Mary's Church, however, indicates that she was born Angela I. Duncan on 26 May 1877. The middle initial "I" is presumably for Isadora, shortened to "Dora" when she was a child. Although Fredrika Blair (*Isadora: Portrait of the Artist as a Woman* [New York: William Morrow, 1986]) identifies Mrs. Duncan as Mary *Isadora,* all other records (including Isadora's birth certificate) and biographies from primary sources refer to her as Mary *Dora;* however, as with her daughter, "Dora" may have been short for "Isadora."

29. See Harry Mulford, "Notes and Items Relating to Joseph Charles Duncan (ca. 1823–1898) Father of Isadora Duncan," Isadora Duncan Collection, Performing Arts Library and Museum, San Francisco, Calif.

30. Duncan, *My Life,* 13.

31. See Kathleen D. McCarthy, *Women's Culture: American Philanthropy and Art, 1830–1930* (Chicago: University of Chicago Press, 1991).

32. "A Craze for Delsarte," *New York World,* 16 August 1891, Richard Hovey Papers, Dartmouth College Library, Hanover, N.H.

33. M. Grace Beckwith, "The Poetry of Motion: Miss Isadora Duncan and Her Remarkable Dance," *New England Home Magazine* 6, no. 6 (5 February 1899): 246. This report of Duncan's success in Newport in Summer 1899 conflicts with Edith Wharton's above. The class distinction implied by Duncan's choice of venue was not lost on an anonymous writer for *Broadway Magazine,* who mocked the pretentiousness of Duncan's elite associations. "Miss Duncan," he wrote, "holds forth at such ultra-fashionable places as the Waldorf-Astoria, Sherry's and Carnegie Lyceum. She spurns Broadway with a large, deep, thick spurn, that almost makes us ashamed of having anything to do with the thoroughfare." Captions for the accompanying photographs read: "How I love my friends, the Vanderbilts" and "Isn't Mrs. Highuppe kind to throw those flowers!" "Isadora Duncan as the Only Real Society Pet," *Broadway Magazine,* June 1899, 143.

34. "American Dancing Girl the New Sensation in Paris: Isadora Duncan, Heroine of the Hotel Windsor Fire, Takes the French by Storm with Her Poetic Rendering of the 'Rubaiyat,'" *World* (16 December 1900). Also: "The Greek dancing of Isidora [*sic*] Duncan has become a fashionable fad in Paris, and she has been invited to many of the drawing rooms of the great houses in the city. Miss Duncan's latest hit was scored at the residence of the Countess de Trobriand, when she danced to the rythm [*sic*] of Greek poetry recited by a venerable professor from the Sorbonne," from "Danced into Paris Society," *Evening Journal,* 11 February 1901. Her next triumph, in Germany, was amply covered as well. One report had Emperor Francis Joseph of Austria and Kaiser William of Germany fighting over her ("Struggle for a Dancer: Beautiful American Girl Rejects the Offer of an Emperor to Accept an Engagement in Berlin," *Pittsburgh Post,* 4 April 1903. Her successes at Bayreuth and in Greece made similar headlines.

35. On the feminist appropriation of Bourdieu's work, see Toril Moi, "Appropriating Bourdieu: Feminist Theory and Pierre Bourdieu's Sociology of Culture," *New Literary History* 22 (1991): 1017–49.

36. Mrs. Lilly Grove, *Dancing* (London: Longmans, Green, and Co., 1895). See Lee J. Vance, "The Evolution of Dancing," *Popular Science Quarterly* 41 (October 1892): 739–56; J. S. Rowbotham, "Dancing as a Fine Art," *Eclectic Magazine* 52, no. 1 (July 1890): 16–23;

Amelia E. Barr, "Characteristic Dances of the World," *Lippincott's* 27 (1881): 330–41; Herbert Spencer, "Professional Institutions. III—Dancer and Musician," *Contemporary Review* 68 (July 1895): 114–24.

37. See Ann Daly, "Dance History and Feminist Theory: Reconsidering Isadora Duncan and the Male Gaze," *Gender in Performance: The Presentation of Difference in the Performing Arts,* ed. Laurence Senelick (Hanover, N.H.: University Press of New England, 1992); Ann Daly, "Done Into Dance: Isadora Duncan and America" (Ph.D. diss., New York University, 1993).

38. Shaemus O'Sheel, "Isadora Duncan, Priestess," *Poet Lore* 21 (1910): 481.

39. Although today "Nature" is set in opposition to "Culture," in Duncan's day the two were elided; the former was used as a justification for the latter by avant-garde artists.

40. Isadora Duncan, "Dancing in Relation to Religion and Love," *Theatre Arts Monthly* 11 (October 1927): 593.

41. The call for a cultural nationalism peaked in the Village during the war years, when artists, radicals, and self-proclaimed Young Intellectuals called for a nationalism that focused not on militarization, but on Culture. Art, they felt, should express American life. *Seven Arts* magazine was founded in 1916 by utopians who believed that America could be regenerated—or, rather, invented—through the expression of art. Herbert Croly, founding editor of the *New Republic* in 1914, wrote about the need for national cultural renewal as early as 1909, with *The Promise of American Life*. And so did Randolph Bourne. "We shall not develop to the fullest as a nation," wrote Mary Fanton Roberts in 1912, "without the enjoyment of these emotional arts, because no people can achieve all that the sensitive among them desire without expressing the hunger for beauty that is deep in their hearts. A nation must sing, must dance, must make its own music to realize its portion of the world's power for beauty." See Robert Henri, "The New York Exhibition of Independent Artists," *Craftsman* 18, no. 2 (May 1910): 160–72; Thomas Bender, *New York Intellect: A History of the Intellectual Life in New York City, From 1750 to the Beginnings of Our Own Time* (New York: Alfred A. Knopf, 1987); Arthur Frank Wertheim, *The New York Little Renaissance: Iconoclasm, Modernism, and Nationalism, 1908–1917* (New York: New York University Press, 1976); Leslie Fishbein, *Rebels in Bohemia: The Radicals of the Masses, 1911–1917* (Chapel Hill: University of North Carolina Press, 1982); Herbert Croly, *The Promise of American Life* (New York: Macmillan Company, 1909); Randolph Bourne, "Our Cultural Humility," *The History of a Literary Radical, and Other Essays* (New York: B. W. Heubsch, 1956); Edward Abrahams, *The Lyrical Left: Randolph Bourne, Alfred Stieglitz, and the Origins of Cultural Radicalism in America* (Charlottesville: University Press of Virginia, 1986); Mary Fanton Roberts, "The Dance of the People," *Craftsman* 22, no. 2 (May 1912): 196.

42. Isadora Duncan, *Art*, 92.

43. Dumesnil, *Amazing Journey*, 153.

44. Duncan, *Art*, 126.

45. Irene and Vernon Castle made their reputation by cleaning up Barbary Coast dances for their exclusive New York clientele.

46. Duncan, *Art*, 102–03.

47. Max Eastman, *Love and Revolution: My Journey through an Epic* (New York: Random House, 1964), 6.

48. "Practical belief is not a 'state of mind,' still less a kind of arbitrary adherence to a set of instituted dogmas and doctrines ('beliefs'), but rather a state of the body" (Bourdieu, *Distinction,* 68). "Bodily hexis is political mythology realized, *em-bodied,* turned into a per-

manent disposition, a durable way of standing, speaking, walking, and thereby of feeling and thinking" (Bourdieu, *Distinction,* 69–70). See Bourdieu, *Logic,* 52–79; Bourdieu, *Distinction,* 169–225.

49. The subfield of dance in the American cultural field shifted, with the tours of Anna Pavlova in 1910 and Diaghilev's Ballets Russes in 1916 and 1917. As ballet took a foothold, and the display of technique came to displace Nature as the generally accepted basis of theatrical dancing, Duncan's claim to naivete worked against her.

50. Allan Ross Macdougall, *Isadora: A Revolutionary in Art and Love* (New York: Thomas Nelson & Sons, 1960), 222. Like many other tidbits of "documented" Duncan lore, this may be apocryphal. In this case, however, the aphorism rings true.

51. See Bourdieu, *Logic,* 122–34.

52. See Jane Desmond, "Dancing Out the Difference: Cultural Imperialism and Ruth St. Denis's *Radha* of 1906," *Signs* 17, no. 1 (Autumn 1991): 28–49.

53. Toni Morrison, *Playing in the Dark: Whiteness and the Literary Imagination* (Cambridge: Harvard University Press, 1992), 51–52.

ISADORA DUNCAN'S DANCE THEORY

1. Edith Wharton, *A Backward Glance* (New York and London: D. Appleton-Century, 1934), 321.

2. Ibid.

3. George Seldes, "What Love Meant to Isadora Duncan," *Mentor,* February 1930, 64.

4. Folder 64, Irma Duncan Collection of Isadora Duncan Materials, Dance Collection, New York Public Library for the Performing Arts, New York City, New York.

5. According to biographer Allan Ross Macdougall, she was heard to say this at various times during her later years, when asked about the origins of her dance. Allan Ross Macdougall, "Isadora Duncan and the Artists," *Dance Index* 5, no. 3 (March 1946): 61.

6. James Oliphant, "Plain Words about Dancing," *Westminster Review* 136, no. 1 (July 1891): 59.

7. Elizabeth Beland, "The Eldest of the Arts," *Cosmopolitan* 10, no. 6 (April 1891): 644.

8. Lady Battersea, "Ethics of Amusement," in *World's Congress of Representative Women,* ed. May Wright Sewall, Vol. 7 (Chicago: Rand, McNally & Company, 1894), 135.

9. "Dancing Literature and Dogma," *Saturday Review* 60 (1 August 1885): 151.

10. Herbert Spencer, "Professional Institutions. III—Dancer and Musician," *Popular Science Monthly* 47 (July 1895): 364–74; Herbert Spencer, "Professional Institutions. III—Dancer and Musician," *Contemporary Review* 68 (July 1895): 114–24.

11. Mrs. Lilly Grove, *Dancing: A Handbook of the Terpsichorean Arts in Diverse Places and Times, Savage and Civilized* (London: Longmans, Green and Co., 1895). Also see Susan Leann Foote, "Lilly Grove Frazer and Her Book *Dancing*" (M.A. thesis, York University, 1986).

12. Lee J. Vance, "The Evolution of Dancing," *Popular Science Monthly* 41 (October 1892): 739–56; J. F. Rowbotham, "Dancing as a Fine Art," *Eclectic Magazine* 52, no. 1 (July 1890): 16–23; Amelia E. Barr, "Characteristic Dances of the World," *Lippincott's* 27 (April 1881): 330–41.

13. Allen Dodworth, *Dancing and Its Relations to Education and Social Life, with a New Method of Instruction* (New York: Harper & Brothers, 1885), 3.

14. Judson Sause, *The Art of Dancing* (Chicago, New York, San Francisco: Belford, Clarke & Co. Publishers, 1889), 128.

15. Philip Hayman, "The Magic of Dancing is Sorcery Sweet," *Theatre* 36 (1 May 1891): 238.

16. Isadora Duncan, *Der Tanz der Zukunft* (Leipzig: Eugen Diederichs, 1903), 23.

17. "Emotional Expression," *New York Herald,* 20 February 1898. Duncan may have picked up her ideas about the character formation of children while in Oakland or San Francisco, where Emma Marwedel, a pioneer of Friedrich Froebel's kindergarten plan as a method of education reform, was laying down its American foundations. Marwedel and other education progressives believed that free kindergartens, as a means of "character training," began the path leading to the emancipation of childhood, the perfection of motherhood, and the regeneration of the human race—Duncan's own concerns, too. Wealthy women such as Mrs. S. B. Crocker and Mrs. Stanwood were underwriting the establishment and maintenance of free kindergartens there. Fletcher Harper Swift, "Emma Warwedel, 1818–1893, Pioneer of the Kindergarten in California," *University of California Publications in Education* 6, no. 3 (1931): 139–216.

18. Quoted in Michael Steven Shapiro, "Froebel in America: A Social and Intellectual History of the Kindergarten Movement, 1848–1918" (Ph.D. diss., Brown University, 1980), 44. Although I have found no evidence directly linking Duncan and Froebel, her ideas seem to echo his. He believed in the correspondence between the evolution of natural forms and the stages of a child's growth, and he stressed an ethics of unity as an expression of God's plan for order. The purpose of children's education, then, was to lead the child toward the "inner law of Divine Unity." Froebel's techniques included singing, marching, and dancing. Shapiro's dissertation establishes the high profile of kindergarten in San Francisco and around the country during the 1880s and 1890s, which further suggests Duncan's likely exposure to these ideas.

19. Stephen Kern, *Anatomy and Destiny: A Cultural History of the Human Body* (Indianapolis and New York: Bobbs-Merrill, 1975), 64–65.

20. "Emotional Expression," *New York Herald,* 20 February 1898.

21. The *Dionysion* pamphlet seems to have been published for performances at the New York Metropolitan Opera House in October 1914 (Dance Collection, New York Public Library for the Performing Arts, New York City, New York).

22. Walt Whitman, *Leaves of Grass* (1892; repr. New York: Bantam Books, 1983), 124.

23. Paul Hertelendy reports this finding from the memoirs of Florence Treadwell Boynton. Paul Hertelendy, "New Light, Old Legend: Isadora's Early Years," *Oakland Tribune,* 18 December 1977, Isadora Duncan Collection, Performing Arts Library and Museum, San Francisco, California.

24. Patricia Albjerg Graham, "Expansion and Exclusion: A History of Women in American Higher Education," *Signs* 3, no. 4 (Summer 1978): 759–73.

25. Isadora Duncan, *The Art of the Dance,* ed. Sheldon Cheney (New York: Theatre Arts, Inc., 1928), 99.

26. Duncan to Ainslie, Berlin to London, Douglas Ainslie Papers, Harry Ransom Humanities Research Center, Austin, Texas.

27. For a consideration of how the manifesto reflected its European and, in particular, German, context, see Claudia Jeschke, "The Dance of the Future," *Proceedings of the Tenth Annual Conference of the Society of Dance History Scholars* (Riverside, Calif.: Dance History Scholars, 1987), 106–18.

28. Duncan, *Der Tanz,* 12.

29. Never mind that Nietzsche rejected Darwin's fatalistic, mechanistic principle of natural selection and supplanted it with the power of the individual free will to create change. This basic incompatibility (among others) between her sources was not impor-

tant to Duncan's purpose. Rather, she drew upon Nietzsche's poetic vision of the future and the power of the will.

30. In 1908, the year of Duncan's first American tour, H. L. Mencken's *The Philosophy of Friedrich Nietzsche* (Boston: Luce and Company, 1908) made an immediate success. By 1925 no European thinker of the nineteenth century, except for Darwin, Spencer, and possibly Thomas Henry Huxley, had been so widely reprinted. There had been two hundred thousand copies of Mencken's works printed in the United States since the first, in 1899. Melville Drimmer, "Nietzsche in American Thought, 1895–1925" (Ph.D. diss., University of Rochester, 1965).

31. Duncan, *Der Tanz*, 26.

32. See John E. Atwell, "The Significance of Dance in Nietzsche's Thought," in *Illuminating Dance: Philosophical Explorations*, ed. Maxine Sheets-Johnstone (Lewisburg, Pa., and London: Bucknell University Press and Associated University Presses, 1984), 19–34; Friedrich Nietzsche, *Thus Spoke Zarathustra*, trans. Walter Kaufmann (1883–85; repr. New York: Viking Press, 1966).

33. Duncan, *Art*, 101.

34. In synthesizing Duncan's theory of dance and tracing its sources, I have built on the sturdy foundation provided by biographers and scholars such as Fredrika Blair, Deborah Jowitt, Elizabeth Kendall, Allan Ross Macdougall, and Nancy Chalfa Ruyter. See Frederika Blair, *Isadora: Portrait of the Artist as a Woman* (New York: William Morrow, 1986); Deborah Jowitt, "The Search for Motion," in *Time and the Dancing Image* (New York: William Morrow, 1988); Elizabeth Kendall, *Where She Danced: The Birth of American Art-Dance* (New York: Alfred A. Knopf, 1979); Allan Ross Macdougall, *Isadora: A Revolutionary in Art and Love* (New York: Thomas Nelson, 1960); Nancy Chalfa Ruyter, *Reformers and Visionaries: The Americanization of the Art of Dance* (New York: Dance Horizons, 1979).

35. Isadora Duncan, blue notebook, 1904, 83–84, Folder 141, Irma Duncan Collection of Isadora Duncan Materials, Dance Collection, New York Public Library for the Performing Arts, New York City, New York.

36. Ibid., 87–89.

37. Whitman, *Leaves*, 315.

38. Nietzsche, *Zarathustra*, 34.

39. Duncan, *Der Tanz*, 24.

40. Duncan, *Art*, 122.

41. Nietzsche, *Zarathustra*, 75.

42. Isadora Duncan, "Form and Movement," *The Theatre Dionysus* notebook, Mary Fanton Roberts Collection of Isadora Duncan materials, Theatre Collection, Museum of the City of New York, New York City, New York.

43. Ibid.

44. Ibid.

45. Duncan, blue notebook, 96–97.

46. Duncan told a reporter: "One works for years to perfect some one artistic thing like that of merging one motion into another, but what difference does it make? Who sees it? Nobody understands." Arthur Ruhl, "Some Ladies Who Dance," *Colliers Weekly*, 5 February 1910, Isadora Duncan Clippings, Dance Collection, New York Public Library for the Performing Arts, New York City, New York.

47. Duncan, *Art*, 69.

48. Ibid., 99.

49. Isadora Duncan, "The Dance," *Theatre Arts* 2, no. 1 (December 1917): 21. See also Duncan, *Art,* 99.

50. Duncan, *Art,* 101.

51. Irma Duncan, *Duncan Dancer: An Autobiography* (Middletown, Conn.: Wesleyan University Press, 1966), 54.

THE BALANCHINE WOMAN: OF HUMMINGBIRDS AND CHANNEL SWIMMERS

The epigraph quotation by George Balanchine is from John Gruen, *The Private World of Ballet* (New York: Penguin Books, 1976), 284.

1. My thanks to Kate Davy and Debra Sowell for helping me formulate my argument and to the Dance Critics Association for the loan of video and audio tapes from its 1985 seminar on *The Four Temperaments.*

2. Sherry B. Ortner and Harriet Whitehead, eds., *Sexual Meanings: The Cultural Construction of Gender and Sexuality* (Cambridge: Cambridge University Press, 1981), 10.

3. E. Ann Kaplan, *Women and Film: Both Sides of the Camera* (London, New York: Methuen, 1983), 29. The pivotal concept of the "male gaze" arises from an examination of the structure of representation, in which the position of the spectator (the gazer) is encoded. Kaplan wrote: "The gaze is not necessarily male (literally), but to own and activate the gaze, given our language and the structure of the unconscious, is to be in the 'masculine' position" (30). Thus, women, too, under patriarchy partake in the acculturated male gaze.

4. Lincoln Kirstein, "Balanchine's Fourth Dimension," in *Ballet: Bias and Belief* (New York: Dance Horizons, 1983), 296.

5. John Berger, *Ways of Seeing* (New York: Viking Press, 1973), 47.

6. John Aschengreen, "The Beautiful Danger: Facets of the Romantic Ballet," *Dance Perspectives* (#58, Summer 1974): 30.

7. John Chapman, "An Unromantic View of Nineteenth-Century Romanticism," *York Dance Review* 7 (Spring 1978): 35.

8. Arlene Croce, "Free and More Than Equal," in *Afterimages* (New York: Vintage Books, 1979), 127. Though I make use of Croce's observations for a feminist critique of Balanchine's ballerina, Croce concludes that "for Balanchine it is the man who sees and follows and it is the woman who acts and guides" (126).

9. Aschengreen, "Beautiful Danger."

10. Kirstein, "Balanchine's Fourth Dimension," 114.

11. Arlene Croce, "Ashley, Balanchine, and 'Ballade,'" in *Going to the Dance* (New York: Alfred A. Knopf, 1982), 277.

12. Ray Birdwhistell et al., "The Male Image," *Dance Perspectives* no. 40 (Winter 1969): 47.

13. See Eugene B. Nadler and W. R. Morrow, "Authoritarian Attitudes toward Women, and Their Correlates," *Journal of Social Psychology* 49 (1959): 113–23.

14. Ibid., 119.

15. Ibid., 114.

16. See Greer Litton Fox, "'Nice Girl': The Behavioral Legacy of a Value Construct," *Signs* 2, no. 4 (Summer 1977): 805–17.

17. Laurel Walum, "The Changing Door Ceremony," *Urban Life and Culture* 2, no. 4 (January 1974): 510.

18. Rolf Garske, "Suzanne Farrell," *Ballett International* 6, no. 9 (September 1983): 22.

19. Flora Lewis, "To Balanchine Dance Is Woman—and His Love," *New York Times,* 6 October 1976, 45.

20. See Suzanne Gordon, *Off Balance: The Real World of Ballet* (New York: McGraw-Hill, 1983).

21. See Cynthia J. Novack, *Sharing the Dance: Contact Improvisation and American Culture* (Madison: University of Wisconsin Press, 1990).

22. See Ann Daly, "Interview with Senta Driver," *Women & Performance: A Journal of Feminist Theory* 3, no. 2 (#6, 1988): 90–96; and Kenneth Laws, *The Physics of Dance* (London: Schirmer Books, 1984).

23. Ann Daly, "Classical Ballet: A Discourse of Difference," *Women & Performance: A Journal of Feminist Theory* 3, no. 2 (#6, 1988): 57–66.

24. Jacques Derrida and Christie V. McDonald, "Choreographies," *Diacritics* 12 (Summer 1982): 76.

25. Ibid.

26. Ray Birdwhistell, *Kinesics and Context* (Philadelphia: University of Pennsylvania Press, 1970), 46.

27. See Albert E. Scheflen, *Body Language and Social Order* (Englewood Cliffs, N.J.: Prentice-Hall, 1972), and *How Behavior Means* (Garden City, N.Y.: Anchor Books, 1974).

CLASSICAL BALLET: A DISCOURSE OF DIFFERENCE

1. Jack Anderson, *Ballet and Modern Dance* (Princeton, N.J.: Princeton Book Company, 1986), 42; Ivor Guest, *The Dancer's Heritage* (London: The Dancing Times, 1977), 17; Parmenia Migel, *The Ballerinas* (New York: Da Capo Press, 1972), 37.

2. In the sixteenth and seventeenth centuries, gender difference was encoded in court spectacles, which adapted social dances in polished and studied form: "Men were assigned jumps and the fancy steps, while the steps for women stressed grace, lightness, and restraint" (Anderson, *Ballet and Modern Dance,* 25). In the earliest years of the Paris Opera (founded in 1669), women's roles were taken by men in travesty. Four ballerinas finally took the stage in 1681 in *Le Triomphe de l'amour,* among them Mlle. de la Fontaine. She was succeeded as prima ballerina by Marie-Thérèse de Subligny and then Françoise Prévost. Still overshadowed by the virtuosic men, neither one drew as much attention as Camargo.

3. Marian Hannah Winter, *The Pre-Romantic Ballet* (New York: Pitman Publishing, 1974), 46.

4. Ibid., 162.

5. Migel, *The Ballerinas,* 37–38.

6. Igor Youskevitch, "The Male Image," *Dance Perspectives,* no. 40 (Winter 1969): 16.

7. Ibid., 23.

8. The ballet dancer's body image is the product of centuries of patriarchal codification about gender difference. In the classic 1828 treatise on dancing, *The Code of Terpsichore,* Carlo Blasis wrote:

> Men must dance in a manner very different from women; the *temps de vigeur,* and bold majestic execution of the former, would have a disagreeable effect in the latter, who must shine and delight by lithsome [*sic*] and graceful motions, by neat and pretty *terre-à-terre* steps, and by a decent voluptuousness and *abandon* in all their attitudes. (94–95)

Blasis, *Code of Terpsichore* (London: James Bulcock, 1828; repr. Brooklyn: Dance Horizons, 1976). The phrase "decent voluptuousness" encapsulates the double bind in which women are placed as erotic/aesthetic objects: they must be erotic enough to titillate but distanced enough not to offend.

9. For further analysis of the pas de deux, see Ann Daly, "The Balanchine Woman: Of Hummingbirds and Channel Swimmers," *TDR: The Journal of Performance Studies* 31, no. 1 (T113, Spring 1987): 8–21. Also reprinted in this volume.

10. Monique Wittig, "The Category of Sex," *Feminist Issues* 2, no. 2 (Fall 1982): 63–68.

11. Théophile Gautier, *The Romantic Ballet as Seen by Théophile Gautier,* trans. Cyril Beaumont (New York: Books for Libraries, 1980), 17.

12. Ibid., 67.

13. Quoted in Igor Guest, *The Romantic Ballet in Paris* (Middletown, Conn.: Wesleyan University Press, 1966), 21.

14. See E. Ann Kaplan's development of the concept of the male gaze in her *Women and Film: Both Sides of the Camera* (London and New York: Methuen, 1983), 23–35. The pivotal concept of the "male gaze" arises from the structure of representation, in which the position of the spectator (the gazer) is encoded. Thus, women, too, under patriarchy can partake in the acculturated male gaze.

15. Anderson, *Ballet and Modern Dance,* 69.

16. Gautier, *The Romantic Ballet,* 15.

17. Lincoln Kirstein, *Ballet: Bias and Belief* (New York: Dance Horizons, 1983), 400.

18. Simone de Beauvoir, *The Second Sex,* trans. and ed. H. M. Parshley (New York: Vintage Books, 1974), xxiii.

19. Clive Barnes, "How Men Have Come to Rule Ballet's Roost," *New York Post,* 22 July 1978, 27.

20. It is interesting to note an opposite stream in the gender conscious 1970s: danseurs in some repertoires had the opportunity to be softer, to display a more pronounced, aesthetic line. Yet women were still not permitted strength. This "androgynous" approach maintained gender difference and asymmetry; it simply reapportioned the polarized attributes allowing men a much larger range of expression.

21. Ray Birdwhistell, "The Male Image," *Dance Perspectives,* no. 40 (Winter 1969): 11.

22. Anna Kisselgoff, "The Dance: Alvin Ailey Performs 'Elephant,'" *New York Times,* 7 December 1985, 14.

23. Laura Mulvey, "Visual Pleasure and Narrative Cinema," *Screen* 16, no. 3 (Autumn 1975): 8.

TO DANCE IS "FEMALE"

1. This symposium, part of the Movement Research Studies Project, was held 19 December 1988 at the Ethnic Folk Arts Center in New York City.

2. This chapter was originally published as an article in *TDR: The Journal of Performance Studies* 31, no. 1 (T113, Spring 1987): 22–47. My response to that article and Hanna's subsequent reply were published in the following issue. See Ann Daly, "Reply to Judith Lynn Hanna's 'Patterns of Dominance: Men, Women, and Homosexuality in Dance,'" *TDR: The Journal of Performance Studies* 31, no. 2 (T114, Summer 1987): 22–24.

3. Hanna explicitly states her reasons "why gender is coterminous with sexuality in dance" (46):

> In contemporary Western society the separation of sex and gender becomes significant when we attempt to make political and economic opportunity relevant to qualifications for positions instead of physical markers with which an individual is born.
>
> However, because a gender role for most people is sexual reproduction, a perceived body in dance, especially when performers appear nude, in anatomically revealing dress, or in stereotypic male or female costume, conflates biological thought and behavior (arousal and sexual identity), gender, and the historical relationship of dance and sex. Of course, people express gender signs in situations unrelated to sexual activity, but in adolescent and adult interaction the manifestation that refers to everyday stereotypes and violations of them is most dramatic. (13)

Apparently, Hanna believes that dance representation is irrelevant in the culture-at-large. And apparently homosexuals and lesbians do not figure into the picture, because, unlike "most people," their gender role does not follow from sexual reproduction. And apparently all dance is sexually arousing to Hanna.

4. See E. Ann Kaplan, *Women and Film: Both Sides of the Camera* (New York: Methuen, 1983); and Laura Mulvey, "Visual Pleasure and Narrative Cinema," *Screen* 16, no. 3 (Autumn 1975):6–18.

5. For the past several years many of my ideas have been sparked, challenged, and encouraged by participants in a study group in feminist theory and dance: Ann Cooper Albright, Judy Burns, Marianne Goldberg, Ellen Graff, Carol Martin, and Leslie Satin.

6. Deborah Hay, "Playing Awake: Letters to My Daughter," *TDR: The Journal of Performance Studies* 33, no. 4 (T124, Winter 1989), 23–27.

7. Jacques Derrida and Christie V. McDonald, "Choreographies," *Diacritics* 12 (Summer 1982): 76.

UNLIMITED PARTNERSHIP: DANCE AND FEMINIST ANALYSIS

1. For an explanation of three basic feminisms—liberal feminism, cultural (or radical) feminism, and materialist feminism—see Jill Dolan, *The Feminist Spectator as Critic* (Ann Arbor, Mich., and London: UMI Research Press, 1988).

2. I am concerned here with the issues of American feminist theory. French feminist theory has developed in a different way. Its preoccupation with the uniqueness of the female body—what has been dubbed "essentialism" on this side of the Atlantic—provides provocative reading for scholars in dance studies. For a comprehensive treatment of the concerns and development of both American and French feminist literary theory, see Toril Moi, *Sexual/Textual Politics: Feminist Literary Theory* (London and New York: Methuen, 1985).

3. The campaign took place in both print and broadcasting. One newspaper advertisement, on the back page of the *New York Times* business section on 26 January 1989, pictured a neatly trimmed mother, with son in sneakers and daughter, in full balletic regalia, stiffly attempting a port de bras. "She's [the new Traditionalist mother] not following a trend," the copy read, in part. "She *is* the trend, now being recognized as the most powerful social movement since the sixties."

4. See Monique Wittig, "The Category of Sex," *Feminist Issues* 2, no. 2 (Fall 1982): 63–68.

5. See Laura Mulvey, "Visual Pleasure and Narrative Cinema," *Screen* 16, no. 3 (Autumn 1975): 6–18; and E. Ann Kaplan, *Women and Film: Both Sides of the Camera* (London and New York: Methuen, 1983).

6. Feminist theorists are now trying to push further and deeper beyond the theory

of the male gaze, and several have proposed alternative or expanded concepts of representation that do allow a space for women. See Jessica Benjamin, "A Desire of One's Own: Psychoanalytic Feminism and Intersubjective Space," in *Feminist Studies/Critical Studies*, ed. Teresa de Lauretis (Bloomington: Indiana University Press, 1986), 78–101; Teresa de Lauretis, *Technologies of Gender: Essays on Theory, Film, and Fiction* (Bloomington and Indianapolis: Indiana University Press, 1987); Julia Kristeva, "Gesture: Practice or Communication?" trans. Jonathan Benthall, in *The Body Reader: Social Aspects of the Human Body*, ed. Ted Polhemus (New York: Pantheon Books, 1978), 264–84; and Kristeva, *Revolution in Poetic Language*, trans. Margaret Waller (New York: Columbia University Press, 1984). Kristeva's ideas are especially suitable to the medium of dance, because they take into account the meaning that is generated by the body. See Ann Daly, "Dance History and Feminist Theory: Reconsidering Isadora Duncan and the Male Gaze," in *Gender in Performance: The Presentation of Difference in the Performing Arts*, ed. Laurence Senelick (Hanover, N.H.: University Press of New England, 1992).

7. Feminist dance scholarship has become a regular feature of annual conferences of the Dance Critics Association, the Society of Dance History Scholars, the Congress on Research in Dance, and the Association for Theatre in Higher Education, whose Women and Theatre program holds its own pre-conference each year. Most of these organizations offer conference transcripts, proceedings, or audiotapes.

8. *Women & Performance: A Journal of Feminist Theory* publishes feminist dance criticism in each of its semiannual volumes.

9. See Johanna Boyce et al., "Movement and Gender: A Roundtable Discussion," *TDR: The Journal of Performance Studies* 32, no. 4 (T120, Winter 1988), 82–101; Ann Daly, "Are Women Reclaiming or Reinforcing Sexist Imagery?" *High Performance* 12, no. 2 (#46, Summer 1989), 18–19; Ann Daly, "The Balanchine Woman: Of Hummingbirds and Channel Swimmers," *TDR: The Journal of Performance Studies* 31, no. 1 (T113, Spring 1987), 8–21; Ann Daly, "Response to: 'Tanztheater: The Thrill of the Lynch Mob or the Rage of a Woman?'" *TDR: The Journal of Performance Studies* 30, no. 2 (T110, Summer 1986), 54–56; Lynn Garafola, "The Travesty Dancer in Nineteenth-Century Ballet," *Dance Research Journal* 17/18, no. 1–2 (Fall 1985/Spring 1986), 35–40; Marianne Goldberg, "She Who Is Possessed No Longer Exists Outside: Martha Graham's *Rite of Spring*," *Women & Performance: A Journal of Feminist Theory* 3, no. 1 (#5, 1986), 17–27.

10. Marianne Goldberg, ed., "The Body as Discourse," *Women & Performance: A Journal of Feminist Theory* 3, no. 2 (#6, 1987/1988).

11. See Susan Leigh Foster, *Reading Dancing: Bodies and Subjects in Contemporary American Dance* (Berkeley, Los Angeles, London: University of California Press, 1986); Lynn Garafola, *Diaghilev's Ballets Russes* (New York and Oxford: Oxford University Press, 1989); Deborah Jowitt, *Time and the Dancing Image* (New York: William Morrow, 1988); and Cynthia J. Novack, *Sharing the Dance: Contact Improvisation and American Culture* (Madison: University of Wisconsin Press, 1990).

DANCE HISTORY AND FEMINIST THEORY: RECONSIDERING ISADORA DUNCAN AND THE MALE GAZE

1. Drafts of this essay were delivered at the 1990 annual conference of the Association for Theatre in Higher Education as well as at a fall 1990 installment of the Women's Studies Research Seminars at the University of Texas at Austin. I appreciate the insight-

ful comments offered to me in those arenas. In particular, I would like to thank Mark Franko, Peter Jelavich, and Amy Koritz for their perceptive responses. Also, thanks to Lori Belilove, Julia Levien, and Hortense Kooluris for sharing their understanding of Duncan dancing and technique. Any shortcomings in the essay, however, are my own.

2. Historically, the term and concept of "feminism" only began to supplant "woman movement," the nineteenth-century phraseology, in the 1910s. However, "feminism" (whose proponents distinguished it from "suffragism") was not entered into the *Oxford English Dictionary* until its 1933 supplement. Duncan spoke mostly in universal terms, rarely referring to specific political situations or movements such as suffragism. See Nancy F. Cott, *The Grounding of Modern Feminism* (New Haven and London: Yale University Press, 1987).

3. Floyd Dell, *Women as World Builders: Studies in Modern Feminism* (Westport, Conn.: Hyperion Press, 1976), 44.

4. Ibid., 49.

5. Ibid.

6. Isadora Duncan, *Der Tanz der Zukunft* (Leipzig: Eugen Diederichs, 1903), 25–26.

7. Elizabeth Kendall's groundbreaking study of early American modern dance, *Where She Danced: The Birth of American Art-Dance* (New York: Alfred A. Knopf, 1979), and Nancy Lee Chalfa Ruyter's study of Delsartism, *Reformers and Visionaries: The Americanization of the Art of Dance* (New York: Dance Horizons, 1979), are notable exceptions. They mined important new historical evidence and made fresh connections between Duncan and American culture. Ironically, however, their originality has now become grist for the mill of recycled history.

8. Isadora Duncan, *My Life* (New York: Boni and Liveright, 1927).

9. Isadora Duncan to Irma Duncan, 10 June 1924, Irma Duncan Collection of Isadora Duncan Materials, Dance Collection, New York Public Library, New York City, New York.

10. That is not to say that the book is an untruth or useless. The work of Duncan's autobiography as historical evidence is not so much in the "truths" it imparts as in how Duncan constructs her vision of those "truths." Without the pretense of being a historical record, *My Life* offers us the seeds of a history, which we must take responsibility for sowing.

11. Rayner Heppenstall, "The Sexual Idiom," in *What Is Dance?* ed. Roger Copeland and Marshall Cohen (Oxford, Toronto, Melbourne: Oxford University Press, 1983), 272–73.

12. At the root of Heppenstall's elaborate objection to Duncan is a near-paranoid fear of female sexuality. Although Heppenstall faults Duncan for being transparently sexual, he builds his own supposedly disinterested theory of dance on implicit models of male versus female orgasm:

> He [the dancer] commits rape and begets lovely forms in his own body, with continual increase of power. His material, the field of his creative experience, is his own muscular and nervous being. And his fulfilment is in the *externalised joy of movement, the release, the building up of inherent tensions into a powerful system of release.* This is the only true freedom. It is the kind of joy and freedom we call dancing. Not the joy of *an inward, an unprotected ecstasy,* which can only be communicated through erotic empathy and sympathy between the Dancer and the onlooker. (Ibid., 288; emphasis mine)

13. The term "choreography" is a twentieth-century phenomenon. A very early, if not the earliest, use of the term was in an article on Duncan entitled "Emotional Expression":

"Her sister reads the poem which she is to interpret choreographically, and an accompaniment harmonizing with the words and sentiments is played on the piano" ("Emotional Expression," *New York Herald* [20 February 1898]). The article was reprinted in *Director,* a magazine of "dancing, deportment, etiquette, aesthetics, physical training" ("Emotional Expression," *Director* 1, no. 4 [March 1898]: 109–11).

14. Heppenstall, "The Sexual Idiom," 272.

15. Lincoln Kirstein, "The Curse of Isadora," *New York Times,* 23 November 1986, sec. 2, pp. 1, 28.

16. A Californian by birth (and temperament), Duncan had originally plied her art in the East, in high society venues, but she went to Europe in 1899 to make her name in the world of legitimate theater. The American tours beginning in 1908 were in effect her "first" appearances here.

17. I borrow the term "feminist subject" from Teresa de Lauretis. It recognizes the postmodern feminist's dilemma in wanting to posit a female subjectivity while also recognizing the myth of the singular subject. See Teresa de Lauretis, *Technologies of Gender: Essays on Theory, Film, and Fiction* (Bloomington and Indianapolis: Indiana University Press, 1987).

18. Laura Mulvey, "Changes: Thoughts on Myth, Narrative and Historical Experience," in *Visual and Other Pleasures* (Bloomington and Indianapolis: Indiana University Press, 1989).

19. See de Lauretis, *Technologies of Gender.*

20. See Jessica Benjamin, "A Desire of One's Own: Psychoanalytic Feminism and Intersubjective Space," in *Feminist Studies/Critical Studies,* ed. Teresa de Lauretis (Bloomington: Indiana University Press, 1986).

21. See Julia Kristeva, *Revolution in Poetic Language,* trans. Margaret Waller (New York: Columbia University Press, 1984).

22. See Laura Mulvey, "Visual Pleasure and Narrative Cinema," *Screen* 16, no. 3 (Autumn 1975): 6–18.

23. See E. Ann Kaplan, *Women and Film: Both Sides of the Camera* (New York and London: Methuen, 1983).

24. Mulvey, "Changes," 162. Not unrelated to this turn toward space as an organizing metaphor is a renewed interest in the body, which creates the very field in and around it, whether on the microlevel (social interaction, choreography) or the macrolevel (culture). But in studying the body and the meanings it generates, feminist and cultural theorists vary widely in their willingness to confront the body as a material as well as symbolic object and to deal with the body as the ground of perception. Dance studies have much to offer feminist and cultural studies precisely because the object of study is the body, that crucial site where culture and nature intersect. The dancing body provides a kind of living laboratory for examining the production of the body: its training, its image, its story, and its ways of creating the world around it.

25. Julia Kristeva, "The System and the Speaking Subject," in *The Tell-Tale Sign: A Survey of Semiotics,* ed. Thomas A. Sebeok (Lisse, Netherlands: The Peter De Ridder Press, 1975). Julia Kristeva, "Gesture: Practice or Communication?" trans. Jonathan Benthall, in *The Body Reader: Social Aspects of the Human Body,* ed. Ted Polhemus, (New York: Pantheon Books, 1978), 264–84.

26. Kristeva, *Revolution.*

27. Quoted in Léon Roudiez's introduction to Julia Kristeva, *Desire in Language, A Semiotic Approach to Literature and Art* (New York: Columbia University Press, 1980), 6.

28. Kristeva, *Revolution,* 29. It should be noted that the semiotic realm is *not* a "feminine" one. The chora corresponds to the pre-Oedipal realm, and the symbolic to the emergence into language. The chora, therefore, cannot be coded as "feminine," because sexual difference does not exist in the pre-Oedipal realm. Kristeva is a staunch anti-essentialist whose idea of the "feminine" is one of position (which is relative) rather than of essence. In fact, those figures whom she cites as exemplary writers of the semiotic (e.g., Artaud, Mallarmé) are men.

29. Kristeva, *Revolution,* 105.

30. Kristeva's theory of the chora is rooted in psychoanalytic theory; the contours of the semiotic and the symbolic are modeled on Lacan's scheme of the imaginary and the symbolic. (Since the publication of *Revolution in Poetic Language,* Kristeva has become a psychoanalyst, and her writings have intensified in that direction.) The problematic question of how her theory of the chora serves both to affirm and to marginalize the nonverbal is extremely complex and beyond the scope of this essay.

31. Daniel Stern, *The Interpersonal World of the Infant: A View from Psychoanalysis and Developmental Psychology* (New York: Basic Books, 1985).

32. Kristeva, "Gesture."

33. Kristeva, "System," 54.

34. Kristeva, "Gesture," 272.

35. "The Vulgarization of Salome," *Current Literature* 45, no. 4 (October 1908): 437–40.

36. The analysis of Duncan's reviews in this article is based on the extensive collection of clippings in the Isadora Duncan Reserve Dance Clipping File at the New York Public Library Dance Collection, New York City, as well as those from other archival and library collections across the country.

37. "Vulgarization," 440.

38. See Mark Gabor, *The Pin-Up: A Modest History* (New York: Bell Publishing Company, 1972).

39. See T. J. Clark, *The Paintings of Modern Life: Paris in the Art of Manet and His Followers* (New York: Knopf, 1985).

40. Abigail Solomon-Godeau, "The Legs of the Countess," *October* 39 (Winter 1986): 104.

41. W. L. Hubbard, "Girl's Art Dance Airy As Her Garb," *Chicago Daily Tribune,* 1 December 1908.

42. There were a few exceptions, notably her 1908 Frohman-produced run at the Criterion Theatre in New York City. At this point, she was in urgent need of money for her school.

43. See Susanne K. Langer, *Feeling and Form* (New York: Charles Scribner's Sons, 1953), 175. Langer asserts that virtual gesture is the essential sign of dance:

> The primary illusion of dance is a virtual realm of Power—not actual, physically exerted power, but appearances of influence and agency created by virtual gesture.
>
> In watching a collective dance—say, an artistically successful ballet—one does not see *people running around;* one sees the dance driving this way, drawn that way, gathering here, spreading there—fleeing, resting, rising, and so forth; and all the motion seems to spring from powers beyond the performers. (175)

Duncan is an embodiment of this principle. Ironically, due to the prevalent modern dance bias against Duncan at the time Langer wrote this passage (Graham and Humphrey and others wanted to distinguish their formalism against what they claimed was Duncan's self-indulgence), she used Duncan as a negative example of the misguided idea that dance is essentially a handmaid to music.

44. Bolton Hall, "Isadora Duncan and Liberty," quoted in *Dionysion*, 1914 performance brochure.

45. Besides Duncan's genius as a performer was her genius as a choreographer. She created that feeling of spontaneity through precisely calculated means. Her technique, while it appeared easy, was actually a physically strenuous and performatively sophisticated one, requiring years' work to perfect.

46. H. T. Parker, *Motion Arrested: Dance Reviews of H. T. Parker*, ed. Olive Holmes (Middletown, Conn.: Wesleyan University Press, 1982), 59.

47. "Triumphs Again," *Philadelphia Telegraph*, 24 November 1908, Isadora Duncan Reserve Dance Clipping File, Dance Collection, New York Public Library, New York City, New York.

48. Shaemus O'Sheel, "Isadora Duncan, Priestess," *Poet Lore* 21 (1910): 482.

49. Jackson Lears, *No Place of Grace: Antimodernism and the Transformation of American Culture 1880-1920* (New York: Pantheon Books, 1981), 32.

50. An extensive variety of these manuals, consulted in research for this essay, are at the Library of Congress.

51. W. R. T., "Classical Dancing in England," *T.P.'s Magazine*, Isadora Duncan Dance Reserve Clipping File, Dance Collection, New York Public Library, New York City, New York.

52. O'Sheel, "Isadora Duncan," 481.

GENDER ISSUES IN DANCE HISTORY PEDAGOGY

I would like to acknowledge the University of Texas dance majors and Marilla Svinicki, of the UT Center for Teaching Effectiveness, for their considerable contributions to this article.

1. See Gerald Graff, *Beyond the Culture Wars: How Teaching the Conflicts Can Revitalize American Education* (New York: W. W. Norton, 1992).

2. See Tony Morrison, *Playing in the Dark: Whiteness and the Literary Imagination* (Cambridge: Harvard University Press, 1992).

3. Christy Adair, *Women and Dance: Sylphs and Sirens* (New York: New York University Press, 1992).

4. Annie Bell, director, *Dancing for Mr. B: Six Balanchine Ballerinas*, VHS videocassette (New York: Seahorse Films and WNET, 1989).

5. Ann Daly, "The Balanchine Woman: Of Hummingbirds and Channel Swimmers," *TDR: The Journal of Performance Studies* 31, no. 1 (T113, Spring 1987): 8–21. Also reprinted in this volume.

6. Nicholas Ferguson, director, *Ballet for All: How Ballet Was Saved*, VHS videocassette (London: Thames, 1975).

7. Lynn Garafola, "The Travesty Dancer in Nineteenth-Century Ballet," *Dance Research Journal* 17/18, no. 1/2 (Fall 1985/Spring 86): 35–40.

"WOMAN," WOMEN, AND SUBVERSION: SOME NAGGING QUESTIONS FROM A DANCE HISTORIAN

1. This paper was delivered as a keynote address to the 1994 annual conference of the Congress on Research in Dance. As a keynote address, it was written specifically for oral delivery. Rather than rewrite the paper, I have chosen to retain its original style.

2. Albert Einstein and Leopold Infeld, *The Evolution of Physics* (New York: Simon and Schuster, 1938), 95.

3. Edwin Denby, "Dancers, Buildings and People in the Streets," in *Dancers, Buildings and People in the Streets* (New York: Popular Library, 1965), 174.

4. See Ann Daly, "An Unlimited Partnership: Dance and Feminist Analysis," *Dance Research Journal* 23, no. 1 (1991): 2–5. Also reprinted in this volume.

5. See Ann Daly, *Done into Dance: Isadora Duncan in America* (Bloomington: Indiana University Press, 1995).

6. See Pierre Bourdieu, *Distinction: A Social Critique of the Judgement of Taste,* trans. Richard Nice (Cambridge: Harvard University Press, 1984), and *The Logic of Practice,* trans. Richard Nice (Stanford: Stanford University Press, 1990).

7. See Ann Daly, "Isadora Duncan and the Distinction of Dance," *American Studies Journal* 35, no. 1 (1994): 5–23. Also reprinted in this volume.

8. See Julia Kristeva, *Revolution in Poetic Language,* trans. Margaret Waller (New York: Columbia University Press, 1984); Daniel Stern, *The Interpersonal World of the Infant: A View from Psychoanalysis and Development Psychology* (New York: Basic Books, 1985); Mark Johnson, *The Body in the Mind: The Bodily Basis of Meaning, Imagination, and Reason* (Chicago: University of Chicago Press, 1987); and Drew Leder, *The Absent Body* (Chicago: University of Chicago Press, 1990).

9. See Annette Kolodny, "Dancing through the Minefield: Some Observations on the Theory, Practice, and Politics of a Feminist Literary Criticism," *Feminist Studies* 6, no. 1 (1980): 1–25.

TRENDS IN DANCE SCHOLARSHIP: FEMINIST THEORY ACROSS THE MILLENNIAL DIVIDE

1. See Ann Daly, "The Balanchine Woman: Of Hummingbirds and Channel Swimmers," *TDR: The Journal of Performance Studies* 31, no. 1 (T113, Spring 1987): 8–21. Also reprinted in this volume.

2. See Ann Daly, "Dance History and Feminist Theory: Reconsidering Isadora Duncan and the Male Gaze," in *Gender in Performance: The Presentation of Difference in the Performing Arts,* ed. Laurence Senelick (Hanover, N.H.: University Press of New England, 1992). Also reprinted in this volume.

3. See Ann Daly, "'Woman,' Women, and Subversion: Nagging Questions from a Dance Historian," *Choreography and Dance* 5, Part 1 (1998): 79–86. Also reprinted in this volume.

4. See Charles Bernstein, "Artifice of Absorption," in *A Poetics* (Cambridge: Harvard University Press, 1992), 9–89.

5. See Ann Daly, *Done into Dance: Isadora Duncan in America* (Bloomington: Indiana University Press, 1995).

6. See Ann Daly, "Mellower Now, A Resolute Romantic Keeps Trying," *New York Times,* 31 October 1999, sec. 2, p. 31. Also reprinted in this volume.

7. See Ann Daly, "Response to 'Tanztheater: The Thrill of the Lynch Mob or the Rage of a Woman?'" *TDR: The Journal of Performance Studies* 30, no. 2 (T110, Summer 1986): 54–56. Also reprinted in this volume as "Tanztheater: The Thrill of the Lynch Mob or the Rage of a Woman?"

ACKNOWLEDGMENTS

ACKNOWLEDGMENTS

"Looking Underneath the Itch to Criticize" originally appeared in the *New York Times,* 2 March 1997, sec. 2, p. 5. Copyright © 1997 by The New York Times Company. Reprinted by permission.

"Writing about Dance: An Urgent, High-Profile Opportunity" originally appeared in *TDR: The Journal of Performance Studies* 30, no. 2 (T110, Summer 1986): 4–5. Reprinted by permission of the author and MIT Press.

"Review: Diana Theodores's *First We Take Manhattan,* Jill Johnston's *Marmalade Me,* and Lynne Conner's *Spreading the Gospel of the Modern Dance*" originally appeared in *TDR: The Journal of Performance Studies* 43, no. 1 (T161, Spring 1999): 184–90. Reprinted by permission of the author and MIT Press.

"Tanztheater: The Thrill of the Lynch Mob or the Rage of a Woman?" originally appeared in *TDR: The Journal of Performance Studies* 30, no. 2 (T110, Summer 1986): 46–56. Reprinted by permission of the author and MIT Press.

"Pina Bausch Goes West to Prospect for Imagery" originally appeared in the *New York Times,* 22 September 1996, sec. 2, pp. 10, 20. Copyright © 1996 by The New York Times Company. Reprinted by permission.

"Love Mysterious and Familiar: Pina Bausch Brings Her Visceral Non Sequiturs to Austin" originally appeared in the *Texas Observer,* 13 September 1996, 28–29. Reprinted by permission of the *Texas Observer.*

"Remembered Gesture" originally appeared in *BAMazine,* no. 3 (Fall 1999): 43–51. Reprinted by permission of the Brooklyn Academy of Music.

"Mellower Now, A Resolute Romantic Keeps Trying" originally appeared in the *New York Times,* 31 October 1999, sec. 2, p. 31. Copyright © 1999 by The New York Times Company. Reprinted by permission.

"Review: *The Man Who Grew Common in Wisdom*" originally appeared in *Theatre Journal* 42, no. 1 (March 1990): 10–11. Reprinted by permission of the author.

"The Play of Dance: An Introduction to *Lamb, Lamb, Lamb, Lamb, Lamb, . . .*" originally appeared in *TDR: The Journal of Performance Studies* 36, no. 4 (T136, Winter 1992): 54–57. Reprinted by permission of the author and MIT Press.

"No Exit: Deborah Hay's Latest Work a Meditation and Celebration in Space and Time" originally appeared in the *Texas Observer,* 8 December 1995, 20–21. Reprinted by permission of the *Texas Observer.*

"An Experimentalist in Soul and Body" originally appeared in the *New York Times,* 30 March

1997, sec. 2, p. 10. Copyright © 1997 by The New York Times Company. Reprinted by permission.

"Horse Rider Woman Playing Dancing: Ann Daly Interviews Deborah Hay" originally appeared in *PAJ: A Journal of Performance and Art* 21, no. 3 (#63, September 1999): 13–23, published by Johns Hopkins University Press. Reprinted by permission of the author.

"Dance at Prospect Park: High Art, Lowbrow Spectacle" originally appeared in the *Prospect Press*, no. 118 (31 July–31 August 1986): 13. Reprinted by permission of the author.

"Review: *Body against Body*, edited by Elizabeth Zimmer and Susan Quasha," originally appeared in *High Performance* 13, no. 3 (#51, Fall 1990): 76–77. Reprinted by permission of Durland Communications.

"Dancing the Unsayable: Bill T. Jones's *Still/Here* Becomes a Meditation on the Possibilities of Postmodern Art" originally appeared in the *Texas Observer*, 22 March 1996, 18–19. Reprinted by permission of the *Texas Observer*.

"When Dancers Move On to Making Dances" originally appeared in the *New York Times*, 6 April 1997, sec. 2, p. 12. Copyright © 1997 by The New York Times Company. Reprinted by permission.

Thanks to The John F. Kennedy Center for the Performing Arts for permission to reprint "The Long Day's Journey of Bill T. Jones," which originally appeared in *America Dancing: The Revolution Goes Worldwide*, season program, John F. Kennedy Center for the Performing Arts, Fall 1997, 7–9.

"Bill T. Jones in Conversation with Ann Daly" originally appeared in *Art Performs Life: Merce Cunningham/Meredith Monk/Bill T. Jones*, exhibit catalogue (Minneapolis, Minn.: Walker Art Center, 1998), 118–24. Reprinted by permission of the Walker Art Center.

Thanks to The John F. Kennedy Center for the Performing Arts for permission to reprint "Voice Lessons," which originally appeared in *America Dancing: From Revolution to Evolution*, season program, John F. Kennedy Center for the Performing Arts, 1999, 20–21.

"Review: Ralph Lemon Repertory Concert" originally appeared in *High Performance* (#44, Winter 1988): 66. Reprinted by permission of Durland Communications.

"Conversations about Race in the Language of Dance" originally appeared in the *New York Times*, 7 December 1997, sec. 2, pp. 1, 44. Copyright © 1997 by The New York Times Company. Reprinted by permission.

"Afterword" originally appeared in Ralph Lemon's *Geography: art/race/exile* (Middletown, Conn.: Wesleyan University Press, 2000), 191–97. Reprinted by permission of the author and Wesleyan University Press.

"Review: Kei Takei's *Light, Part 20 & 21 (Diary of the Dream)* and *Tetsu Maeda's Evocations*" originally appeared in *High Performance* 8, no. 3 (#31, 1985): 106. Reprinted by permission of Durland Communications.

"Review: Fred Holland's *Harbor/Cement*" originally appeared in *High Performance* 8, no. 3 (#31, 1985): 106–07. Reprinted by permission of Durland Communications.

"Review: Jane Comfort's *TV Love*" originally appeared in *High Performance* 8, no. 4 (#32, 1985): 74. Reprinted by permission of Durland Communications.

"Review: Kazuo Ohno's *Admiring La Argentina* and Kuniko Kisanuki's *Tefu Tefu*" originally appeared in *High Performance* 9, no. 1 (#33, 1986): 76–77. Reprinted by permission of Durland Communications.

"Review: Molissa Fenley Repertory Concert" originally appeared in *High Performance* 9, no. 1 (#33, 1986): 77–78. Reprinted by permission of Durland Communications.

"Review: Gwall's *Exit*" originally appeared in *High Performance* 9, no. 1 (#33, 1986): 78. Reprinted by permission of Durland Communications.

"Review: Lucinda Childs Repertory Concert" originally appeared in *High Performance* 9, no. 2 (#34, 1986): 82. Reprinted by permission of Durland Communications.

"Review: Merce Cunningham's *Roaratorio: An Irish Circus on Finnegans Wake*" originally appeared in *High Performance* 9, no. 4 (#36, 1986): 77. Reprinted by permission of Durland Communications.

"New York (USA): Experimental Dance" originally appeared in *Ballett International* 10, no. 3 (March 1987): 4. Reprinted by permission of Ballett Tanz International.

"Review: John Kelly's *Ode to a Cube*" originally appeared in *High Performance* 12, no. 1 (#45, Spring 1989): 57–58. Reprinted by permission of Durland Communications.

"Review: Ralf Ralf's *The Summit*" originally appeared in *High Performance* 12, no. 1 (#45, Spring 1989): 58. Reprinted by permission of Durland Communications.

"Molissa Fenley's State of Darkness" originally appeared in *High Performance* 12, no. 1 (#45, Spring 1989): 32. Reprinted by permission of Durland Communications.

"Review: Susan Marshall's *Interior with Seven Figures*" originally appeared in *High Performance* 12, no. 3 (#47, Fall 1989): 61. Reprinted by permission of Durland Communications.

"Review: Dana Reitz's *Suspect Terrain*" originally appeared in *High Performance* 12, no. 4 (#48, Winter 1989): 64. Reprinted by permission of Durland Communications.

"Review: Nina Martin's *Changing Face* and *Date with Fate*" originally appeared in *High*

Performance 13, no. 2 (#50, Summer 1990): 73. Reprinted by permission of Durland Communications.

"Susan Marshall Choreography Explores Tragedy, Joy" originally appeared in the *Austin American-Statesman,* 26 September 1994, B10. Reprinted by permission of the author.

"The Choreography of Crisis: Women, Machines, and Utopia Lost" originally appeared in the *Texas Observer,* 24 February 1995, 20. Reprinted by permission of the *Texas Observer.*

"Ballet with Attitude (or The Ballet of the Sexes)" originally appeared in the *Texas Observer,* 10 March 1995, 21–22. Reprinted by permission of the *Texas Observer.*

"Margery Segal's Primal Emotions" originally appeared in the *Texas Observer,* 8 March 1996, 20–21. Reprinted by permission of the *Texas Observer.*

"No Gravity No Boundary" originally appeared in the *Texas Observer,* 6 April 1996, 15. Reprinted by permission of the *Texas Observer.*

"The Freedom of Tradition" originally appeared in the *Texas Observer,* 3 May 1996, 21. Reprinted by permission of the *Texas Observer.*

"A Chronicle Faces Death and Celebrates Life" originally appeared in the *New York Times,* 28 March 1998, sec. 2, p. 52. Copyright © 1998 by The New York Times Company. Reprinted by permission.

"A Dancer Discovers a World of Profit and Daredevil Feats" originally appeared in the *New York Times,* 6 August 2000, sec. 2, pp. 9, 16. Copyright © 2000 by The New York Times Company. Reprinted by permission.

"New York (USA): Dance and Fashion" originally appeared in *Ballett International* 10, no. 4 (April 1987): 41. Reprinted by permission of Ballett Tanz International.

"John Singer Sargent and the Dance" originally appeared in *DanceView* 10, no. 1 (Autumn 1992): 8–13. Reprinted by permission of the author and *DanceView.*

"Lois Greenfield, the Frames That Bind, and the Metaphysics of Dance" originally appeared in *DanceView* 10, no. 3 (Spring 1993): 17–20. Reprinted by permission of the author and *DanceView.*

"Becoming Artaud: Solo Performances at Drawing Center Expand MOMA Exhibit" originally appeared in the *Village Voice,* 26 November 1996, 90. Copyright © 1996 by Village Voice Media, Inc. Reprinted with permission of the *Village Voice.*

"Body of Evidence: Schneemann Retrospective Exposes Subversive Gestures" originally appeared in the *Village Voice,* 15 January 1997, pp. 48–49. Copyright © 1997 by Village Voice Media, Inc. Reprinted with permission of the *Village Voice.*

"An Inspiration Compounded of Hands and Feet" originally appeared in the *New York Times,* 31 January 1999, sec. 2, p. 25. Copyright © 1999 by The New York Times Company. Reprinted by permission.

"Turning a Photographer's Vision into Choreography" originally appeared in the *New York Times,* 27 June 1999, sec. 2, pp. 28–29. Copyright © 1999 by The New York Times Company. Reprinted by permission.

"What Dance Has to Say about Beauty" originally appeared in the *New York Times,* 23 July 2000, sec. 2, pp. 26–27. Copyright © 2000 by The New York Times Company. Reprinted by permission.

"Review: Sondra Horton Fraleigh's *Dance and the Lived Body: A Descriptive Aesthetics*" originally appeared in *Theatre Journal* 41, no. 3 (October 1989): 421–22. Reprinted by permission of the author.

"'What Revolution?': The New Dance Scholarship in America" originally appeared in *Ballett International* 14, no. 1 (January 1991): 49–50. Reprinted by permission of Ballett Tanz International.

"Review: Martha Graham's *Blood Memory* and Agnes de Mille's *Martha*" originally appeared in *Journal of American History* 79, no. 3 (December 1992): 1228–29. Reprinted by permission of the the Organization of American Historians.

"Review: *A Cultural History of Gesture,* edited by Jan Bremmer and Herman Roodenburg," originally appeared in *TDR: The Journal of Performance Studies* 39, no. 1 (T145, Spring 1995): 156–58. Reprinted by permission of the author and MIT Press.

"Alvin Ailey Revealed" originally appeared in the *Texas Observer,* 7 April 1995, 15. Reprinted by permission of the *Texas Observer.*

"Postmodernism and American New Dance" originally appeared in the program of the Festival international de nouvelle danse (Montreal: Parachute, 1987), 40–42. Reprinted by permission of the Festival international de nouvelle danse.

"BAM and Beyond: The Postmoderns Get Balleticized" originally appeared in *High Performance* 10, no. 2 (#38, 1987): 46–49. Reprinted by permission of Durland Communications.

"The Closet Classicist" originally appeared in *DanceView* 11, no. 2 (Winter 1993–94): 2–6. Reprinted by permission of the author and *DanceView.*

"Darkness into Light: A Decade in the West Transforms a Butoh Troupe" originally appeared in the *Village Voice,* 19 November 1996, 84. Copyright © 1996 by Village Voice Media, Inc. Reprinted with permission of the *Village Voice.*

"Finding the Logic of Difference" was originally published in *Dance Theatre Journal* 13, no. 3 (Spring 1997): 18–21. Reprinted by permission of *Dance Theatre Journal*.

"Dancing: A Letter from New York City" originally appeared in *TDR: The Journal of Performance Studies* 42, no. 1 (T157, Spring 1998): 15–23. Reprinted by permission of the author and MIT Press.

"New World A-Comin': A Century of Jazz and Modern Dance" originally appeared in *Modern Dance, Jazz Music and American Culture,* season program. Durham, N.C., and Washington, D.C.: American Dance Festival and the Kennedy Center, 2000, 31–39. Reprinted by permission of the American Dance Festival.

"In Dance, Preserving a Precarious Legacy Begins Onstage" originally appeared in the *New York Times,* 18 February 2001, sec. 2, p. 29. Copyright © 2001 by The New York Times Company. Reprinted by permission.

"Review: From the Repertory of Isadora Duncan's 'Soviet Workers' Songs'" originally appeared in *Theatre Journal* 42, no. 3 (October 1990): 368–69. Reprinted by permission of the author.

"The Continuing Beauty of the Curve: Isadora Duncan and Her Last Compositions" originally appeared in *Ballett International* 3, no. 8 (August 1990): 11–15. Reprinted by permission of Ballett Tanz International.

"Review: Millicent Dillon's *After Egypt*" originally appeared in *Dance Research Journal* 23, no. 1 (Spring 1991): 41–43. Reprinted by permission of the Congress on Research in Dance.

"Review: Lillian Loewenthal's *The Search for Isadora*" originally appeared in *Dance Research Journal* 26, no. 1 (Spring 1994): 30–31. Reprinted by permission of the Congress on Research in Dance.

"Isadora Duncan and the Distinction of Dance" originally appeared in *American Studies* 35, no. 1 (Spring 1994): 5–23. Reprinted by permission of *American Studies.*

"Isadora Duncan's Dance Theory" originally appeared in *Dance Research Journal* 26, no. 2 (Fall 1994): 24–31. Reprinted by permission of the Congress on Research in Dance.

"A Fearless Confession Heard Round the World" originally appeared in the *New York Times,* 20 December 1998, sec. 2, p. 38. Copyright © 1998 by The New York Times Company. Reprinted by permission.

"The Balanchine Woman: Of Hummingbirds and Channel Swimmers" originally appeared in *TDR: The Journal of Performance Studies* 31, no. 1 (T113, Spring 1987): 8–21. Reprinted by permission of the author and MIT Press.

ACKNOWLEDGMENTS

"Classical Ballet: A Discourse of Difference" originally appeared in *Women & Performance: A Journal of Feminist Theory* 3, no. 2 (#6, 1988): 57–64. Reprinted by permission of *Women & Performance: A Journal of Feminist Theory.*

"To Dance Is 'Female'" originally appeared in *TDR: The Journal of Performance Studies* 33, no. 4 (T124, Winter 1989): 23–27. Reprinted by permission of the author and MIT Press.

"Unlimited Partnership: Dance and Feminist Analysis" originally appeared in *Dance Research Journal* 23, no. 1 (Spring 1991): 2–5. Reprinted by permission of the Congress on Research in Dance.

"Dance History and Feminist Theory: Reconsidering Isadora Duncan and the Male Gaze" originally appeared in *Gender and Performance: The Presentation of Difference in the Performing Arts,* ed. Laurence Senelick (Hanover, N.H.: University Press of New England, 1992), 239–59. Copyright © by University Press of New England, reprinted with permission.

"About Interpretation: Joann McNamara Interviews Ann Daly" is excerpted from Joann McNamara, "From Dance to Text and Back to Dance: A Hermeneutics of Dance Interpretive Discourse" (Ph.D. diss., Texas Woman's University, 1994). Reprinted by permission of Joann McNamara, Ph.D.

"Gender Issues in Dance History Pedagogy" originally appeared in the *Journal of Physical Education, Recreation, and Dance* 65, no. 2 (February 1994): 34–35, 39. Reprinted with permission from the *Journal of Physical Education, Recreation, and Dance,* a publication of the American Alliance for Health, Physical Education, Recreation and Dance, 1900 Association Dr., Reston, Virginia 20191.

"'Woman,' Women, and Subversion: Some Nagging Questions from a Dance Historian" originally appeared in *Choreography and Dance* 5, Part 1 (1998): 79–86. Copyright © 1998 by Taylor & Francis, Ltd. Reprinted by permission of Wesleyan University Press.

"Trends in Dance Scholarship: Feminist Theory across the Millennial Divide" originally appeared in *Dance Research Journal* 32, no. 1 (Summer 2000): 39–42. Reprinted by permission of the Congress on Research in Dance.

INDEX

INDEX